Ephemeral city

Ephemeral city

Cheap print and urban culture in Renaissance Venice

ROSA SALZBERG

Manchester University Press

Copyright © Rosa Salzberg 2014

The right of Rosa Salzberg to be identified as the author of this work has been asserted by her in accordance with the Copyright, Designs and Patents Act 1988.

Published by Manchester University Press
Altrincham Street, Manchester M1 7JA, UK
www.manchesteruniversitypress.co.uk

British Library Cataloguing-in-Publication Data
A catalogue record for this book is available from the British Library

Library of Congress Cataloging-in-Publication Data applied for

ISBN   978 0 7190 8703 5   hardback

First published 2014

The publisher has no responsibility for the persistence or accuracy of URLs for any external or third-party internet websites referred to in this book, and does not guarantee that any content on such websites is, or will remain, accurate or appropriate.

Typeset in Minion and Gill by
Servis Filmsetting Ltd, Stockport, Cheshire
Printed in Great Britain by
TJ International Ltd, Padstow

Contents

List of figures	*page* vi
Acknowledgements	viii
List of abbreviations	x
A note on the text	xii
A note on currency	xiii
Introduction	1
1 'Every piece of rubbish given to the press': defining and debating cheap print	18
2 'Through the piazzas and on the Rialto Bridge': the landscape of the ephemeral city	47
3 'A trade open to any mortal man': mobility and versatility in the Venetian printing industry	73
4 'In the mouths of charlatans': pamphlets from print shop to piazza	98
5 'Extreme disorder and confusion': policing the ephemeral city	129
Conclusion	158
Bibliography	167
Index	192

Figures

1 A charlatan's pamphlet: G. Greci, *Operetta noua di auree sententie & vtilissimi documenti ...* ([Venice?, c.1545] for Leonardo il Furlano). BMV Misc. 2231.3. Su concessione del Ministero dei Beni e delle Attività Culturali e del Turismo – Biblioteca Nazionale Marciana. Divieto di riproduzione *page* 22
2 A street singer's chivalric tale: *Canto primo del cavalier dal leon d'oro, d'Hippolito Ferrarese, qual seguita Orlando Furioso* (Venice: V. Ruffinelli for Ippolito Ferrarese, 1538). BEM alfa. Y.7.30/5   23
3 Lament for a dead performer: *Lamento d'Hyppolito detto il Ferrarese che cantaua in bancha* (n.p.d.). BMV Misc. 2231.8. Su concessione del Ministero dei Beni e delle Attività Culturali e del Turismo – Biblioteca Nazionale Marciana. Divieto di riproduzione   25
4 A pamphlet evoking performance: *Frottole nuoue di Lazaro da Cruzola. Con vna barzelletta, & alcune stanze ala schiauonescha ...* (Venice, 1547). BMV Misc. 2231.4. Su concessione del Ministero dei Beni e delle Attività Culturali e del Turismo – Biblioteca Nazionale Marciana. Divieto di riproduzione   26
5 An attention-grabbing title: E. Celebrino, *Questo e lo modo da guarir del mal francioso novo, & vechio ...* (Venice: G. A. Niccolini da Sabbio, 1526)   27
6 J. de' Barbari, *Bird's-eye View of Venice* (Venice, 1500) (with important locations for cheap print production and sale indicated). ©Trustees of the British Museum   48
7 Song against the housekeepers of Venice: *Canzonetta delle massarette, cosa piaceuole da ridere, con la brauata del signor Hieronymo ...* (Venice: M. Pagan, n.d.). BMV Misc. 2213.13. Su concessione del Ministero dei Beni e delle Attività Culturali e del Turismo – Biblioteca Nazionale Marciana. Divieto di riproduzione   60
8 Performers onstage near the clocktower in Piazza San Marco, plus two in foreground, from N. Bianco, *Viaggio da Venetia al Santo*

	Sepolcro, et al monte Sinai … (Venice: A. De' Vecchi, 1606), c. Aiv^v. Getty Institute Library, Los Angeles, 2951–716	62
9	Recycling Aretino: Ippolito Ferrarese's *Opera nova del superbo Rodamonte re de Sarza* … (Venice: G. Fontaneto, 1532). BLCR 132 D 2.3	103
10	A patriotic news song: *La nova de Bressa con una barzelletta in laude del Re de Franza e de San Marco* (Venice: P. Danza, c.1516). ©British Library Board. BL C.20.c.22.55	107
11	A religious work in verse with a woodcut copy of a famous painting: E. Celebrino, *Li stupendi et maravigliosi miracoli del Glorioso Christo de Sancto Roccho Novamente Impressa* (Venice, c.1525). BGC 639	115
12	A horrendous case of murder: *Copia di una lettera venuta novamente da Ravenna, nellaquale si contiene l'horrendo caso* … (Venice: B. and G. A. Bindoni, 1551). BSM Crim. 294,4	137
13	A bawdy pamphlet on Venice's prostitutes: *Pronostico alla villota sopra le putane* … (Venice: M. Pagan, 1558). BMV Misc. 2213.7. Su concessione del Ministero dei Beni e delle Attività Culturali e del Turismo – Biblioteca Nazionale Marciana. Divieto di riproduzione	140
14	An oration offering protection from plague: *Questo è quel gran secreto da esser sicuro à tempo di peste* … (Venice: P. De' Farri, 1575). From ASV, *SU*, b. 39, fasc. 7	159

Acknowledgements

This book is the product of many itinerant years, which would have been infinitely more difficult without a great deal of support, friendship and hospitality. It is a long-awaited pleasure to be able to acknowledge some of my debts here. My doctoral research in London and Italy, from which this book evolved, was made possible by the generous support of the Rae and Edith Bennett Travelling Scholarship, and aided by an Overseas Research Student award from the British government and grants from the Gladys Krieble Delma's Foundation, the University of London Central Research Fund, the UK Society for Renaissance Studies and the Stretton Fund. Post-Ph.D., I was able to explore new avenues and develop the thesis into a book thanks to fellowships from the Australian European University Institute Association and, again, the UK Society for Renaissance Studies. In the home stretch, I have been extremely lucky to find myself in the congenial surroundings of the History Department at the University of Warwick, and I am very grateful to my colleagues there (and in Warwick's Centre for the Study of the Renaissance) for their advice and encouragement. I also add my thanks to the dedicated and obliging staff of all the institutions whose rich collections I have (respectfully) plundered, in particular, the Biblioteca Marciana and the Archivio di Stato in Venice, and the British Library in London.

My wanderings have carried me through a series of supportive and stimulating intellectual environments, each of which have influenced the path my research has taken. My first forays into this field took place in Melbourne, where I was spurred along by the friendship and guidance of Catherine Kovesi, Charles Zika, Andrea Rizzi and Camilla Russell, among others. In London, I was very fortunate to find Kate Lowe as a doctoral supervisor; she has been a conscientious guide and an inspiring model. Miri Rubin, Evelyn Welch, Dilwyn Knox and Brian Richardson also provided valuable assistance and criticism. I add my thanks to Eleanor Davey, Erin Davey, Clare Carlin and Marie Eshuys, particularly patient and generous friends in London. In or around Venice, I crossed paths with a delightful group of scholars including Alex Bamji, Jane Stevens Crawshaw, Esther Brummer Gabel, Chriscinda Henry and Allison Sherman, who helped to cement my attachment to the city and to its history over the requisite spritzes, *polpette* and

Nomboli *panini* as well as sharing with me their thoughts and insights. Courtney Quaintance and Krystina Stermole deserve special mention for offering their different disciplinary perspectives, continually extending their hospitality and making my time in Venice such a pleasure. I am also especially grateful to Claire Judde de Larivière, who read and commented on most of the book manuscript, and who continues to be a boundless source of ideas, enthusiasm and encouragement. For generously sharing with me their thoughts or writings over the years, I also offer sincere thanks to Niall Atkinson, Laura Carnelos, Samuel K. Cohn Jr, Julia DeLancey, Filippo De Vivo, Alessandro Giacomello, Neil Harris, Robert Henke, Mario Infelise, Innes Keighren, Piero Lucchi, Stephen Milner, Dennis Rhodes, Silvana Seidel Menchi, Kevin M. Stevens, Tessa Storey, Jo Wheeler and Andrea Zannini.

On a more personal note, I dedicate this book to my beloved family, particularly to my grandmother Sarah Szental and to my parents, Susan Lefroy and Michael Salzberg, also extremely perceptive and valuable readers of my work. This is a small recompense for their love, support and encouragement, which has been lasting and limitless. I also dedicate the book to Massimo Rospocher – for sharing my enthusiasms, reading everything, providing me every day with intelligent advice, love and moral support, and being the perfect companion for my journeys.

Some parts of this book, now revised and reworked, have appeared elsewhere. Revised parts of Chapter 2 are reprinted here with permission of the publishers from '"Per le piazze & sopra il ponte": Reconstructing the geography of popular print in sixteenth-century Venice', in Miles Ogborn and Charles W. J. Withers (eds), *Geographies of the Book* (Farnham, UK: Ashgate, 2010), pp. 111–31. Copyright © 2010. Revised parts of Chapters 3 and 4 are reprinted here with permission of the publishers from 'The lyre, the pen and the press: performers and cheap print in Cinquecento Venice', in Craig Kallendorf and Lisa Pon (eds), *The Books of Venice*, special issue of *Miscellanea Marciana*, vol. XX (Delaware and Venice: La musa Talìa and Oak Knoll Press, 2008), pp. 251–76; and 'In the mouth of charlatans: street performers and the dissemination of pamphlets in Renaissance Italy', *Renaissance Studies*, 24:5 (2010), 638–53. Revised sections from 'Selling stories and many other things in and through the city: peddling print in sixteenth-century Florence and Venice', *Sixteenth-Century Journal*, 42:3 (2011), 737–59; and 'Print peddling and urban culture in Renaissance Italy', in Joad Raymond, Jeroen L. Salman and Roland J. Harms (eds), *Not Dead Things: The Distribution and Dissemination of Popular Print* (Leiden: Brill, 2013), also are reprinted here with permission from the publishers.

Abbreviations

Archives/libraries

ASF	Archivio di Stato, Florence
AMS	*Arte dei medici e speziali*
OSMN	*Ospedale di Santa Maria Nuova*
ASV	Archivio di Stato, Venice
AC	*Avogaria di Comun*
ALS	*Arte dei librai, stampatori e ligatori*
CCX	*Capi del Consiglio dei Dieci*
CX	*Consiglio dei Dieci*
Decime	*Dieci savi sopra la Decime*
ECB	*Esecutori contro la bestemmia*
PSM	*Procuratorie di San Marco de supra*
Reformatori	*Reformatori dello studio di Padova*
Sanità	*Provveditori alla Sanità*
ST	*Senato Terra*
SU	*Sant'Uffizio*
BBM	Biblioteca Braidense, Milan
BEM	Biblioteca Estense Universitaria, Modena
BGC	Biblioteca Giorgio Cini, Venice
BL	British Library, London
BLCR	Biblioteca dell'Accademia nazionale dei Lincei e Corsiniana, Rome
BMCV	Biblioteca del Museo Correr, Venice
BMV	Biblioteca Marciana, Venice
BNCF	Biblioteca Nazionale Centrale, Florence
BNR	Biblioteca Nazionale, Rome
BRF	Biblioteca Riccardiana, Florence
BSM	Bayerische StaatsBibliothek, Munich
BTM	Biblioteca Trivulziana, Milan

BUP   Biblioteca Universitaria, Padua
BV   Biblioteca Vaticana, Vatican City
Wellcome   Wellcome Library, London

Printed publications and databases

DBI   *Dizionario biografico degli italiani.* Rome: Istituto della Enciclopedia italiana, 1960–
DMS   M. Sanudo. *I diarii (1496–1533).* Edited by R. Fulin *et al.* 58 vols. Venice: Visentini, 1879–1903
DTEI   Menato, M., E. Sandal and G. Zappella, eds. *Dizionario dei tipografi e degli editori italiani. Il Cinquecento.* Vol. 1: A–F. Milan: Editrice Bibliografia, 1997
Edit16 Istituto Centrale per il Catalogo Unico delle biblioteche italiane e per le informazioni bibliografiche (ICCU). *Edit 16. Censimento Nazionale delle edizione italiane del XVI secolo*
GOR   *Guerre in ottava rima.* 4 vols. Ferrara: Istituto di Studi Rinascimentali; Modena: Panini, 1989
STC   *Short-Title Catalogue of Books Printed in Italy and of Italian books Printed in Other Countries from 1465 to 1600 Now in the British Library.* London: British Library, 1958

Other abbreviations

b.   *busta*
c./cc. leaf/ves
f.   *filza*
Not.   notary
r.   registro
s.v.   *sub voce*

A note on the text

All translations into English are my own unless stated. In the transcriptions from early modern Italian texts I have expanded abbreviations, added spaces or apostrophes to separate words, modernised the punctuation, capitalisation and accentuation and changed 'u' to 'v' and vice versa to distinguish respectively vocalic and consonantal 'u'. I have not otherwise modernised the spelling. I have, however, preserved the original spelling of book titles from the period in order to facilitate finding them in catalogues, although I have abbreviated long titles. I also give publication details where possible; attributed publication details are inserted in square brackets. For rare editions, I include the library and shelfmark of the copy I have consulted.

The Venetian calendar began on 1 March. Unless otherwise stated, I have adapted *more veneto* dates to the modern style. The Florentine calendar began on 25 March, and I have likewise adapted dates to the common style.

A note on currency

A Venetian ducat was worth six *lire* and four *soldi*, or 124 *soldi*, in this period. There were twelve *denari* in a *soldo*. A number of smaller coins are mentioned in this book: *quattrino* (worth three *denari*); *bezzo* (worth six *denari*); *gazzetta* (worth two *soldi*); *grossetto* (worth four *soldi*). A *denaro* was also known as a *bagattino* while a *soldo* was also known as a *marchetto*. See M. Sanudo, *De origine, situ et magistratibus urbis venetae ovvero La città di Venetia (1493–1530)* (Milan: Cisalpino-La Goliardica, 1980), pp. 63–4; and also A. Cairola, *Le monete del rinascimento* (Rome: Editalia, 1973), p. 241.

Introduction

In the summer of 1545, a few months before the Council of Trent was to debate the response of the Catholic Church to the Protestant Reformation, a street singer (*cantimbanco*) was arrested in Venice. Like many other performers, Francesco Faentino – his name suggesting that he hailed from Faenza in central Italy – must have been attracted to the city by its reputation as a centre of consumption and commerce; by its large audiences eager for entertainment and novelty. In a central area, perhaps around the Rialto market area or Piazza San Marco, he set up his bench, or *banco*, and from there sold a scurrilous printed work about the phallic Roman god Priapus. He would likely have performed some part of the text, the audience who drew around him then buying the printed version. He may have embellished his performance with suggestive gestures. If the crowd in the streets were delighted by this, however, the authorities were not: Francesco was thrown into prison by the officers of the Esecutori contro la bestemmia, the Venetian blasphemy magistrates. Although eventually released, he was fined three ducats, not a trifling sum.[1] The pamphlet, which Francesco had been selling without the required permission of the local authorities – not that he was likely to have been granted it – was ordered to be burned. Following this incident, there is no sign that the singer ever was active in Venice again, although he had worked there continually in the preceding years.

This small instance of urban crime and punishment captures, for a moment, the movement of people, words and money before these ephemeral, usually anonymous individuals, interactions and transactions disappeared into the crowd. Apart from a couple of lines in one of the few surviving registers of the blasphemy magistrates, the episode left no other material trace, as far as I have been able to tell. No edition has been found identifiable as the one Faentino was selling.

However, the significance of this fleeting moment emerges when we pin it down more precisely within the broader cultural landscape of Renaissance Venice. For instance, it is probable that the work Faentino sold (described as *Il dio Priapo*) was some part of the *Priapea* by the prolific and controversial contemporary writer Niccolò Franco, a protégé, and later enemy, of Pietro Aretino. Franco's translation of these obscene classical poems, usually attributed to Virgil, was first published in 1541 and later prohibited.[2] Furthermore, alongside the street performer, the blasphemy magistrates also fined Giovanni Padovano who printed the illicit text (three ducats), and Guglielmo Fontaneto da Monferrato, who paid for the publication (five ducats). So Faentino was not a marginal, unconnected figure on the fringes of the printing industry; there were existing links between these three men. The singer had commissioned at least four pamphlets in Venice in the few years preceding this incident, two of them attributed to the press of Giovanni Padovano.[3] Fontaneto had worked with Padovano and with other performer-publishers (if not Faentino himself, as far as we know); he had also printed the Latin original of the *Priapea* in 1522.[4] Padovano and Fontaneto, while not the most eminent members of the Venetian printing industry, nonetheless can be anchored more securely in the trade than can the itinerant performer Faentino. Although their names suggest they were immigrants to Venice from the mainland cities of Padua and Monferrato (in Lombardy), by 1545 both had been in the city for some years printing and publishing and continued on working after this incident.[5] Each was able to call on the help of more senior members of their profession, powerful heads of printing dynasties, to act as pledge (*piezo*) for their fines (Fontaneto enlisted the support of Melchiore Sessa, publisher and bookseller at the sign of the Cat; Padovano was aided by Tomaso Giunta, publisher and bookseller at the Lily).[6] Thus, fine webs of association begin to materialise, weaving their way from the street, where Francesco Faentino plied his trade from his temporary *banco*, to the shops of the most powerful members of the Venetian printing industry and the most innovative literary circles in the city. Here, as in so many other quotidian interactions, the ephemeral life of the city revealed itself to be intimately connected to the more stable and lasting structures of Venetian life.

Capturing the ephemeral city

The so-called 'Myth of Venice' long celebrated the city's stability and serenity, its extraordinary durability and beauty. In the sixteenth century, Venice, 'La Serenissima', was envied and renowned for having one of the most secure ruling regimes in Europe, an aristocratic government that would endure, never seriously challenged, until the arrival of Napoleon's troops in the last years of the eighteenth century. But the stability of Venice always relied on movement: on the stream of the first refugees, the fabled founders of the city, into the lagoon in search of safety; on the arrival and departure of ships carrying a cornucopia of goods into and out of the port; on the gush of money and credit through some of Europe's first banks; on the ebb and flow of people bringing goods to trade, money to invest, skills, labour and ideas to sell.[7] Just as Venice's buildings need flexibility in their foundations to be able to stand upon the tides of the lagoon, the city had to absorb and direct these flows in order to survive the centuries. The attentions of historians (and of visitors) tend to be paid to the lasting cultural edifices – the Piazza San Marco with its basilica and ducal palace; the heavy neo-classical structures of the architects Sansovino and Palladio; the patrician *palazzi* that line the Grand Canal – as to the famous literary and artistic products of the Renaissance. And, yet, we must not forget the mobile and ephemeral matter of everyday life that flowed around, fed and sustained these enduring monuments.

This book sets out to capture something of this 'ephemeral city'. It began as a study of some of the smallest, cheapest, most humble products of the spectacularly successful Venetian printing trade. But it soon became apparent that the pamphlets and broadsheets that survive now, often only in single copies, scattered through libraries and archives, had been unpicked from the fabric of city life in which they were once closely woven.[8] It seemed essential to try to place them back into this context in order to understand something of how the new technology of print was entering Venetian life, and lives, but also to offer a different perspective on the history of the city at one of its greatest moments of cultural energy and productivity.

Trying to capture the ephemeral (objects, practices, people) is of course a most challenging task for a historian. However, it is a task worth pursuing, for things that were not necessarily supposed to survive, such as cheap prints, offer a uniquely privileged way into the transient, the quotidian, as well as the extraordinary, life of the city that is challenging to access by other means. The importance of ephemera is also a pressing question in own our day, when technological change and digital culture are making us more acutely aware of all that is lost as societies transition between different modes of communication, and ask what evidence of our lives will be preserved into the future, by design or by chance.[9]

In fact, new technologies are a vital aid to the scholar wishing to study the flotsam of the first age of print. While the vast majority of early Italian cheap print is certainly lost, online catalogues and digitisations rapidly are making what survives of this scattered patrimony more accessible to scholars.[10] Despite the difficulty of making systematic surveys, since the 1990s a number of significant works have explored aspects of Italian cheap print.[11] And, yet, there are still many vital questions to answer about the nature of this material, how it circulated and what part it played in cultural life, particularly in the fifteenth and sixteenth centuries. Italy's cultural heritage in the Renaissance period is so fantastically rich that it has taken a long time for scholars to divert their attention away from the canonical works towards objects and practices that must have been much more ubiquitous and familiar to most people.

Scholars of Italian material can take inspiration from a growing body of works that has challenged what Peter Stallybrass called 'the conceptual gluttony of "the book"' and asserted the importance of ephemeral matter in assessing the historical impact of the printing press.[12] This scholarship argues that cheap print was critical to the European printing trade from its earliest beginnings, as when Gutenberg interrupted the production of his famous forty-two-line Bible to run off two thousand single-sheet indulgences for the church.[13] These studies suggest that cheap print needs to be taken seriously for many reasons. Compared to larger books it was more likely to be produced in large quantities, and to be sold, stuck up or handed out in public spaces, sometimes given away for free. Closely associated with quotidian events and communal experiences, cheap print was very often read out loud or performed in some way. It also commonly made use of simple and easily 'read' images. A rapid and responsive medium, it could be used to quickly make information known to the public, to spread ideas and opinions. In other words, it was both very accessible, acting as a crucial threshold into the world of print for the less literate, and at the same time, potentially, an extremely powerful tool of mass communication.[14]

I add 'potentially' because recent work on early modern communication has convincingly problematised the view of print as an unstoppable 'agent of change' in the progress of history, as suggested by the seminal work of Elizabeth Eisenstein.[15] For one thing, print remained closely intertwined with oral and manuscript modes of transmission, acting, as Joad Raymond stresses, as just 'one particularly noisy strand in a network of communications … [so that] the meaning and the efficacy of print lay in its connectivity'.[16] Moreover, early modern people did not necessarily see printed texts as any more authoritative or reliable than traditional forms of communication, and often less so.[17] As a result, in this book I have found it necessary to consider one category of print – the smallest, cheapest works, frequently sold on the streets – within a precise temporal and physical context, and in relation to other forms of communication and cultural practices. Nonetheless, in doing so, I aim to provide grist for larger comparisons across time and space and contribute to deeper understanding about how print permeated early modern European society, and what part it played in longer term transitions.

Above all, the material I examine here adds further definition to a view emphasised in recent scholarship of the early modern period, and particularly of the Renaissance, as an era characterised and animated by a great deal of movement: not just across the seas with the discovery of new lands and the expansion of global trade routes, but also all over the continent with the migrations of ordinary people, objects and ideas.[18] Print was one of the aspects of early modernity that speeded up the tempo of life, allowing ideas and texts to flow more quickly and widely than ever before. But it was disseminated by mobile people, around cities and between them; it interacted with other fast and fluid forms of communication, oral and handwritten; it benefited from an expanding infrastructure of trade and travel and a more rapid and regular postal system, which put together would radically change people's sense of time and space. Again, print needs to be seen as one critically important strand in this constellation of change and movement.[19]

The Venetian case

Venice, where printing began around 1470 and swiftly flourished, is an extremely important case study both for the impact of early print and for Renaissance urban culture more broadly. It is – as Venice tends to be – both unique and exemplary. Here the new technology of the press fell on extremely fertile ground. The combination of a vigorous, receptive and well-connected commercial environment; an open and cosmopolitan city that welcomed those who could contribute ideas, innovations and capital; a blossoming literary, artistic and performance culture capable of providing abundant original fodder for the press: all these factors contributed to an ideal milieu for the growth of printing. And, indeed, for much of the first century after Gutenberg's invention, the city hosted one of Europe's largest and most productive printing industries. As many as 50,000 to 60,000 editions may have been published in Venice in the sixteenth century, more than all the other Italian centres combined.[20]

Although scholars have focused mostly on the elegant and prestigious editions of the city's top printers, pioneers like Nicholas Jenson and Aldo Manuzio, many forms of very cheap, or even free, print appeared there from the first days of the industry. Producing cheap, quick runs of broadsheets (single sheets printed on one side only) or pamphlets, on commission or for the market, in between larger undertakings was fundamental to the survival of many printers including some of the city's most esteemed, as was the case elsewhere in Europe.[21]

Following Gutenberg's example, much early Venetian cheap print was religious in nature. In 1474, for example, the press of Nicholas Jenson, more renowned for large, expensive editions of the classics, printed a single-sheet papal bull that promised indulgences to those who contributed to the building of a new hospital in Venice.[22] Jenson also was among those who began to produce small religious works in the vernacular, such as confessional aids and verse lives of the saints.[23] Other modest publications quickly began to address topical events and issues. Venice, as the great 'centre of information and communication', strategically located between the Mediterranean and Europe, was particularly precocious in this regard, although other Italian and European cities quickly followed.[24] As early as 1470, the fall of the Venetian colony of Negroponte to the Ottomans provoked an outpouring of publications ranging from small vernacular verse pamphlets to more sophisticated and lengthy Latin works, indicating interest in this topic across the social spectrum.[25] A few years later, in 1475, the Venetian doge reiterated a papal prohibition against anyone who dared to write and sell stories concerning the inflammatory recent case of the murder of the child Simon of Trent, which had been blamed on the Jews. Despite this warning, pamphlets of verse on the topic were printed in the city soon after, as well as numerous cheap woodcut images.[26]

By the time Venice became embroiled in the Italian Wars in the first decade of the sixteenth century, printers in the city already were accustomed to producing cheap and accessible publications to feed the broad public interest in events on the mainland. Indeed, the period of the War of the League of Cambrai (1509–17) might be considered the moment when cheap print cemented its place in Venetian urban life.[27] In 1510, for example, Venetians could purchase a copy of Pope Julius II's excommunication of the French, in Latin and translated into the vernacular, on the Rialto Bridge for the modest price of one *soldo*.[28] The patrician

Girolamo Priuli noted with disapproval in his diary that other works damning Venice's enemies and celebrating fleeting successes also were being peddled 'through the piazzas and on the Rialto Bridge' in the heart of the city.[29] Priuli believed that the government should intervene to stop these publications, which he considered deleterious to civic morale.

Not only visible on the streets and bridges, cheap print was becoming tangible, and audible. As well as being sold publicly, much of this printed production was deeply woven into the oral culture of urban life. For example, after the Imperial army gave up their siege of Padua in October 1509 and that city remained one of the last surviving parts of the Venetian *terraferma* empire, songs about the episode circulated 'throughout all of Padua and Venice, day and night ... sung by children and others in contempt of the enemies'. But these compositions also were beginning to pass into print, quickly run off the presses and hawked around the city.[30] Priuli recorded that, across Italy, street singers hastily were composing accounts of incidents in the war and performing them in the public squares, no doubt followed by the sale of printed copies.[31] The circulation of cheap political prints also fuelled intense discussions and murmurings of dissent among Venetians against their patrician rulers, which in turn fed into further circulation of unofficial political discourse in print and manuscript.[32]

In this period, too, we see other indications of the forms that cheap print would take in the sixteenth century. Many of the ephemeral works produced blurred the lines between official and unofficial publication. Printers published editions of decrees and laws, sometimes on commission of the government or local institutions, sometimes of their own accord. In order to reach a wider public, papal bulls and decrees of the Venetian Senate were rendered into easily obtainable printed forms, for example by the writer Giorgio Sommariva, who translated various political documents, including apostolic bulls, into verse for the presses.[33]

The crisis period of the wars also provides us with some indication of how the Venetian governing oligarchy would react to the flood of print beginning to issue from the city's presses. Already we can observe the government's ambivalence towards the new medium of print, torn between the instincts to exploit or repress it. Certainly, Venice's rulers began to discern the usefulness of the press for communicating with their subjects, starting, as mentioned, to print laws and decrees around this time. However, particularly at sensitive moments such as during the Cambrai War, they looked for ways to stem the printed tide, in this way hoping to inhibit widespread political discussion and speculation. For instance, in 1510, the magistracy concerned with state security, the Council of Ten, acted swiftly to repress the circulation of some broadsheet printed letters from the Holy Roman Emperor Maximilian I to the people of Venice, inciting them to rebel against their government.[34] A few months later, once alliances shifted and Maximilian became Venice's ally, the Ten acted as censors again, but this time by confiscating from sale a printed song criticising the Emperor, worrying it would cause offence. In the meantime they encouraged the circulation of songs against other enemies, the Ferrarese.[35] The government also kept a worried eye on anti-Venetian songs printed elsewhere in Italy, such as some printed in Milan, brought by a messenger from Bergamo in 1509.[36] Confirming the association between cheap print, oral performance and public space, in 1519, after the crisis had subsided, the Council of Ten passed a law decreeing that no one could sell printed verses 'on the piazzas, nor on the Rialto Bridge, nor elsewhere in this city'.[37] As we will see, this decree clearly was not obeyed, and the government, along with the church, would continue to struggle to control forms of communication deemed illicit.

These examples suggest how print was permeating the urban culture of Venice by the early decades of the sixteenth century, a 'sudden explosion in [the] vitals' of the city that would continue to spread and reverberate.[38] A dynamic three-way interaction was materialising that would continue to shape Venetian literary culture: between political and religious authorities divining the benefits, as well as the dangers, of print for communicating messages to the people in one corner; printers, publishers, pedlars and performers discerning a large potential market and a new source of profit in another; and finally the populace starting to seek news, information and instruction in printed form. At the same time, print remained intertwined with more traditional oral and manuscript modes of communication. As a result, the circulation of print emerged as a prominent part of urban culture: in streets, squares, taverns and churches, broadsheets were stuck up and handed out, pamphlets bought and sold, their contents declaimed and discussed.

Many of these developments can be seen in other European cities in the early modern period: from the official and unlicensed structures developed to spread print widely throughout the urban community, to the acculturation to printed texts, especially as a function of their close association with orality, to the creative, catalytic roles of printers as well as performers and pedlars in shaping the print market and determining what texts people would be exposed to. Similarly, the debates ignited by the proliferation and social penetration of print echoed resoundingly throughout the continent.[39] What was exceptional about Venice was the speed and scale of this initial explosion, with the consequence that not only the possibilities but also the problems (as they were perceived by some) of printing were sensed particularly acutely, and particularly early. As well as fostering some of the most acclaimed advances of the early age of print, Venice was one of the very first places where a need to rein in and diminish the capacities of the press was recognised and acted upon, with some of the earliest legislation on censorship and copyright enacted there.[40] This book explores how these possibilities, problems and potential solutions were expressed, between the late fifteenth century and the end of the sixteenth, via the medium of cheap print. It follows the trajectories of this material through Venetian urban space and culture, and the itineraries of the people who produced, sold and consumed it. Pursuing these paths, we can see the early potential for rapid social and cultural change as a result of the press, but also observe how that explosive potential was, to some degree, defused and stifled.

Outline of the book

As I explore in Chapter 1, Venice was the site of some of the most animated debate about the potentially great changes heralded by the press, prefiguring arguments that would continue to take place in other European milieux at least until the eighteenth century.[41] Some residents and visitors to the lagoon city recorded their feelings – a mix of joy, fear and uncertainty – about the consequences of the new medium. Cheap print in particular elicited ambivalent reactions because of its extreme fluidity and mobility, and thus its special capacity to seep across and undermine cultural and social divisions within the population of Venice. As such, it and its producers became lightning rods for fears aroused by the press.[42]

The effect of printing in Venice was also notably intense because of the city's unusual topography and social composition: a great crossroads on the road to everywhere, but at the same time a contained, crowded physical and social space. As I suggest in Chapter 2, the particular physical environment of the city, coupled with its effervescent commercial and cultural life and dynamic, diverse society, meant that cheap print could circulate especially quickly and widely, and intersect in unexpected and creative ways with other cultural, political, religious and economic itineraries.[43] Rather than as a timeless and static corpus of 'folk' literature, cheap print needs to be seen as an element of the changeable urban environment, part of the living history of the city at a particular moment.[44] As a result, it is necessary to look beyond the more familiar sources for printing history (for example, private and print shop inventories which often ignore the presence of cheap print because of its low value, or mask it under casual or vague headings).[45] Opening up a wider range of evidence – from contemporary literary texts to government records concerning the regulation of city space – cheap print and its producers and purveyors (also, but more rarely, its consumers) begin to appear from the shadows.

Exploring the production and dissemination of cheap print also casts new light on a uniquely vibrant cultural moment in Venice, when relative freedom and safety and the booming printing industry helped to make the city a magnet for many kinds of artists, writers and performers. The boom in cheap print was part of a shift in early modern public life, which made it easier for many more people to become producers and consumers of literature, to be heard in the cultural arena, to connect and communicate with others with similar interests or beliefs.[46] Some of the most prominent authors on the Venetian literary scene were, for the first time, women, as well as men of humble origins.[47] In Chapter 3, an even more diverse array of figures comes into view: not only migrant printers who set up shop in Venice, but numerous other more or less recent arrivals who became involved in the printing industry as part-time publishers and pedlars. They brought with them their experiences and texts from other places and took away with them the cultural baggage they had picked up in Venice if they moved on. Rarely highly educated or trained in the print trade, these jacks of all trades might combine publishing and selling print with other activities, such as performing (singing or playing instruments) and peddling other inexpensive consumer goods like soap, medicines or haberdashery. For them, the printed text was just another item to sell in the city's bustling marketplace. And, yet, with a printed pamphlet that could be performed and sold in the street, passed around and broadcast by further oral recitations, these figures were essential mediators in Venetian and Italian Renaissance literary culture, helping to make it less restricted, and more inclusive.

Examining these printed products and their promiscuous and often unexpected trajectories reinforces again the view, established by over thirty years of scholarly debate about the concept of 'popular culture', that we must be wary of using the term to assign particular cultural products or practices exclusively to the lower classes or to brand them as inferior quality.[48] The public for cheap print certainly was not limited to those of low social status. The Venetian patrician Marin Sanudo and the son of Christopher Columbus, Hernan Colòn, were among the eminent collectors of pamphlets and broadsheets in this period, buying and reading cheap print 'in addition to, rather than as a substitute for, more substantial reading matter'.[49] But a much larger potential market existed below this elite crust, which we can assume was principally composed of the 'middling sort' of artisans and shopkeepers, with some degree of literacy and a small amount of expendable income, a group that in a prosperous city like Venice composed a good part of the population.[50] To be sure, it remains frustratingly difficult to document the moments in which consumers encountered and engaged with these texts; to understand the alchemy of individual readers' and listeners' experiences. We have only rare glimpses, as in the 1580s, when, on the fringes of the Venetian Empire in rural Friuli, the miller Menocchio testified how he had owned, borrowed or read a number of familiar cheap works of the kind examined here (religious poems, chivalric tales, almanacs).[51] The survival of Menocchio's trial provides rich and rare evidence of how this unusual individual consumed printed texts, however, we will encounter other examples of how ordinary people in Venice itself engaged frequently with printed texts – buying or borrowing them, copying them or having them copied, hearing them read aloud or sung – showing that even 'those on the margins of literacy hoped to or actually did find ways to penetrate the world of books'.[52] Further systematic study of sources such as Inquisition trials will no doubt continue to illuminate how print permeated the fabric of Venetian society.

The evidence I survey here certainly suggests that the size of the market for cheap print was not entirely limited by the barrier of literacy. While only a minority of people may have been formally educated to read and write in Venice in this period (c.33 per cent of boys and 12–13 per cent of girls), such a city constituted a 'hothouse' environment par excellence, the high presence of books, writing and literate people encouraging some degree of literacy to permeate much further into the population.⁵³ In an urban centre such as Venice, people of different backgrounds and social statuses shared a good deal of common ground, often, if not always, occupying some of the same spaces, participating in the same rituals, witnessing the same performances and reading (or listening to) the same texts. At the same time, Venice was linked into larger networks of cultural exchange with cities like Rome, Florence, Naples, Lyons or Nuremberg, with a great deal of movement and cultural interaction between them. The kinds of cheap print that could be found on the streets of Venice in the sixteenth century, as I suggest in Chapter 4, were eloquent expressions of this distinct Venetian urban culture that was at the same time wired into wider cultural circuits. The easy mobility of ephemeral texts, their rapid and cheap production, meant that they moved very freely between different cultural milieux within Venice, as well as between Venice and other cities.

But shifts in Venetian culture also were under way in the sixteenth century, under the pressure of domestic affairs and broader currents. The spread of printing coincided with other profound transitions in European society that challenged and undermined traditional certainties about what it was possible to think, believe and know, even if did not cause those changes.⁵⁴ Contact with the New World not only expanded Europeans' mental horizons, it also represented an early stage in a larger political and geographic shift that would see Venice lose its strategic centrality in European and Mediterranean trade. Likewise, the challenge of Protestantism to the Catholic Church that convulsed Europe in the sixteenth century had an acute significance for Venice, a principal connector between northern and southern Europe, with strong ties to southern Germany. These threats to Venice's great wealth, power and importance did not result in immediate decline, but they provoked a climate of increasing uncertainty and unease in the Serenissima, raising questions about the proper ordering of the state and society, about economic and social policy, about the behaviour and morals of the populace and the organisation and control of urban space.⁵⁵

In this context, as I suggest in Chapter 5, the potentially destabilising power of print became a cause of escalating concern. Cheap print was especially problematic because it could spread swiftly, widely and often anonymously, and because, for the same reasons, it was extremely hard to control. Alongside initiatives to more clearly define and discipline Venetian society and urban space, efforts were made to bring some degree of order to the circulation of texts, even down to the smallest or most ephemeral. These efforts never were entirely successful, and the will to enforce them waxed and waned as time went on according to a variety of other circumstances. However, they altered Venetian urban culture and the place of cheap print within it in certain marked ways. With the creation of a guild of printers and booksellers in the middle of the sixteenth century and the combined efforts of other state and church bodies, stronger limits were imposed on who could participate in the production and circulation of print, and on what could be printed at all. Print was directed into a series of more clearly demarcated channels, greater distinction emerging between texts intended for the educated and discerning and those suitable for the 'masses'.[56] Ultimately, as we will see, Venice was able to harness the tides of printed material and keep them in check.

Notes

1. ASV, *ECB*, Notatorio, b. 56, vol. 1, c. 49^r. Three ducats was about the monthly wage of a skilled workman in this period. On wages and costs of living, see Chapter 1.
2. On the *Priapea*, studied by many scholars in the Renaissance as part of the works of Virgil, see C. Kallendorf, *Virgil and the Myth of Venice: Books and Readers in the Italian Renaissance* (Oxford: Clarendon Press, 1999), pp. 84–9.
3. For Faentino's publications, see *Edit16*; M. Sander, *Le livre à figures italien depuis 1467 jusqu'à 1530: essai de sa bibliographie et de son histoire* (Nendeln, Lichtenstein: Kraus Reprint, 1969), vol. 3, p. 1344, Addenda no. 155; and C. Valenti, *Comici artigiani. Mestiere e forme dello spettacolo a Siena nella prima metà del Cinquecento* (Ferrara: Panini, 1992), pp. 274–5, 300, 327, 417–18, 459. See also D. Rhodes, 'Francesco detto il Faventino', *Gutenberg Jahrbuch* 52 (1977), 144–5.
4. On Fontaneto's connections with performers, see Chapter 3.
5. See F. Ascarelli and M. Menato, *La tipografia del '500 in Italia* (Florence: Olschki, 1989), pp. 356, 365. Until at least 1544, Padovano had been working with his partner, Venturino Ruffinelli, to whom a 1546 Mantuan edition of Franco's *Priapea* is attributed; see R. L. Bruni, 'Le tre edizioni cinquecentesche delle *Rime contro l'Aretino* e la *Priapea* di Nicolò Franco', in *Libri, tipografi, biblioteche: ricerche storiche dedicate a Luigi Balsamo* (Florence: Olschki, 1997), p. 133.
6. On Sessa and Giunta, see Ascarelli and Menato, *La tipografia del '500*, pp. 327, 329.
7. On the key aspects of the myth, see J. S. Grubb, 'When myths lose power: four decades of Venetian historiography', *Journal of Modern History* 58:1 (1986), 43–94; J. Martin and D. Romano, 'Reconsidering Venice', in J. Martin and D. Romano (eds), *Venice Reconsidered: The History and Civilisation of an Italian City-State, 1297–1799* (Baltimore, MD: Johns Hopkins University Press, 2000), pp. 1–38.
8. See R. M. San Juan, *Rome: A City Out of Print* (Minneapolis: University of Minnesota Press, 2001), p. 26.
9. J. Mussell, 'The passing of print', *Media History*, 18:1 (2012), 77–92.
10. Problems of survival are suggested by the title of U. Rozzo's important work *La strage ignorata: I fogli volanti a stampa nell'Italia dei secoli XV e XVI* (Udine: Forum, 2008). See also N. Harris, 'Marin Sanudo, forerunner of Melzi. Parte I', *La Bibliofilía* 95 (1993), 1–37. The online database *Edit16*, by the Istituto centrale per il catalogo unico delle biblioteche italiane e per le informazioni bibliografiche (ICCU), including Italian sixteenth-century editions in Italian libraries (and some elsewhere), is an invaluable resource, however it provides no means to search specifically for ephemeral material. The Universal short title catalogue (www.ustc.ac.uk), another valuable recent addition, has the same limitation.
11. For an overview of scholarship on Italian cheap print up to the present, see L. Braida, 'Gli studi italiani sui "libri per tutti" in antico regime. Tra storia sociale, storia del libro e storia della censura', in L. Braida and M. Infelise (eds), *Libri per tutti. I generi editoriali di larga circolazione tra antico regime ed età contemporanea* (Turin: Utet, 2010),

pp. 326–44; and O. Niccoli, 'Italy', in *The Oxford History of Popular Print Culture*, vol. 1, ed. J. Raymond (Oxford: Oxford University Press, 2011), pp. 187–95. Important studies of particular genres or typologies of print include *Guerre in ottava rima*, 4 vols (Ferrara: Istituto di Studi Rinascimentali; Modena: Edizioni Panini, 1989); O. Niccoli, *Prophecy and People in Renaissance Italy*, trans. L. G. Cochrane (Princeton, NJ: Princeton University Press, 1990); R. Wilhelm, *Italienische flugschriften des cinquecento (1500–1550). Gattungsgeschichte und sprachgeschichte* (Tübingen: Niemeyer, 1996); Rozzo, *La strage ignorata*; and for the later period, L. Braida, *Le guide del tempo. Produzione, contenuti e forme degli almanacchi piemontesi nel settecento* (Turin: Deputazione subalpina di storia patria, 1989); L. Carnelos, *I libri da risma. Catalogo delle edizioni Remondini a larga diffusione (1650–1850)* (Milan: FrancoAngeli, 2008); L. Carnelos, *'Con libri alla mano'. L'editoria di larga diffusione a Venezia tra Sei e Settecento* (Milan: Unicopli, 2012). These works build upon a rich tradition of erudite scholarship that, from the late nineteenth century, began to explore and catalogue the great mass of Italian 'popular' print. See, in particular, F. Novati, *Scritti sull'editoria popolare nell'Italia di antico regime*, eds E. Barbieri and A. Brambilla (Rome: Archivio Guido Izzi, 2004); A. D'Ancona, *La poesia popolare italiana*, 2nd edn (Leghorn: Giusti, 1906). For some of the Venetian material, see A. Segarizzi (ed.), *Bibliografia delle stampe poplare italiane della R. Biblioteca nazionale di S. Marco di Venezia* (Bergamo: Istituto Italiano d'Arti Grafiche, 1913).

12 P. Stallybrass, '"Little jobs": Broadsides and the printing revolution', in S. Alcorn Baron, E. N. Lindquist and E. F. Shevlin (eds), *Agent of Change: Print Culture Studies after Elizabeth L. Eisenstein* (Amherst, MA and Washington, DC: University of Massachusetts Press/Center for the Book, Library of Congress, 2007), p. 340. Pioneering works in this field include H.-J. Kohler (ed.), *Flugschriften als Massenmedium der Reformationszeit: Beiträge zum Tübinger Symposion 1980* (Stuttgart: Ernst Klett, 1981); R. W. Scribner, *For the Sake of the Simple Folk: Popular Propaganda for the German Reformation* (Cambridge: Cambridge University Press, 1981); M. Spufford, *Small Books and Pleasant Histories: Popular Fiction and Its Readership in Seventeenth-Century England* (Cambridge: Cambridge University Press, 1985; first published 1981); R. Chartier, *The Cultural Uses of Print in Early Modern France*, trans. L. G. Cochrane (Princeton, NJ: Princeton University Press, 1987); T. Watt, *Cheap Print and Popular Piety 1550–1640* (Cambridge: Cambridge University Press, 1991). A recent prominent survey stressing the importance of cheap print is A. Pettegree, *The Book in the Renaissance* (New Haven and London: Yale University Press, 2010).

13 Stallybrass, '"Little jobs"', p. 316. See also J. L. Flood, 'The printed book as a commercial commodity in the fifteenth and early sixteenth centuries', *Gutenberg Jahrbuch*, 76 (2001), 179; D. F. McKenzie, 'The economies of print, 1550–1750: scales of production and conditions of constraint', in S. Cavaciocchi (ed.), *Produzione e commercio della carta e del libro, secc. XIII–XVIII* (Prato: Le Monnier, 1992), pp. 389–425.

14 On the 'acculturation' of people to print, see in particular R. Chartier 'Publishing strategies and what the people read, 1530–1660', in Chartier, *Cultural Uses of Print*, pp. 145–82. Printed images are not a focus of this book, although they could be very cheap and often were sold via the same circuits that I describe here. See D. Landau and P. Parshall, *The Renaissance Print, 1470–1550* (London: Yale University Press, 1994); G. Jan van der Sman, 'Print publication in Venice in the second half of the

sixteenth century', *Print Quarterly*, 17 (2000), 235–47; M. Bury, *The Print in Italy, 1550-1620* (London: British Museum, 2001); B. Wilson, *The World in Venice: Print, the City and Early Modern Identity* (Toronto: University of Toronto Press, 2005); D. S. Areford, *The Viewer and the Printed Image in Late Medieval Europe* (Burlington, VT: Ashgate, 2010). It is important to note that not every small printed item, every pamphlet or broadsheet, was cheap, low quality and intended for a wide public via street sale. Particularly in the first decades of print we see ephemeral publications in Latin or in short print runs intended to circulate within a more restricted and learned public. See F. Eisermann, 'Mixing pop and politics: Origins, transmission, and readers of illustrated broadsides in fifteenth-century Germany', in K. Jensen (ed.), *Incunabula and Their Readers: Printing, Selling and Reading Books in the Fifteenth Century* (London: British Library, 2003), pp. 159–77.

15 E. L. Eisenstein, *The Printing Press as an Agent of Change: Communications and Cultural Transformations in Early Modern Europe*, 2 vols (Cambridge: Cambridge University Press, 1979). For a summary of the main arguments surrounding Eisenstein's work, see the articles by Eisenstein, A. Johns and A. Grafton in the debate: 'How revolutionary was the print revolution?', *American Historical Review* 107:1 (2002); and Baron *et al.*, *Agent of Change*. Another important contribution is W. Behringer, 'Communications revolutions: a historiographical concept', *German History*, 24:3 (2006), 333–74.

16 J. Raymond, 'The origins of popular print culture', in Raymond, *Oxford History of Popular Print Culture*, vol. 1, p. 9. Other key works on the interaction of oral, printed and written cultures in this period include D. F. McKenzie, 'Speech–manuscript–print', in his *Making Meaning: Printers of the Mind and Other Essays*, ed. P. D. McDonald and M. F. Suarez (Amherst and Boston, MA: University of Massachusetts Press, 2002), pp. 237–58; A. Fox, *Oral and Literate Culture in England, 1500-1700* (Oxford: Oxford University Press, 2000); F. De Vivo, *Information and Communication in Venice: Rethinking Early Modern Politics* (Oxford: Oxford University Press, 2007); B. Richardson, *Manuscript Culture in Renaissance Italy* (Cambridge: Cambridge University Press, 2009).

17 See, in particular, A. Johns, *The Nature of the Book: Print and Knowledge in the Making* (London and Chicago, IL: University of Chicago Press, 1998); D. McKitterick, *Print, Manuscript and the Search for Order, 1450 – 1830* (Cambridge: Cambridge University Press, 2003).

18 L. Page Moch, *Moving Europeans: Migration in Western Europe since 1650* (Bloomington, IN: Indiana University Press, 1992); P. Fumerton, *Unsettled: The Culture of Mobility and the Working Poor in Early Modern England* (Chicago, IL and London: University of Chicago Press, 2006); S. Greenblatt (ed.), *Cultural Mobility: A Manifesto* (Cambridge: Cambridge University Press, 2010).

19 See T. Cresswell, *On the Move: Mobility in the Modern Western World* (New York: Taylor & Francis, 2006), pp. 12–13.

20 This estimate was made by U. Rozzo, *Linee per una storia dell'editoria religiosa in Italia (1465-1600)* (Udine: Arti Grafiche Friulane, 1993), pp. 21–2, taking into account potentially lost editions and ephemera ignored in some other estimates. *Edit16* currently lists 27,148 editions produced in or attributed to Venice between 1501 and 1600 out of a total of 64,247 from that period. Fundamental works surveying the early history of the Venetian trade include H. F. Brown, *The Venetian Printing*

Press (London: Nimmo, 1891); M. Lowry, *The World of Aldus Manutius: Business and Scholarship in Renaissance Venice* (Ithaca, NY: Cornell University Press, 1979); M. Lowry, *Nicholas Jenson and the Rise of Venetian Publishing in Renaissance Europe* (Oxford and Cambridge, MA: Blackwell, 1991); A. Nuovo and C. Coppens, *I Giolito e la stampa nell'Italia del XVI secolo* (Geneva: Librairie Droz, 2005).

21 See the works cited above, n. 13.

22 D. Fattori, 'Incunaboli sconosciuti ed incunaboli semisconosciuti all'Archivio di stato di Venezia', *La Bibliofilía*, 102:3 (2000), 253–7.

23 M. Lowry, '"Nel beretin convento": The Franciscans and the Venetian press (1474–78)', *La Bibliofilía*, 85 (1983), 27–40. Cheap religious woodcut images had been widely diffused from the early fifteenth century; see R. Cobianchi, 'The use of woodcuts in fifteenth-century Italy', *Print Quarterly*, 23:1 (2006), 47–54; Areford, *The Viewer and the Printed Image*.

24 P. Burke, 'Early modern Venice as a center of information and communication', in Martin and Romano, *Venice Reconsidered*, pp. 390–408.

25 M. Meserve, 'News from Negroponte: Politics, popular opinion, and information exchange in the first decade of the Italian press', *Renaissance Quarterly*, 59:2 (2006), 440–80.

26 U. Rozzo, 'Il presunto "omicidio rituale" di Simonino di Trento e il primo santo tipografico', *Atti dell'Accademia udinese di scienze, lettere e arti*, 90 (1997), 197, 216; Areford, *The Viewer and the Printed Image*, ch. 4.

27 See R. Salzberg and M. Rospocher, 'The evanescent public sphere: Voices, spaces, and publics in Venice during the Italian wars', in M. Rospocher (ed.), *Beyond the Public Sphere: Opinions, Publics, Spaces in Early Modern Europe (XVI–XVIII)* (Bologna and Berlin: Il Mulino/Duncker & Humblot, 2012), pp. 93–114.

28 'La scomunicha, fata per il papa contra il gran maistro e altri francesi, ozi vidi vender su el Ponte di Rialto, a stampa, latina et vulgar, un soldo l'una'. *DMS*, vol. 11, col. 615 (19 November 1510).

29 'Se vendeva a Venetia per le piaze e sopra il Ponte d'il Rialto segondo il solito li frotoli li verssi in rima et le canzoni dele ruyne … nel teritorio ferarexe e de l'armata veneta in Pado[a] contra il Ducha ferarexe' (G. Priuli, *Diarii*, BMCV, MS. Prov. Div. 252-c, vol. 5, cc. 55^{r-v} (end of December 1509)).

30 'Per tuta Padoa et Venetia il giorno et nocte dali putti et altri hera cantata questa canzone per disprectio deli inimici' (G. Priuli, *I diarii di Girolamo Priuli, 1499–1512*, ed. R. Cessi (Bologna: Zanichelli, 1938), vol. 4, p. 359 (25 September 1509)). The printing of these songs is mentioned in *DMS*, vol. 9, col. 335 (22 November 1509). See also V. Rossi, 'Su, su, su chi vuol la gatta', *Giornale storico della letteratura italiana*, 5 (1885), 504–7.

31 'Per tutta la Italia se cantavano et recitavano sopra le piazze per li zarlatani, che vivevano cum questo' (Priuli, *I diarii*, vol. 4, pp. 56–7 (June 1509)).

32 See L. Da Porto, *Lettere storiche di Luigi da Porto vicentino dall'anno 1509 al 1528*, ed. B. Bressan (Florence: Le Monnier, 1857), pp. 127–37. For examples of (handwritten?) fliers posted up in public places, complaining about the nobility, see *DMS*, vol. 18, cols 44–5 (18 March 1514); vol. 58, col. 247 (3 June 1533).

33 See G. Petrella, *Fra testo e immagine. Edizioni popolari del Rinascimento in una miscellanea ottocentesca* (Udine: Forum, 2009), pp. 34, 46–7. For examples of official printed laws, see *DMS*, vol. 50, cols 140–1, 306–7; vol. 58, cols 107–14.

34 *DMS*, vol. 12, col. 291 (November 1510). On these letters, a precocious example of printed political propaganda, see M. Rospocher, '"Non vedete la libertà di voi stessi essere posta nelle proprie mani vostre?" Guerre di scritture e cambi di regime al tempo di Cambrai', in M. Bonazza and S. Seidel Menchi (eds), *Dal leone all'aquila. Comunità, territori e cambi di regime nell'età di Massimiliano I* (Rovereto: Accademia roveretana degli Agiati-Edizioni Osiride, 2012), pp. 127–47.

35 *DMS*, vol. 9, col. 335 (22 November 1509). For other examples of the perceived political power of poetry and song, see M. Rospocher, 'Versi pericolosi? Controllo delle opinioni e ricerca del consenso nelle guerre d'Italia', in D. Ramada Curto *et al.* (eds), *From Florence to the Mediterranean and Beyond: Essays in Honour of Anthony Molho* (Florence: Olschki, 2009), vol. 1, pp. 394–402.

36 'Alcune canzone, stampade a Milano in disprecio nostro, chome fu la cota e presa dil signor Bortolo, e poi uno lamento di venitiani, composto per uno Symone di Bitti' (*DMS*, vol. 8, cols 544–5 (23 July 1509)).

37 '[Nessuno] ardisca, né presuma de stampar aut far stampar opera alchuna, né grande né picola, né soneto ne verso, né stantie … né quelli vender, né far vender, né in botege, né sule piaze, né sopra el ponte de Rialto' (ASV, *CX*, Minuti dei proclami, f. 2, fasc. 33 (3 July 1519)). I would like to thank Claire Judde de Larivière for alerting me to this reference.

38 Lowry, *Nicholas Jenson*, p. 177, referring to the earlier period of the 1480s.

39 For an overview of developments across Europe, see the works cited above, n. 12.

40 On the beginnings of censorship and copyright, see P. F. Grendler, *The Roman Inquisition and the Venetian Press, 1540–1605* (Princeton, NJ: Princeton University Press, 1977); and C. L. C. E. Witcombe, *Copyright in the Renaissance: Prints and the* Privilegio *in Sixteenth-Century Venice and Rome* (Leiden: Brill, 2004).

41 See, in particular, Johns, *Nature of the Book*; E. L. Eisenstein, *Divine Art, Infernal Machine: The Reception of Printing in the West from First Impressions to the Sense of an Ending* (Philadelphia, PA: University of Pennsylvania Press, 2011).

42 As was also the case in England: see A. Halasz, *The Marketplace of Print: Pamphlets and the Public Sphere in Early Modern England* (Cambridge: Cambridge University Press, 1997), pp. 4, 14–15; Raymond, 'Origins of popular print culture', pp. 8–9.

43 There has been growing attention to the geography of print since the important study of L. Febvre and H. J. Martin, *The Coming of the Book: The Impact of Printing 1450–1800*, eds G. Nowell-Smith and D. Wootton, trans. D. Gerrard, new edn (London: NLB, 1976), esp. pp. 167–215. For a recent overview, see M. Ogborn and C. W. J. Withers, 'Introduction: book geography, book history', in M. Ogborn and C. W. J. Withers (eds), *Geographies of the Book* (Farnham, UK and Burlington, VT: Ashgate, 2010), pp. 1–25.

44 Niccoli, 'Italy', p. 197.

45 For a few examples, see A. Nuovo, *Il commercio librario nell'Italia del Rinascimento* (Milan: FrancoAngeli, 1998), pp. 50–1. From the later sixteenth century and the seventeenth century, more inventories are being unearthed which suggest the vast quantities of cheap print in circulation. See G. L. Masetti Zannini, *Stampatori e librai a Roma nella seconda metà del cinquecento: documenti inediti* (Rome: Palombi, 1980), pp. 140–1, 215–16; K. M. Stevens, 'Vincenzo Girardone and the popular press in Counter-Reformation Milan: A case study (1570)', *Sixteenth Century Journal*, 26:3 (1995), 639–59; K. M. Stevens and P. F. Gehl, 'Cheap print: A look inside the

Lucini–Sirtori stationary shop at Milan (1597–1613)', *La Bibliofilía*, 92:3 (2010), 281–327; S. Minuzzi, *Il secolo di carta: Antonio Bosio artigiano di testi e immagini nella Venezia del Seicento* (Milan: FrancoAngeli, 2009)

46 See the introduction by P. Yachnin and B. Wilson to their edited volume, *Making Publics in Early Modern Europe: People, Things, Forms of Knowledge* (New York: Routledge, 2009), pp. 1–21.

47 C. Dionisotti, 'La letteratura italiana nell'età del Concilio di Trento', in his *Geografia e storia della letteratura italiana* (Turin: Einaudi, 1967), pp. 227–54.

48 Two seminal works on this theme are P. Burke, *Popular Culture in Early Modern Europe*, 3rd edn (Farnham, UK: Ashgate, 2009; first published, 1978), and C. Ginzburg, *The Cheese and the Worms: The Cosmos of a Sixteenth-Century Miller*, trans. J. and A. Tedeschi (London: Routledge & Kegan Paul, 1980; first published in Italian, 1976). For an overview of debates on this topic, see S. Wiseman, '"Popular culture": A category for analysis?', in M. Dimmock and A. Hadfield (eds), *Literature and Popular Culture in Early Modern England* (Farnham, UK: Ashgate, 2009), pp. 15–28.

49 Watt, *Cheap Print*, p. 265.

50 On Venetian society, see D. Romano, *Patricians and Popolani: The Social Foundations of the Venetian Renaissance State* (Baltimore, MD: Johns Hopkins University Press, 1987). On the 'middling sort', defined as independent householders who had to work for an income but who were generally self-employed, see J. Barry and C. Brooks (eds), *The Middling Sort of People: Culture, Society and Politics in England, 1550–1800* (Houndmills, UK: Macmillan, 1994). On the prices of cheap print in relation to wages, see Chapter 1.

51 Ginzburg, *The Cheese and the Worms*, pp. 29–32. Menocchio's books included an almanac (*lunario*) once published in Venice by the *cantimbanco* Ippolito Ferrarese, cited in Chapter 3, n. 70.

52 J. J. Martin, *Venice's Hidden Enemies: Italian Heretics in a Renaissance City* (Berkeley, CA: University of California Press, 1993), p. 83. See also X. von Tippelskirch, 'Lettrici e lettori sospetti davanti al tribunale dell'Inquisizione nella Venezia post-tridentina', *Mélanges de l'école française de Rome: Italie et méditerranée*, 115:1 (2003), 315–44.

53 R. A. Houston, *Literacy in Early Modern Europe: Culture and Education 1500–1800*, 2nd edn (Harlow, UK: Pearson Education, 2002), pp. 150–1; see also H. Brayman Hackel, 'Rhetorics and practices of illiteracy or the marketing of illiteracy', in I. F., Moulton (ed.), *Reading and Literacy in the Middle Ages and the Renaissance* (Turnhout, Belgium: Brepols, 2004), pp. 169–83. On literacy rates, see P. F. Grendler, *Schooling in Renaissance Italy: Literacy and Learning, 1300–1600* (Baltimore, MD: Johns Hopkins University Press, 1989), pp. 43–6. Grendler admits that functional literacy probably extended into a relatively broad segment of the male population at least (p. 47). In contrast, illiteracy remained much more widespread in the Italian countryside, well into the nineteenth century. See M. Roggero, *L'alfabeto conquistato. Apprendere e insegnare nell'Italia tra sette e ottocento* (Bologna: Il Mulino, 1999), p. 19.

54 S. Landi, *Stampa, censura e opinione pubblica in età moderna* (Bologna: Il Mulino, 2011), p. 14.

55 On debates about the nature of Venetian decline, see Grubb, 'When myths lose power'.

56 On widening cultural divisions and attempts to reform popular practices from the later sixteenth century, see Burke, *Popular Culture*, pp. 207–43; and also P. Camporesi, 'Cultura popolare e cultura d'élite, fra Medioevo ed età moderna', in *Storia d'Italia:*

Annali, vol. 4: *Intellettuali e potere*, ed. C. Viviani (Turin: Einaudi, 1981), esp. p. 86. Despite the questioning of rigid divisions between popular and elite, most historians still recognise a movement in this direction. See, for example, G. Sullivan and L. Woodbridge, 'Popular culture in print', in A. Kinney (ed.), *The Cambridge Companion to English Literature 1500–1600* (Cambridge: Cambridge University Press, 2000), pp. 277–8.

'Every piece of rubbish given to the press': defining and debating cheap print

In a dialogue by Niccolò Franco, first printed in Venice in 1539, two characters discussed the inundation of new printed products and deliberated how an aspiring bookseller might navigate the choppy waters of this emerging market and hope to make a profit from it. Sannio, the mouthpiece for Franco, advised his friend Cautano that a successful bookseller should stock a very diverse range of works, including small, cheap and humble ones. But how could one ever stock so many books, Cautano queried, when these days 'two thirds of men' are involved in writing and printing? Sannio quibbled with his friend's definition: 'every written paper, every shitty booklet, and every piece of rubbish given to the press you call a book?'.[1]

As this exchange suggests, what was meant by the term 'book', all of its traditional social and cultural associations, were coming under stress in this period, because of the emergence of so much printed matter covering the spectrum of size, price and quality. In Venice, the presses were booming, the city producing around 65 per cent of Italian print in the second quarter of the sixteenth century, several times as much as the next largest Italian printing centre, Rome.[2] Customary notions of writers and readers, of their identities and motivations, were being challenged by the accessibility of print, while printers, publishers and booksellers assumed a new, powerful role in the circulation of texts and thus in the wider culture.

Franco himself was one of numerous writers who converged on the city at this time (in his case, after an unsuccessful career as a courtier in Naples and Rome), attracted by the promise of literary glory. In reality, many of these furious scribblers had to be ready to traverse multiple genres and to sell their services as correctors, translators and editors for the presses, hence becoming known as *poligrafi*. Not all of them found success; after a brief stint as secretary to Venice's greatest literary celebrity, Pietro Aretino, Franco fell out with his employer and ended up fleeing the city after a knife attack by one of Aretino's followers. Franco, like others discussed below, would eventually fall foul of the Inquisition.[3]

This chapter focuses on the words of Franco and other sixteenth-century commentators, many of whom worked closely with the presses, as they capture something of the intoxicating sense of excitement and upheaval that pervaded the period. They suggest the ways in which the book, more commonly associated with exclusive social spheres and spaces, was entering the marketplace, literally and figuratively, becoming a ubiquitous commodity on the streets of Venice and other cities alongside a proliferation of other more or less disposable consumer goods. As a result, what exactly a book was, what it was worth and who it was for, became acutely contentious questions.[4]

As I propose here, much of the controversy focused on the lower end of the print spectrum, and on the qualities that were particularly associated with the kind of material considered in this book: its cheapness (or worthlessness), its abundance (or ubiquity) and the inferior quality (both material and literary) that resulted from the speed of its production and the commercial aspirations of its purveyors. Although there was much continuity between manuscripts and early printed books, cheap printed broadsheets and booklets were a novel presence in urban culture and sometimes a troubling one. For many, they represented the first opportunity to own a text, the first possibility to enter the community of readers, and must have been welcomed. But for some commentators, they were the most visible manifestation of the sheer proliferation of texts unleashed by the press, of the enormous potential power of print to spread ideas and information, for good or ill, and as a result they represented a challenge to established cultural order.

Defining cheap print

Before examining these different points of view, we need to look more closely at the category of material I am calling cheap print, to consider its physical characteristics and cultural associations. In the sixteenth century, people were less likely to refer to the type of ephemeral material that concerns me as *libri* (books), than to use diminutive terms such as *libriccini*, *libretti* (little books), or *opuscoli*, *operette*, *operine* (little works). They might also refer to this loose category by naming the genres of text usually printed in this form and the modes and spaces of its sale. For example, a 1543 edict of the Venetian Council of Ten stated that no one could print or sell any work without first obtaining a licence, extending this to all those 'who sell such books and works, prognostications, stories, songs, letters, and other similar things on the bridge of the Rialto, and in other places of this city'.[5]

I adopt the comprehensive term 'cheap print' for this material, in order to stress what I believe to be its most important characteristic in the context of the period. Because these works were small, they were cheap, as paper was the most expensive component of print production.[6] The terminology for cheap print in contemporary historiography is not settled. Italian historians are now less likely to use the potentially problematic term *stampe popolari* (popular prints) than more neutral formulations like *libri per tutti* or *libri di larga circolazione* (books for all/of wide circulation) and *fogli volanti* ('flying sheets'), for broadsheets and fliers. In English, I prefer to use 'cheap print' to encompass the broad category from broadsheets to small pamphlets.[7]

The information we have regarding prices suggests that a good deal of printed matter was very cheap indeed. Although it is difficult to establish a standard price for small books and broadsheets in Renaissance Venice, fragments of evidence suggest that from early on these were much more affordable than 'proper' books, which, according to Grendler, cost an average of about one to two *lire* in this period.[8] Already in the sales register of the bookseller Francesco de' Madiis in the 1480s, Lowry observed book prices dropping as the numbers of copies rose. Among the cheapest works was the small literacy primer the *Psalteriolo*, being sold by the dozen for as little as two *quattrini* (half a *soldo*) per copy.[9] By the early sixteenth century, some works were even cheaper. For instance, the diarist Sanudo recorded that in 1509 printed songs about the War of the League of Cambrai were being sold around the city for one *bezzo*, or half a *soldo*, each.[10] As noted in the Introduction, the following year the text of the Pope's excommunication of the French could be bought on the Rialto for one *soldo*.[11] This was also the suggested price for a two-leaf quarto of sonnets by the Venetian poet Leonardo Giustinian, and for a four-leaf oration by the Imperial ambassador printed in Venice in the same period.[12] Evidence from the purchases of the collector Hernan Colòn suggests similarly cheap prices for print (including Venetian print) in other Italian cities in the period.[13]

These prices were certainly very low, however it remains difficult to ascertain what they meant to ordinary people, rather than to wealthy collectors such as Colòn, who could presumably buy hundreds of pamphlets without batting an eyelid. Information on the ordinary costs of living is scarce. However, cheap print prices seem to compare to those of basic foodstuffs and frequently used services. Two *soldi* was the price of a loaf of bread in a time of grain shortage (1534), or of one mackerel.[14] A pound of oil or candles at the Rialto market in the late fifteenth century should have cost no more than four *soldi*, the same maximum price set for a visit to a barber.[15] For those not wealthy enough to own a gondola, crossing the Grand Canal on a *traghetto* or ferry boat cost a *bagattino* (worth one-twelfth of a *soldo*) – an unremarkable expense at a time when there was only one bridge across the city's main waterway, but dozens of *traghetti* stops.[16]

Thus half a *soldo* for a printed pamphlet was not an unimaginable luxury for a skilled workman (like a print shop compositor, who earned about three to four ducats a month) or a shop assistant in a mercer's store (sixteen to eighteen *soldi* a day).[17] Although not negligible, the price of a *soldo* or less for many small printed items was far from prohibitive. Buying such a work was significantly cheaper than going to a play, for example. In 1515, entry to a production of Plautus's *Asinaria* in the vernacular at the refectory of the convent of Santo Stefano cost ten *soldi*, which one historian suggests was a 'modest price … accessible to a large public'.[18] By the early sixteenth century, then, a burgeoning category of cheaper printed matter was appearing in the Venetian marketplace, at prices accessible to a large proportion of the population.[19]

The economics of cheap print generally meant that large quantities had to be printed at low cost in order for the producers to make a profit.[20] The physical form of these works was geared entirely towards keeping their costs low. Most of the works I consider could have been printed on one sheet of paper, folded into an octavo of eight leaves or a quarto of four. Some are even smaller – a single printed flier or broadsheet. Paper was often of poor quality, particularly from later in the sixteenth century. These works almost never feature printing with red ink or other adornments that made the printing process more complicated and thus expensive. Simple woodcut illustrations were common especially earlier in the century but rarely were produced specifically for the text. A generic image on the title page served to give some indication of the type of text presented, for example a combat scene could indicate either a chivalric tale or an account of a recent battle.[21] Easy and inexpensive to assemble, these works were held together at most by a couple of stab-stitches and, increasingly, with cheap cardboard covers.[22] They were unlikely to be bound in leather, except by the odd collector who might gather together a miscellany of small works.

So the physical form in itself usually signalled low cost and thus availability to a diverse public. But Grendler has suggested that some of these characteristics also communicated that a work was popular in a broader cultural sense, that is easily accessible to all sorts of people even those with a low level of education, or 'intended for a non-critical audience which read for pleasure'. Grendler stresses the fact that printers largely stuck to traditional and familiar styles of presentation – old-fashioned typefaces such as Gothic or an early version of Roman type – to indicate popular texts, at least until the 1530s when they increasingly began to use italic type to indicate new works by living authors to readers looking for novelty or innovation.[23] However, it is important to emphasise that, particularly in the first half of the sixteenth century, a great variety of material was presented with some or all of the physical characteristics that Grendler says expressed a work's 'popularity', from conservative and familiar texts to newer, more innovative ones. The same decorative woodcut borders, for example, were reused across very different genres of texts, from religious works to chivalric tales, suggesting that readers did not always immediately identify the type of text from the physical presentation (see Figures 1 and 2). (As Niccoli notes, these booklets also were distinguished by a 'distinct heterogeneity' of content; for example, bawdy poetry might be printed alongside devotional material.)[24] The inhabitants of Venice, including the less affluent and educated, encountered a wide range of different texts on the market at affordable prices and in manageable forms, and had to decide what did and did not interest them, what they could or could not understand. Physical form and presentation were important in helping them make these decisions but so too were the spaces and the ways in which they were sold, and the role of pedlars and performers in advertising the works and communicating their qualities to potential consumers.

It is worth reflecting briefly on a few further implications of the way in which these texts were presented, which give indications of their modes of sale and use.

1 A charlatan's pamphlet: Greci, *Operetta noua di auree sententie & vtilissimi documenti*

2 A street singer's chivalric tale: *Canto primo del cavalier dal leon d'oro, d'Hippolito Ferrarese*

The titles often were displayed prominently, frequently in larger letters and/or in Gothic typeface to make them stand out from the text which followed. These titles, and the woodcut illustrations that often accompanied them, increased the commercial possibilities of the text, and illustrate how printers and publishers actively sought new ways to entice buyers; they could not just rely on word of mouth or the established reputation of an author or a work. In some instances an author's name was advertised on the title page – sometimes the name of a famous figure who had never given permission for their works to be printed or whose works were not even actually included within the text – and occasionally we find a portrait of the author if they were sufficiently renowned and perhaps even visually recognisable. At times, this approach was designed to evoke the memory of, and make it clear that the text derived from, a performance, as in the title-page reference to Ippolito Ferrarese *che cantava in banca* ('who sang on a bench') (Figure 3) or the inclusion of images of music-making (Figure 4).[25]

The titles suggest the words likely used by street vendors to advertise the texts; as Niccoli points out, they often start with the word *questo* ('this'), as the vendor would have indicated to the text, as in Eustachio Celebrino's anti-syphilis booklet *This Is the Way to Cure the French Disease* (Figure 5).[26] The commercial possibilities of titles were discussed in a 1542 preface letter in which the printer of the work distanced himself from others in his trade who by these means enticed readers to buy old or poor-quality works: 'It is enough for them with the title alone to spur an appetite to buy, when they have some young rascal go through the streets and piazzas crying "New work newly printed! Gentlemen, buy this lovely new story!"'[27] The verbal and visual proclamation of a work as novel, useful, funny, beautiful, horrifying or pious was intended to lure potential buyers, as printers pioneered the art of printed advertisement and experimented with sensationalism. Moreover, the very fact that the majority of such editions were in the vernacular and that they were short, simple texts, often in verse, immediately communicated their accessibility to a much larger public than those who could approach large works of densely printed Latin prose, for example.[28]

It is imperative to imagine these small and often very humble-looking items within an original context that must have been very much richer and multisensory. Works in verse in particular would have been performed both by professionals and amateurs, to a popular tune, although we can almost never recover the refrains because the music was not printed alongside the words.[29] They might have been recited with vigorous gestures and exaggerated expressions, sometimes by performers in evocative costumes. They were as likely to have been sold and consumed within public and communal contexts, in the piazza, tavern or workshop, as to be found in restricted spaces like the bookshop or study. If the materiality of manuscript communication in the period evoked a sense of intimacy, of belonging to a select in-group and 'of close communication between the like-minded',[30] many of these texts were more likely to spur a sense of community with the crowd, with the potentially very large public of readers and listeners, both in Venice and beyond. Many were tied to specific

3 Lament for a dead performer: *Lamento d'Hyppolito detto il Ferrarese che cantaua in bancha*

Frottole nuoue de Lazaro da Cruzola. Con vna Barzelletta, & alcune Stanze ala Schiauonesca & due Barzellette alla Bergamascha. Cosa da Ridere.

A Scolta questa cantera
de Lazaro da Curzola
che ha fatto questa struzzola
per vogia che gauanzera.
Non bisogna sindunia
chi n'ha dinar da spendere
non mi dara 'dintendere
nisciun con tromba o piferi
Bisogna hauer di spiteri
chi vol viuer contenti

4 A pamphlet evoking performance: *Frottole nuoue di Lazaro da Cruzola*

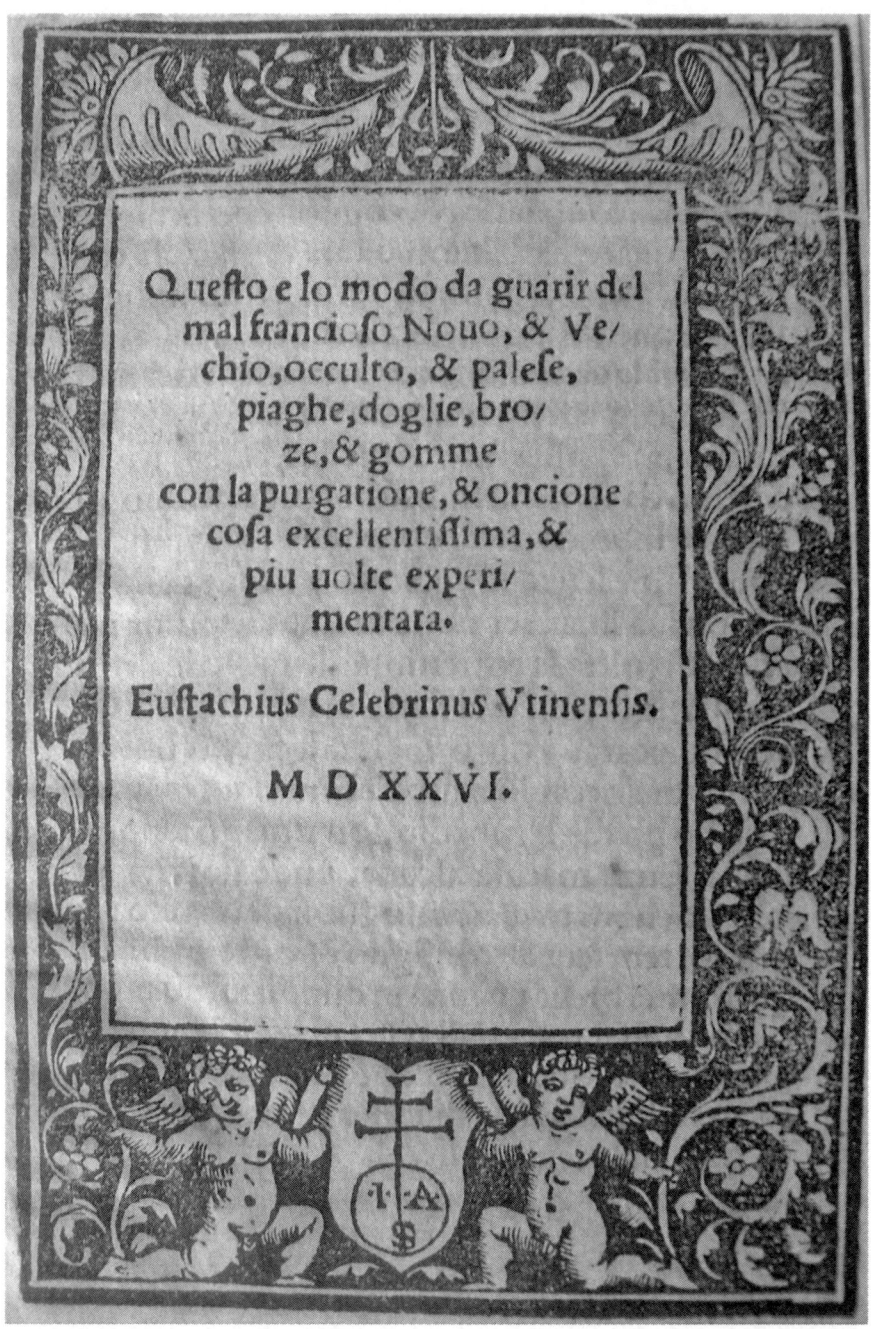

5 An attention-grabbing title: Celebrino, *Questo e lo modo da guarir del mal francioso novo, & vechio ...*

moments and contexts, and designed for obsolescence, to be used and discarded. At the same time, they could be employed in intimate and personal ways, for example the printed poems, orations and images that were folded into amulets, carried in a pocket or on the body. Just because these works were cheap and widely available did not mean that they were not valued by those who bought them.[31]

So, at least until the seventeenth century, when publishers like the Remondini began to produce more uniform series of cheap *libri da risma* – booklets transmitted to pedlars in sheet form, by weight, and priced by the ream of 500 unbound sheets – cheap print was a category with blurred edges, its cultural associations not clearly fixed.[32] Nevertheless, from quite early in the sixteenth century we can see emerging a category of print at the bottom end of the market which was becoming more or less clearly separated in people's minds from 'proper' books, characterised by low material value and quality. In 1537, for example, the Venetian Senate passed a law attempting to counter slipping standards in the printing trade. Threatening to fine those printers who did not use good-quality paper for their works, the Senate exempted 'small things that are sold up to the sum of ten *soldi* each'.[33] As we have seen, this would have included almost the entire category of works I call cheap print: the smallest editions at the lower end of the market which were expected to be produced quickly and cheaply.

Although this printed form hosted a diverse range of texts and was consumed by a heterogeneous public, increasingly it was associated with inferior social status and low intellectual and material worth, with cultural as well as physical ephemerality. For some critics, cheap print was troubling because it seemed closer to the essence of a pure commodity than to the hallowed and almost sacred nature of a book. This was expressed by the fact that commonly it was sold in open, public spaces by poor, even indigent individuals, alongside other kinds of small ephemeral luxuries such as ribbons, soap or perfumes. Because of this, its ultimate worth, and its presence and impact in urban life, were a matter of hot dispute.

A gift from God or the work of the devil?

In *The Printing Press as an Agent of Change*, Eisenstein argued that, 'whether the new art was considered a blessing or a curse; whether it was consigned to the Devil or attributed to God; the fact remains, that the initial increase in output did strike contemporary observers as sufficiently remarkable to suggest supernatural intervention'.[34] And, indeed, the benefits and dangers of the press were a subject of heated debate from the earliest days of printing in Italy. Despite many continuities in both the texts printed and the physical characteristics of early printed books, the speed of the press to mass-produce literature and lower prices, disseminating texts throughout society, provoked extreme reactions from various cultural commentators. From the late fifteenth and throughout the sixteenth century, a number of prominent social commentators, particularly humanists and popular writers, expressed a fear of print's uncontrollable disseminative ability and thus its potential to break down the social, political, cultural and religious boundaries which organised Venetian and Italian society. Others, particularly those who worked closely with the presses, rather rejoiced, for more or less the same reasons (and the press itself gave them the means to record and disseminate their opinions). Often these fears and hopes crystallised around cheap print, its producers, distributors and consumers, as the ultimate expressions of the capacity of the medium for mass production. Furthermore, cheap print represented a class of commodity with fewer precedents, a more distinct novelty.[35] It is difficult to know to what degree ordinary individuals shared these views. Many simply must have enjoyed the new range of printed products available to them, others not been interested at all. But these views are significant, because they were heard and sometimes shared by those in positions of power who would ultimately decide how to react to the spread of printing.

Many of the most vocal commentators on the impact of printing in Italy lived in Venice, or spent some time working there. This is not surprising, since the growth of the Venetian printing industry was so explosive; foreign printers and publishers poured into the city to try their luck, and new print and bookshops sprouted rapidly in the central urban areas. There were a few voices of outspoken opposition to this development. Already in the early 1470s, a Dominican scribe named Fra Filippo de Strata passionately urged the Venetians to regulate the foreign printers (mostly Germans at this point), whom he described as 'utterly uncouth types of people', drunken and greedy for profit.[36] The Venetian government initially granted an exclusive privilege over the new art of printing to the German John of Speyer, but after John's death in 1470 the monopoly was allowed to lapse and the industry permitted to grow with little restraint. De Strata, writing to the doge, also raised other concerns that would echo throughout the following century, about the degradation of moral and scholarly standards as a result of the press. He complained that the presses were flooding the city with books, exposing young and tender minds to works of an inappropriate nature and letting all and sundry think themselves learned.[37] 'Writing [argued de Strata] ... should be respected and held to be nobler than all goods, unless she has suffered degradation in the brothel of the printing presses. She is a maiden with a pen, a harlot in print.'[38] De Strata's feeling that print commercialised and thus corrupted the book tapped into a long tradition of thinking about books as rare, precious repositories of knowledge, to be exchanged as gifts, not within the framework of the market, and continued to be shared.[39]

As printing boomed to unprecedented levels in the sixteenth century, especially the production of cheaper books in the vernacular, the discussion continued unabated. Many of those who wrote on this topic were involved with the printing industry directly, particularly writers who published their works and/or edited or corrected the editions of others. While some praised the benefits of printing wholeheartedly, many betrayed a conflicted ambivalence towards the new technology, which offered them new possibilities for publicising their works and making a living less dependent on patronage, at the same time as it commercialised the production of literature and fundamentally restructured the world of books and learning.

Three main areas of concern are evident in the critical or satirical remarks expressed throughout the late fifteenth and sixteenth centuries about the proliferation of print and printers, all interrelated. The first regards the status and motivations of printers, as men with control over the dissemination of literature but often with little education and few scholarly ideals. The second concerns the uncontrolled proliferation and thus commercialisation of texts inherent in the expansion of printing. A final concern was for the way in which these other developments were allowing new writers and new readers into the literary sphere, undermining traditional distinctions between the learned and unlearned. All of these anxieties are inflected with notions of class, of the right and proper ordering of society and culture, and the pressure that print was placing on it. An escalating sense of instability and disruption is apparent in the views of many commentators, reaching a crescendo around the middle of the sixteenth century at the same time as civic and religious authorities began to institute mechanisms aiming to bring the press under control.

The northern humanist Erasmus is considered one of the first authors to have taken full advantage of the promotional possibilities of print to further his career, however he is also exemplary of the ambivalence of many writers towards the press in this period.[40] When Erasmus published an edition of his *Adages* in Venice in 1508, he used the occasion to lavish praise on his Venetian printer, Aldo Manuzio, whose reputation had attracted him to Italy. Aldo's famous trademark of the dolphin and anchor, stamped on his books and probably hanging above the door of his shop in the parish of San Paternian, 'is now [wrote Erasmus] not only famous but beloved wherever Good Letters are known or cherished'. Aldo was accorded the highest praise for his commitment to publishing the classics of Greek and Roman literature, thereby making them easily available to scholars everywhere. 'This man seems born to restore [classical learning], and shaped for that destiny by the Fates themselves; all his desires are turned to one thing, all his tireless efforts are spent on it, no labour is too great, if only literature in all its glory may be restored pure and unsullied to honest minds.'[41] When Erasmus updated his work in 1525, however, he felt moved to insert some extra comments into this section. Aldo had died in 1515, Venetian printed books were snapped up everywhere because of the fame of the Aldine press, and yet 'rascally printers' were abusing this reputation by printing shamelessly inaccurate works. 'The law sees to it that no one may make shoes or boxes without the approbation of the masters' guild', Erasmus complained, and yet the greatest authors

> are handed out to the public by people so illiterate that they cannot even read, or so lazy that they don't trouble to go over what has been printed, or so mean that they

would rather let a good book get choked up with six thousand mistakes than spend a few coins on paying someone to supervise the proof-reading … Not everyone may have leave to be a baker, but printing is a trade open to any mortal man.[42]

This variety of criticism was recurrent. The printer held in his hands the keys to literature and learning but often had no particular training or vocation for the task. As Erasmus said, in Venice it was easier to become a printer than a baker, and he was right, for there would be no printers' guild until the second half of the sixteenth century.[43] A printer like Manuzio managed to rise above the fray and attain unrivalled authority and prestige because of his elite intellectual pedigree, eminent patrons and clearly articulated scholarly ideals. Most printers could not claim these attributes, nor did they necessarily want to. Such qualities were not essential for someone who, for example, simply aimed to make a living producing popular, vernacular works for a wider market. However, it is still notable that comments such as those of Erasmus were inflected with strong connotations of class and social distinction.

As the century progressed, this critique was fed by a growing snobbery towards the 'mechanical' arts, as Venetian and Italian culture in general took on a more aristocratic stripe.[44] One of the characters in Anton Francesco Doni's dialogue on printing (1552–53) described the trade as a 'mechanical, sordid activity', a 'job for commoners', compared to the more honourable scribal arts.[45] As Doni worked for a time as a printer himself, and collaborated continuously with the presses in Venice, this probably did not reflect his own opinion, however the dialogue form allowed him to air the sorts of views in circulation at the time. Tomaso Garzoni, the Lateran canon and writer who described the spectrum of urban professions in his *Piazza universale di tutte le professioni del mondo* (first published in Venice in 1585) voiced particular praise for bookselling precisely because it was not a mechanical art: 'it is not at all dirty in itself, but clean and polite'.[46]

Criticism of printers focused not only on their lack of education and training. The printer became the scapegoat for many authors disturbed by an inevitable consequence of printing with movable type: the commercialisation of textual transactions. Laudable printers were those, like Manuzio, who were (or claimed to be) concerned only to benefit the cause of 'Good Letters'. Less praiseworthy were the many who entered the industry to make a profit, so that they might, as Erasmus implied, just as well be producing loaves of bread as books. This distinction was evident in Erasmus's satirical representation of Aldo's business partner, the printer Andrea Torresani d'Asola, in the colloquy *Opulentia sordida*. Torresani was presented in the guise of Antronius, a 'Mr Moneybags' who was cheap, mean and cared only for making money. 'That's the way it is with people who go from rags to riches', remarked the character standing in for Erasmus in the colloquy.[47] The critique of printers thus evoked the distinction between the sacrality of the book as a cultural entity and the mass-produced printed product, harder to distinguish from any other commercial commodity.

It was not only scholars who bemoaned printers' single-minded pursuit of profit, and the concern that their greed led inevitably to the lowering of standards of quality, and the deception of customers with inferior or faulty copies of works. A popular poem printed in Venice in the 1520s warned its readers and listeners about a long list of urban professions, including printers and booksellers, who found devious ways to dupe unwary customers out of their money.[48] 'I am not speaking about all of them, worthy listener', the author wrote, 'but of those who employ great deceit', such as selling books with missing or incorrect pages. 'And never trust their words', he urged, 'because their habit is to talk up their wares'.[49] According to a speaker in Doni's dialogue about printing, 'many printers lay honesty aside for lucre, so indifferent and error-ridden is their printing, so poor their choice of paper and the type that is chipped, rammed in and forced to fit'.[50] Even Garzoni, who was a great advocate of the press, noted that booksellers could be unscrupulous salesmen, prone to overcharge and to 'sell to peasants and rustics with their sales prattle some foolish thing they have in their shop, and … [to] talk up a piece of nonsense composed by a shoemaker more than some good and useful work written by a gentleman'. Printers, meanwhile, could be very careless with corrections, devoting their attention to useless trifles while neglecting worthy works.[51]

Printers but also others involved in the production, dissemination and consumption of print (including hack writers, booksellers and ordinary readers) were blamed for what many sixteenth-century commentators saw as a glut of printed matter, a vertiginous increase in the quantity of texts but not in their quality. Erasmus, for example, showed great concern for the bewildering proliferation of print issuing uncontrolled from the presses, the 'swarms of new books … rubbish written by all and sundry'.[52] Characters in Doni's dialogue about printing echoed this feeling of information overload. One character remarked that 'there's such an abundance of stuff to read about our feet, we find ourselves climbing a rubbish heap', also likening the situation to confronting a table laden with a bounty of food that turned out to be mostly inedible.[53] Writers with unjustified pretensions were partly to blame for this; the character of Coccio, for instance, complained that 'every last pedant seems bent on bringing out half-baked legends of dubious origin filched from a thousand other tall tales' in a two-sheet pamphlet, then considering himself a rival to great writers such as Bembo and Ariosto.[54] But new types of readers also contributed to the problem, according to Giuliano de' Ricci, who complained that 'the good authors are no longer valued since the ignorant pleb goes more for those books which deal with lascivious things than those which deal with continence and sobriety'. As a result of this consumer demand, he suggested, 'the world is filled with despicable and licentious books'.[55]

Two cultural systems were rubbing up against each other, causing friction and heat: the more exclusive system of literary circulation among small groups of elites and scholars, which favoured the language of patronage, friendship and gift-giving, and the newer commercial culture of the press. In practice many writers signed up to the new creed while continuing to proclaim the old in their public presentations of themselves, particularly in dedication letters and prefaces. Pietro Aretino exemplified this shifting terrain. Coming to Venice after the sack of Rome and rapidly embedding himself at the centre of the city's booming printing trade, the writer and son of a cobbler recognised the self-promotional possibilities of the press like few before him. Despite his lowly origins and little formal education, Aretino was the first writer to publish his own letters in the vernacular, proclaiming the power of his printed words of praise or censure to make him the 'scourge of princes'. Yet he also carried on more traditional practices, using print to win the patronage of princes and noblemen.[56] However, Aretino reserved his criticism for the figure of the writer rather than the printer. In a letter to his printer Marcolini, he declared himself repelled by what he perceived to be the cold commercialisation of creativity entailed in the mass production and sale of books, pronouncing that a writer 'who goes to the [book]shop in the evening to collect the money from the day's sales smacks of the pimp who empties his woman's purse before he goes to bed. Please God, I wish that the favours of our princes and not the poverty of those who buy them will pay me for my trouble in writing.'[57] In Aretino's words, some common cultural associations emerge, stretching back at least to De Strata. Print was connected with the public spaces of the street or marketplace, with the common, cheap and sordid. In implied opposition to this were more exclusive forms of communication (such as the manuscript) in more exclusive spaces (such as the academy or elite literary circle), where texts might circulate as gifts among the elite and educated.

In a similar vein, ambulant pedlars (sometimes also performers) of print, those who disseminated the cheapest forms of print to the widest audience in open public sites, at times could be portrayed as embodiments of the most crassly commercialistic effects of printing. In another poem by the scribe De Strata, a seller with a basketload of books offered them all 'for three or two *grossetti*, / As if he wanted to sell me a sack of cats'.[58] The hack writer Giovan Battista Dragoncino tried to ennoble some of his poems by claiming that he had them printed, 'not to lay them out venally on the piazzas on some bench or another, as I have done with many other of my little works in the past', but so that they could be shared among the exclusive friendship circle of the dedicatee.[59] In Franco's 1539 dialogue about bookselling, the character Sannio stands on a bench, crying out his wares, which are also written out on a large board (*cartone*). With the characteristic hyperbole of the charlatan, he calls out to customers to 'come to me if you want to make something of yourself. I, I, I, and no one else, possess the true art of making any man a Solomon ... [Come to me] whoever wants to learn letters without having to learn from pedants'.[60] After seven fruitless hours on his bench, Sannio complains to his friend Cautano, he has sold nothing, and starts to knock down the price of his wares. From offering a work that will make buyers into 'a Pope, or a Bishop, or a Cardinal' for ten *scudi*, he eventually drops down to peddling 'a good poet for half a *soldo*'.[61] What has the world come to, he asks Cautano

> that today … for the price of a salad you cannot sell off Poetry? If I were a charmer selling pills and roots, or a charlatan who shows off asps and snakes, you can be sure that right now I would not be wanting for business. But … today the avarice of the world is such, that one appreciates a *quattrino* more than to learn a thousand pieces of wisdom.[62]

Literature was being taken out onto the streets and hawked alongside ordinary products like food; the secrets of the arts and sciences, of elite manners and customs, sold at rock-bottom prices to all and sundry. Street sellers and performers were depicted as emblematic figures of an age when everything seemed to be up for sale. They were often poor and uneducated; they jostled for space and vied for attention with the rest of the rabble in the squares; they were seen to reduce the printed text to just one more item for sale in the marketplace. Moreover, they sold publicly that which had once been mainly the reserve of the educated and the wealthy.

The social snobbery often applied to printers and pedlars was present too when some writers surveyed the entry of new readers into the circle of literate communication as a result of print. Richardson writes of how, in the sixteenth century, 'the frontiers of the world of letters were now being pushed back to include parts of the population to whom *letterati* had previously been able to feel superior: access to the ideas of others and the ability to diffuse one's own ideas were, in other words, no longer reserved for an elite'.[63] Many writers commented with ambivalence, or outright disapproval, that the abundance of cheap print in the vernacular was admitting many new groups into the circle of readers. Doni's character Coccio argued that

> Many people of low extraction who, once upon a time and to the greater advantage of the world, would have devoted their efforts to mechanical crafts in keeping with their abilities, are now lured by how easy it is to study and have begun to take up reading … The dignity and good reputation of literature have been belittled and the rewards too have dwindled, given the ease and paltry effort required to become a man of learning nowadays.[64]

Similarly, one of Franco's characters lamented the decline of letters and of *letterati*, while 'manual labourers, and artisans … triumph in this world'.[65] Ricci sneered that 'any *ciabattino* [shoemaker], as long as he knows how to read', might put his 'filthy hands' on a copy of the great authors, now translated into the vernacular, while 'every vile little merchant wants to debate the highest secrets of philosophy'.[66]

However, this negative point of view was not the only one expressed in the period. For many of those who made a living in the various branches of the printing industry, the desire to open up print to an ever wider market of consumers made good commercial sense, even if they had some reservations about the cultural consequences. As Franco's Sannio suggested in the 1540s, a successful bookseller needed to keep his shop stocked with all kinds of little works (*operine*) translated into the vernacular, 'because the manual labourers, who are not lettered [i.e. do not know Greek and Latin], in order to learn *De agibilibus mundi*, will want Pliny. The soldiers, who do not understand Latin, will want the wars of Appian with the Commentaries of Caesar.'[67] It was in the bookseller's interests to cater to these new consumers, to *far concorso col popolazzo* (do business with the plebs), since 'the swarms of the vulgar are greater than the academies of the learned'.[68] Similarly tongue-in-cheek, Anton Francesco Doni wrote in his satirical preface to the illiterate in his *Seconda Libraria* of 1551 of how it was the unenviable task of he and his fellow *poligrafi* to produce all kinds of writings, 'every quality of meat' for readers to devour. Works had to be published that might please 'Lords, gentlemen, ladies, workers, peasants and porters ... because every sort of person reads'. Writers like Doni must be able to speak to the masses; like preachers, they were 'listened to by all of the trades, and our scribblings read by all of the professions'.[69]

Others celebrated, more wholeheartedly than Doni, this capacity of the press to break the monopoly on learning and initiate new readers and writers. One vocal advocate was the Bolognese charlatan and writer Leonardo Fioravanti who was attracted to Venice partly by the possibilities of the printing industry. As he wrote in his paean to the art of printing:

> since this blessed press appeared, the majority of people, women as well as men, know how to read; and what is more important is that philosophy and medicine, and all the other branches of knowledge, are abridged and printed in this our mother tongue, in such a way that every one can know his part of it ... I see that the majority, even including women, speak about philosophy, medicine, astrology, mathematics and about as many sciences as there are in the world without being doctors; and so no one can be deceived any more, since every one who wants to work his brain a little can be learned, and the cause of this has been the press.[70]

In the past, the *povera plebe* had been beguiled by the complicated speeches of the learned. Now, Fioravanti wrote, 'the kittens have opened their eyes, so that everyone can see and understand of his own accord, so that we the doctors can no longer deceive the people' as before.[71] Fioravanti was echoed by Tomaso Garzoni, who believed that the press had 'opened the eyes of the blind, and brought light to the ignorant', who could no longer be deceived.[72]

As the comments of writers like Franco and Fioravanti suggest, it was not printing alone that was perceived to be an agent of change, but the press in concert with the move to translate works into the vernacular 'mother tongue' and to publish abridgements and shorter, easier texts. These changes were celebrated from early on in the history of printing, particularly by the first writers and printers to champion the use of the vernacular. The Ferrarese printer, publisher and performer Niccolò Zoppino who based his business in Venice in the early decades of the sixteenth century used the prefaces of his works to trumpet his plan to publish numerous vernacular translations in order to cater to the great numbers of readers who could not read Latin or Greek. For example, Zoppino's letter to the reader of the 1524 edition of the Roman historian Justin celebrated the many recent translations from Latin, 'so that both the learned and the unlearned might have perfect knowledge' of the ancient histories.[73] In the same years, other printers and hack writers incorporated similar ideas into their advertising rhetoric in titles and other paratexts that addressed readers directly. For instance, the anonymous translator of the *Vernacular Herbal* (1522) praised the public-spiritedness of the printer Alessandro Bindoni who commissioned the work and wrote of his own motivation: to help the 'many needy ... and especially the poor' by translating this work 'so that those who do not possess the Latin language might understand the secrets of nature for themselves'.[74] 'Moved by charity', the hack writer Eustachio Celebrino claimed that he had published an account of his own experience of syphilis and his own cure in order to benefit 'the health of the infinite poor infected with the French disease who, not having the way, or the capacity, to pay for doctors and medicine, can by themselves and at little expense in a short time free themselves from such a disease and inflagration'.[75]

Many publications explicitly spoke to classes of readers who previously had little access to books. Giovan Antonio Tagliente's brief writing manual (1525) promised to instruct 'both the masculine sex and the feminine, both gentle spirits and rough ones' to write beautifully.[76] Zoppino addressed some of his books specifically to female readers and advertised one embroidery handbook as a means for lowly born women to better themselves and their prospects by mastering the skills taught in the book.[77] Countless other cheap works in the vernacular advertised themselves as keys to discrete bodies of practical or arcane knowledge that previously had been more restricted and secret.[78] Celebrino alone published pamphlets instructing how to lay a dinner table, write love letters, learn the *mercantesca* handwriting style, concoct various cosmetics that would 'make any woman beautiful', cure syphilis and preserve one's health in a time of plague.[79] It was clearly in the interests of printers and writers working at the lower end of the market to celebrate the proliferation of cheap print and of texts, particularly vernacular texts, that could reach many different readers. These individuals had less need to bother with social and intellectual prejudices and more to gain from turning their attention to new constituencies of readers and consumers.

In the case of Zoppino and others, this advocacy of the press was linked to a strong belief in the social benefits of spreading writings in the vernacular, particularly religious works.[80] Indeed, from early on in the history of printing, some prominent figures rejoiced in its capacities to open up religious teaching to many more people. The Ferrarese preacher Girolamo Savonarola had been one of the earliest religious reformers to make extensive use of the press and he frequently celebrated how his many translations into the vernacular would make his teachings accessible to the 'unlettered faithful' (*fideli illiterati*).[81] 'So that ordinary people (*il vulgo*) might taste these fruits / they have been translated from Latin into the vernacular', was the more humble claim of Fra Giovanni da Firenze in his edition of penitential psalms in octave verses published in Venice around 1490.[82] Similarly, the cleric and writer Giuliano Dati wrote in his *Story of Saint Job* that he had translated the work into vernacular verse voluntarily in the hope that someone 'will be able to own this work / who cannot have the great Bible at home'.[83] Several decades later, when such notions were becoming more explicitly controversial, the *poligrafo* Antonio Brucioli still reiterated the conviction, in the dedication to his vernacular translation of the New Testament, that the word of God should be heard (and, indeed, read) by 'the beggar, the smith, the peasant, the mason, the fisherman, the publicans, and all the conditions of men, and of women'.[84]

While many readers embraced this idea, nonetheless such statements would help to crystallise a belief that something had to be done to stem the uncontrolled spread of print. Particularly in the 1530s and 1540s, many prominent churchmen expressed their concern that the new availability of religious works in the vernacular was encouraging the uneducated to sing Bible stories and debate religious ideas freely 'on every street corner'.[85] More generally, a number of writers around this time suggested the need for some restraint to be extended over the press, to filter more carefully the quality and content of works. The opinions voiced in works from the middle decades of the century suggest that such calls were reaching a climax at this time and reinforcing the drive to implement a more effective system of censorship. The character Lollio in Doni's *Dialogue* frowned particularly upon the writers who shared their 'heretical views' in print, while Coccio chimed in to bemoan the appearance of 'so much foul rubbish in print that speaks ill of Christ, of the Pope, of the Church'. Henceforth, there should be a 'universal law that would state that not every worthless little book is allowed to go to the press'.[86] Lodovico Domenichi, in his 1562 dialogue on printing, which closely followed Doni's, expanded on the shameful availability of 'dishonest texts' like the *Priapea* of Niccolò Franco, the text which may have been responsible for Francesco Faentino's arrest described in the Introduction. Such works were laid out in bookstalls, read and openly discussed in cities like Venice, 'giving a very bad and damaging example to those simple people who waste their time reading them'.[87] In tune with the change of attitude around the middle of the century, Ricci proclaimed that secular rulers as well as churchmen should prohibit translations from Greek into Latin or from Latin into the vernacular.[88] Thus, all of the hallmarks of the new print market – cheapness, abundance, vernacular translation, open and easy sales on the streets – were the subject of criticism in this period.

As will be discussed in Chapter 5, it was in these middle decades of the century that secular and religious authorities began to make more serious efforts to bring the printing industry under control, part of a wider climate of increasing social discipline. Indeed, many of the writers cited above, who had registered their alarm as well as their exhilaration as they witnessed the expansion of the print market, were among those whose works would fall prey to the censors, sometimes with very serious consequences for themselves. For example, Doni's works were condemned to be expurgated in 1593, the same year that Niccolò Franco's entire works were banned. Franco himself had been tried and hanged for writing anti-papal libels in 1570.[89]

As we have seen, there was incessant debate about the merits of the press in Venice continuing from the 1470s throughout the sixteenth century and beyond. Ultimately, most of the commentators accepted that the press was there to stay, and that it brought benefits to Italian society as well as potential dangers. But many shared the belief that some sort of control was needed; if not outright censorship, then a way to distinguish the worthy publications from the rest. In parallel with the promulgation of the Indices of Prohibited Books in the second half of the sixteenth century, a broader cultural movement, both satirical and serious, attempted to catalogue and categorise the enormous quantity of books on the market; to distinguish good, canonical literature from rubbish for the masses. Examples of this trend range from Anton Francesco Doni's first and second *Libraria* (1550 and 1551) – respectively, a catalogue of vernacular books in print and a satirical list of fake vernacular titles – to the playful *Convito universale* (1592) of the Bolognese singer Giulio Cesare Croce in which contemporary classics like Castiglione's *Book of the Courtier* and Ariosto's *Satires* 'dined' alongside canonical Greek and Roman texts (Homer, Virgil, Plutarch *et al.*) at a banquet of books, waited upon by characters from 'second class' popular titles.[90]

However exaggerated some of the views expressed in the period may have been, collectively they register the perception of a pervasive cultural shift taking place in sixteenth-century Italy, particularly in Venice, with the appearance of so many new texts, readers and writers. The explosion detonated in the late fifteenth century continued to resonate into the sixteenth and many commentators recognised that, for good or ill, it could have profound long-term consequences, not only in cultural terms but also for society, politics and religion. As we will see, their hopes and fears were not to be entirely realised, but first we must descend from the perspective of writers and other cultural commentators to examine what changes could be seen, felt and heard on the street.

Notes

1 'Ogni carta scritta, ogni scartaffo merdoso, et ogni cosaccia data a le stampe tu chiami libro?' N. Franco, *Dialogo del venditore di libri* (1539–93) (Venice: Marsilio, 2005), p. 36. This dialogue was published in Franco's *Dialogi piacevoli* … (Venice: G. Giolito, 1539).

2 L. Baldacchini, 'I centri di produzione del libro nell'Italia del Cinquecento', in M. Guerrini (ed.), *Il linguaggio della biblioteca. Scritti in onore di Diego Maltese* (Milan: Editrice Bibliografica, 1996), pp. 501–2.

3 On Franco, see C. Di Filippo Bareggi, *Il mestiere dello scrivere. Lavoro intellettuale e mercato librario a Venezia nel Cinquecento* (Rome: Bulzoni, 1988); P. F. Grendler, *Critics of the Italian World, 1530–1560: Anton Francesco Doni, Nicolò Franco and*

Ortensio Lando (Madison, MI and London: University of Wisconsin Press, 1969). These books are also essential reading on the wider group of the *poligrafi*.

4 On these debates, see also N. Bonazzi, *Il carnevale delle idee: l'antipedanteria nell'età della stampa, Venezia, 1538–1553* (Bologna: Gedit, 2007).

5 'Quelle veramente che vendeno de tal libri et opere pronostici, hystorie, canzone, lettere, et altre simel cose sul Ponte de Rialto et in altri loci de questa cità' (ASV, *CX*, Parte comuni, f. 32, fasc. 234).

6 See Watt, *Cheap Print*, p. 1.

7 The term 'pamphlet' could suggest a topical work by the late sixteenth century, but I use it here in a more neutral bibliographical sense to indicate a short, unbound book. See J. Raymond, *Pamphlets and Pamphleteering in Early Modern Britain* (Cambridge: Cambridge University Press, 2003), p. 8; Watt, *Cheap Print*, p. 264. I also consider examples of 'free print', such as printed laws and advertisements, because they were also widely available and accessible.

8 Grendler, *Roman Inquisition*, p. 14.

9 Lowry, *Nicholas Jenson*, p. 191. On the publication of literacy aids, see P. Lucchi, 'La Santacroce, il Salterio e il Babuino. Libri per imparare a leggere nel primo secolo della stampa', *Quaderni storici*, 38 (1978), 593–630.

10 *DMS*, vol. 9, col. 335 (22 November 1509). One *bezzo* was also the advertised price of a two-sheet quarto pamphlet *Esortazione all'imperator Massimiliano* printed in Rome in these years, however it was bought by Hernan Colòn for only half a *quattrino*; see K. Wagner and M. Carrera, *Catalogo dei libri a stampa in lingua italiana della Biblioteca Colombina di Siviglia/Catalogo de los impresos en lengua italiana de la Biblioteca Colombina de Sevilla* (Ferrara: Panini, 1991), p. 135, n. 226.

11 Cited in the Introduction, n. 28.

12 *Questi sonetti scrissi con sua mano in proposito de ciaschum [sic] amatore il nobil miser Leonardo Iustiniano* makes reference to its price of one *marchetto*, equal to one *soldo*. Listed in M. Zorzi (ed.), *La vita nei libri. Edizioni illustrate a stampa del Quattro e Cinquecento dalla Fondazione Giorgio Cini* (Venice: Edizioni della Laguna, 2003), p. 244. The pamphlet oration for one *soldo* is mentioned in *DMS*, vol. 7, col. 132 (16 August 1507).

13 Colòn first visited Italy in 1512 and acquired dozens of small printed pamphlets of songs, stories, religious orations and many other subjects, many of them printed in Venice, commonly paying between one and two *quattrini* for a four-leaf quarto. He helpfully annotated many of his texts with the price, date and place of purchase. See Wagner and Carrera, *Catalogo dei libri*.

14 P. Pavanini, 'Abitazioni popolari e borghesi nella Venezia cinquecentesca', *Studi veneziani*, 5 (1981), 71; R. C. Davis, *Shipbuilders of the Venetian Arsenal: Workers and Workplace in the Preindustrial City* (Baltimore, MD: Johns Hopkins University Press, 1991), p. 103.

15 M. Sanudo, 'Praise of the city of Venice', in D. Chambers and B. Pullan (eds), *Venice: A Documentary History: 1450–1630* (Oxford: Blackwell, 1992), p. 13.

16 D. Romano, 'The gondola as a marker of station in Venetian society', *Renaissance Studies*, 8:4 (1994), 361.

17 On the compositor's wage, see Lowry, *Nicholas Jenson*, p. 186; on the shop assistant's (1567), Mackenney, *Tradesmen and Traders*, p. 95. These wages are comparable with those of a worker in the building industry who earned around twenty *soldi* a day or a

master builder earning around thirty *soldi* (in 1551–65): B. Pullan, 'Wage-earners and the Venetian economy, 1550–1630', *Economic History Review*, 16:3 (1964), 415.

18 G. Padoan, 'La commedia rinascimentale a Venezia dalla sperimentazione umanistica alla commedia "regolare"', in G. Arnaldi and M. Pastore Stocchi (eds), *Storia della cultura veneta* (Vicenza: Neri Pozza, 1981), p. 399.

19 By the time of the Interdict crisis of 1606–07, small polemical pamphlets were selling for around four *soldi* each, which De Vivo concludes brought them within reach of 'a great many readers indeed' (*Information and Communication*, pp. 226–7).

20 Print runs could vary greatly, from a couple of hundred to many thousands for some indulgences, for example. L. Baldacchini, 'I centri di produzione', pp. 503–4, suggested an estimate of 1,000 copies for Italian sixteenth-century books and ephemera, while N. Cannata, *Il canzoniere a stampa (1470–1530). Tradizione e fortuna di un genere fra storia del libro e letteratura* (Rome: Bagatto, 2000), p. 9, suggested *c*.850 copies on average for small books of verse. Pedlars commissioned runs of 500 to 1,000 pamphlets and broadsides from the Ripoli press in Florence (discussed in Chapter 3) in the 1480s; see M. Conway, *The Diario of the Printing Press of San Jacopo di Ripoli, 1476–1484: Commentary and Transcription* (Florence: Olschki, 1999).

21 On the use of images that did not illustrate the text, see M. Rothstein, 'Disjunctive images in Renaissance books', *Renaissance and Reformation*, 14:2 (1990), 101–20. For a sensitive analysis of the interaction of texts and images in early cheap print, see Petrella, *Fra testo e immagine*.

22 Carnelos, *I libri da risma*, p. 13; M. I. Palazzolo, 'Banchi, botteghe, muricciuoli. Luoghi e figure del commercio del libro a Roma nel settecento', in *Editoria e istituzioni a Roma tra settecento e ottocento. Saggi e documenti* (Rome: Archivio Guido Izzi, 1994), p. 10.

23 P. F. Grendler, 'Form and function in Italian Renaissance popular books', *Renaissance Quarterly*, 46:3 (1993), 476–8.

24 Niccoli, 'Italy', p. 189.

25 See Chapter 3 for these examples, and on the relationship between cheap print and performance. See also the portrait of the buffoon Zuan Polo from his *Libero del Rado Stixoso* (1533) reproduced in R. Henke, *Performance and Literature in the Commedia dell'arte* (Cambridge: Cambridge University Press, 2002), p. 53.

26 E. Celebrino, *Questo e lo modo da guarir del mal francioso novo, & vechio, occulto, & palese, piaghe, doglie, broze, & gomme con la purgatione, & oncione cosa excellentissima, & piu volte experimentata...* (Venice: G. A. Niccolini da Sabbio, 1526), BGC 998. Niccoli, 'Italy', p. 190.

27 'Basta loro col titolo solo movervi l'appetito al comprarla, quando da qualche forfantello fanno per le vie et per le piazze gridare, "Opera nova novamente stampata! Compratela, gentilhomini, questa bella legenda nova!"' (G. Landi, *Formaggiata*, cited in L. Severi, *Sitibondo nel stampar de' libri: Niccolò Zoppino tra libro volgare, letteratura cortigiana e questione della lingua* (Manziana: Vecchiarelli, 2009), pp. 42–3).

28 Niccoli, 'Italy', p. 190.

29 On the performance of works to familiar tunes, see B. Wilson, *Singing Poetry in Renaissance Florence: The* Cantasi come *Tradition (1375–1550)* (Florence: Olschki, 2009), p. 9; C. Marsh, 'The sound of print in early modern England: the broadside ballad as song', in J. Crick and A. Walsham (eds), *The Uses of Script and Print, 1300–1700* (Cambridge: Cambridge University Press, 2004), pp. 171–90.

30 B. Richardson, 'Print or pen? Modes of written publication in sixteenth-century Italy', *Italian Studies*, 59 (2004), 43.
31 On the intimate use of printed ephemera, see E. Barbieri, 'Per il *Vangelo di S. Giovanni* e qualche altra edizione di S. Jacopo a Ripoli', *Italia medioevale et umanistica*, 43 (2002), 384–5; Areford, *The Viewer and the Printed Image*.
32 Carnelos, *I libri da risma*. On the blurred edges of this category, see Braida, 'Gli studi italiani sui "libri per tutti"', pp. 331–2.
33 'Non si comprehendono però sotto el presente ordine le cose minute, che si vendessero fino alla summa de soldi 10 l'una' (ASV, *ST*, r. 29, cc. 129^v–130^r (4 June 1537)).
34 Eisenstein, *Printing Press*, vol. 1, p. 50. See also her recent *Divine Art, Infernal Machine*; and B. Richardson, 'The debates on printing in Renaissance Italy', *La Bibliofilía*, 100 (1998), 135–55.
35 As A. Petrucci has noted, small printed books descended from what he calls *libri da bisaccia*, simple, pocket-sized manuscripts often written in the vernacular and carried in the sacks of travelling preachers, merchants and artisans before the invention of print. However, as Petrucci acknowledges, print allowed for an inordinately greater proliferation of works of this kind, reaching a much wider audience. See his 'Alle origini del libro moderno. Libri da banco, libri da bisaccia, libretti da mano', *Italia medioevale e umanistica*, 12 (1969), 301–2.
36 See F. de Strata, *Polemic against Printing*, ed. M. Lowry, trans. S. Grier (Birmingham: Hayloft, 1986) [unpaginated].
37 *Ibid*. On de Strata's criticisms, see Lowry, *World of Aldus Manutius*, pp. 26–7.
38 'Scriptura est equidem veneranda, bonisque ferenda / Nobilior cunctis, quae nobis congerat aurum, / Ni sit prostibulo stamparum turpia passa. / Est virgo haec penna: meretrix est stampificata' (de Strata, *Polemic against Printing*).
39 See. N. Zemon Davis, 'Beyond the market: books as gifts in sixteenth-century France', *Transactions of the Royal Historical Society*, 33 (1983), 69–88.
40 L. Jardine, *Erasmus, Man of Letters: The Construction of Charisma in Print* (Princeton, NJ: Princeton University Press, 1993).
41 D. Erasmus, *Erasmus on his Times: A Shortened Version of the 'Adages' of Erasmus*, ed. M. Mann Phillips (Cambridge: Cambridge University Press, 1967), p. 9, from his explication of the adage 'Festina lente' (Hasten slowly), Aldo's motto.
42 *Ibid*., pp. 10–12.
43 See Chapter 5 on the establishment of the guild.
44 See A. Zannini, 'Il "pregiudizio meccanico" a Venezia in età moderna. Significato e trasformazione di una frontiera sociale', in M. Meriggi and A. Pastore (eds), *Le regole dei mestieri e delle professioni (secoli XV–XIX)* (Milan: FrancoAngeli, 2000), pp. 36–51; A. Cowan, '"Not carrying out the vile and mechanical arts": touch as a measure of social distinction in early modern Venice', in A. Cowan and J. Steward (eds), *The City and the Senses: Urban Culture since 1500* (Aldershot, UK: Ashgate, 2007), pp. 39–59.
45 A. F. Doni, *A Discussion about Printing which Took Place at 'I Marmi' in Florence*, trans. D. Brancaleone (Turin: Tallone, 2003), p. 17. Machiavelli's grandson, Giuliano de' Ricci, addressing an academy in Perugia on the evils of the press in 1567, was less equivocal, arguing that printing was an especially ignoble art, 'alle mane di houmini [*sic*] meno che ordinari et di mercanti vilissimi che non per altro l'han fatta che per guadagnare' (cited in G. Sapori, 'Giuliano de' Ricci e la polemica sulla stampa nel Cinquecento', *Nuova rivista storica*, 56 (1972), 162).

46 'Non è sporca niente in se stessa, ma netta, et polita' (T. Garzoni, *La piazza universale di tutte le professioni del mondo*, ed. G. B. Bronzini (Florence: Olschki, 1996), vol. 2, p. 1020).

47 D. Erasmus, 'Penny-pinching (*Opulentia sordida*)', in his *Colloquies*, trans. and annotated by C. R. Thompson, in *The Collected Works of Erasmus* (Toronto: University of Toronto Press, 1997), vol. 40, pp. 979–95.

48 *Opera nuova de le malitie che usa ciascheduna arte ... Novamente Stampata ...* (Venice: P. Danza, [c.1525]), cc. Ai–iv. BL, 11426.e. The suggestion of date comes from the STC. Another edition of the work is included in a miscellany thought to have been owned and performed by a Roman street singer in this period. See A. M. Adorisio, 'Cultura in lingua volgare a Roma fra Quattro e Cinquecento', in G. de Gregori and M. Valenti (eds), *Studi di biblioteconomia e storia del libro in onore di Francesco Barberi* (Rome: Associazione italiana biblioteche, 1976), p. 32.

49 'Convien che segua d'alcun stampadore / o ver de quelli che libri venderanno / non dico de tutti degno auditore / ma de quelli che usan cotal inganno / e se tu non apri li occhi comperatore / in qualche modo te la caleranno / ma se odientia alquanto me darai / dirote la rason se tu non la fai. // Qualuncha vora libri comparare / convien che habbia mente t'imprometto / di dover in carta in carta guardare / acciò non sia caduco né scoretto / o qualche carta non havesse a mancare / o fusse straciato o qualche difetto / e in le parole mai non te fidare / ch'usanza è la sua roba avantare' (*Opera nuova de le malitie ...*, c. Aii^r). *Cartolai* (stationers) were accused of selling badly bound and poorly illustrated works.

50 Doni, *Dialogue on Printing*, pp. 45–6.

51 Garzoni, *La piazza universale*, vol. 2. On booksellers: 'vendono a' contadini, et a' villani con ciancie quanto di sciocco hanno in bottega, et sopra tutto magnificano talhora più una castroneria composta da un ciavattino, che qualche opera bella, et utile composta da un galanthuomo' (p. 1021). On printers: 'nelle cose inutile mettono sovente studio grandissimo, et nelle giovevoli sono scioperati, et negligenti affatto' (p. 1024).

52 Erasmus, *Erasmus on His Times*, p. 12.

53 Doni, *Dialogue on Printing*, pp. 32–3. For a similar refrain in a 1590 dialogue, see C. Lucas, 'Vers une nouvelle image de l'écrivain: *Della dedicatione de' libri* de Giovanni Fratta', in C. A. Fiorato and J.-C. Margolin (eds), *L'écrivain face à son public en France et en Italie à la renaissance* (Paris: J. Vrin, 1989), p. 87. More broadly on the sense of 'information overload' in early modern Europe, see A. M. Blair, *Too Much to Know: Managing Scholarly Information before the Modern Age* (New Haven, CT and London: Yale University Press, 2010).

54 Doni, *Dialogue on Printing*, p. 34. According to Giovanni Fratta, 'libri dati a vilissimo pretio sono occasione, che molti, che dovriano attendere alla zappa, e seguir le vestigia de' padri loro, ardiscano con ogni stravagante maniera nutrirsi con la penna' (cited in Lucas, 'Vers une nouvelle image de l'écrivain', p. 100). See also Bonazzi, *Il carnevale delle idee*, pp. 132–5.

55 'Non sono più in pregio li buoni autori perché il volgo ignorante va più drieto a quei libri che trattano di lascivie che a quelli che trattano di continentia et sobrietà; più abbraccia quelli che biasimano che quelli che lodano, et ogni vil pedantuzzo vuol mandare a stampa, et non ci si provvede, et son cagione che si riempie il mondo di libri licentiosi et scelerati' (quoted in Sapori, 'Giuliano de' Ricci', p. 154).

56 See G. Aquilecchia, 'Pietro Aretino e altri poligrafi a Venezia', in *Storia della cultura veneta*, vol. 4, *Dal primo Quattrocento al concilio di Trento* (Vicenza: Neri Pozza, 1981), pp. 61–98; A. Quondam, 'Nel giardino dei Marcolini: Un editore veneziano tra Aretino e Doni', *Giornale storico della letteratura italiana*, 157 (1980), 75–116; F. M. Bertolo, *Aretino e la stampa. Strategie di autopromozione a Venezia nel Cinquecento* (Rome: Salerno, 2003); R. B. Waddington, *Aretino's Satyr: Sexuality, Satire, and Self-Projection in Sixteenth-Century Literature and Art* (Toronto: University of Toronto Press, 2004), esp. pp. 33–56.

57 'Colui che la sera va a la bottega per torre i danari de la vendita del giorno, pizzica de la natura del Roffiano, che prima che se ne va a letto vota la borsa de la sua femina. Io voglio, con il favor di Dio, che la cortesia de i Principi mi paghi le fatiche de lo scrivere, e non la miseria di chi le compra' (P. Aretino, *Lettere*, ed. P. Procaccioli (Rome: Salerno, 1999), vol. 1, p. 513 (22 June 1537)).

58 'Vuottu comprare questa corba intiera, / piena de libri in stampa ben ligati? / … Se li dasessi per tri o dui grossetti, / comme che in sacco me volessi vender gatti' (quoted in A. Segarizzi, 'Un calligrafo milanese', *Ateneo veneto*, 32:1 (1909), 70).

59 'M'è venuto pensato di farne stampare alquante copie nella presente forma, non per esponerle venali sulle piazze in questo et in quell'altro panco, come di più altre mie operette (quali elle si siano) ho fatto ne' passati tempi. Ma solo, essendo cosa vostra particolare, per tutte in dono mandarlevi, come le vi mando, acciò che di quelle possiate far partecipi solamente alcuni de vostri amici, et parenti' (G. B. Dragoncino, *[Lugubris est titulus, lacrimosaque carmina …]* (Venice: M. Vitali, 1526), c. Civ^v. BMV 2147.7, copy missing title page).

60 'Vegniate a me se volete essere da qualche cosa. Io, io, io, e null'altro, ho la ver'arte da fare tutti gli huomini Salamoni … chi vuole imparare lettere senza prattica di pedanti' (Franco, *Dialogo del venditore*, p. 26).

61 'Venga con diece scudi, chi vuole imparare di farsi o Papa, o Vescovo, o Cardinale'; 'un buon poeta per mezzo soldo' (*ibid.*, pp. 48, 54). Similarly, in Aretino's play *La Cortigiana*, one character buys an 'orazione ch'insegna a diventare cortigiano' from a street seller for the trifling sum of two *quattrini* (P. Aretino, *La Cortigiana* (Turin: Einaudi, 1970), act 1, scene 7, pp. 44–5).

62 'Che hoggi … al prezzo d'un'insalata non si possa stravendere la Poesia? S'io fussi incantatore di pillole, e di radici, o ciurmatore, che avessi mostro sordaspi, e biscie, sia tu certo, che a quest'hora non mi mancarebbe de le faccende. Ma … hoggi l'avaritia del mondo è tale, che piu s'appezza un quatrino, che l'imparare mille scienze' (Franco, *Dialogo del venditore*, p. 54).

63 Richardson, 'Debates on printing', 154.

64 Doni, *Dialogue on Printing*, p. 29.

65 'Le lettre hoggi … sono ite tanto al basso, che tristo chi pensa haverne … Hoggi i mecanici, e gli artigiani, per quanto veggo, triomphano di questo mondo' (Franco, *Dialogo del venditore*, p. 30).

66 'A ogni ciabattino pur che sappi leggere sia hoggi lecito tramenarsi per le vil mani l'opere d'Aristotile, di Platone, di Cicerone et di tanti altri … hoggi ogni vil mercantuzzo vuol disputare de' più alti segreti della filosofia' (quoted in Sapori, 'Giuliano de' Ricci', 153).

67 'Importerà di tenere la bottega fornita di quelle operine, che in questa lingua so state tradutte, e si traducono di mano in mano. Perche i mecanici; che non hanno lettere,

per imparare *de agibilibus mundi*, voranno Plinio. I soldati; che non intendono latinamente, vorranno le guerre d'Appiano con i Comentari di Cesare' (Franco, *Dialogo del venditore*, p. 38).

68 'Non sai; che sono più le ciurme del volgo; che l'accademie de i dotti?' (*ibid.*). Similarly, Doni's character Lollio opined that, 'since the mass of the ignorant is more numerous than the Academy of the erudite, surely those who put just about anything in the press make a bigger profit than do men of discrimination from printing good books' (*Dialogue on Printing*, p. 45).

69 'Ci bisogna a questa mensa, d'ogni qualità di carne, per nutrire Signori, Gentil'huomini, Donne, lavoratori, contadini, et facchini ... Adunque noi apparecchiaremo, cose dotte, artificiate, mediocri, pure, semplici, et naturali, non voglio dire in tutto goffe. Bisogna adunque, poi che siamo condannati a questo, havere un certo discorso generale, perche ogni sorte di gente, legge ... noi siamo della lega de' Predicatori (per non ci mettere nel branco de' ciurmadori) iquali sono ascoltati da tutte l'arti, et i nostri scartabelli son letti da tutte le professioni' (A. F. Doni, *La seconda libraria del Doni* (Venice: Marcolini, 1555), cc. 9–10. BL 271b23). On Doni's ambivalent attitude to the proliferation of books in print, particularly well expressed in this preface, see also J. D. Bradbury, 'Anton Francesco Doni and his *Librarie*: Bibliographical friend or fiend?', *Forum for Modern Language Studies*, 45:1 (2009), 90–107.

70 'Dipoi che questa benedetta stampa è suscitata, la maggior parte delle genti tanto huomini quanto donne sanno leggiere; et quello che più importa è che la filosofia e la medicina, e tutte l'altre scientie sono ridotte et stampate in questa nostra lingua materna: di modo che ogni uno ne può sapere la parte sua ... vedo che la maggior parte, anzi fino alle donne parlano di filosofia, di medicina, di astrologia, di matematica e di quante scientie sono al mondo senza esser dottori; et cosi nissuno può esser più gabbato; poi che ogni uno che voglia affaticarsi un poco il cervello, può esser dotto: e la causa di ciò è stata la Stampa' (L. Fioravanti, *Dello specchio di scientia universale* ... (Venice: A. Ravenoldo, 1567), c. 62^r).

71 'I gattisini hanno aperti gli occhi perchè ciascuno puo vedere e intendere il fatto suo, in modo che noi altri medici non possiamo piu cacciar carotte alle genti'. This was added to the 1583 edition of Fioravanti, *Dello specchio di scientia universale*, c. 41^{r-v}, cited in P. Camporesi, *Camminare il mondo: Vita e avventure di Leonardo Fioravanti, medico del Cinquecento* (Milan: Garzanti, 1997), p. 64. For further discussion of this rhetoric about the opening up of knowledge via print, see Chapter 4.

72 'Avanti a questa miracolosa arte della stampa, si trovavano, in comparatione del tempo d'hoggi, molti pochi letterati; il che non derivava d'altro, se non dalla spesa de' libri intolerabile ... La stampa ancora è stata a guisa dell'anello d'Angelica, c'ha rotto gli incanti di molti filosofi antichi, i quali tanto altamente, et profondamente parlavano ... che la povera plebe come incantata, et stordita stava del continuo intenta a que' ragionamenti senza moversi punto ... tutto nasce, et procede dalla stampa, la quale ha aperto gli occhi a' ciechi, et dato il lume agli ignoranti' (Garzoni, *La piazza universale*, vol. 2, pp. 1022–3).

73 'Acciò che parimente gli dotti et gl'indotti possino sì dell'historie barbare et esterne, come delle romane havere perfetta cognitione'. This, wrote Zoppino, would allow the unlearned reader to feel at ease among the more educated: 'ritrovandoti poi fra huomini saputi et dotti, anchor tu possi alcuna volta parlare, et disputare dell'historie greche et latine' (M. I. Iustinus, *Iustino Historico Clarissimo* ..., cited

in Severi, *Sitibondo nel stampar de' libri*, p. 390). For more examples, see *ibid.*, pp. 55–69.

74 'Conossendo molti bisognosi a commune utilità e massime delli poveri del mio redemptore Iesu Christo molto più volentieri queste fatiche fidelmente traducendo ho fatte aciò anchora quelli che non hanno la lingua Latina possino da per se li secreti della natura intendere' (*Herbolario volgare. Nel quale le virtu delle herbe e molti altri simplici se dechiarano con alcune belle aggionte novamente de latino in volgare tradotto* (Venice: Alessandro Bindoni, 1522), c. Ai^v. BL 453.c.8).

75 'Spinto de caritade ho voluto stampare questa operetta, acciòche la ditta sia causa della salute de infiniti poveri infetti del mal francioso, quali non havendo il modo, né la facultade, a supplimento di medici, e medicine, possano da se medesmi cum poco dispendio in breve tempo da tanta egrirudine [*sic*], e incendio liberarsi' (Celebrino, *Questo e lo modo ...*, c. Ai^v).

76 'Con grandissima sua utilitade e satisfatione de l'animo, si al sexo masculino quanto al femminino si ali spiriti gentili quanti ali rozi sempre tal thesauro sera guida et a quello timone' (G. A. Tagliente, *Lo presente libro insegna la vera arte de lo Excellente scrivere ... Con la presente opera ognuno le potra imparare impochi giorni per lo amaistramento ragioni, essempi, come qui seguente vedrai* ([Venice], 1525), c. 40^v, BL C.31.f.7). On Tagliente, see A. J. Schutte, 'Teaching adults to read in sixteenth-century Venice: Giovanni Antonio Tagliente's *Libro maistrevole*', *Sixteenth Century Journal*, 17:1 (1986), 3–16.

77 'Quelle che per sua sorte di patre et matre di non tanta conditione sono nasciute, et altre d'infimo grado, con le vivande di questo mio delicatissimo *Convivio* per la virtù loro non invidiano quelle che non miglior fortuna in quanto a' beni temporali sono nate et cresciute, anzi possano andare altere, gloriandosi che quelle di tanta altezza senze le virtù di sue mani nobilitar si possano, ne tra le nobile comparere' (*Convivio delle belle donne ...*, cited in Severi, *Sitibondo nel stampar de' libri*, p. 395). On the new public of women readers, see T. Plebani, *Il 'genere' dei libri. Storie e rappresentazioni della lettura al femminile e al maschile tra medioevo e età moderna* (Milan: FrancoAngeli, 2001); M. P. Donato and X. von Tippelskirch, '"Il tanto leggere mi fa doler la testa". Appunti sulle lettrici alla soglia del pubblico', in B. Borello (ed.), *Pubblico e pubblici di antico regime* (Pisa: Pacini, 2009), pp. 1–20.

78 On the genre of instructional manuals, see R. M. Bell, *How to Do It: Guides to Good Living for Renaissance Italians* (Chicago, IL and London: University of Chicago Press, 1999).

79 *Opera noua che insegna a parecchiar una mensa a vno conuito ... Intitulata Refetorio ...* (Cesena, [1527]); *Formulario de lettere amorose, intitulato Chiaue damore* (Venice: F. Bindoni and M. Pasini, 1527); *Il modo d'imparare di scriuere lettera merchantescha ... composto per lo ingenioso maistro Eustachio Cellebrino ...* ([Venice], 1525); *Opera noua piaceuole la quale insegna di far varie compositioni odorifere per far bella ciascuna dona et etiam agiontoui molti secreti necessarij alla salute humana ...* (Venice: F. Bindoni and M. Pasini, 1526); *Regimento mirabile, et verissimo a conseruar la sanita in tempo di peste ... intitulato Optimo remedio de sanita* (Cesena: H. Soncino, 1527).

80 On Zoppino's reformist religious leanings, expressed in his publications of Erasmian and Lutheran works, see Severi, *Sitibondo nel stampar de' libri*, pp. 67–85, and my discussion in Chapter 4. More generally, see M. Firpo, 'Riforma religiosa e lingua volgare nell'Italia del '500', *Belfagor*, 57:5 (2002), 517–39.

81 See G. Savonarola, *Triumpho della croce di Christo volgare* ... (Venice: F. Bindoni and M. Pasini, 1535), c. Ai^v. BL 3901aaa71.
82 'Perchè 'l vulgo gusti questi frutti / di latini in vulgar gli abian tradutti' (*Psalmi poenitentiales* (Venice: A. Calabrensis, *c.* 1490), cited in R. Rusconi, 'Pratica culturale ed istruzione religiosa nelle confraternite italiane del tardo medioevo: "libri di compagnia" e libri di pietà', in *Le mouvement confraternel au Moyen Age: France, Italie, Suisse* (Geneva: Droz, 1987), p. 138).
83 'I'te l'ho messe in versi per amore / che sono a qualchedun più dilettose / poi tal potrà quest'opera tenere / che non può la gran Bibia in casa avere' (cited in P. Farenga, 'Giuliano Dati', in *DBI*, vol. 33, p. 33).
84 'E perchè non potrà venire al pasco di quel nostro gran Giesù Christo il mendicante, il fabbro, il contadino, il muratore, il pescatore, i pubblicani et tutte le conditioni degli huomini, et de le donne' (Brucioli's 1538 edition, dedicated to Anna d'Este, quoted in G. Spini, *Tra Rinascimento e Riforma: Antonio Brucioli* (Florence: La Nuova Italia, 1940), pp. 216-17).
85 The papal nuncio Girolamo Aleandro in 1534 lamented the circulation of heretical books and ideas in Venice, noting that 'di parlarse etiam tra artegiani et vil canaglia della fede et sacramenti per ogni canton è cosa publica' (F. Gaeta (ed.), *Nunziature di Venezia. Vol. 1 (12 marzo 1533-14 agosto 1535)* (Rome: Istituto storico italiano per l'età moderna e contemporanea, 1958), p. 177). See also Firpo, 'Riforma religiosa', 534.
86 Doni, *Dialogue on Printing*, pp. 34, 36-7.
87 L. Domenichi, *Dialoghi di m. Lodouico Domenichi* ... (Venice: G. Giolito, 1562), cc. 389-90. BMV C068C197. Coccio: 'Non vi pare egli cosa infame, e vituperosa, che si leggano a stampa tante dishonestà, come noi veggiamo? Non havete voi letto, o veduto al meno la *Priapea* del Franco, la *Cortigiana* con le figure, e mille altre opere lascive ... È impossibile, che voi passando dalle librarie di questa città, non habbiate veduto su per li banchi, a esser lordate dalle mosche, le librerie, le invettive sporche contra la fama, e l'honor de' virtuosi e buoni, e vivi, e morti, con pessimo, e dannoso essempio di quelle persone semplici, che a leggerle vi perdono quel tempo'.
88 Sapori, 'Giuliano de' Ricci', 160.
89 See Grendler, *Roman Inquisition*, pp. 258, 262. Franco's dialogue on bookselling, quoted above, was eventually allowed to circulate in expurgated form.
90 G. C. Croce, *La libraria, conuito uniuersale doue s'inuita grandissimo numero di libri, tanto antichi, quanto moderni* ... (Ferrara and Bologna, [1592?]). See also Croce's *Indice uniuersale della libraria, o studio del celebratiss. eccellentiss. eruditiss. et plusquam opulentiss. arcidottor Gratian Furbson da Francolino* ... (Ferrara, 1600). See also D. Shemek, 'Books at banquet: commodities, canon and culture in Giulio Cesare Croce's *Convito universale*', *Annali d'italianistica*, 16 (1998), 89-91. On Doni's works, see Bradbury, 'Anton Francesco Doni'. On the broader sense of a need for order in the world of books from the later sixteenth century, see R. Chartier, *The Order of Books* (Stanford, CA: Stanford University Press, 1994).

2

'Through the piazzas and on the Rialto Bridge': the landscape of the ephemeral city

The fabric of Venice is famously permeable. The intertwining of land and water, of narrow streets and canals, engineers collisions and encounters. Voices and music travel easily between indoor and outdoor spaces. Webs of tiny streets, or *calli*, are punctuated by *campi*, or small squares; bridges link one neighbourhood to another almost seamlessly. As in many Italian cities, squares and streets are important places of gathering and encounter, but here the interaction between different people, between interiors and exteriors, public and private spaces is particularly intense because the city is so densely woven.

From around 1500, images like Jacopo de' Barbari's bird's-eye-view woodcut cityscape began to fix an iconic, and remarkably enduring, vision of this labyrinthine city in print and in the minds of people both at home and abroad (Figure 6).[1] At ground level, though, Venice was a space of constant flux. The central areas and particularly Piazza San Marco were refashioned in this period, made more formal, ordered and imposing; at the margins, the population pushed out to the edges of the inhabited islands. Meanwhile, the fortunes of the Republic were shifting as a consequence of deeper political and economic transitions, while the population itself saw continuous turnover, growing by a third largely from immigration in the first half of the sixteenth century before being cut back by a similar amount by the plague of the mid 1570s.[2]

The social world of Renaissance Venice, too, was more fluid and dynamic than it has sometimes been portrayed. While nominally divided into three distinct classes – the small, hereditary patrician and citizen castes who monopolised political and bureaucratic power and the large and undifferentiated *popolani*, comprising around 90 per cent of the population – in fact social boundaries were more indistinct. This was especially so because of the large numbers of migrants and travellers, from permanent settlers to those just passing through, who lent a strongly cosmopolitan flavour to urban life.[3] Although the peripheral neighbourhoods had a more distinctly working class character, with large clusters of sailors, Arsenal workers, and recent immigrants, the central areas were highly variegated, the 'cities of the rich and poor fused together' so that people of every different background, economic and social status lived side by side or on top of each other.[4]

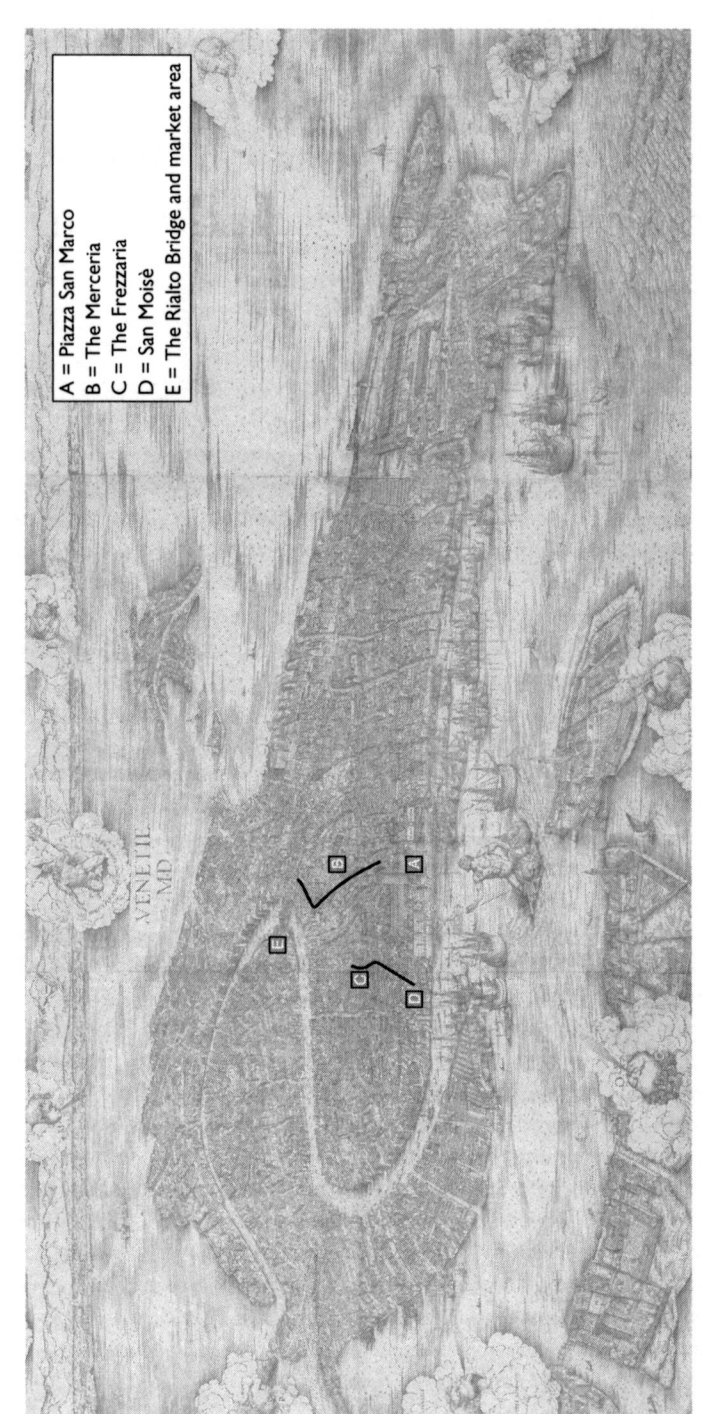

6 J. de'Barbari, *Bird's-eye View of Venice* (1500)

It was into this complex and variegated urban environment that print entered in the late fifteenth century, and that environment intimately shaped the kinds of texts produced and the ways in which they circulated.[5] In this chapter, I suggest how the form of the city acted as an agent itself in the dissemination of print, or at least of texts. An examination of the spaces and places of the print trade highlights the vitality and complexity of Venetian urban culture, shaped by government edicts from above as well as by the actions of ordinary people at street level. By applying a geographical lens, we can bring to light the dissemination of cheap print in particular, an aspect of print culture that tends to be hidden by more traditional approaches to book history. To find cheap print, we need to look beyond the city's restricted literary circles and the houses and workshops (*botteghe*) of the most celebrated representatives of the new printing trade, and out into the streets.[6] Printed texts flowed through the city of Venice along numerous, sometimes unforeseen, paths, reaching people across the social spectrum. In many ways, the landscape of cheap print mapped onto the larger 'geography of the book' in Venice, focused on some of the same central spaces.[7] However, it was also more specifically associated with the city's public life as much of the advertising and selling of cheap print took place outdoors, and also because it was so closely bound up with oral cultural practices such as street performance, hawking and announcing.

A first step is to survey the operations of those who specialised in the production and dissemination of cheap print, both from shops and on the street. I then look beyond the spatial topography of print production and distribution at other ways in which print penetrated the visual and sonic landscape of the city. Print was not only sold in shops and the streets but also performed, recited, posted up and handed out for free, to advertise other products or to inform the public about important issues or new laws. It was at once just another product of industrial and commercial activity in a city that offered a profuse array of goods and services; at the same time, it possessed a more profound significance as it intersected with and changed the shape of other cultural geographies in the city: performative, political, informative, devotional.

The emergence of print in the urban landscape

Before the arrival of the press, the presence of books in Venice was relatively restricted. The city had no large-scale book trade before 1469, which is thought to have made it easier for printing to flourish there as rapidly as it did. This can be compared to Florence, where a very strong manuscript trade seems to have stifled the beginnings of the printing industry, which remained one of the less important in Italy.[8] In Venice, books were expensive and prized, and moved among scholars and the social elite by means of lending and borrowing, helping to forge networks and reinforce friendships.[9] In the fifteenth century one might have witnessed auctions of books from deceased estates taking place in Piazza San Marco and at Rialto, but these were held sporadically and the manuscript books sold were costly. There were also some bookshops and *cartolai* (stationers) who sold books located around Rialto and Santa Maria Formosa, the parish to the north of San Marco.[10]

As happened in other cities, the dissemination of printed books in Venice, starting from the 1470s, grew from and fed upon an existing circuit of manuscript dissemination.[11] As there continued to be a market both for manuscripts and print, the two kinds of book distribution could coexist, even collaborate. When a section of the Rialto Bridge collapsed in 1524, Sanudo recorded the great damage done to the shops on the bridge that had thereby lost much of their stock in the water, which included two *cartolai* and two sellers of 'libri a stampa'.[12] Although sometimes there was dispute about the right of *cartolai* to sell finished books, they were the natural collaborators of printers and booksellers, serving as suppliers of paper and offering complementary services in binding and embellishment. Nuovo suggested that the presence of *cartolai* diminished the rupture between manuscript and print, as many *cartolai* moved quickly into the binding, hand-illustration, and sale of printed books and frequently into the role of publisher themselves.[13] Customers used to buying manuscripts could now find printed books in some of the same prominent and central spaces, and sometimes buy them from the same people.

However, a visible change in the urban landscape was registered quickly after the introduction of print in the 1470s. As a large printing trade developed into one of the most important commercial and industrial facets of the city, Venetians and visitors were exposed to an ever-widening panorama of print. In the early 1490s, the humanist Marc'Antonio Sabellico famously described a friend becoming distracted and entranced by the many bookstalls displaying their wares as he walked down the great commercial artery of the Merceria that weaves from the Rialto Bridge to Piazza San Marco. As well as exhibiting their goods out of doors, bookshops began to post up stock lists outside to lure in customers.[14]

As time passed, print became a much more visible presence in the city than the manuscript trade had ever been. The production of printed books escalated rapidly, necessitating new ways of distributing texts, especially for the growing numbers of small, cheap, unbound pamphlets and *fogli volanti* that had few precedents in the manuscript era. As described in the Introduction, Venetian observers recorded printed pamphlets and fliers being peddled 'through the piazzas and on the Rialto Bridge' during the War of the League of Cambrai. By 1533 a list of printers and booksellers active in the city named sixteen dedicated booksellers, and at least thirteen printers who may also have sold books.[15] About half of the figures listed were identified only by their sign; about half also by their locations, which were principally in the parishes between Rialto and San Marco. But these fixed points do not offer a comprehensive picture of Venetian print-selling at this moment. As well as omitting several prominent characters active at the time, the list includes no stallholders or street sellers who had continued to proliferate from the first decade of the century.

These elusive figures were more evident in 1549 in the comments of a young scribe, Angelo Lion, to the Venetian branch of the Holy Office regarding his possession of prohibited books. Lion testified that 'wishing to read some nice things' ('desideroso de lezer qualche bella cosa') he had both borrowed and bought some prohibited works. He had purchased them in one of the city's key civic spaces: Piazza San Marco, specifically under the clocktower and under the porticoes of the grand buildings that surrounded the square, 'from those booksellers who sell on feast days'.[16] Others, he noted defiantly, he had bought 'publicly in the Merceria' ('publicamente in merzaria'), which could have meant from one of the shops displaying their wares along the thoroughfare or from a temporary stall or pedlar's basket encountered there.[17]

The testimony of contemporaries like Sabellico and Lion indicates the appearance of a range of possible places and methods to obtain printed material in Venice during the first century of the industry's development. Below the upper level of merchant booksellers, with sophisticated Italian and even broader European distribution systems, a rank of lesser-known figures toiled to meet the needs of a more exclusively local market. At the bottom end of this spectrum existed the vendors without their own *botteghe*, such as those who sold on feast days under the porticoes of Piazza San Marco to Lion. At certain times, public spaces such as the Piazza were co-opted for a variety of ephemeral sales operations – temporary but nevertheless important sites for the dissemination of printed texts to the city's reading public. However, it is important to consider these different retailing operations as part of the same system; they were linked not only by spatial proximity but functionally at many points.

The topography of print commerce and production

The printing trade was fuelled by migration from northern Europe and later from mainland Italy, profiting from the skills, capital, labour and entrepreneurialism of migrants – similar to, although to an even greater degree than, many other trades in Venice. One of the ways in which printers embedded themselves in the city was by choosing prominent locations for their shops with strong associations with commercial production and the retail of luxury (in the sense of non-necessary) goods, and settled communities of foreigners. This meant between the zones of Rialto and San Marco, and down the thoroughfare of the Merceria which joined them, where, soon after the advent of printing, the shops of printers and booksellers rapidly came to be clustered (see Figure 6). Zorzi noted twelve printers active in Venice in 1473, nearly all German and mostly living in the parishes of San Paternian and San Giuliano, thus around the Merceria. These parishes hosted an established German community and were proximate to the German trading house, the Fondaco dei Tedeschi, off Campo San Bartolomeo.[18] By the early sixteenth century, although the majority of those involved with print in Venice now were Italians of relatively recent arrival from the mainland, they continued to group in this area.

Rialto, Piazza San Marco and the zone in between them were also the chief loci of trade and commerce in Renaissance Venice, as well as the most densely populated areas of the city through which many people had to pass on daily business of various kinds. At Rialto and San Marco merchants and noblemen gathered daily to negotiate and gossip, along with a great variety of other Venetians and foreigners come to trade, buy and transport goods around the city. The location of the city's two chief food markets in these places also made them essential stops. As Marin Sanudo wrote of Rialto in the late fifteenth century, although nothing was grown in Venice, 'everything – and whatever you might want – is found there in abundance ... because everything, from every land, and part of the world ... comes here'.[19] Meanwhile, down the length of the Merceria, the famous winding street which joined the main Piazza to the Rialto Bridge, 'everything known, or that you might ever seek' could be found.[20] Around San Bartolomeo in particular, on the eastern side of the Bridge, were shops offering specialist goods of use to printers and booksellers, for example *speziali*, or spice-dealers who sold the ingredients for ink and *vende colori*, or colour sellers who sold pigments for illustration.[21]

San Marco had the added significance of being the main centre of government and religious ritual, the site of the Ducal Palace and the Basilica of San Marco. In the sixteenth century it was undergoing progressive renovation, mostly under the guidance of the architect Jacopo Sansovino, to make it fit to be the spiritual and political heart of the Republic.[22] As in other European cities, the areas that attracted printers and booksellers also had established associations with politics and education, and thus with the circulation of ideas and texts. Venice made use of the university in the mainland subject town of Padua at this time, but the city's official schools were located at Rialto and San Marco, and while San Marco was the seat of the major councils and the more informal discussions of the *broglio*, other magistracies had their seats at Rialto.[23]

These were prestigious and prominent locations, often with expensive rents to match; the prime real estate of shops on the Rialto Bridge, for example, might go for as much as 100 ducats a year.[24] Perhaps as a result, newly launched printers in the sixteenth century increasingly clustered in other areas, although still close by to Rialto and San Marco. One area that emerges prominently is the parish of San Moisè, immediately to the west of Piazza San Marco, which became a particular focus for the production of cheap print in the sixteenth century. The densely packed lattice of streets around San Moisè was an area, like the Merceria, devoted to the production and sale of fine artisanal goods, such as arrows (*frezze* – hence the name of its main street, the Frezzaria). The printers and print-sellers who located themselves there, however, could expect a very mixed potential clientele to pass their doors. Some very grand patrician palaces were located nearby but so were dilapidated buildings and courtyards reputed for their poverty.[25] San Moisè has been described as the Venetian parish *'per eccellenza'* for foreigners, and indeed most of the printers to have worked there came from the *terraferma*.²⁶ Evidently, one could find cheap premises there, such as the Giustiniani houses which rented for between five and twenty ducats a year.²⁷ Close to the centres of power and the port beyond San Marco where ships arrived, bringing travellers, news and commodities, San Moisè also was a natural hub of information gathering and dissemination. By the seventeenth century it would become the focal point for writers of manuscript newssheets, demonstrating the continued proximity of different media in Venetian urban space.²⁸

By the 1520s or 1530s, a person walking through this small parish could have encountered the shops and workshops of some of the most productive printers and publishers of cheap material active at the time. One of the most active was the *bottega* of Francesco Bindoni and Maffeo Pasini at the sign of the Archangel Raphael. This workshop was located more precisely *'nelle case nuove Giustiniani'* (in the new houses owned by the noble Giustiniani family) in San Moisè, although it is not known whether these were the same houses mentioned above, for the Giustiniani owned a good deal of property in this parish. Nonetheless, the address reminds us how *popolani* artisans and retailers often rented their shops and houses from Venetian patricians.²⁹ In the same period, the printers Giorgio Rusconi from Milan and Guglielmo Fontaneto from Monferrato, also in Lombardy, both worked in San Moisè, although the precise locations of their shops are not known.³⁰ The presence of immigrant printers from northern Italy may have encouraged others from the same region to settle in the area and it remained a focal point of cheap print production throughout the century, as in the case of the De' Franceschi family of printers who ran a *bottega* in the Frezzaria, at the sign of the Queen, between the 1550s and 1570s.³¹

Other new arrivals to the print trade settled in the neighbouring parishes to San Moisè, including the brothers Nicolini (from Sabbio on the banks of Lake Garda), Niccolò Zoppino from Ferrara and another member of the Bindoni family, Benedetto, in San Fantin, and Benedetto's brother Agostino in San Paternian, immediately north-east of San Fantin.³² A few minutes' walk away, near the Ponte dei Fuseri in San Luca, one could find the engraver and printer Giovan Andrea Valvassore.³³ A more wealthy and powerful figure such as the publisher and bookseller Melchiore Sessa could afford a shop in the prominent and prestigious location of the Merceria in the parish of San Giuliano, just north of Piazza San Marco. And yet, despite this spatial distinction, Sessa was still located near the smaller printers just mentioned, with whom he had numerous business connections.³⁴ In the same period, the Merceria and the Frezzaria also became the site of many print shops specialising in printed images and maps, from large and expensive ones to cheaper varieties.³⁵

For the members of the new trade, the rather intimate, parochial context in which many of them lived and worked mirrored, and must have reinforced, the close-knit nature of the industry from its early days. As mentioned, these central neighbourhoods were very close to the hubs of political and commercial information in the city, particularly useful for those printing items of news. But helpful technical and business information could also pass quickly between shops, as printers socialised with each other and formed short-term partnerships, and their workers shared their grievances at the tavern or left one shop to work in another.[36] It is unsurprising that piracy of texts, images and ideas was rife, as well as a more congenial sharing and bartering of materials. Geographical proximity may have brought a stronger sense of identity and community to a trade that encompassed a broad spectrum of specialisations and socio-economic levels, and which until the later sixteenth century had no official guild to bring it together. The concentration of members of the print trade in these neighbourhoods also provided strong bases for new arrivals to access, particularly networks of fellow migrants from the same regions of the mainland who were connected further by ties of marriage and business.

Aside from a few printers located in more peripheral parts of the city,[37] the majority were thus located in Venice's most central, frequented areas. This suggests that the presence of print in Venice by the sixteenth century was difficult to ignore, encountered whenever one passed through the central arteries of the city. A prime position on the Merceria, or Rialto Bridge, may have signalled a more prestigious, high-end business and there must have been other cultural associations with certain areas and particular sellers who gained a reputation for particular goods. The writer Tomaso Garzoni, for example, distinguished between the market area of Rialto, where one was more likely to find a charlatan's flimsy prognostication for sale, and the Merceria where you would go to buy 'some compositions by a gentleman'.[38] But producers and distributors of cheap print and of the most expensive editions could be found in more or less the same central areas, while a wandering pedlar or a temporary stall could appear almost anywhere, including in the most prominent positions in the city.[39] In the crowded centre of Venice, it was difficult to maintain clear distinctions between different activities, products and social groups. The streets, squares and bridges were 'socially levelling spaces' where a variety of lowly quotidian activities occurred alongside the grander pursuits of state politics and international trade, and people of all backgrounds and levels of wealth rubbed shoulders.[40]

On the streets

Street-selling of all kinds of goods was a fixture of European cities from the Middle Ages, an ephemeral commercial culture that recent historiography has begun to restore to light.[41] Hence it is not surprising that when printing developed the products of the press started to find their way to customers in this manner. Extensive networks of print pedlars would not emerge in Italy and other parts of Europe until the seventeenth and eighteenth centuries, however individual street sellers quickly perceived small printed items to be a valuable supplement to their baskets, often alongside consumer trifles such as ribbons, soap and perfumes.[42] While cheap print also was sold in bookshops, street-selling played an essential role in the dissemination of this kind of material. Some of the earliest government edicts in Venice which specifically mention cheap print particularly associated this type of product with outdoor spaces, as in the 1519 Council of Ten declaration that no one could sell printed verses 'on the piazzas, nor on the Rialto Bridge, nor elsewhere in this city'.[43]

We must not draw too great a distinction between bookshops and the street trade in print, however. In the words of Evelyn Welch, the boundary between shops and street in Italian cities of this period was 'defined yet permeable', not absolute.[44] Bookshops could be open to the street, and advertise their wares outside. Furthermore some stalls were semi-permanent fixtures of the urban landscape, occupying the same position for a number of years, such as those of Giacomo da Trino under the portico at Rialto and Battista Furlan in Piazza San Marco in the 1560s and 1570s.[45]

Some booksellers may have graduated from being street sellers to stallholders to shopkeepers as their economic status became more secure; however, the various activities were not mutually exclusive. Sigismondo Bordogna for some years had a stall near the north-east corner of the Piazza, near the church of San Basso, in addition to his shop, as well as publishing various cheap pamphlets.[46] The bookseller Francesco Rocca had both a shop and a stall in San Polo, for both of which he registered the sign of the 'The Glowing Bride'.[47] In Florence in the same period, the printer Giorgio Marescotti was among those who petitioned for the right to peddle cheap print in the streets on feast days, even after he established his own *bottega*.[48] After its establishment in the middle of the sixteenth century, the printers' guild struggled continuously to stop masters with shops from selling their wares in the streets, or sending them out with ambulant pedlars or their own *garzoni* (apprentices), in an effort to maintain the propriety of the trade and to marginalise poor and untrained practitioners. However, before and after this it seems that various kinds of mutually beneficial relationships were forged between printers, booksellers and street vendors.[49]

On the streets of Venice, clearly there was an array of different print sellers of varying levels of status, permanence and experience, vending a profusion of printed products, but clustered around the same central areas already highlighted. Our fragmentary snapshots of these figures in action do not always allow us to distinguish the more established stallholders from the lowliest print pedlars with baskets. For example, a list of book and print sellers to whom a censorship decree was communicated in 1567 by the Holy Office indicates a landscape of semi-permanent stalls and street sellers clustered around Rialto and San Marco. These included stallholders, such as 'Julio Bressanin di Bortolomeo the Brescian, [who] has a bench in Piazza San Marco'. Others were listed who may have held a stall, a chest or even a basket, but who were reliably associated with a particular location. These included 'Jacomo di Simon di Venezia, bookseller who sells under the portico at Rialto', 'Zuane de Anzolo *erbariol* [*erbarolo* = seller of greens] ... [who] sells books at San Salvador, without a shop'; and 'Nicolò di Bortolomeo Pierio Toschan from Bergamo, sells books on feast days in the Merceria'.[50]

Stalls carried not only cheaper print but sometimes also larger and more expensive items, although probably not the newest and most prestigious publications. Some stallholders sold second-hand works, such as Bartolomeo da Sabbio, a poor old bookseller with a chest at Rialto, who was caught selling prohibited second-hand books there in 1574.[51] One could also find printed images on sale outdoors. According to Vasari, the artist Marc'Antonio Raimondi encountered prints by Albrecht Dürer being sold in Piazza San Marco around 1506, which Raimondi later copied.[52]

Within this relatively static landscape, there moved a host of more mobile sellers on the streets of Venice, who carried works in their arms or a basket. These may often have been young boys employed by booksellers to cry and sell their works in the streets. (In Rome, there seems also to have been the custom of advertising small printed works for sale on poles, carried around the city, but I have not found a reference to this occurring in Venice.)[53] In 1512, Sanudo reported an incident that had taken place in the piazza, when a young boy selling 'certain songs against France' was slapped by an angry passerby who disputed the song's version of events. Uncowed, the boy went to the authorities to complain.[54] By 1568, the practice had proliferated, for the Venetian blasphemy magistrates at that point tried to control the selling of unlicensed cheap works 'by boys [*puti*] and others on the Rialto Bridge and in other places'.[55] Such a character, a street urchin (*furfante*) selling stories, appears in Aretino's play *La Cortigiana*. He enters the scene shouting about his 'lovely stories' for sale ('Alle belle Istorie!') and offering a range of typical items including letters or poems about recent events ('*La pace tra il Cristianissimo e l'Imperatore! La presa del re!*') and popular poetry ('*I Capricci de fra Mariano in ottava rima! Egloghe del Trasinio!*').[56] Although Aretino set his play in Rome, and the first version circulated there in the mid 1520s, he must have encountered similar characters in Venice where he moved in 1527 and where the play was first published in 1534. In the poem *Il trent'uno della Zaffetta* (*The Zaffetta's Thirty-One*), by Aretino's pupil Lorenzo Venier, published in the early 1530s, the courtesan-victim lamented that the news of her malicious gang rape described in the poem was being spread rapidly around the city. Already she could 'hear the loud cry of the boys / on the Rialto Bridge [shouting]: / "Who wants [to buy] the story of the Zaffetta?".'[57]

The emerging geography of street-selling of cheap print clearly maps on to more or less the same areas mentioned in the survey of shops, for many of the same reasons already discussed. Most importantly, these were places that could guarantee passing trade. The obligatory passage in the city was the Rialto Bridge, especially for those without their own gondola. The bridge was the only way then possible to cross on foot the Grand Canal that cut the city in half.

It created a bottleneck for foot traffic in the city, and thus was an obvious place for selling and begging, while the nearby Rialto market area was also a focal point for ambulant selling of all sorts of goods.[58] Sure enough the Rialto became a key location particularly associated with the sale of cheap print from early on in the history of the printing trade. The 1543 Council of Ten law regarding printing licences confirms that the presence of street sellers of print operating in Venice 'on the bridge of the Rialto, and in other places of this city', already was significant.[59]

Pamphlet sellers on the Rialto appear repeatedly in contemporary poems that depict the bustle of life in this most frenetic part of Venice. Later in the sixteenth century, the poet Maffio Venier (Lorenzo's son) described sellers on the Rialto hawking devotional booklets, prognostications and cheap pamphlets of poetry.[60] Another work depicted among the many items for sale on the Rialto Bridge – 'so crowded / with people and shops and stalls' – small books of hours, almanacs, and the printed 'song of San Martino / twenty for a *quattrino*'.[61] We should note how these accounts emphasise the abundance and cheapness of the print available in the streets of Venice, twenty pamphlets of verses offered (probably hyperbolically) for the tiny sum of one *quattrino*. Other bridges, places of transition and movement, were places for pamphlet selling as well. In a short poem published in the early decades of the century in Venice, claiming to be the lament of a priest's concubine over her lover's imprisonment for blasphemy, the 'femena' of Father Agostino complained that her lover's plight had become fodder for the pamphlet writers of Venice, and now the stories about him 'are sold on the bridges / and through the *piazze* of every parish'.[62] Print-selling by this point had occupied the very heart of Venice, an ephemeral but not insignificant aspect of life.

The presence of sellers of cheap print was greater not just in certain spaces but at certain times. Street sellers of cheap print were drawn to the times and places when buying and selling were most common, particularly market days and fairs, as in the aforementioned case of Nicolò da Bergamo who sold books on feast days. Great markets were held weekly at the city's two largest open spaces, Campo San Polo (Wednesdays) and Piazza San Marco (Saturdays), while every May the Venetian Ascension festival, the Sensa, was accompanied by a famous fair, during which Piazza San Marco was filled with temporary stalls, but also attracted many street vendors.[63] In one Holy Office trial, a soldier was questioned for possessing some obscene pictures, which he claimed to have bought in Piazza San Marco during the Sensa, where vendors were 'selling them outside, publicly' ('le vendevano li fuori pubblicamente').[64]

Religious holidays or *feste* seem to have been particularly common times for print-selling in the streets, even if local authorities increasingly tried to clamp down on this practice, since in theory all commercial activity was meant to cease on these days.[65] In 1565, the magistrates in charge of small-time commerce, the Giustizia Vecchia, instructed that on feast days under the portico of the Rialto market square known as the Drapparia it was permitted only to sell 'images of saints, books of the epistles, the evangelists, and legends of the saints, offices, bibles, and similar devout works', and not 'dirty books, plays, and [works] of any other sort that be profane'. Down the commercial thoroughfare of the Merceria, and under the portico at San Marco, there might be sold only images of saints and other 'honest and devout' subjects, and not of 'dishonest and shameful things'.[66] This activity evidently did not cease, however, and in 1598, the guild of printers and booksellers tried at least to control feast day peddling by issuing four licences per *festa* to poor masters to sell in the streets. The places where they could operate were strictly regulated, with two sellers with stalls permitted at Rialto and two at San Marco, and a particular instruction that no one was to display their wares down the Merceria. However, there were so many poor guildsmen wishing to sell in these streets on these days that the guild received many more than four petitions.[67] As well as being a prominent public activity, street-selling of print was also one of crucial importance to poor vendors who relied on it to survive. Although it ebbed and flowed at certain times and there were periodic attempts to repress it, print peddling would remain an ineradicable feature of Venice and other Italian cities throughout the early modern period.[68]

This was also a result of consumer demand. It needs to be emphasised that, even in a large city like Venice with many bookshops, numerous street sellers of print were able to eke a living; hence they must have offered something that the established booksellers did not. They may not have stocked a wide range of works, but they could use aggressive forms of verbal and visual advertising to draw customers who made their way through the streets. Vendors working in public spaces were a 'crucial extension' of established bookselling structures, bringing new printed products, which could be very cheap, within the grasp of many more people than might have crossed the threshold of a bookshop to buy a printed a book, and certainly many more than would have sought out a manuscript from a scribe or a stationer.[69]

Hearing and seeing print

Venetians did not actually have to buy a printed product from one of this multitude of vendors in order to gain some exposure to the texts they contained. Printed stock lists and displays of books and prints were designed to catch the eyes of passersby, while hawking and performing snatches of text aimed to catch their ears. In addition, print was not only sold but also was given away as part of more sophisticated promotional strategies, used to advertise other goods and events and circulated freely in order to communicate official and unofficial political information. While Venice thus was a highly literate society by the standards of the time, visual and oral forms of communication remained absolutely vital. Song, for instance, has been described as the 'connective tissue' of early modern society, a powerful form of communication open to all, and this applied equally in Venice.[70]

Many of the sources considered thus far suggest how closely the sale of cheap print was associated with oral performance, hawking and singing. This is illustrated well by a sixteenth-century comical song in the voice of the *massare* (housekeepers) of the city, calling for retribution against the singing pamphlet sellers who slandered them in song (see Figure 7: the frontispiece of what seems to be the original song aimed at the *massare*).[71] Again, the Rialto is the key space for performing and selling cheap print. The lead *massara* calls out to her comrades:

> Let's go first to that fool,
> who, on the Rialto Bridge,
> sells and cries out loudly
> our lament, or song.
> Let's throw him in the water ...
> We'll teach him for making up
> a new song every day ...[72]

Performance and print-peddling obviously became strongly associated activities in Venice by the sixteenth century. This was a natural development when the advertised item was a printed pamphlet, containing stories or songs that might hook the attention of listeners. Selling printed pamphlets quickly became a common feature of the appearances of charlatans and other street performers.

Contemporary with the expansion of printing, Venice was experiencing an exceptionally vibrant period in the development of public spectacle and performance. Frequent, lavish festivals and processions involved a large proportion of the populace as participants or observers, and increasingly worked to frame and direct attention towards Piazza San Marco as the chief site of secular and spiritual power.[73] Theatrical performances held in private palaces or official spectacles within the ducal palace often spilled out into the streets, squares and canals, opening themselves up to a wider audience, moving amphibiously between interior and exterior spaces. This permeability allowed for widespread participation in cultural events. Enjoyment of spectacles was not confined to those with the status or means to be part of a select audience in a private location; the use of public space opened up participation to a broader public.[74]

Street performances of various kinds also were becoming a much more common sight, particularly, but not only, during the period of Carnival and the Ascension fair in May. These entertainments ranged from the impromptu to the sophisticatedly staged, from blind beggars to famous actors, singers and charlatans, but they generally, and increasingly, had a strong commercial flavour – either selling the performance itself (collecting contributions at the end), or peddling other products alongside, or via, the performance. This should not be surprising when so many of the co-opted performance spaces were also marketplaces, where spectacle and commerce constantly intermingled. Tomaso

7 Song against the housekeepers of Venice: *Canzonetta delle massarette, cosa piaceuole da ridere*

Garzoni's *Piazza universale*, first published in 1585, described charlatans and performers competing for attention on platforms in Piazza San Marco. According to Garzoni, buffoons and charlatans could be seen in the piazza 'every evening from the twenty-second to the twenty-fourth hours of the day [i.e., the two hours before sunset], acting out tales, inventing stories, making up dialogues ... singing impromptu, getting angry at each other, making peace, dying from laughter, becoming angry again, brawling on the stage, making a fuss together, and finally passing out the collection boxes, and coming to the little matter of the coins, which they want to swindle out of you with this most polite and courteous chatter of theirs'.[75] Hyperbolic though it might have been, Garzoni's depiction of the piazza was rooted in reality. By the end of the sixteenth century, Venice was renowned for the street entertainments that could be witnessed there, and visitors to the city often reported on this phenomenon. In the early seventeenth century, the Englishman Thomas Coryate wrote that, although there were mountebanks elsewhere in Italy, 'there is a greater concurse of them in Venice than elsewhere' and 'a larger toleration of them here than in other Cities'. Coryate described five or six stages erected in the Piazza for charlatans' performances that took place twice a day, plus more humble performers working on the ground.[76]

The two flourishing cultures of print and performance, unfolding in the same city spaces at the same time, were linked at many points. A number of the performers Garzoni mentioned, for instance, can be identified as authors or publishers of pamphlets from the few decades prior to his writing.[77] Most probably they sold or even gave away such works in the context of performances in these most public spaces of the city. But this tradition was established earlier in the century, as in 1533 when the famous buffoon Zuan Polo set up a platform next to the clocktower in Piazza San Marco, performed for the crowd, then sold copies of his *Book of Rado Stizoso*, a parody of chivalric verse for which previously he had sought a printing privilege.[78] A 1543 edict by the Venetian health magistrates, the Provveditori alla Sanità, circumscribed the places in which entertainers could operate in Piazza San Marco to precisely the area where Zuan Polo had erected his bench: towards the clocktower at the northern edge rather than in the Piazzetta that gave onto the waterfront at the south, closer to the important sites of the Ducal Palace and the Basilica of San Marco (see Figure 8).[79] Another edict of a few months later described the activities of those 'mounting the benches' as singing, distributing stories and medicines and pulling teeth.[80] Over half a century later, Coryate recorded the mountebanks of Venice performing in precisely the same place and doing very similar things, peddling 'oyles, soveraigne waters, amorous songs printed, Apothecary drugs, and a Commonweale of other trifles'.[81] The records of the Venetian health magistrates throughout the century confirm that printed pamphlets and fliers containing medical remedies and 'secrets' were given away or sold by charlatans as a key promotional strategy.[82]

8 Performers onstage near the clocktower in Piazza San Marco, plus two in foreground, from Bianco, *Viaggio da Venetia al Santo Sepolcro, et al monte Sinai* …

Information centres

Ephemeral print also was beginning to be widely used in Venice to communicate many kinds of information. Traditional forms of oral advertisement and announcement quickly were supplemented by print, perceived as an effective way to communicate with large numbers of people, who would either read it themselves or hear it read out loud. Again these activities were focused around the key 'information centres' of the city, Rialto and San Marco, where it was presumed that a good number of Venetians frequently would pass through in person, or that news would rapidly make its way from there to the more outlying quarters of the city.[83] In 1522, for example, Sanudo described an upcoming lottery being advertised one morning in Rialto with 'trumpets and pipes', while printed notices also were used.[84] Charlatans commissioned handbills or posters to advertise their presence in town, like the one that Tomaso Cazola da Como 'medico et astrologo' had put up in public around Rialto, San Marco and elsewhere in the city. Cazola noted that under his own poster there had been affixed other advertisements for healers and an astrologer.[85]

The organs of government themselves also began to employ print to communicate edicts and laws to the populace. By the early sixteenth century, laws started to be routinely posted up at Rialto and San Marco and also read out loud from the two columns designated for this purpose, the *pietre delle bande*, along with court summons and banishments. Furthermore, the publication of other types of political information occurred as early as 1496, when Sanudo recorded that news of Venice's involvement in an international alliance was 'thrown into print' (*butada in stampa*) for the purpose of public information.[86] The printer Paolo Danza, who wrote and printed songs about recent events from his shop near Rialto, also was employed in the 1520s and 1530s to print some government laws.[87] Ecclesiastical authorities contributed to the proliferation of print for public information, as in the publication of an indulgence granted on the occasion of the Sensa festival, which was 'thrown into print, posted up and published throughout the churches so that everyone would know'.[88]

Less official forms of communication also began to be 'thrown into print' and distributed publicly in the same central city spaces. The Rialto area was the favoured site for defamatory graffiti and the posting of libels, as in 1532 when pasquinades against Pietro Aretino and various courtesans were posted up in the area and copied down by many. After it was erected in 1541, the hunch-backed statue of the Gobbo in the market square of San Giacomo, at the heart of the commercial district, became the chosen site for libels previously stuck to the *pietra delle bande*.[89] While manuscript continued to be used for these kinds of semi-licit publications, they also began to appear in cheap printed form, presumably to amplify their diffusion. In 1499, some defamatory sonnets concerning the death of the King of France were printed and 'sold throughout this city', only to be confiscated by a Venetian government agent concerned about the political ramifications.[90] Cheap print was permeating the political culture of the city, and like the oral circulation of songs and poems, it reached a great variety of people, many of whom did not belong to the classes officially permitted to play a political role. Although it would take the Venetian government another century or so to adopt a more open domestic 'media strategy', already it was recognising both the potential power of cheap print to communicate to its subjects, as well as the danger that this would turn those subjects into a public – one that expected to be continually informed about and even involved in political life.[91]

Other cheap publications recorded other types of news, including the more quotidian, and were produced in close relation to the ebb and flow of daily events. The speed of the pamphleteers to spread news of local interest was a recurring literary trope, as in the example of the poem about the courtesan La Zaffetta. Pamphlet writers recorded events of local significance such as the fire that ripped through the Rialto market in 1514, commemorated in a pamphlet by the singer Perosino della Rotonda, or the festivities of Carnival.[92] Pamphlets were issued to tap into popular enthusiasm for occasions such as the Sensa festival and the feast day of San Martino.[93] Later in the century, there were huge outpourings of cheap printed pamphlets, maps and images informing the public about, and commemorating, major events such as the Venetian victory over the Ottomans at Lepanto or the French King Henry III's visit to Venice.[94] Some of these promoted precisely the official government line about the power and glories of the Republic, but the circulation of other such publications caused great concern to the authorities. Such was the case with the pamphlets confiscated from ambulant vendors on the Rialto Bridge in the 1540s which discussed the imprisonment of the heretical monk Fra Baldo Lupetino. The printers responsible were pursued energetically by the Council of Ten and the Inquisition.[95]

What made cheap print so potentially powerful in the dissemination of news and other information was its continued and close interaction with manuscript and oral modes of communication, as when printed laws were read out loud by the government heralds or *comandadori*, or when a street singer rendered the latest news into verse form and performed it in the public square. Although mostly lost, enough survives to show that cheap printed matter was an integral aspect of the urban culture of Venice in this period, becoming part of the temporary geography of the city. The pulsing of print through other cultural circuits in the city, carrying ordinary and extraordinary information, through political, social and religious life, through performance and retail, set it apart from other cheap commodities with which it was lumped by some sixteenth-century commentators.

Some time ago, Roger Chartier suggested that printed matter displayed in the streets and read out loud in various group settings was crucial to 'acculturating' the illiterate or partially literate to the written word in the early years of printing.[96] Reconstructing the presence of these activities in the urban environment does indeed show how, at street level, the expansion of printing impinged on the lives of many, if not most, Venetians. The ubiquity of ephemeral printed matter and its connections to public performance and oral culture indicate that even if a majority of the Venetian population did not possess full functional literacy, or did not wish to part with the few coins necessary to buy a pamphlet, they still participated to some degree in the same shared public culture. The implications of this were that the circulation of various kinds of texts was now much harder to restrict; as we saw in the previous chapter, it was precisely the public, commercial and accessible nature of cheap print – personified by the figure of the street pedlar or print-peddling charlatan – that disturbed some observers.

This chapter has suggested how the mechanisms of producing and disseminating cheap print insinuated themselves right into the economic, political and ritual heart of Venice by the early years of the sixteenth century. The city's canals, bridges, public squares and alleyways described an urban geography of production, circulation and consumption of printed texts. More ephemeral means of diffusion were far from marginal in Venetian life. While the shops of prolific printers and publishers of cheap material were clustered tightly around the main commercial thoroughfares of the city, the sellers of print that were probably the most visible and most familiar to the majority of city dwellers were those now most invisible to modern scholars. Stallholders and street sellers who sold a variety of goods including print operated in strategic, central locations, putting themselves in the path of many Venetians going about their everyday business. By taking to the streets, these print pedlars and performers not only found a way to earn a living but also staked out a place in the urban culture of Venice, their often unlicensed and uncontrolled presence a continuous challenge to the officially sanctioned activities of the city.[97]

Notes

1 See Wilson, *World in Venice*, esp. ch. 1.
2 On the physical and cultural renovation of the city, see D. Calabi, 'Il rinnovamento urbano del primo Cinquecento', in *Storia di Venezia dalle origini alla caduta della Serenissima*, vol. 5, *Il Rinascimento: società ed economia*, eds A. Tenenti and U. Tucci (Rome: Istituto della Enciclopedia Italiana, 1996), pp. 101–63; M. Tafuri (ed.), '*Renovatio urbis*'. *Venezia nell'eta di Andrea Gritti (1523–1538)* (Rome: Officina edizioni, 1984). Venice's population grew from around 115,000 in 1509 to around 158,000 in 1552; D. Beltrami, *Storia della popolazione di Venezia dalla fine del secolo XVI alla caduta della Repubblica* (Padua: Cedam, 1954), p. 59.
3 See C. Judde de Larivière and R. Salzberg, 'Le peuple est la cité. L'idée de popolo et la condition des popolani à Venise (XVe–XVIe siècles)', *Annales ESC*, 68:4 (2013): 1113–40.
4 P. F. Brown, '"Not one but many separate cities": housing diversity in Renaissance Venice', in N. Howe (ed.), *Home and Homelessness in the Medieval and Renaissance Worlds* (Notre Dame, IN: University of Notre Dame Press, 2004), p. 16. On peripheral neighbourhoods with high numbers of migrants, see P. Braunstein, 'Cannaregio, zona di transito?', and J.-F. Chauvard, 'Scale di osservazione e inserimento degli stranieri nello spazio veneziano tra XVII e XVIII secolo', both in D. Calabi and P. Lanaro (eds), *La città italiana e i luoghi degli stranieri. XIV–XVIII secolo* (Rome: Laterza, 1998), pp. 52–62, 85–107.
5 Cf. Johns, *Nature of the Book*, esp. ch. 2.
6 Important works on these more exclusive spaces include A. Quondam, '"Mercanzia d'onore", "mercanzia d'utile". Produzione libraria e lavoro intellettuale a Venezia nel Cinquecento', in A. Petrucci (ed.), *Libri, editori e pubblico nell'Europa moderna. Guida storica e critica* (Rome: Laterza, 1977), pp. 51–104; Quondam, 'Nel giardino dei Marcolini'; M. Zorzi, 'La circolazione del libro a Venezia nel Cinquecento: biblioteche private e pubbliche', *Ateneo veneto*, 28 (1990), 117–90. See also Nuovo's discussion of bookshops as important places of intellectual exchange in *Il commercio librario nell'Italia*, pp. 266–72. A more comprehensive overview of the spaces of Venetian cultural life is provided by F. De Vivo, 'I luoghi della cultura a Venezia nel primo Cinquecento', in *Atlante della letteratura italiana*, vol. 1: *Dalle origini al Rinascimento*, ed. A. De Vincentiis (Turin: Einaudi, 2010), pp. 708–18.
7 On the idea of the 'geography of the book', see Ogborn and Withers, 'Introduction: book geography, book history'.
8 M. A. Rouse and R. H. Rouse, Cartolai, *Illuminators, and Printers in Fifteenth-Century*

Italy (Los Angeles: Department of Special Collections, University Research Library, University of California, 1988), p. 32.
9 Lowry, *Nicholas Jenson*, esp. ch. 2.
10 For records of auctions, see S. Connell, 'Books and their owners in Venice, 1345–1480', *Journal of the Warburg and Courtauld Institutes*, 35 (1972), 163–86.
11 See P. Cherubini, 'Note sul commercio librario a Roma nel '400', *Studi romani*, 33:3–4 (1985), 217–18; M. L. Bianchi and M. L. Grossi, 'Botteghe, economia e spazio urbano', in F. Franceschi and G. Fossi (eds), *Arti fiorentine. La grande storia dell'artigianato* (Florence: Giunti, 1999), p. 45.
12 'Et quelli de le botege haveno gran danno, maxime quelle botege verso la riva d'il Ferro, qual era do cartoleri, [e] do librari di libri a stampa'. *DMS*, vol. 36, col. 526 (14 August 1524). On the continued market for manuscripts in the sixteenth century, see Zorzi, 'La circolazione del libro'; Richardson, *Manuscript Culture*.
13 Nuovo, *Il commercio librario nell'Italia*, p. 36. See also Rouse and Rouse, *Cartolai, Illuminators, and Printers*; and A. Melograni, 'The illuminated manuscript as a commodity: production, consumption and the *cartolaio*'s role in fifteenth-century Italy', in M. O'Malley and E. Welch (eds), *The Material Renaissance* (Manchester: Manchester University Press, 2007), pp. 71–84. Printers and booksellers also cemented mutually beneficial ties with *cartolai* by intermarriage.
14 M. A. Sabellico, *De latinae linguae reparatione* (1493), discussed in Lowry, *World of Aldus Manutius*, pp. 36–7; Nuovo, *Il commercio librario nell'Italia*, p. 114.
15 ASV, *AC*, Notatorio, r. 2054, c. 40^v (29 March 1533).
16 'Sotto el relogio di San Marco'; 'sotto i portigi a San Marco da quelli librari che vendeno la festa'. ASV, *SU*, b. 7, fasc. 18, cc. 1^v–2^v (22 May 1549).
17 *Ibid*, c. 2^v.
18 M. Zorzi, 'Stampatori tedeschi a Venezia', in his *Venezia e la Germania* (Milan: Electa, 1986), p. 122. See also M. Lowry, 'The social world of Nicholas Jenson and John of Cologne', *La Bibliofilía*, 83:3 (1981), 193–218; M. Lowry, 'Venetian capital, German technology and Renaissance culture in the later fifteenth century', *Renaissance Studies*, 2:1 (1988), 1–13; and C. Dondi, 'Printers and guilds in fifteenth-century Venice', *La Bibliofilía*, 106:3 (2004), 229–65, for what is known about the locations of early printers' homes and shops.
19 'Tutto – e sia qual si voglia – se ne trova abbondantemente ... perchè di ogni cossa, et di ogni terra, et parte del mondo che possa vegnir robba ... qui vi viene' (M. Sanudo, *De origine, situ et magistratibus urbis venetae ovvero La città di Venetia* (1493–1530) (Milan: Cisalpino-La Goliardica, 1980), p. 30).
20 'Qui tutte cosse che si sa, et vol dimandar vi si trova' (*ibid*., p. 25).
21 Mackenney, *Tradesmen and Traders*, pp. 88–9; J. Delancey, '"In the streets where they sell colors': placing *vendecolori* in the urban fabric of early modern Venice', *Wallraf-Richartz-Jahrbuch*, 72 (2011), 193–232.
22 Calabi, 'Il rinnovamento urbano'.
23 See Febvre and Martin, *Coming of the Book*, pp. 176–7, on the clustering of bookshops around the neighbourhoods of universities and *parlements* in French cities.
24 For the rent at Rialto, see Sanudo, 'Praise of the city of Venice', p. 12.
25 One patrician landlord, Lorenzo di Bernardo Giustiniani, in 1514 declared his ownership of a number of houses in the parish, where he himself lived, some of which,

he claimed, 'per essere in loco disonestissimo come è publico veramente la mita de l'ano sono desafita' (ASV, *Decime*, b. 51, *condizione* of Lorenzo Giustiniani, c. 1ᵛ (1514)).

26 A. Zannini, *Venezia, città aperta. Gli stranieri e la Serenissima XIV–XVIII sec.* (Venice: Marcianum, 2009), p. 149.

27 For the rent of the Giustiniani houses, see the *condizione* cited above, n. 25.

28 M. Infelise, *Prima dei giornali. Alla origine della publica informazione (secoli XVI e XVII)* (Rome and Bari: Laterza, 2002), pp. 25–6.

29 Bindoni and Pasini were active from around 1525 until the 1550s (*DTEI*, s.v). On at least one occasion, the location of this print shop also was described as 'presso il bastione di San Moisè', a *bastione* being a type of wine shop or tavern, potentially an important site for the distribution, recitation and display of cheap printed songs and verses. See G. Tassini, *Curiosità veneziane, ovvero origini delle denominazioni stradali di Venezia*, ed. L. Moretti, rev. edn (Venice: Filippi, 1970), p. 67.

30 Rusconi is documented in the parish from 1514 and was active until the 1520s; E. Pastorello, *Tipografi, editori, librai a Venezia nel secolo XVI* (Florence: Olschki, 1924), p. 76. Fontaneto was active from around 1514 until the 1540s and recorded at San Moisè in the 1533 list cited above, n. 15.

31 On the De' Franceschi, see *DTEI*, s.v. Other printers in the area in this period include Francesco Bindoni's uncle Bernardino (active c.1532–63), with a shop at the sign of Saint Peter in the Frezzaria, although by 1534 he moved to the parish of Santa Marina to the north-east of San Marco; *DTEI*, s.v. Matteo Pagan (active c.1543–60), one-time partner of Bernardino's brother Agostino, worked in the same street as a printer and engraver at the sign of Faith (Ascarelli and Menato, *La tipografia del '500*, p. 383).

32 The Nicolini worked in San Fantin from c.1512 until mid-century (Ascarelli and Menato, *La tipografia del '500*, p. 354). Zoppino was publishing in Venice (located at least some of that time 'sul campo della Madonna di San Fantino') from 1507 until the mid 1540s; N. Harris, *Bibliografia dell'Orlando innamorato* (Ferrara: Istituto di studi rinascimentali; Modena: Panini, 1988), vol. 2, p. 87. Benedetto Bindoni, active c.1520–41, was recorded in San Fantin in the 1533 list cited in n. 15. although in 1538 he relocated, renting a *bottega* next to the church of San Geminiano on Piazza San Marco for twenty ducats per annum (ASV, *PSM*, Affittanza, r. 174, c. 52ʳ; *DTEI*, s.v). Agostino Bindoni had his shop in San Paternian, immediately north-east of San Fantin, according to the 1533 list and was active c.1523–58 (*DTEI*, s.v). For further discussion of these printers, see Chapter 3.

33 Active c.1530–72. Valvassore's shop location is noted in J. D. Passavant, *Le peintre-graveur* (Leipzig: Weigel, 1864), vol. 5, pp. 88–9; see also Ascarelli and Menato, *La tipografia del '500*, p. 363.

34 Sessa was active from 1505 to c.1562, when his heirs carried on in the same shop (Ascarelli and Menato, *La tipografia del '500*, p. 327).

35 Van der Sman, 'Print publication in Venice', 235; see also D. Woodward, *Maps as Prints in the Italian Renaissance: Makers, Distributors and Consumers* (London: British Library, 1996), p. 45.

36 On the close-knit environment of the Roman print shops, see C. L. C. E. Witcombe, *Print Publishing in Sixteenth Century Rome: Growth and Expansion, Rivalry and Murder* (Turnhout: Brepols, 2008), esp. ch. 4.

37 For example, the printers Aurelio Pincio at San Giovanni in Bragora in the eastern *sestiere* of Castello and Tomaso Ballarin at San Giacomo dell'Orio, west of Rialto, both recorded in the 1533 list cited in n. 15.
38 'A Rialto si spaccia più un pronostico d'un ceretano, che in merciaria qualche compositione fatta da un valent'huomo' (Garzoni, *La piazza universale*, vol. 1, p. 157).
39 It should be noted that even the geography of the print shops could be a shifting one, as in the relocations of Benedetto Bindoni noted above, n. 32.
40 W. Eamon, 'Markets, piazzas, and villages', in K. Park and L. Daston (eds), *The Cambridge History of Science*, vol. 3, *Early Modern Science* (Cambridge: Cambridge University Press, 2008), p. 215, referring to piazzas.
41 For a useful overview of the historiography, see D. van den Heuvel, 'Selling in the shadows: peddlers and hawkers in early modern Europe', in M. van der Linden and L. Lucassen (eds), *Working on Labour: Essays in Honour of Jan Lucassen* (Leiden and Boston, MA: Brill, 2012), pp. 125–51.
42 On later developments of peddling networks, see L. Fontaine, *History of Pedlars in Europe*, trans. V. Whittaker (Cambridge: Polity, 1996); R. Chartier and H.-J. Lüsebrink (eds), *Colportage et lecture populaire. Imprimés de large circulation en Europe XVIe–XIXe siècles (Actes du colloque des 21–24 avril 1991, Wolfenbüttel)* (Paris: Institut mémoires de l'édition contemporaine/Maison des Sciences de l'Homme, 1996); R. Myers, M. Harris and G. Mandelbrote (eds), *Fairs, Markets and the Itinerant Book Trade* (London: British Library, 2007); Carnelos, *I libri da risma*; J. Raymond, J. Salman and R. Harms (eds), *Not Dead Things: The Dissemination of Popular Print in Britain, Italy, and the Low Countries, 1500–1900* (Leiden: Brill, 2013). On the beginnings of print peddling, see G. Bertoli, 'Librai, cartolai e ambulanti immatricolati nell'Arte dei medici e speziali di Firenze dal 1490 al 1600', pts 1 and 2, *La Bibliofilía*, 94:2–3 (1992), 125–64, 227–62; and R. Salzberg, '"Selling stories and many other things in and through the city": peddling print in sixteenth-century Florence and Venice', *Sixteenth Century Journal*, 42:3 (2011), 737–59.
43 Cited in the Introduction, n. 37.
44 E. Welch, *Shopping in the Renaissance: Consumer Cultures in Italy 1400–1600* (New Haven, CT: Yale University Press, 2005), p. 97.
45 'Ser Iacomo da Trini quondam Alberto sartor libraro vende sotto il portego de Rialto' was recorded in a 1567 list of booksellers to whom a decree of the Holy Office was communicated (ASV, *SU*, b. 156, unnumbered sheet dated 13 September 1567). In 1571, still working in this location, Giacomo was questioned by the Holy Office about selling prohibited books (ASV, *SU*, b. 156, c. 27^r). 'Ser Batista furlan quondam Tomaso Zanier, ha il banco in Piaza de San Marco' was recorded in the same 1567 list and in 1575 was picked up for selling unlicensed printed orations: see ASV, *SU*, b. 39, fasc. 7, and the Conclusion of this book. On repeated attempts to unencumber the piazza of stalls, see Carnelos, *'Con libri alla mano'*, pp. 186–7.
46 Bordogna was active in Venice from *c.*1555 to 1602 and listed as keeping a 'banchetto a San Marco' in 1571 (*DTEI*, s.v.; ASV, *SU*, b. 156, c. 34^v). In the 1567 list cited in the previous note, he appears as 'Ser Sigismondo quondam Zuane bressan vende libri a la chiesia de San Basso'.
47 Rocca registered 'per insegna della sua bottega et suo bancho la novizza in lustro' in 1568 although he was active on and off from 1549–76 (G. Moro, 'Insegne librarie e

marche tipografiche in un registro veneziano del '500', *La Bibliofilía*, 91:1 (1989), 69; Ascarelli and Menato, *La tipografia del '500*, p. 391).

48 T. Carter, 'Music-printing in late sixteenth- and early seventeenth-century Florence: Giorgio Marescotti, Cristofano Marescotti and Zanobi Pignoni', *Early Music History*, 9 (1990), 41–2.

49 On later relations between the guild and street sellers, see L. Carnelos, 'La corporazione e gli esterni stampatori e librai a Venezia tra norma e contraffazione (XVI–XVIII)', *Società e storia*, 33:130 (2010), 657–88.

50 'Julio Bressanin de Bortolomio bresan ... a il banco in piaza'; 'Jacomo de Simon da Venezia libraro vende sotto il portego de Rialto'; 'Nicolo de Bortolamio Pierio Toschan da Bergamo vende libri la festa in Marzaria'; 'Zuane de Anzolo erbariol ... vende libri a San Salvador non ha botega'. *Erbariol* could also be from *erbolaio*, a seller of medicinal herbs; see G. Boerio, *Dizionario del dialetto veneziano* (Venice: Cecchini, 1867), s.v. The list is in ASV, *SU*, b. 156, unnumbered sheet dated 13 September 1567. The others listed who were almost certainly street sellers include: 'Ser Bonadio de Filippo Tagiapiera da Venezia vende libri in Rialto', 'Ser Piero francese quondam Jane Feriero francese vende libri in Rialto sotto il portego', 'Ser Ulivier quondam Lunardo da Vizenza vende libri in Rialto sotto il portego', 'Ser Zuane del quondam Nicolò bergamasco vende libri in Rialto sotto il portego', 'Ser Bortolomio del quondam Bernardin di Salò vende libri a San Marco soto li portegi', 'Ser Antonio de Alvise da Venetia vende libri a San Marco apreso il Ponte dela Palgia [i.e., Paglia]', 'Ser Lorenzo da Bergamo di ser Bortolomio di Maffei vende in Piaza de San Marco'.

51 For further discussion of the connection between poverty and street-selling, and of this case, see Chapter 3.

52 L. Pon, *Raphael, Durer and Marcantonio Raimondi: Copying and the Renaissance Print* (New Haven, CT: Yale University Press, 2004), pp. 38–40. See also, Bury, *Print in Italy*, p. 170.

53 See A. Reynolds, *Renaissance Humanism at the Court of Clement VII. Francesco Berni's* Dialogue Against Poets *in Context* (New York and London: Garland, 1997), p. 192.

54 'Accidit in piaza che era uno puto vendeva a stampa certe canzon contra Franza, dicendo englesi à roto il campo di Franza, et fo uno che li zafò di man con dir "tu menti per la gola", e corse via; e il puto vene in palazo a dolersi. Li capitani andò per piar quel tristo fe' tal atto; ma non fu trovato' (*DMS*, vol. 14, col. 475 (11 July 1512)).

55 'Molti librari et stampadori contra la forma delle parte et ordini dell'illustrissimo Consiglio di Dieci ... si fano lecito stampare in questa città libri, istorie, frotole, canzon, lettere, et pronostichi senza le debite licentia et liberamente venderli over per puti et altri far vender sul Ponte di Rialto et altri lochi' (ASV, *ECB*, Notatorio, b. 56, vol. 2, c. 38^v (2 March 1568)).

56 Aretino, *La Cortigiana*, act 1, scene 4, p. 71. The shouting of titles by a *forfantello* is also mentioned in Giulio Landi's *Formaggiata* (cited in Chapter 1, n. 27).

57 'E parmi udir da i putti gridar forte, / Sul Ponte di Rialto, acciò s'intenda: / Chi vuol della Zaffetta legenda?' (L. Venier, *La Zaffetta* (Catania: Guaitolini, 1929), p. 47).

58 D. Calabi and P. Morachiello, *Rialto: le fabbriche e il Ponte (1514–91)* (Turin: Einaudi, 1987), p. 176. The other two bridges that now span the Grand Canal, the Accademia

and the Scalzi, were built in the nineteenth and twentieth centuries respectively. Nevertheless, there were numerous ferry stations (*traghetti*) along the Grand Canal. On the social distinctions reinforced by various means of transport, see Romano, 'The gondola', 359–74.

59 Cited above, Chapter 1, n. 5. Established printers and booksellers who contravened this law were to be fined twenty-five ducats, street vendors to be whipped publicly along the prominent route between Rialto and San Marco, then imprisoned for six months. This may have been because they were expected to be too poor to pay the fine, as well as to make a very public example of them in precisely the spaces in which they tended to operate.

60 'Sul ponte de Rialto chi ghe cria: / ... A chi dàghio sti bei officietti? / Un pronostico nuovo ... / che ve mostra i pianetti / ... La barceletta de Missier Sbruffaldo!' (M. Venier, *Canzoni e sonetti* (Venice: Corbo e Fiore, 1993), pp. 177–8).

61 'A un pont che tug de legn fondat senz arch, / e quand o'l vid si carch / de zent e de boteghi, e de banchet / ... Puri qui è la canzon de San Martin, / vinti per un quatrin ... / Chi vol un officietto ...?/ Lunari novi e beli' (*Viaggio de Zan Padella, cosa ridiculosa e bela, dond es descrif tug le cose ches vende sul punt de Rialt in Venesia* (Modena, [c.1580]), cc. Aii^r–Aiii^r. BL 1071.c.63.20).

62 'Si vendeno le hystorie per li ponti, / et per le piazze in ciascadun confino' (*Il lamento della femena di pre Augustino, qual si duol di esser viua vedendolo in tante angustie* ... [Venice: c.1520s?], c. Aii^r. BMV 2231.5).

63 Welch, *Shopping in the Renaissance*, pp. 166, 177–84.

64 Trial of Capitano Annibale da Perugia (1585), held in ASV, SU, b. 55, quoted in M. Milani, *Piccole storie di stregoneria nella Venezia del '500* (Verona: Essedue, 1989), p. 180.

65 On the attitudes of church and state authorities to working, trading and displaying goods on the many movable and immovable feasts of the Italian calendar, see Welch, *Shopping in the Renaissance*, pp. 111–15.

66 'Sotto il portego di Rialto della Drapparia, non sia lecito ad alcuno di tenir in tal zorni, salvo che santi, et libri de epistole, et evangelii, et lezende de santi, offitii, bibie, et simil opere devote, et non libri immondi, comedie, et d'altra sorte, che siano profano, et così altra sorte de robba non s'habbi da vender sotto il detto portego. Per la Marzaria veramente se possi tenir santi, et carte de dissegni, et depente de cose divote, et honeste, et non cose dishoneste, et vergognose, et così sotto il portego de San Marco'. Law copied into the *Matricola dell'Arte dei stampatori e librari di Venezia*, BMCV, MS. Cicogna 3044/ Mariegola no. 119, c. 42^r.

67 ASV, ALS, Atti, b. 163, r. 2, c. 8^r (5 November 1598). For more on attempts to regulate the street trade, see Chapter 5.

68 See Salzberg, 'Selling stories'. See also Carnelos, '*Con libri alla mano*', esp. ch. 5.

69 See J. Salman, 'Watching the pedlar's movements: itinerant distribution in the urban Netherlands', in Myers et al., *Fairs, Markets and the Itinerant Book Trade*, p. 137.

70 T. Plebani, 'Voci tra le carte. Libri di canzone, leggere per cantare', in Braida and Infelise (eds), *Libri per tutti*, p. 72. For other important works on oral culture, see the Introduction, n. 16.

71 *La congivra che fanno le massare, contra coloro che cantano la sua canzone* ... (Venice: A. Facol, [c.1600]). BL 1071.a.37. *Edit16* lists two earlier editions of this text (1584, 1593) but there were probably earlier lost editions.

72 'Demo in prima a quel giotton, / che, sul Ponte de Rialto, / nostro pianto, o sia canzon, / vende, e cria con parlar alto. / Femo farlo in acqua un salto ... / Insegnemoghe a trovar / ogni dì nuovo cantare' (*La congivra che fanno le massare* ..., c. A1^v).

73 E. Muir, *Civic Ritual in Renaissance Venice* (Princeton, NJ: Princeton University Press, 1981), pp. 154, 209-11.

74 R. Guarino, *Teatro e mutamenti. Rinascimento e spettacolo a Venezia* (Bologna: Il Mulino, 1995); R. Ferguson, 'Staging scripted comedy in Renaissance Venice (1500-1560): a survey of the evidence', in B. Richardson, S. Gilson and C. Keen (eds), *Theatre, Opera, and Performance from the Fifteenth Century to the Present. Essays in Honour of Richard Andrews* (London: Society for Italian Studies, 2004), pp. 47-8. A very useful overview of the kinds of festivities occurring in Venice in this period is the collection of *Articoli estratti dai Diarii di Marino Sanudo concernenti notizie storiche di Commedie, Mumarie, Feste e Compagnie della Calza*, held in BMCV, MS. Cicogna 1650/XV.

75 'Ogni sera dalle vintidue fino alle vintiquattro hore di giorno, finger novelle, trovare historie, formar dialoghi ... cantare all'improviso, corrucciarsi insieme, far la pace, morir dalle risa, alterarsi di nuovo, urtarsi in sul banco, far questione insieme, e finalmente buttar fuora i bussoli, et venire al quanquam delle gazette soldi, che vogliono carpire con queste loro gentilissime, et garbatissime chiachiere' (Garzoni, *La piazza universale*, vol. 2, p. 910).

76 T. Coryate and G. Coryate, *Coryate's Crudities* (Glasgow: MacLehose, 1905; repr. of 1611 edn) vol. 1, pp. 409-10.

77 Henke, *Performance and Literature*, pp. 117-20.

78 *DMS*, vol. 58, col. 542 (10 August 1533): 'havendo Zuan Polo piacevole buffon preparado un soler appresso el Relogio, vestito da poeta con zoia de lauro in testa, suo fiol et uno altro travestidi, fè un sermon a tuti e dete fuora l'opera composta per lui a stampa di Rado Stizoso'. For more on the performances and prints of the Venetian buffoons, see D. Vianello, *L'arte del buffone. Maschere e spettacolo tra Italia e Baviera nel xvi secolo* (Rome: Bulzoni, 2005). On Zuan Polo's privilege for the work, see Chapter 3, n. 63.

79 'Alcuno che canta in bancho per l'avenir non debbi più montar in bancho per cantar, o altro, dalla Piera del Bando verso le colone in loco alcuno, ma debano star da lì verso il relogio' (ASV, *Sanità*, Notatorio, b. 729, c. 21^r (4 January 1543)). The use of the piazza for such performances already was traditional by the late fifteenth century, when Sanudo recorded that 'in questa sera sopra la piaza di San Marcho, per uno orbo con la lira, a l'improvisa fu cantato verso la loza di le cosse di Milan e dil parti dil signor Lodovico [il Moro]' (*DMS*, vol. 2, col. 1198 (3 September 1499)).

80 'Non sia persona alcuna ... che ardisca montar sopra bancho alcuno per cantar, dar via balote, historie, o ... a cavar denti' (ASV, *Sanità*, Notatorio, b. 729, c. 26^r (law of 2 May 1543)).

81 Coryate, *Coryate's Crudities*, vol. 1, p. 410.

82 See Chapter 4.

83 See De Vivo, *Information and Communication*, pp. 89-119. See also Burke, 'Early modern Venice as a center of information'; Infelise, *Prima dei giornali*; C. Neerfeld, *Historia per forma di diaria: la cronachistica veneziana contemporanea a cavallo tra il Quattro e il Cinquecento* (Venice: Istituto Veneto di Scienze, Lettere ed Arti, 2006), pp. 147-73. S. J. Milner explores what he calls the 'information gateways' of Florence in

his '"... Fanno bandire, notificare, et expressamente comandare". Town criers and the information economy of Renaissance Florence', *I Tatti Studies*, 16: 1–2 (2013), 107–51.
84 *DMS*, vol. 33, col. 408 (8 August 1522). On the running of lotteries, see E. Welch, 'Lotteries in early modern Italy', *Past and Present*, 91:1 (2008), 71–111.
85 ASV, *SU*, b. 50 (1583–84).
86 *DMS*, vol. 1, col. 252 (31 July 1496).
87 Some of these are preserved in *DMS*, vol. 50, cols 140–1, 306–7; vol. 58, cols 107–14.
88 *DMS*, vol. 2, cols 691–2 (5 July 1499): 'Copia dil brieve di la confirmation dil Perdon di la Sensa ... ditta bolla fo butada a stampa, posta et publicata per le chiesie acciò tutti sapi'.
89 A. Marzo, 'Pasquino e il Gobbo di Rialto', in C. Damianaki, P. Procaccioli and A. Romano (eds), *Ex marmore. Pasquini, pasquinisti, pasquinate nell'Europa moderna* (Manziana: Vecchiarelli, 2006), p. 123. See also A. Moschetti, 'Il Gobbo di Rialto e le sue relazioni con Pasquino', *Nuovo archivio veneto*, 5:1 (1893), 5–93. For the pasquinades against Aretino, see *DMS*, vol. 57, col. 288 (29 November 1532).
90 *DMS*, vol. 2, col. 366 (24 January 1499).
91 De Vivo, *Information and Communication*.
92 P. della Rotonda, *Lo incendio de Realto in Venetia nel anno M.D.XIIII. Novamente composto* (n.p.d.), bought by Hernan Colòn in Rome in November 1515 (listed in Wagner and Carrera, *Catalogo dei libri*, p. 397, no. 745). A four-leaf octavo *Dimostration fatta il giovedì di Carnevale in Venetia sopra la Piazza di Santo Marco ...* (Venice, 1528), also was owned by Colòn (listed in *ibid.*, p. 450, no. 855). For further discussion of news pamphlets, see Chapter 4.
93 See, for example, the pamphlet, thought to have been produced in Venice in the early sixteenth century, entitled *El triompho e festa che fanno le garzone alegrandosi de la Sensa ...* (listed in E. Picot, 'La raccolta di poemetti italiani della Biblioteca di Chantilly', *Rassegna bibliografica della letteratura italiana*, 2 (1894), 122).
94 D. Rhodes, 'La battaglia di Lepanto e la stampa popolare a Venezia. Studio bibliografico', *Miscellanea marciana*, 10–11 (1995–96), 9–63; U. Rozzo, 'La battaglia di Lepanto nell'editoria dell'epoca e una miscellanea fontaniniana', *Rara volumina*, 1–2 (2000), 41–69; I. Fenlon, *The Ceremonial City. History, Memory and Myth in Renaissance Venice* (New Haven, CT and London: Yale University Press, 2007), esp. ch. 9. See also the discussion of ephemeral print concerning the plague of 1575–77 in the Conclusion, below.
95 See ASV, *SU*, b. 10, fasc. 15, documents X and XIII. A copy of the offending six-leaf quarto pamphlet, *Articoli proposti à Fra Baldo, preggione in San Marco, con la risposta de esso frate*, is held in this file. On this case, see S. Cavazza, 'Libri in volgare e propaganda eterodossa: Venezia 1543–47', in *Libri, idee e sentimenti religiosi nel Cinquecento italiano* (Ferrara: Istituto di Studi Rinascimentali; Modena: Panini, 1986), p. 23.
96 Chartier, 'Publishing strategies'.
97 See the forthcoming book of Niall Atkinson, *The Noisy Renaissance: Sound, Architecture and Florentine Urban Life*, on the competition between official and unofficial sounds and narratives in urban public space. I am grateful to Niall for allowing me to see a part of his monograph before its publication.

3

'A trade open to any mortal man': mobility and versatility in the Venetian printing industry

For about a century after the initial flux of printers into the city, the Venetian printing industry remained a dynamic and fluid community composed of more or less mobile individuals. With this physically mobility went a good deal of professional versatility, as people tried their hand at different aspects of print production or dissemination, without necessarily possessing a great deal of training or experience. At least until the guild began to restrict entry from the 1570s, the trade was still, in the words of Erasmus, 'open to any mortal man'.[1] This was particularly the case with the production and dissemination of cheap print; the shorter and cheaper the texts, the lower the barriers to participating.

With their marked mobility, members of the print trade were exemplary of what is increasingly seen to be a common characteristic of the experiences of non-elite people across early modern Europe. Mobility was not just a strategy of the very poor seeking to survive; many others from the world of artisans and small-time traders moved at some point in their lives, if not several times. While most people's moves were small-scale (frequently intra-regional) and temporary, they are crucial to our understanding of early modern life and processes of cultural, economic, religious and social change that occurred in the period.[2] Furthermore, with these moves often came changes of career; professional flexibility needs to be seen as another useful asset for working people in this period.[3] Until recently, these factors have not been adequately emphasised in studies of the early Italian printing trade. The regional focus of much printing history, concentrating on the successful practitioners who settled in one place and established themselves as printers, publishers or booksellers, long obscured the degree to which many members of the trade continued to be highly mobile.[4] Likewise, the retrospective, and anachronistic, attribution of fixed professional identities meant that the multifaceted careers of many figures remained in the shade.

This chapter places the themes of mobility and professional versatility at its centre, and examines how they run through the lives and careers of various individuals involved in the production and dissemination of cheap print in Renaissance Venice. The focus on cheap print brings a wider and more heterogeneous array of characters into view than those few eminent figures who have dominated histories of Venetian printing, such as Aldo Manuzio, Nicholas Jenson and Gabriele Giolito (although of course they, too, were migrants – from the vicinity of Rome, from France and from Lombardy respectively).[5] Here I examine other, less renowned immigrant printers who set up shop in the city, at least temporarily, as well as more itinerant characters who moved through Venice commissioning and selling cheap print. The distinction between these two categories is somewhat artificial, since, as noted in the previous chapter, some individuals operated both from shops and on the streets and most careers encompassed periods of stability and mobility. But by examining the social and economic lives of individuals at different points along the spectrum of mobility, their actions and strategies to survive and prosper in the metropolis, I want to suggest how their choices and movements brought diversity and creative energy to Venetian urban culture, especially in the first half of the sixteenth century, and how they were instrumental in disseminating print widely throughout the community. At the same time, we must remain aware of how their paths were shaped by the benevolent or repressive actions of local authorities, by commissions from institutions or individuals and by changing economic and political conditions both in Venice and elsewhere.[6]

Immigrant printers

In the previous chapter, I suggested how printers first from northern Europe and then principally from the Italian mainland settled into the central neighbourhoods of the city where they could tap into networks of fellow immigrants and locals to access the commercial, technical, and artistic contacts they needed. There were occasional protests about this influx, for example those of the scribe Fra Filippo de Strata calling for measures to rein in the 'utterly uncouth' German printers.[7] However, such objections had little effect. The Venetian *popolani* already was a resolutely cosmopolitan group. As the Vicentine writer Luigi Da Porto commented in 1509, many *popolani* came to work as sailors or in the city's numerous trades, and 'very few of them have fathers born in Venice'.[8] In the same month, the Venetian patrician diarist Priuli claimed proudly that, despite the threat of war on Venice's doorstep, the city had remained 'always open to foreigners, who could go and stay and return and pass through every place without any obstacle'.[9] Indeed, traditionally Venice welcomed anyone who could bring some economic benefit; from the fifteenth century the government was especially keen to attract valuable skilled migrants for the city's growing industries. A relatively open migration policy encouraged a great deal of movement into and through Venice, largely unchecked by restriction.

However, Venice's openness to foreigners would be tested severely in the sixteenth century, as new flows of people were unleashed by war, famine, religious persecution and epidemic disease. Even Priuli admitted that in the worst moment of the Cambrai War Venice briefly closed itself to foreigners and expelled some who were there, although he again stressed the Venetians' desire to remain open to merchants and trade.[10] The tension between welcoming some immigrants and repelling others, between receptivity to the skills and innovations brought by new arrivals and the wish to protect the fortunes of Venetian residents, would shape the experiences of many working migrants in Venice, as well as the development of the printing trade across its first century.[11]

After the devastating Italian Wars began in the 1490s, more than ever Venice seemed a place of great opportunity and relative serenity, excepting the few years of turmoil that marked the War of the League of Cambrai. Many printers who pioneered the production of cheap print in the early sixteenth century came from the Venetian *terraferma* state. Some hailed from areas with shifting allegiances, but where people naturally looked towards Venice when contemplating a move, like the paper-producing region of the Riviera di Salò on Lake Garda (part of Venetian territory prior to 1509).[12] Others came from the neighbouring region of Lombardy, like the Bindoni family who I discuss below, or Guglielmo Fontaneto and Comin da Trino, from small towns in the March of Monferrato, connected to Venice by the winding course of the Po River. Melchiore Sessa, one of the most powerful publishers of the first half of the sixteenth century, was the son of a migrant who came from Lugano at the end of the fifteenth century, before it passed from Lombard to Swiss dominion in 1513. New families continued to arrive throughout the century, some establishing themselves as successful printers in Venice and others moving on to greener pastures. The brothers Pietro and Domenico De' Franceschi, for example, printers at the sign of the Queen in the Frezzaria between the 1550s and 1570s, came to Venice from Brescia, although Pietro also worked in Pesaro.[13] While Venice seemed an ideal place to settle and try to make one's fortune in the booming printing trade, printers and publishers, like other migrants, were used to adapting themselves to new circumstances and, if necessary, moving on in search of further opportunities.

Many of these individuals, particularly in the early period, came to Venice with little experience in the still new trade of printing. Without a guild to regulate their entry until after the middle of the sixteenth century, however, there were few obstacles to 'having a go', even if a certain amount of capital was required to set up a printing establishment and buy a press, paper and other equipment. Although most were too humble to consider applying for Venetian citizenship – primarily the province of elite merchants who could benefit from the trading privileges that came with it – these men used other well-tested strategies to embed themselves in their adopted environment.[14] As mentioned, many settled close to each other in a few parishes in the *sestiere* of San Marco, particularly around San Moisè. Shared provenance was a crucial binding factor for many in the print trades at this time, as for those in other trades, leading to some clustering of immigrant groups in certain localities. Moving into these areas helped printers access networks of fellow immigrants and they were often followed by other members of their families. Regional connections not only provided points of first reference for the new arrival in the city, but also valuable links back to the home territory, for example for immigrant printers from the Riviera di Salò back to the many paper dealers operating in that area.¹⁵ This encouraged the kind of 'multiple identities' highlighted by Zannini: many of the Venetian *popolani*, foreign born, kept one foot in Venice and the other in their home territory, so that news, money and people flowed constantly between the capital and the provinces.¹⁶

The physical proximity of many in the print trade quickly was overlaid with a tangled web of personal, familial and business connections that facilitated their establishment in the city and in the business of printing and print-selling. While Romano noted low rates of endogamy within professions in Renaissance Venice, intermarriage was marked in the print trade from its earliest days.¹⁷ An early example is Paola, the widow of Venice's first printer, John of Speyer, a 'matrimonial phoenix' who remarried the publisher John of Cologne and, after his death, another master printer, as well as marrying her daughter Hieronima to a bookseller. In the early sixteenth century, the printer Giorgio Rusconi's daughter, Daria, married the printer Alessandro Paganino. Daria in turn wed one of her own daughters to a paper dealer (*cartaio*) in the Riviera di Salò and another to the bookseller Giovanni Varisco in Venice, while Paganino's sister Anna also married a printer.¹⁸ Women were important transmitters of knowledge, capital and equipment; furthermore, this form of social cement must have been particularly important in a new trade not gathered together into a guild until later in the sixteenth century.¹⁹

Printers, publishers and booksellers also reinforced their personal and economic connections via a variety of other kinds of social bonds. They asked their colleagues to act as testamentary executors or pledges, sometimes reflecting horizontal bonds of friendship, sometimes more hierarchical and clientelistic associations. For example, I noted in the Introduction how the printer Guglielmo Fontaneto called on the powerful publisher Melchiore Sessa to stand as pledge when he fell foul of the blasphemy magistrates in 1545. Fontaneto printed many works on Sessa's commission, but also appointed Sessa as an executor of his will in 1542.²⁰ Lay confraternities, aside from their pious functions, offered useful artistic, financial and technological contacts for men in the print trade. For example, Giorgio Rusconi and Paganino Paganini, fathers of the aforementioned spouses Daria and Alessandro, might have consolidated a friendship as members of the Scuola Grande di San Rocco.²¹ In other words, members of the printing and print-selling trades pursued similar strategies to many other migrants in Venice and other Italian cities in their quest to make a career for themselves in a new city.²² A closer look at one family of printers shows also how cheap print played a role in that process.

The Bindoni: a family business

The Bindoni family of printers, among the most prolific and pioneering producers of cheap print in sixteenth-century Venice, exemplify many of the processes just described.²³ Several branches of the family ran printing outfits in Venice throughout the length of the century, and their careers demonstrate both the importance of the kinds of social strategies already discussed and the crucial role played by cheap print. The Bindoni brothers progressively relocated to Venice from the tiny island of Isola Bella in Lake Maggiore from the first decade of the sixteenth century. The first brother to start printing in Venice, Alessandro, set up shop in the street of the Frezzaria in the parish of San Moisè by 1506 and printed close to one hundred surviving editions before he died around 1522.[24] His brothers Benedetto, Agostino, and Bernardino soon followed, and also began to work as printers, sometimes in collaboration with each other, sometimes on their own.[25]

A vital factor in the success of the Bindoni brothers in Venice was the production of small, cheap pamphlets in the vernacular that catered to the widening market for print. While many of these occupied the traditional territory of late medieval Italian vernacular culture – bawdy songs and poems, familiar devotional works – others pushed at the boundaries of the market with new and sometimes innovative content, often occupying the borders between oral and literate culture and thus helping to make print accessible to less confident readers.[26] This kind of cheap print would have also made perfect business sense to the Bindoni, as to many starting out. It required little time and investment, was easy to sell, and could be a stepping stone to undertaking larger works. As a character in Anton Francesco Doni's *Dialogue on Printing* noted, 'some printers first grow rich by printing trash, and then, turning to finer things, grow wealthier still'.[27]

Alessandro Bindoni, for example, began to intersperse larger undertakings like a folio edition of Ovid's *Metamorphoses*, financed by the wealthy publisher Luc'Antonio Giunta, with small topical pamphlets and news-poems which he appears to have financed himself, recounting events in the Cambrai wars and promoting a jingoistic pro-Venetian view.[28] Such publications undoubtedly found a welcome reception with Venetian audiences hungry for information and commentary about the war presented in a way that played to pre-existing sympathies. But they also were a shrewd choice, potentially pleasing the Venetian authorities by promoting their political agenda of the time.

As well as printing a range of works on their own account and others on commission, the Bindoni consolidated their position in the community and the printing industry by strategic marriages, as when Alessandro's widow Orsia married a publisher from the territory of Brescia, Maffeo Pasini, who established a very fruitful partnership with Alessandro's son Francesco from about 1524.[29] The Bindoni–Pasini partnership would be one of the most productive of the second quarter of the sixteenth century in Venice, unleashing a flood of modest vernacular editions ranging from pamphlets to larger books, including numerous reprints of contemporary writers like Aretino and Ariosto.[30] Although not as innovative as the contemporary publisher Niccolò Zoppino, discussed below, Bindoni and Pasini were responsible for making a great deal of the contemporary literature of the period, as well as more traditional vernacular works, available to the Venetian public cheaply and easily.

However, their partnership also reflects a broader transition over time in the Bindoni family's publishing output. The cultural climate was changing, as censorship efforts increasingly extended not only to tomes of serious Protestant theology, but also to frivolous vernacular works seen to transgress moral and religious propriety. In the 1540s, Francesco Bindoni's uncle Bernardino fell under suspicion for printing unlicensed works, some of which flirted with the ideas of religious reform widespread in Venice at the time.[31] Francesco Bindoni and Maffeo Pasini, however, chose instead to turn towards a more educated readership, producing fewer works of cheap print and a rise in the proportion of Latin titles.[32] Although Francesco himself was implicated in the shipping of some prohibited books to a Sienese bookseller in 1564 he was cleared of suspicion and pronounced to be 'religioso catholico et da bene' (a religious Catholic and a good man).[33] The prudent choices of Francesco Bindoni also meant that, by mid-century, his part of the family had secured a central place for themselves in the Venetian printing community, having achieved a position as respectable businessmen, modest holders of land and founding members of the guild. Francesco's son Gaspare was regularly elected to positions of responsibility in the guild in the 1570s and 1580s, while in 1580 and 1584 Francesco himself was elected to the *zonta* or body of guild advisers.[34] Gaspare and his brother Francesco the younger would on the whole leave the printing of cheap, vernacular pamphlets to newly arrived printing families like the De' Franceschi and the De' Farri.

Later generations, however, failed to demonstrate the adaptability of their forbears as the print market changed. By the early seventeenth century, the Bindoni were losing the moderate stature they had achieved in the trade, in tandem with the beginning of a decline in the absolute dominance of Venetian printing in Italy. However, here again, cheap print played a significant role. In 1613, Agostino Bindoni the younger, a grandson of one of the original migrants from Isola Bella, was among several poor guildsmen who applied for special permission to sell on feast days.[35] Like growing numbers of guild members from the late sixteenth century, this Bindoni peddled cheap print in the streets, to supplement the presumably meagre income from his shop in the parish of San Luca. Cheap pamphlets and broadsheets increasingly were associated with the poor members of the guild (and outside the guild) who hawked them from benches and baskets outdoors.[36] A century or so after their arrival in Venice, the Bindoni were no longer the drivers of a dynamic and productive print culture, although cheap print remained important to them as a way to eke out a living on the margins of the industry.

Niccolò Zoppino: between print and performance

The story of a family like the Bindoni who came and settled in Venice should not obscure the element of continuous mobility that characterised the printing industry in Venice, particularly in the earlier sixteenth century. The move to

Venice and into the community of the Venetian *popolani* was not necessarily a permanent one for many printers, publishers and booksellers. Their own travels, as well as the transmission of their products, etched out a web of connections spreading across mainland Italy and sometimes further. These bonds were reinforced by further migrations into the industry, particularly of young apprentices who came mostly from the *terraferma*.[37] In this way, the body of the print trade continually was infused with foreign blood, growing and feeding off ideas and skills from the rest of Italy and beyond. At the same time, printers and other members of the trade were not immune to the allure of other places, and were ready to up and move if a better opportunity presented itself, particularly as the Venetian trade became ever more crowded and competitive in the sixteenth century.

A primary example of this continuous mobility is the protean figure of Niccolò Zoppino, originally from Ferrara, a bookseller and publisher who in the first decades of the sixteenth century worked in Bologna, Milan, Pesaro, Ancona and Perugia before opening a shop in the parish of San Fantin in Venice where he produced the majority of his works. Yet, although he continued to have business concerns in the lagoon city until at least 1544, Zoppino did not concentrate all his efforts on settling there, but went off in search of other commercial opportunities. In 1536, in order to sell books in Florence, he enrolled in the Florentine guild that encompassed sellers of print.[38] In 1542, Zoppino petitioned the local authorities to open a bookshop in Ravenna. The petition noted that 'wandering for so many years through the cities of Italy, as he has done', Zoppino had observed the need in Ravenna for a good bookshop, which he promised to provide for the benefit of the city.[39] Despite, or perhaps partly because of, his unceasing personal peregrinations, Zoppino was one of the most prolific publishers of the time. He also played what is now recognised to have been a major cultural role in the promotion of the Italian vernacular as a literary language, with his publication of a great deal of contemporary literature, from plays and poetry to religious tracts.[40]

However, Zoppino also personifies another trait that I highlight in this chapter: professional versatility. After many years of speculation, evidence is now coming to light that proves Zoppino was certainly also active as a performer, and continued to be so even as his publishing career took off. A recently discovered document reveals that, in 1510, Zoppino was imprisoned briefly and threatened with banishment from Venice for singing and selling printed songs critical of the Serenissima ('in vituperium Status veneti') back in his native Ferrara, at a time when the two states were at war.[41] This brush with the law did not discourage Zoppino from continuing his dual career; in 1521 and 1526, a 'Zupin che canta in banco' performed his services at the court of Ferrara. This had to be the same figure as the publisher as he was paid by the court not only for singing but for selling books, and there is mention of his son Sebastiano.[42] These documents are supplemented by many tangential pieces of evidence from the same period which refer to a piazza performer called Zoppino, active in Venice and elsewhere, including a description of him performing in Piazza San Marco in Teofilo Folengo's *Baldo*.[43]

While some scholars still doubt that Zoppino could have combined the two careers of publishing and performance, the confirmation that he certainly did is of great significance to our understanding of the early Italian printing industry, and of the ways in which texts reached their audiences in this period. We can surmise that Zoppino may have at times played a double function in promoting the texts he published: both in print and by his own performances. Some of the authors he worked with may have favoured him precisely for this reason. One wrote that he had entrusted Zoppino with his composition so that the publisher could carry it far and wide, spreading its fame in song.[44] As a consequence of his travelling and his performative experience, Zoppino must have possessed an excellent knowledge of what would gain favour with an audience and what would sell. Furthermore, a good number of his publications were directly linked to performance, both plays and the kinds of songs and poems habitually performed by popular entertainers, while in Ferrara he is recorded selling song books (*libri di canto*).

However, the fault lines that Zoppino crossed in his career and on his travels could also be shifting and dangerous. As mentioned, he found himself in very hot water in 1510, over his performance and sale of a song in the popular *barzelletta* form about the war between Venice and Ferrara.[45] The episode suggests Zoppino's flexible and shifting loyalties; the song was a hearty attack on Venice's conduct in the war with his native Ferrara, rejoicing in the Republic's losses on the *terraferma*. Unlike Alessandro Bindoni, who would print pro-Venetian poems during the war, Zoppino in this case chose instead to cater to a Ferrarese audience, assuming that the Venetian government would never find out. He was wrong. Although he and his partner Vincenzo di Paolo eventually were let off after an appeal, initially they were imprisoned and sentenced to banishment from the Venetian state for three years. Nonetheless, perhaps because of the support of powerful friends, this incident does not seem to have impeded Zoppino's career in Venice, where he resumed publishing works throughout the period of the war.

So while there are many similarities between his publication list and those of the first generations of the Bindoni, Zoppino's career also suggests that it was not necessary to follow exactly the same social and business strategies in order to prosper in Venice at this time. He collaborated professionally with other members of the printing trade more rooted in Venice, including Giorgio Rusconi, Giovanni Padovano and the Nicolini brothers, but he did not seek to integrate into the trade in the same way. For his most important and long-term partnership Zoppino instead turned to a fellow performer, the Venetian Vincenzo di Paolo, who was described as a bookseller and street singer ('bibliopola ac cantor circumforaneus') in his 1524 testament. The two publishers signed works together from between 1513 and 1524, although the recent discovery of the 1510 document shows that they were in fact collaborating already by that date. Theirs was a strong bond: Vincenzo appointed Zoppino his heir, and a 1543 contract shows

Zoppino working with Vincenzo's son Paolo.[46] It was not unusual to find business relationships between street performers and publishers in Venice and other Italian cities in the sixteenth century, but Zoppino stands out as one of the earliest and most important mediators between the worlds of performance and printing, taking advantage of the commercial possibilities of the Venetian trade as well as linking Venice into wider circuits of cultural communication.

Zoppino's career indicates that mobility (and also professional versatility) were not obstacles to finding success in the printing trade in Venice in the first half of the sixteenth century. They could be great assets, although we have seen how they could bring with them attendant risks. These risks became more pronounced with the establishment of dedicated organs to monitor the print trade around mid-century. Thus it may also be significant that Zoppino ceased publishing in the mid 1540s (his last recorded publications are from 1544), as he was an important promoter of ideas of religious reform in cheap, vernacular editions, which became a particular target of repression at precisely this time. Although he would have been quite old at this point and may have died or simply ceased working, it is unlikely that his career could have continued in the same vein in the years that followed.[47]

The lowest corner of the piazza

While Zoppino is a prominent example of a highly mobile printer and publisher with close associations to the world of street performance, he was not unique. Other performers worked as printers or publishers, including the singer Zanobi della Barba in Florence and possibly also Paolo Danza in Venice.[48] Indeed, Italian piazzas and streets in this period were peopled by a motley array of other figures who combined print peddling, performing and occasionally commissioning pamphlet publications. Again, we need to conceive of a spectrum of activity: from those who took up these endeavours as part of a continuous scrape to survive, to others who carried on a more successful and established trade, or used print as a sophisticated means of self-promotion. The edges of these activities also were blurred in the sense that print-selling overlapped with other forms of commerce; it was especially common to encounter print peddled alongside other goods such as perfumes, medicines, soap and haberdashery.[49] Here, I am especially interested in those who combined print peddling with some kind of performance, because of their particular role in bringing print into the experience of the mass of city dwellers via the potent combination of printed, verbal and visual forms of communication.

Pursuing these figures is clearly challenging, due to their frequent mobility, the ephemeral and transient nature of their activities, and of the goods they sold. Just as they could dismantle their benches, pick up their baskets and flee the authorities searching for prohibited or unlicensed print, so they now evade the historian, leaving few documentary traces of their actions and itineraries. But the evidence that does survive reveals irrefutably that there was a web of connections linking shop-based printers, publishers and booksellers with stationary or mobile street sellers and performers of various kinds. No consideration of how print reached its audiences can be complete without trying to follow these threads.

How such connections worked is suggested by the rich resource that is the logbook of the Ripoli Press near Florence from the 1470s and 1480s. The logbook demonstrates how the Dominican-run press frequently took commissions from itinerant performers and pedlars, mostly for *fogli volanti* or small pamphlets. These itinerant vendors shifted large quantities of prints, picking up a batch at a time and leaving objects such as bedsheets and spoons as tokens of credit before they could come back with their profits and pay in cash.[50] As Martin Lowry commented some time ago, the Ripoli records 'prove beyond any doubt that investment in printing reached from the top of the *palazzo* to the lowest corner of the piazza', adding that the same must certainly have been true for Venice.[51] The fragmented nature of the Venetian guild system also means there is no equivalent source to the valuable registers of the Florentine guild which encompassed print sellers, the Arte dei medici e speziali. These registers cast further refracted light on Venice, testifying to the presence of numerous print pedlars, performers and publishers who hailed from or were also active in Venice, including the aforementioned Zoppino.[52] In Venice, there was no guild which could encompass these elusive figures; they belonged to the 'dark side of the urban economy that lay outside the official guild structures'.[53] It was only after the corporation of printers and booksellers became functional from the 1570s that there began, sporadically, the pursuit of outsiders who encroached on the guild's turf.

On the other hand, strong evidence of similar interactions between printers and performer-pedlars in Venice derives from the survival of substantial numbers of printed texts commissioned by itinerant publishers and performers. Even if a great many of these ephemeral publications have been lost over time, certainly enough survive to testify to the collaborations of performers with the Venetian presses even from the earliest days of the industry. For example, the blind singer Francesco da Firenze had his translation of the chivalric tale *Persiano* printed in Venice in 1483, while another singer called Antonio Farina in the early 1490s put his name to several ephemeral publications similar to those commissioned by performers and pedlars from the Ripoli press, including a broadsheet oration to the archangel Raphael and some short prophecies.[54] By the early sixteenth century, it became more common for performers and other occasional publishers to indicate their involvement on the pamphlets themselves with the formula *ad instantia di* ('on commission of'), perhaps an indication that some were more intent to promote their name in association with signature works. However, many cheap pamphlets were issued without any or all identifying information, so it is not always possible to name their printers or publishers or be certain of the involvement of performers in their production or distribution. Nonetheless, this again may be suggestive of the dynamics of distribution, the absence of publication details allowing the works to be sold in other places and at a later time without seeming out of date.⁵⁵

Although no contracts that I am aware of have come to light between performers and printers in Venice, the surviving pamphlets indicate that there were a number of printers there who specialised in the production of cheap publications designed for street sale, and who repeatedly printed works at the request of street performers.⁵⁶ Either these printers actively sought out performers who came to Venice and offered to print works for them or, more likely, performers were apprised of the specialty of these printers when or before they arrived in town, and knew where to go to make the arrangements for publication. The proximity of the places in which performers and printers tended to operate in Venice facilitated the making of such connections.⁵⁷ In Venice, printers who worked repeatedly with performers included Francesco Bindoni and Maffeo Pasini (with the street singers Ippolito Ferrarese and Baldassare Faentino), Giovanni Padovano and Guglielmo Fontaneto di Monferrato (with Francesco Faentino and others) and Venturino Ruffinelli (again with Ippolito Ferrarese).⁵⁸ After mid-century, Domenico De' Franceschi also published several contemporary works by buffoons and *commedia dell'arte* actors, although it is not known if the performers themselves commissioned these publications.⁵⁹

The surviving editions also alert us that performers sometimes formed partnerships to help gather the capital necessary to finance a run of small works. For example, the singer Francesco Faentino with an unknown partner commissioned the publication of several pastoral comedies in Siena and Venice in the late 1530s.⁶⁰ Such partners may have at times been fellow performers, as when Leonardo Furlano, another itinerant publisher and probably a charlatan, collaborated with Ippolito Ferrarese to publish a pamphlet of Ariosto's poetry.⁶¹ I have also mentioned the prolific and long-lasting partnership between Niccolò Zoppino and Vincenzo di Polo. However, short-term relations of mutual expediency, as in the case of the Ripoli Press, probably were more common. From the printers' point of view, maintaining a successful business was a precarious matter, and they sought investment from many sources. Additionally, sending works out with itinerant sellers of print was another useful outlet of sale for small publications.

As the sixteenth century progressed, expanding mechanisms of control over printing and public space in Venice generated more records of these activities. Civic authorities such as the Health Board (the Provveditori alla Sanità) and the Procurators of Piazza San Marco granted licences to perform and sell particular goods and regulated precisely when and where entertainers and pedlars could operate.⁶² The more prominent performers, such as the Florentine singer l'Altissimo, the renowned Venetian buffoon Zuan Polo and the charlatan Iacopo Coppa, sought privileges for published editions of their work from the Venetian government, to protect them from piracy and probably to add prestige.⁶³ Many, however, trusted that their humble publications and fleeting appearances in the streets would evade the scrutiny of the censors and the patrols of the police – although, as we will see in Chapter 5, some were not so lucky.

What is not documented – and what we must surmise – are the interactions that took place on the streets, between the sellers, the texts and their customers. Here it is necessary to stress that street performers (particularly the singers known as *canterini, cantastorie* and later *cantimbanchi*) had played a part in medieval society as, apart from the church, perhaps the most important transmitters of information, entertainment and ideas to large audiences.[64] Moving into print was a logical step for these professional communicators, although it added a new dimension to their traditional activities. Their mastery of the arts of oral communication to large and diverse audiences must have been of great use in the dissemination of early print. They possessed a unique power to attract and hold the attention of the crowd with only their voice and gestures, and perhaps with an instrument such as a *lira da braccio*. Because of this, performers were closely attuned to what appealed to an urban public, and could help to turn that public of listeners and watchers into a public of buyers and readers. The Ripoli logbook demonstrates that performers and pedlars chose works with strong and established performative possibilities (orations, laments), often of topical interest to a diverse audience. As shown in the next chapter, the same occurred in Venice.

I have continually stressed how the printed word latched onto established forms of communication, old media for a long time coexisting and interacting with the new. Thus the skills of pedlars and performers in working the streets, in reading a crowd, should be considered alongside the more familiar 'tools' of printers and publishers – equipment, technical know-how, access to capital – that helped the new trade to grow. In all likelihood, such figures were especially important in the early decades of the print trade when customers needed to be familiarised with the attractions of the new products of the press. They showed (or recited or sung) the work directly to the customer and this relationship also made them useful as 'intermediaries transmitting necessary information about demand and supply in both directions, between the printer and the public'.[65]

Ippolito Ferrarese: a cantimbanco publisher

To get more of a sense of the career of an itinerant performer and his relations with the press in this period, we can look at the figure of Ippolito Ferrarese.[66] This singer from Ferrara exemplifies the sustained mobility of many performer-publisher-pedlars involved with the printing industry. For him and others like him there was a continual need to be on the move, in order not to wear out the appetite for new entertainment or novel products in each town.[67] Plainly, this mobility earned Ferrarese widespread popularity for when he died around the middle of the sixteenth century, at least three pamphlets were published purporting to record his dying words (see Figure 3).[68] Ferrarese's career also testifies to a continuous and fruitful collaboration with the presses in many of the cities he visited, and his role as a publisher in bringing both original and more derivative works onto the marketplace, and in carrying them from city to city.

He published at least twenty small booklets in various genres in Venice and other cities across northern Italy including Brescia, Bologna, Parma, Pesaro and Milan, over the two decades prior to his death.[69]

What remains of Ferrarese's published output is poor in the material sense: a scattering of small works mostly of fewer than twelve leaves, scarcely illustrated and rarely surviving in more than one copy (see, for example, Figures 2 and 9). However, they were undeniably important to his career, as a new source of earning and a way to promote his reputation as a performer. Moreover, they form a diverse and eclectic collection which gives a sense of the range of material that one could have encountered freely, hawked and performed on the Italian piazzas: from the singer's first surviving publication, a verse account of the 1530 siege of Florence published soon after that traumatic event, to an astrological almanac, to the first known edition of some of Ariosto's vernacular lyrics under the title *Forze d'amore*.[70] In the same year, 1538, he seems to have published cheap booklet editions both of a pornographic parody of the chivalric epic by a Venetian patrician and follower of Aretino (*La puttana errante*) and a work of religious instruction dedicated to the famously pious noblewoman Vittoria Colonna.[71] These editions alone suggest how performer-publishers like Ferrarese were not just recyclers of traditional and familiar material for popular consumption but could also be channels for innovative and challenging works to find a broad audience in the piazza.

We cannot know exactly what Ferrarese's role was in these publications, beyond commissioning a run of them from a local printer and paying at least some of the expenses, as indicated by the formula *ad instantia di* on the title page or as a colophon. None of Ferrarese's publications are known certainly to have been his own work as author; frequently their authorship is unidentified, some are by famous names advertised on the title page and some were taken from other authors without acknowledgement. Often the texts were adapted, cut or versified for their new published form, and the same textual elements turn up in various combinations in one or other of Ferrarese's pamphlets. Given Ferrarese's renown as a street singer, he must have performed at least some of the texts he had printed, and sold the pamphlets in the course of his public appearances in the main squares of the cities he visited. His deathbed lament suggests that he was particularly beloved for his singing, playing the stringed *lira da braccio* and also famous for selling soap.[72]

The publications by and about Ferrarese indicate how performers adapted their repertoires and engaged with local printers as they moved around. For instance, commissioning new editions of pamphlets or poems in each place they visited, as Ferrarese did, was a practical way to avoid having to transport a stock of pamphlets from town to town; the traveller could rather carry a sample and have a local printer copy it.[73] Ippolito's sometime partner Leonardo Furlano followed a similar practice, commissioning editions of a pamphlet on writing in code in Venice (1543, 1547), in Milan (1544) and in Brescia (1546).[74] At the same time, performers like Ferrarese and Furlano did not need to adapt the language of their publications a great deal as they moved around the peninsula. In their speech (or song) most *cantimbanchi* and charlatans appear to have used a pan-Italian language rather than local dialects which, like travelling preachers, allowed them to transfer their operations easily from place to place. This was reflected in their publications, which, at least after the 1530s generally followed the Tuscanised Italian norm established by Venetian editors.[75]

Nevertheless, the reprinting of works in different cities liberated the performer to adapt his works as he went along, reflecting the continual updating of his performative repertoire, and allowed him to appeal to the sympathies and interests of local audiences. Flattery seems to have played a part in winning over local audiences.[76] For example, in his deathbed lament, Ferrarese instructed his beloved *lira* to pass on his regards to the city

> above all the others, most pleasing to me
> … Venice, whose name in a thousand pages
> always guarded by the winged Lion [of Saint Mark],
> [is] upheld and revered everywhere.
> I know that the people [there], knowing of my death,
> since they always love me, will be greatly pained.[77]

We do not know how or if such works were performed for the Venetian public or governors. However, flattering the local authorities who might determine a performer's tenure in town, and playing to the sympathies of the home crowd were useful tactics. Their works suggest that performers knew how to appeal to a local market but also to adjust themselves to new circumstances in different places. Cheap printed pamphlets offered them a novel commercial sideline – in Ferrarese's case, he sold them alongside soap – but also proved themselves to be a flexible medium that could be modified as needed as one travelled from town to town. From the audience's point of view, print preserved the ephemeral experience of a performance they had enjoyed, or at least some hint of it. It provided a new possibility to buy and keep a memento of the singer's repertoire, and permitted further, ad hoc renditions of his songs in the home, tavern or workplace.

'Poveri meschini'

Ippolito Ferrarese is an example of a relatively successful performer who turned to publishing and print peddling to supplement his career as an entertainer and soap seller. However, for many others, peddling cheap print was quite simply essential to their survival. At the bottom end of the spectrum, the most lowly performers and small-time hawkers of print and other goods could be hard to distinguish from beggars. With war, famine and severe economic pressures, the sixteenth century offered recurrent crises of the kind that threw people on the margins of poverty over the edge, forcing them to seek new ways to survive and sometimes to hit the roads. Print peddling was a new option in this period, and it tended to escalate in hard times, becoming a common strand in the 'makeshift economy' of the early modern poor, both in Italy and elsewhere in Europe.[78] When local authorities tried to control the street trade in print, they found it was almost impossible; peddling was irrepressible because endemic poverty was a persistent (and indeed a growing) problem.

This is attested by the permissions granted for the right to sell print in the streets on feast days which survive in the records of the Venetian printers' guild from the end of the sixteenth century onwards. The numerous sellers who applied for these licences were referred to as *poveri* and many seem genuinely to have been in a wretched position. Allowing them to operate in a restricted way was considered an act of charity towards the least fortunate members of the guild.[79] The petitioners for these licences presented themselves as close to destitute, 'not just poor but extremely poor', as one Andrea Ravanello described himself.[80] In Florence, the more detailed petitions that survive addressed to the Florentine duke may have exaggerated the poverty and desperation of the petitioners in a bid to win his sympathy, but the guild officials there often confirmed their claims, and referred to the print pedlars as 'poor wretches' (*poveri meschini*).[81]

Peddling print also was an activity that workers might turn to later in life, never having managed to establish their own shops and no other form of support. Such was the case with two old men reprimanded by the Venetian Holy Office for selling prohibited books from street stalls in the 1560s and 1570s. Giacomo da Trino was described as a *poveretto*, who sold books to earn a few *soldi*. The Inquisitors, considerate of his old age and reputation as a devout Christian, let him be released.[82] Bartolomeo da Sabbio had worked as an apprentice in several printing shops, yet claimed not to be able to read or write. He was prohibited from buying and selling books in future, although the Holy Office later took pity on his family, his poverty and age and gave him licence to continue to buy and sell books as long as he frequently consulted the Index of prohibitions.[83] It is particularly notable that many of the street vendors in this position were more or less recent migrants to the city – in these cases, presumably from Trino in Lombardy and Sabbio near Lake Garda. These figures likely had less capacity to call on local networks of support at difficult times, and they remind us that migration was not always followed by integration and social mobility.

The often improvised act of setting up a small bookstall or taking to the streets with a basket of cheap print made it a viable choice for many people on the threshold of destitution in this period. (Singing a song, playing an instrument and collecting a few coins after an impromptu performance was another one.) The Venetian authorities, like those elsewhere, generally recognised this need and allowed small-time sellers to persist, even if this brought them into conflict with other interest groups such as the printers' guild. In 1588, for example, the Provveditori di Comun who oversaw the Venetian guild refused to completely enforce a ban by the guild on unlicensed sellers, adding the condition that ambulant sellers of cheap print ('quelli che vendono istorie per la città') be exempt.

The Provveditori evidently took the view that it was better if such individuals were employed in this way than turning to begging or crime.[84]

Despite debates about how, where, when or whether these humble figures should be allowed to operate, there is no doubt that they were becoming a permanent presence in the public spaces of Venice. So too, their voices can occasionally be heard via the medium of cheap print, albeit often in a caricatured or mediated way. Poverty was a common theme of popular poems and songs, and occasionally the performer-composer described his own experiences of indigence and need. For example, an ordinary-looking octavo pamphlet containing 'pleasant and ingenious' (and ribald) songs about melons and grapes published in Venice in 1557 by a blind singer called Giovanni di Giorgio *veneto* includes an interesting addition on the final page. Here, presumably Giovanni himself lamented the 'cruel and vicious poverty / which has made me become a dark shadow, / disformed, and uglier than fear'. He speaks of sitting all day on the Rialto Bridge in Venice 'like an invisible spirit ... no one sees me, no one takes care of me any more. / ... friends, and even my relatives / pass in front and behind me, and do not see me ... / Since poverty makes me invisible'.[85] Another pamphlet published by Giovanni di Giorgio, a sensational *capitolo* in the voice of a murdered woman, concluded with the plea for all who read the story to make an offering 'to this blindman who composed this in print / ... this poor Job and father of a family'.[86]

Venetians may have read or listened to such stories and songs for pleasure, just as they laughed at the antics of the starving Bergamask immigrant Zanni in the early *commedia dell'arte* and numerous related pamphlets.[87] But putting these words in print also made them marginally more difficult to ignore, as well as preserving them through time, an alternative record of life on the streets of Venice. In fact, as an act of charity, the poor and particularly the blind were permitted to sing and peddle print on the streets of Venice for many centuries, as elsewhere in Europe. In the seventeenth century, the prolific Venetian *cantastorie* Paolo Britti, who described himself as 'rich in poverty, and in children' ('riccho di povertà, de fantolini'), produced numerous songs about the low lives of Venice, including his own.[88] Given the involvement of figures like Giovanni di Giorgio and Britti in publishing and peddling cheap print in the streets of Venice, we should not simply dismiss such works as caricatured creations, and recognise their part in the conception, production and dissemination of cheap print.

This chapter has suggested a variety of reasons why people became involved in producing and selling cheap print in Renaissance Venice and Italy. For printers, it might be a way to get started in the business and to supplement one's income between larger jobs; for performers, a commercial sideline and a means to promote one's reputation; and for the lowliest pedlars, an opportunity to eke out a living that was marginally more respectable than begging. These motives all in one way or another shared a commercial imperative, and encouraged the common desire to reach as many people as possible with cheap printed products. The search for profit drove the circulation of all kinds of cheap print aimed at people across the social spectrum, including those with low levels of literacy who might nonetheless be attracted to simple, familiar texts particularly if they lent themselves to being performed or read aloud. Moreover, despite the varying social and economic levels of the people surveyed here, many of them were connected to each other, in one way or another, by the medium of cheap print. A family like the Bindoni, over time, incorporated successful printers as well as less prosperous street pedlars. Niccolò Zoppino and Ippolito Ferrarese encompassed the roles of performer, publisher and print seller, although to varying degrees. Because of this kind of versatility, and thanks to the temporary and more long-term collaborations of printers, publishers, pedlars and performers, cheap print made its way from the print shop out into the piazza and the streets and became an inescapable part of urban culture in Venice.

This chapter also has stressed the importance of physical mobility in the careers of many of the people involved in cheap print production and dissemination in Venice. The nature of documentary sources tends to illuminate the stationary and obscure the more mobile, but the flowing in and out of fresh blood, ideas and capital was essential to the vitality of the Venetian printing scene in the sixteenth century.[89] Books and other printed matter did not just move by themselves, in consignments of boxes on carts or ships. They were also carried by people, in baskets and sacks, and those people's unpredictable itineraries allowed printed matter to infiltrate more broadly and deeply into the cultural terrain.

Notes

1 Cited in Chapter 1, n. 42. On the actions of the guild, see Chapter 5.
2 Widespread and more continuous mobility, rather than just migration from one point to another, has been stressed by many recent studies. See, in particular, L. Fontaine, 'Gli studi sulla mobilità in Europa nell'età moderna: Problemi e prospettive di ricerca', *Quaderni storici*, 93:3 (1996), 739–56; G. Pizzorusso, 'Le migrazioni degli italiani all'interno della penisola e in Europa in età moderna', in A. Eiras Roel and D. L. González Lopo (eds), *Movilidad y migraciones internas en la Europa latina* (Santiago de Compostela: Universidad de Santiago de Compostela, 2002), pp. 55–85; Page Moch, *Moving Europeans*; C. Moatti and W. Kaiser, 'Mobilità umana e circolazione culturale nel mediterraneo dall'età classica all'età moderna', in P. Corti and M. Sanfilippo (eds), *Storia d'Italia: Annali 24, Migrazioni* (Turin: Einaudi, 2009), pp. 5–20.
3 See, for example, E. Canepari, *Stare in compagnia. Strategie di inurbamento e forme associative nella Roma del Seicento* (Soveria Mannelli: Rubettino Università, 2008), p. 41.
4 A research project under the leadership of Professor Marco Santoro has begun to direct more attention to the mobility of members of the printing trade in this period. See M. Santoro and S. Segatori (eds), *Mobilità dei mestieri del libro tra Quattrocento*

  e Seicento: Convegno internazionale, Roma, 14–16 marzo 2012 (Pisa and Rome: Fabrizio Serra, 2013).
5 See Lowry, *World of Aldus Manutius*; Lowry, *Nicholas Jenson*; Nuovo and Coppens, *I Giolito*.
6 On some of the 'push and pull' factors influencing the movement of people in the print trade, see M. Santoro, 'La mobilità dei mestieri del libro: caratteristiche e valenze', in Santoro and Segatori, *Mobilità dei mestieri del libro*, p. 288.
7 Cited in Chapter 1, n. 36.
8 'Pochissimi sono ch'abbiano il padre nato in Vinegia' (Da Porto, *Lettere storiche*, p. 127). On the composition of the *popolani*, see de Larivière and Salzberg, 'Le peuple est la cité'.
9 'Sempre la citade veneta fu aperta ali forestieri, che chadauno potesse andare et stare et ritornare et passare per ogni locho senza obstaculo alchuno' (Priuli, *Diarii*, p. 385 (4 October 1509)).
10 *Ibid.*
11 See C. M. Belfanti, 'Guilds, patents and the circulation of technical knowledge: northern Italy during the early modern age', *Technology and Culture*, 45:3 (2004), 577–8; P. Lanaro, 'Corporations et confréries: les étrangers et le marché du travail à Venise (XVe–XVIIIe siècles)', *Histoire urbaine*, 21 (2008), 31–48; R. C. Mueller, *Immigrazione e cittidinanza nella Venezia medievale* (Rome: Viella, 2010). For a general survey of immigrant communities in Venice, see D. Calabi, 'Gli stranieri e la città', in Tenenti and Tucci, *Storia di Venezia*, vol. 5, pp. 913–46.
12 The printers Paolo Danza and the Nicolini brothers came from this region. See E. Sandal (ed.), *Il mestier de le stamperie e de i libri. Le vicende e i percorsi dei tipografi di Sabbio Chiese tra Cinque e Seicento e l'opera dei Nicolini* (Brescia: Grafo, 2002), pp. 14–15; E. Sandal, '"Folli da papir" e "merchantia de libri". Il caso della Riviera di Salò', in A. Nuovo and E. Sandal (eds), *Il libro nell'Italia del rinascimento* (Brescia: Graf, 1998), p. 176.
13 See *DTEI*, s.v. These are not to be confused with another family of printers called De' Franceschi active in the same period who hailed from Siena.
14 Among the few exceptions were the printer Vincenzo Valgrisi, although his privilege of citizenship was never confirmed by the Senate, and Gabriele Giolito. See A. Bellavitis, *Identité, mariage, mobilité sociale. Citoyennes et citoyens à Venise au XVIe siècle* (Rome: École Française de Rome, 2001), p. 44; and S. Bongi, *Annali di Gabriel Giolito de' Ferrari da Trino di Monferrato, stampatore in Venezia* (Rome: Ministero della Pubblica Istruzione, 1890), vol. 1, p. lix. On the costly and time-consuming process of applying for citizenship, see L. Molà and R. C. Mueller, 'Essere straniero a Venezia nel tardo Medioevo: accoglienza e rifiuto nei privilegi di cittadinanza e nelle sentenze criminali', in S. Cavaciocchi (ed.), *Le migrazioni in Europa, secc. XIII–XVIII* (Florence: Le Monnier, 1994), pp. 839–51; and Mueller, *Immigrazione e cittidinanza*.
15 Sandal, '"Folli da papir"'.
16 A. Zannini, 'L'identità multipla: Essere popolo in una capitale (Venezia, sec. xvi–xviii)', *Ricerche storiche*, 32:2–3 (2002), 252.
17 Romano, *Patricians and Popolani*, pp. 77–8.
18 On Paola, see V. Scholderer, 'Printing at Venice to the end of 1481', in his *Fifty Essays in Fifteenth- and Sixteenth-Century Bibliography*, ed. D. E. Rhodes (Amsterdam: Hertzberger, 1966), p. 84. On the Rusconi/Paganini connections, see ASV, Notarile,

Testamenti, Not. A. de Canali, b. 209, fasc. 155 (testament of Daria Rusconi, 14 July 1556) and *ibid.*, Not. A. Marcon, b. 1203, fasc. 22 (testament of Anna 'consorte di Comin stampador', 1551).

19 D. Parker, 'Women in the book trade in Italy, 1475–1620', *Renaissance Quarterly*, 49:3 (1996), 509–41; Plebani, *Il 'genere' dei libri*, pp. 78–80.

20 Fontaneto's will of 1542 is in ASV, Notarile, Testamenti, Not. A. Marcon, b. 1203, fasc. 92. See also the will of the engraver and printer Giovan Andrea Valvassore, in which he requested that the printer Paolo Danza organise his burial, published in A. Markham Schulz, 'Giovanni Andrea Valvassore and his family in four unpublished testaments', in *Artes atque humaniora. Studia Stanislao Mossakowski sexagenario dicata* (Warsaw: Instytut Sztuki Polskiej Akademii Nauk, 1998), pp. 120–1.

21 See Dondi, 'Printers and guilds', 260–1, 264; Lowry, 'Social world'. In the 1530s and 1540s, the printers Niccolò Nicolini and Paolo Danza were among the members of the Scuola Grande di San Marco alongside powerful publishers such as Giovan Maria and Tomaso Giunta. See ASV, Scuola di San Marco, b. 40, Libro di Morti.

22 See E. Canepari, 'Immigrati, spazi urbani e reti sociali nell'Italia d'antico regime', in Corti and Sanfilippo, *Storia d'Italia: Annali 24, Migrazioni*, pp. 55–74.

23 P. Burke in his 'Oral culture and print culture in Renaissance Italy', *ARV: Scandinavian Yearbook of Folklore* (1998), 9–10, pointed out the particular interest of the Bindoni among the printers of Venice, but they have not been the subject of a dedicated published study. However, see I. Menis, 'I Bindoni: Materiali storico-documentari per una ricostruzione biografica e annalistica' (*tesi di laurea*, Università degli studi di Udine, 1992–93), for an overview of their career and output.

24 See *DTEI*, s.v., and A. Cioni, 'Alessandro Bindoni', in *DBI*, vol. 10, pp. 498–9.

25 On the other brothers, see *DTEI*, s.v.; A. Cioni, 'Agostino Bindoni', 'Benedetto Bindoni', 'Bernardino Bindoni', in *DBI*, vol. 10, pp. 496–501; and E. Motta, 'Uno stampatore del Lago Maggiore a Venezia', *Bollettino storico della svizzera italiana*, 14:9–10 (1892), 199–200. See Menis, 'I Bindoni', p. 84, on the brothers' subtly different publishing strategies.

26 Burke, 'Oral culture'.

27 Doni, *Dialogue on Printing*, p. 45. On the importance of cheap print in fledgling businesses, see Flood, 'Printed book', 179.

28 See, for example, *La obsidione di Padua*, about the reconquest of Padua after it had been lost to the Holy Roman Emperor (first printed in 1510 in Venice, anonymously, and reprinted under Bindoni's name in 1515; *GOR*, vol. 1, pp. 60–1, nos 72–3); *La vera nova de Bressa de punto in punto come andata ...*, on the recapture of Brescia from the French (attributed to Bindoni c.1512; *GOR*, vol. 1, pp. 68–9, no. 85); and *La historia de tutte le guerre facte el facto darme fato in Geradada ...* (n.p.d.), attributed to Bindoni in Petrella, *Fra testo e immagine*, pp. 50–69; also in *GOR*, vol. 1, pp. 51–2, no. 54, vol. 2, pp. 273–80. For more on these kinds of news-poems, see Chapter 4.

29 Pasini describes himself as 'Maphio fi[glio] di quondam ser Francisci di Pasini di sopra Torso [?], territorio bressan stampador in Venettia in contrada di San Patturnian' in his 1549 testament (ASV, Notarile, Testamenti, Not. B. Marino, b. 641, fasc. 295).

30 *Edit16* lists 429 editions by the Bindoni–Pasini partnership, as well as fifty by Francesco alone.

31 See Chapter 5.

32 Menis calculates that the proportion of their Latin titles rose from 10.6 per cent between 1524–39 to 31.4 per cent in 1540–51 ('I Bindoni', pp. 77–8). On the broader change in the output of the Bindoni family towards more conservative works for more educated readers, see *ibid.*, pp. 79–81, 106–7.
33 See G. Catoni, 'Processi a librai senesi del Cinquecento', in *Studi di storia medievale e moderna per Ernesto Sestan* (Florence: Olschki, 1980), vol. 2, p. 522.
34 On Gaspare, see *DTEI*, s.v; and for their guild positions, ASV, *ALS*, Atti, b. 163. The grandsons of the original migrant, Alessandro, were successful enough to have to submit *condizioni* for the Decima tax of 1566, showing minor holdings of land and houses in Venice and its hinterland (ASV, *Decime*, b. 126, fasc. 311 and 315).
35 ASV, *ALS*, Atti, r. 2, cc. 87^v, 91^v. See also 'Notizie: Sul famoso libraio veneziano Gaspare Bindoni', *La Bibliofilía*, 35:8–9 (1933), 359, on another Bindoni who ran into financial troubles at this time.
36 See below.
37 For more on the presence of immigrant workers in Venetian print shops, see I. Mattozzi, '"Mondo del libro" e decadenza a Venezia (1570–1730)', *Quaderni storici*, 72:3 (1989), 754–5; and R. Salzberg, 'Masculine republics: establishing authority in the early modern Venetian print shop', in S. Broomhall and J. Van Gent (eds), *Governing Masculinities in the Early Modern Period* (Farnham, UK: Ashgate, 2011), pp. 47–64.
38 Bertoli, 'Librai, cartolai e ambulanti', pt 1, p. 157, no. 84. See also A. Serra-Zanetti, *L'àrte della stampa in Bologna nel primo ventennio del Cinquecento* (Bologna: Alle spese del Comune, 1959), pp. 40–1; J. M. Potter, 'Nicolò Zoppino and the book-trade network of Perugia', in D. V. Reidy (ed.), *The Italian Book, 1465–1800: Studies Presented to Dennis E. Rhodes on His 70th Birthday* (London: British Library, 1993), pp. 135–59.
39 'Discorendo per tanti e tanti anni come ha fatto per le città d'Italia … ha visto havere bisogno de una bottega fornita de libri comodamente servirsi et suvenirsi' (quoted in S. Bernicoli, 'Librai e tipografi in Ravenna a tutto il secolo XVI', *L'Archiginnasio*, 30:4 (1935), 174–5). The petition also records that Zoppino held bookshops in Faenza and other cities.
40 A. Quondam, 'Letteratura in tipografia', in A. Asor Rosa (ed.), *Letteratura italiana*, vol. 2: *Produzione e consumo* (Turin: Einaudi, 1983), pp. 639–40. Lorenzo Baldacchini's recently compiled *annali* of Zoppino list 438 editions: *Alle origini dell'editoria in volgare: Niccolò Zoppino da Ferrara a Venezia. Annali (1503–1544)* (Manziana: Vecchiarelli, 2011), although on omissions from this total, and the likely large number of completely lost editions, see N. Harris's review of Baldacchini's book in *The Library: The Transactions of the Bibliographical Society*, 14:2 (2013), 213–17.
41 ASV, *AC*, Raspe 3661 (22 June 1510). I would like to thank Claire Judde de Larivière for alerting me to this important document, which will be the subject of a forthcoming article by Massimo Rospocher in *The Italianist*. Zoppino could have passed through Ferrara on his way to Pesaro, where he also printed several works in this period. For Venice's monitoring of derogatory songs, see the Introduction.
42 The references are as follows: 'Al Zuppino che canta per tanti libri di canto havuti per li figlioli illustri li portò Sebastiano suo figliolo lire 3.16.0' (Archivio di Stato, Modena, Libri camerali diversi, r. 274, 1521 c. 5^r (5 February 1521)); 'Al Zupin che canta in banco a conto de suo credito lire 1.2.02' (*ibid.*, r. 300, 1525–29, c. 152 (27 March 1526)). Cited in C. Cavicchi, 'Musici, cantor e "cantimbanchi" a corte al tempo dell'*Orlando*

Furioso', in G. Venturi (ed.), *L'uno e l'altro Ariosto in corte e nelle delizie* (Florence: Olschki, 2011), p. 282.

43 T. Folengo, *Baldo*, trans. A. E. Mullaney (Cambridge, MA and London: Harvard University Press, 2007), vol. 1, pp. 360–1. See also L. Baldacchini, 'Chi ha paura di Nicolò Zoppino? Ovvero: la bibliologia e una "coraggiosa disciplina"?', *Bibliotheca. Rivista di studi bibliografici*, 1 (2002), 193–4.

44 'Posto l'ho in man a Nicolò Zoppino / aciò che la traporta in ogni clima / e aciò se alza el tuo nome pellegrino / e vada appresso Iove in l'alta cima / e là per te se canta sta idioma / non che Milan, Venecia, Napol, Roma' (R. Valcieco, *Quinto libro dell'Orlando Innamorato* (1514), cited in Severi, *Sitibondo nel stampar de' libri*, p. 92). Likewise, the writer Nicolò degli Agostini claimed to have composed his own continuation of the *Orlando innamorato* (1524) 'per il mio Zopino: / Nicolo saggio, accorto et peregrino' (cited in N. Harris, 'L'avventura editoriale dell'*Orlando innamorato*', in *I libri di Orlando innamorato* (Ferrara and Modena: Panini, 1987), p. 94).

45 This must be the *Barzoletta novamente composta de la mossa facta per Venetiani contra alo illustrissimo Signore Alphonso duca terzo de Ferrara* ([Ferrara?, 1510]), c. Aii^v. BL 11426.c.93.

46 Vincenzo's will is transcribed in G. Rossini, 'Ulteriori notizie su la cartiera, i librai e le prime stampe faentine', *Studi romagnoli*, 7 (1956), 287. Zoppino's collaboration with Paolo is recorded in ASV, Notarile, Not. A. Pellestrina, b. 10638, cc. 73^v–74^r, cited in Harris, *Bibliografia dell'*Orlando innamorato, vol. 2, p. 87. A pair of brothers, Agostino and Fabio Zoppini, were active in Venice as printers in the second half of the sixteenth century, but there is no indication that they were related to Niccolò.

47 See Chapter 5 on the increasingly hostile attitude to the physically and professionally mobile later in the sixteenth century. On Zoppino's reformist publications, see Chapter 4.

48 M. Villoresi, 'Zanobi della Barba, canterino ed editore del rinascimento', in M. Picone and L. Rubini (eds), *Il cantare italiano fra folklore e letteratura. Atti del convegno internazionale, Landesmuseum Zürich, 23–25 Giugno 2005* (Florence: Olschki, 2007), pp. 461–73. Danza is thought by some to have been a performer as he composed some of the poems and songs he printed. See F. Novati, 'La storia e la stampa nella produzione popolare italiana', first published 1906, reprinted in his *Scritti sull'editoria popolare*, p. 97; Niccoli, *Prophecy and People*, p. 17. The role of street performers as publishers and pedlars of early print was signalled long ago by Bongi, *Annali di Gabriel Giolito*, vol. 2, pp. 27–36; and in Novati's just cited essay. See also R. Salzberg, 'In the mouths of charlatans: street performers and the dissemination of pamphlets in Renaissance Italy', *Renaissance Studies*, 24:5 (2010), 638–53.

49 This is evident from the records of the Florentine Arte dei medici e speziali which enrolled print pedlars, published in Bertoli, 'Librai, cartolai e ambulanti'. See also below and Salzberg, 'Selling stories'.

50 See S. Noakes, 'The development of the book market in late Quattrocento Italy: printers' failures and the role of the middleman', *Journal of Medieval and Renaissance Studies*, 11:1 (1981), 45–52; Rouse and Rouse, *Cartolai, Illuminators, Printers*, pp. 71–89; Nuovo, *Il commercio librario nell'Italia*, pp. 106–10; Barbieri, 'Per il *Vangelo di S. Giovanni*'. The logbook is published in Conway, *Diario of the Printing Press*.

51 M. Lowry, 'La produzione del libro', in Cavaciocchi, *Produzione e commercio*, pp. 371, 385.

52 These include the street singers Baldassare Faentino and Benedetto Clario, who both published several short works in Venice in the 1540s. Baldassare was also listed as selling soap (ASF, AMS, r. 11, c. 166^v (23 December 1544); r. 12, c. 38^r (3 June 1549)).

53 J. E. Shaw, *The Justice of Venice: Authorities and Liberties in the Urban Economy, 1550–1700* (Oxford: Oxford University Press for the British Academy, 2006), p. 2. Unfortunately, the records of the Giustizia Vecchia, that Shaw used to illuminate elements of this economy, are mostly lost for the sixteenth century. The fragmented nature of the Venetian guild system meant that jurisdiction over particular forms of commerce was unclear and subject to continuous negotiation (*ibid.*, pp. 27, 109–37).

54 Farina's *Oratione dell'Arcangelo Raffaele* ([Venice]: G. Anima Mia, [1491–92]) is reproduced in Zorzi, *La vita nei libri*, p. 47, from a copy held in the BGC. On Farina, see A. Cioni, ed., *La poesia religiosa. I cantari agiografici e le rime di argomento sacro* (Florence: Sansoni antiquariato, 1963), pp. 249–50. The *Persiano* is cited in A. Melzi and P. A. Tosi, *Bibliografia dei romanzi e poemi cavallereschi italiani*, 2nd edn (Milan: Tosi, 1838), p. 39. On Francesco, see G. Frasso, 'Una poeta improvvisatore nella "familia" del Cardinale Francesco Gonzaga: Francesco Cieco da Firenze', *Italia medioevale e umanistica*, 20 (1977), 395–400.

55 As suggested by L. Rubini, 'Fiabe in ottava rima: il cantare fiabesco a stampa (1475–1530)', in Picone and Rubini, *Il cantare italiano*, p. 414. On the frequency of anonymous printing in Cinquecento Venice, see D. Rhodes, *Silent Printers: Anonymous Printing at Venice in the Sixteenth Century* (London: British Library, 1995).

56 Contracts between performers and printers must have been primarily verbal, as was the case between *poligrafi* and printers in Venice at this time. See Di Filippo Bareggi, *Il mestiere di scrivere*, p. 248. However, for a contract between one performer and a printer in Perugia, see M. Beer, *Romanzi di cavalleria. Il Furioso e il romanzo italiano del primo Cinquecento* (Rome: Bulzoni, 1987), p. 177.

57 See D. Gentilcore, *Medical Charlatanism in Early Modern Italy* (Oxford: Oxford University Press, 2006), p. 349.

58 Fontaneto also seems to have worked with the Florentine singer l'Altissimo, Ippolito Ferrarese and Leonardo Furlano. Ruffinelli, in 1538, may have printed a now lost second edition of the pornographic poem *La puttana errante* for Ippolito Ferrarese, on which see below, n. 71. Outside of Venice, printers who specialised in works written or commissioned by performers included Luca Bini and Cosimo Bianchino del Leone in Perugia, Giovanni Landi in Siena, and Giovan Battista Faelli in Bologna. On printers who specialised in these kinds of works in England and the Netherlands, see N. Würzbach, *The Rise of the English Street Ballad, 1550–1650*, trans. G. Walls (Cambridge: Cambridge University Press, 1990; first published in German 1981), p. 19; Salman, 'Watching the pedlar's movements', p. 145.

59 On these sorts of publications, see Henke, *Performance and Literature*, ch. 7.

60 See, for example, the *Egloga pastorale di Lylia* … ([Venice], 'ad instantia di Francesco detto Faentino e Compagno', 1538) (BMV Rari 810.5). See also Rhodes, 'Francesco detto il Faventino', 144–5.

61 *Stanze transmutate dell'Ariosto con una bellissima canzone* ([Venice]: 'Per Leonardo detto il Furlano, et il Ferrarese compagni', 1545), listed in G. Agnelli and G. Ravegnani, *Annali delle edizioni Ariostee* (Bologna: Zanichelli, 1933), vol. 2, pp. 200–2.

62 See Chapter 5.

63 See R. Fulin, 'Documenti per servire alla storia della tipografia veneziana', *Archivio veneto*, 12 (1882), 193–4 (2 September 1519) (for l'Altissimo's privilege); ASV, CCX, Notatorio, r. 9, c. 78ʳ (11 January 1532); *ibid.*, r. 11, c. 57ʳ (29 November 1535) (for Zuan Polo's); G. Fatini, 'Su la fortuna e l'autenticità delle liriche di Lodovico Ariosto', *Giornale storico della letteratura italiana*, supp. 22–3 (1924), 148–59 (on Coppa's).

64 Camporesi, 'Cultura popolare'; G. R. Cardona, 'Culture dell'oralità e culture della scrittura', in Asor Rosa, *Letteratura italiana*, vol. 2, pp. 56–8. On the developing role of these figures in fifteenth and sixteenth centuries, see Salzberg, 'In the mouths of charlatans'; R. Salzberg and M. Rospocher, 'Street singers in Italian Renaissance culture and communication', *Cultural and Social History*, 9:1 (2012), 9–26; Gentilcore, *Medical Charlatanism*; L. Degl'Innocenti, *I Reali dell'Altissimo: Un ciclo di cantari tra oralità e storia* (Florence: Società Editrice Fiorentina, 2008).

65 Noakes, 'Development', 40, 54.

66 On Ferrarese, see V. Rossi, 'Di un cantastorie ferrarese del secolo XVI', *Rassegna emiliana*, 2 (1890), 435–46; F. Cirilli, 'Ippolito Ferrarese', in *DBI*, vol. 42, pp. 576–88; Salzberg, 'In the mouths of charlatans'; and more recently G. Petrella, '"Ad instantia d'Hippolito Ferrarese". Un cantimbanco editore nell'Italia del Cinquecento', *Paratesto*, 8 (2011), 23–79.

67 See Gentilcore, *Medical Charlatanism*, pp. 279–83.

68 These are *Il pianto e gran lamento fatto per il Ferrarese, in Luca, un giorno auanti la sua morte* ... (n.p.d.), BL 1071.g.22.5; *Il pianto e lamento fatto per Hippolito Ferrarese in Luca vn giorno auanti la morte sua* ... (n.p.d.), BMV Misc. 2208.14; and *Lamento d'Hyppolito detto il Ferrarese che cantaua in bancha* (n.p.d.), BMV Misc. 2231.8. Ferrarese's death (and thus these pamphlets) probably can be dated to the mid 1540s.

69 For the most up-to-date list of his publications, see Petrella, '"Ad instantia d'Hippolito Ferrarese"'.

70 [*Lamento di Firenze*] (Pesaro, 1531), BMV Misc. 2405.6, copy missing title page; C. Leonardis, *Lunario nouo perpetuo al modo de Italia. Composto per lo excellentissimo dottore maestro Camillo de Leonardis* ... (Venice, 1532) (BL 1395.a.29); *Forze d'amore. Opera nova nella quale si contiene sei capitoli di messer Ludouico Ariosto* ... (1537). Petrella thinks that this last edition, which survives in several copies, was printed in Venice by Zoppino ('"Ad instantia d'Hippolito Ferrarese"', 42).

71 Petrella, '"Ad instantia d'Hippolito Ferrarese"', 49–54. The lost edition of the *Puttana errante* by Lorenzo Venier, attributed to the printer Venturino Ruffinelli in Venice, is described in Bongi, *Annali di Gabriel Giolito*, vol. 2, p. 30. The other work, *All'illustre Signora Vittoria dignissima Marchesa di Pescara. Opera santissima ed utile a qualunque fidel christiano de trenta documenti di frate Cherubino da Spoliti heremita. Donato per il detto a Hyppolito detto Ferrarese e stampata novamente ad instantia sua* ([Venice?]; for Ippolito Ferrarese, 1538) (BUP 112.b.147/2), is discussed further in Chapter 4.

72 Of the Venetians, Ferrarese lamented: 'O che bella audientia hebbi da loro; / o quanto li fu grato el suono il canto; / quanto li piacque a tutti il mio lavoro. / Io portabo fra gli altri il pregio il vanto, / facendo di savone argento et oro' (*Il pianto e lamento fatto per Hippolito Ferrarese*, c. Aiiʳ). Ferrarese bid a tearful farewell to his *lira* in the opening stanzas of this work.

73 Ferrarese commissioned multiple editions of the *Canto primo del cavalier del lion d'oro* and a collection of *Sonetti e strambotti* (listed in Petrella, '"Ad instantia d'Hippolito Ferrarese"').

74 *Opera nova la quale insegna scrivere e leggere in vintisette modi di zifere* ... For these editions, see *Edit16* and A. Giacomello, 'Ad instantia di Leonardo il Furlano. I libri di un editore del XVI secolo', in *Cultura in Friuli. Omaggio a Giuseppe Marchetti* (Udine: Società Filolgica Friulana, 1988), p. 134. The Brescian edition is held in BMV Misc. 2369.1, but not listed in *Edit16*.

75 On the language used by travelling performers, see D. Gentilcore, 'Il sapere ciarlatanesco. Ciarlatani, "fogli volanti" e medicina nell'Italia moderna', in M. P. Paoli (ed.), *Saperi a confronto nell'Europa dei secoli XIII–XIX* (Pisa: Edizioni della Normale, 2009), pp. 384–5. For some interesting reflections on the language in texts intended for a wide audience, closely tied to orality, see Carnelos, 'Con libri alla mano', pp. 103–16. On the imposition of Tuscan norms, see B. Richardson, *Print Culture in Renaissance Italy: The Editor and the Vernacular Text, 1470–1600* (Cambridge and New York: Cambridge University Press, 2004).

76 See R. Henke, 'Towards reconstructing the audiences of the Commedia dell'arte', *Études théâtrales / Essays in Theatre*, 15:2 (1997), 208. The Florentine singer l'Altissimo played to the local crowd when he performed near the ducal palace in Venice in 1518: according to Sanudo, 'comenzò prima voler dir in laude di questa terra' (*DMS*, vol. 25, col. 391 (10 May 1518)). See also Damonfido Pastore, *Opera nvova nellaquale sicontiene un capitolo in laude della città di Fiorenza* ... (Florence, n.d.) (BNCF Palat. E.6.6.119).

77 'Sopra tutte l'altre a me più grata ..., / Venetia di cui nome in mille carte, / dallo alato Leon sempre guardata, / tenuta, e reverita in ogni parte. / So che'l popolo inteso la mia morte, / perche sempre mi amò, si dorrà forte' (*Il pianto e lamento fatto per Hippolito Ferrarese*, c.Aii^r). There were also similar hymns for the city of Florence, 'che tanto voluntier sempre mi udia', and for his hometown of Ferrara (*ibid*, cc. Aiiv, Aiii^v). Ferrarese seems to have mined this vein of flattery continually. The *Lamento d'Hyppolito* contains 'Stamze [*sic*] che cantava'l Ferrarese in lode de Vinitiani', in which he called upon the god Phoebus to give him the skill to play and sing the praises of the Venetians (*ibid.*, cc. Aiii^v–iv^r).

78 Salzberg, 'Selling stories'. See Salman, 'Watching the pedlar's movements', p. 139. Peddling's role in the 'economy of makeshifts' is described in O. H. Hufton, *The Poor of Eighteenth-Century France, 1750–1789* (Oxford: Clarendon, 1974), pp. 83–4, 120–1.

79 On these *poveri* see, for example, ASV, *ALS*, b. 163, r. 2, c. 8^r (5 November 1598).

80 *Ibid.*, c. 7^v (1 October 1598).

81 See, for example, ASF, *OSMN*, b. 195, c. [20^r] (15 February 1569).

82 ASV, *SU*, b. 22, fasc. 25, cc. 1^r, 3^v–4^r (22 May 1567). Giacomo, mentioned in the Holy Office list of booksellers in ASV, *SU*, b. 156, unnumbered sheet dated 13 September 1567, also bound books.

83 ASV, *SU*, b. 37, fasc. 3 (October–November 1574), cc. 3^{r-v}. This is probably the same 'Bortolomio del quondam Bernardin de Salò vende libri a San Marco soto li portegi' listed in the 1567 list cited in the previous note.

84 ASV, *ALS*, Atti, b. 163, r. 1, c. 75^v (15 March 1588). The guild's original ruling is in *ibid.*, c. 74^r (4 September 1586).

85 'La povertà malvaggia, e ria / qual m'ha fatto venir un'ombra scura, / disforme, e brutto più che la paura ... / Ma come spirto ch'invisibil sia, / niun mi vede, niun di me più cura. / Su'l Rialto giorno e notte tengo il piede, / dove gli amici, e anchor parenti miei, / passano inanci, e adietro, e non mi vede / ... Pero che povertà mi fa

invisibile' (G. di Giorgio il cieco, *Lamento di meloni, in barcelletta. Et vn capitulo in lode de l'vua* ... (Venice: M. Pagan, 1557), c. Aiv^v. BL 1071.c.65.18). For some of Giovanni's other publications, see *Edit16*. For other street performers who included plaints of poverty in their compositions, see P. Camporesi, *Bread of Dreams: Food and Fantasy in Early Modern Europe*, trans. D. Gentilcore (Chicago, IL: University of Chicago Press, 1989; paperback edn 1996), p. 65; G. Caravale, 'Censura e pauperismo tra Cinque e Seicento. Controriforma e cultura dei "senza lettere"', *Rivista di storia e letteratura religiosa*, 38:1 (2002), 39–77.

86 'Prego ogni donna non si faccia schiva / ogni vecchio, o gargion non si disdegna / a legger quest'historia santa e diva, / A dapoi letta a porger qui si degna / offerta a questo cieco che in la stampa, / Questa compose ch'al ben far s'ingegna / Questo bon Cieco in la virtute avampa / pover qual Giobbe di famiglia padre / e chi questo non crede al tutto inciampa' (*Il pianto, e'l lamento che fa il famoso censor mastro Pasquino, per la morte de la Signora Lucretia Milanese ditta Romana ... Composta per Giouanni di Georgi cieco Venetiano* (Venice: 1550), BNR 69.7.C.19.3, c. Aiv^v).

87 See, for example, the *Lamento dun Bergamasco venuto in pouerta per la carestia, con diuerse altre canzoni alla bergamasca, Cosa nuoua da ridere, & pigliarsi piacere* (n.p., 1554). BL 11427.b.20. See also R. Henke, 'Representations of poverty in the Commedia dell'arte', *Theatre Survey*, 48:2 (2007), 229–46.

88 P. Britti, *Canzoneta nova nella qual se intende li auisi, che manda Paolo Briti à i suoi confederati amici dandoli noua come non è vero che lui sia morto* ... (Treviso, 1641), c. Ai^v, BMV 95.C.278.18. On Britti and other blind singers in Venice, see Carnelos, 'Con libri alla mano', pp. 208–25. On Spain, see J.-F. Botrel, 'Les aveugles colporteurs d'imprimés en Espagne', *Mélanges de la casa de Velázquez*, 9-10 (1973-74), 417–82, 233–71.

89 See D. Rollison, 'Exploding England: the dialectics of mobility and settlement in early modern England', *Social History*, 24:1 (1999), 1–16.

4 'In the mouths of charlatans': pamphlets from print shop to piazza

In 1545, a few months after the street singer Francesco Faentino was arrested by the Esecutori contro la Bestemmia, Pietro Aretino wrote a letter from Venice. The recipient was Iacopo Coppa, a famous charlatan and performer who a few years later would have his own troubles with the Venetian blasphemy magistrates. In 1545, however, Coppa was in Ferrara, where he had been busy praising Aretino's work as he sold it in the piazza. Among his enthralled audience were the painter Titian and another friend of Aretino's, who reported back to the writer in Venice. In contrast to some who disparaged the showmanship and mendacious prattle of street performers, Aretino claimed to be delighted that his work and reputation were being disseminated in this manner, 'in the mouths of charlatans'.[1] The power of the charlatan to pull in an audience and to convince them of the merit of his wares was unrivalled:

> Who is so busy, so needy, or so stingy, [asked Aretino] that at the first touch of [the performer's] *lira*, at the first sound of their voice, at the first advertisement of their merchandise, he would not stop himself, not engage himself, and not throw himself into buying the remedies, the *bossoletti*, and the stories, that they sell even to those who are certain that they are worth nothing, that they matter nothing, and that they say nothing?[2]

As well as giving a rare glimpse of performers' techniques on the piazza, this rather backhanded compliment is typical of Aretino, who embodied the ambivalence that many felt regarding the cultural impact of print.[3] Yet, as someone who relished flouting social mores, he sometimes professed admiration for figures who embraced the mercenary spirit of the times, the need to sell one's 'wares', be they charlatans, courtesans or professional writers.[4] In this vein, Aretino claimed pleasure in hearing of his work disseminated in the streets, with the most attention possible drawn to it by the performative techniques of the charlatan.

This episode is significant for a number of reasons. It shows how the writings of one of the most innovative and prominent writers of the period could be encountered by anyone who passed through the public square of an average-sized city like Ferrara, his words reaching their audience via the mouth of a singing and peddling charlatan, just one part of an elaborate and attention-seeking spectacle and an exuberant sales pitch. This is yet another example of how closely entwined print and oral practices of performance and communication continued to be throughout the sixteenth century, and of how many connections existed between the seemingly separate spaces of the more exclusive literary milieux, the print shops and the piazzas.

If the last chapter emphasised physical mobility, this one is concerned with what has been called cultural mobility; with the interactions between different social groups, spaces and media, between art, spectacle and commerce, that were particularly characteristic of Renaissance culture and which were both thrilling and unsettling to people at the time.[5] This was no more so the case than in Venice, where the boundaries between elite and popular, learned and unlearned spheres were difficult to trace; a city where charlatans and street singers performed a great variety of texts publicly and people of all kinds encountered cheap print for sale in the streets. The cheap print disseminated in Venice in this period expressed this very complex and diverse urban culture in which a great variety of people participated, patricians and *popolani*, locals and foreigners, although we will also see some of the ways in which this culture was changing across the sixteenth century.

The production of cheap print in sixteenth-century Venice and Italy was vast and it would be extremely difficult to give a summary overview. Here I focus on some of the most common genres of literature that could be found peddled and performed in the streets of the city. Many are works that were commissioned, written or sold by travelling performers or itinerant publishers, which issued from the presses of Venice – texts, to echo Aretino, that were in the mouths (and hands) of charlatans.[6] A survey of some of these texts allows us to cut a path through the thick forest of cheap printed matter produced in the period and to gain some sense of its rich diversity, which would be much more difficult to observe were we to focus on just one printer, author or genre of text. The literature published in this form was extremely varied: it embraced conservative and traditional elements as well as more innovative and provocative ones; it offered fantasy and escapism as well as reflecting anxieties about pressing contemporary issues such as war, poverty and religious change. It ranged from obscure and anonymous pieces to some of the future classics of Renaissance literature (or bits of them, at least). But it was united by being published in small, cheap printed forms, by appearing almost entirely in the vernacular language, by its often close associations with oral modes of communication and by being made easily available on the streets.

This form and these modes of dissemination lent these small and humble objects a particular power, intensifying the speed and ease with which words could move. They created a rapid and responsive medium that registered the quotidian rhythms of life in the city as well as the surges and ripples of more extraordinary events. Ephemerality is again a key term here for, as we will see, many texts were not fixed in one printed form but continued to move and change, reflecting fluid and flexible notions of authorship, authority and possession, and closely implicated in ephemeral transactions, interactions and performances.

Books of battles

Chivalric tales in verse form had been at the centre of the *cantastorie*'s repertoire since the Middle Ages, and with their proven popularity with an extremely broad public they were carried rapidly into print. Venice became the predominant Italian centre of publication for such works – sometimes known as *libri di batagia* (*battaglia*), or books of battles – from the early years of printing, even though the literary tradition had stronger roots in the Padana region and Tuscany. Venetian printers quickly recognised the popularity of the tales with audiences and pursued their publication. Hack writers or *poligrafi* also got in on the act, helping to feed the market by producing new chivalric tales or continuations of old ones.[7] Yet, this was also a genre where performers played a crucial early role in providing material, driving production and helping their audiences make the transition from listening to reading; a role they continued to perform throughout the sixteenth century.[8] The early history of the chivalric genre in print was not simply that of a popular, oral genre transforming into a more elevated, literary one. The genre always had been at the crossroads between oral and written communication, between educated and uneducated audiences, and its fortune through the sixteenth century was characterised by a complicated, multi-directional cycling of texts through various media, via hands, mouths, press and pen. In some ways, it is the ultimate expression of the circularity of Italian Renaissance urban culture and the interpenetration of different media in the period.

This can be demonstrated by no better example than Lodovico Ariosto's phenomenally popular *Orlando furioso* (first published in 1516 and in a revised version in 1532). Ariosto played with the popular, oral associations of the chivalric genre yet infused it with a thoroughly literary and learned spirit. His poem became one of the bestsellers of the sixteenth century in Italy and scholars such as Javitch have chronicled how it became encased in a critical armour that established its status as a literary classic and distanced the chivalric genre from its roots in the piazza.[9] It also encouraged a cavalcade of imitators. However, the publication history of the *Furioso* is not one of simple progression up the literary ladder. Throughout the century the poem was printed in a wide variety of typographical forms, from small and cheap to large and lavishly illustrated, and as such it reached an exceptionally broad reading public, 'momentarily united in listening to the great voice of the humanist in the guise of *cantastorie*'.[10] Ariosto also echoed the customs of travelling performers in his use of a supra-regional vernacular, rather than a particular dialect, which further promoted the text's accessibility and popularity.[11]

Ariosto's poem was particularly valued for how enjoyable it was to *hear*, as well as to read, and how well it could be set to music. There is much contemporary testimony of the widespread diffusion of the poem outside of the elite courtly circles in which it first circulated, into the streets, houses, taverns and workshops, especially via oral recitations or song versions.[12] The poem also was among those taught in Venetian vernacular schools in the sixteenth century, where pupils valued it as an exciting chivalric romance rather than a contemporary literary classic.[13] Like the plays of Shakespeare, this text appealed widely less because it was quickly hailed as a classic and a masterpiece but because it was entertaining and accessible to those of different levels of education. The heroes of the tale also became ubiquitous in material culture, images of them appearing in paintings and tapestries, on fabrics, fans and playing cards.[14]

The extensive diffusion of the poem and its very popularity both were spurred and evidenced by the flood of pamphlet texts printed from the 1530s on that presented, adapted or parodied some part of the long poem. Piazza performers made a notable contribution to this post-publication history of Ariosto's poem. The popularity of Ariosto made him an obvious source to plunder for material that could be recycled into a public performance or a printed pamphlet. His name had great public appeal, as evinced by its liberal use on the title pages of a horde of cheap imitatory pamphlets, not to mention the many copycat titles that linked themselves explicitly to the stories of Orlando and Charlemagne's knights. Despite the humble form and often limited literary merit of these texts, their cultural significance cannot be dismissed. The music of the *cantastorie* is thought to have influenced polyphonic settings of Ariosto's verse, while there has even been suggestion that Ariosto revised his poem for the second edition after hearing it performed in the piazza by street singers.[15] Moreover, cheap copycat editions plainly were welcomed by ordinary readers and listeners still entranced by the stories of Orlando and the other knights of Charlemagne.

A typical example of the kinds of texts produced in an attempt to cling to the coattails of the *Furioso* is the short verse work entitled the *First Canto of the Knight of the Golden Lion*. This is thought to be a reworking of a text by the contemporary Trevisan notary and poet Bartolomeo Oriolo, author of two other compositions inspired by the *Furioso*; a reworking seemingly done by the singer Ippolito Ferrarese, whom I discussed in the Chapter 3.[16] Clearly the publication of this text was fashioned to target fans of Ariosto, as the title pages of the 1538 editions declare that it 'follows the *Orlando furioso*'. In seventy-two octaves, the poem relates the adventures of one of Charlemagne's knights, who earns his name by fighting a formidable lion. It then segues to an episode involving Charlemagne and some of the most popular characters of the *Furioso*: the brave warrior Marfisa and the evil pagan king Rodomonte. The story cuts off abruptly and the narrator promises to continue in another poem, a common ploy of the piazza entertainer leaving his audience wanting more.[17]

Although no continuation is known to have been published, the poem found some success as it was reprinted at least four times in four years. It must have been incorporated into the repertoires of piazza performers, as the only identified editions of this text to survive were published by *cantimbanchi*: two each by

Ippolito Ferrarese and by Baldassare Faentino, another *cantimbanco*-publisher. At least two of these, probably three, were printed in Venice.[18] All were modest productions in octavo, with generic decorative woodcut borders on the title pages but with no other illustrations (see Figure 2). Notably, the same woodcut borders were used in other publications by performers (see Figure 1).[19] All make use of the same old-fashioned Roman typeface that Grendler has identified as a common feature of printed chivalric romances in the sixteenth century.[20] In other words, the performer-publishers and the printers were not aiming for the cutting edge. They presented their works in a familiar visual form for cheap print, and positioned them within the genre of works dominated by Ariosto, as well as linking them visually with other works associated with performance and street sale. These editions are a representative instance of how diffuse the culture of the chivalric romance was, and how fluid the boundaries between the soon-to-be canonical text and the cheap knock-off, between prestige and popularity, and between the written and the recited or sung.[21]

This was not the first occasion that the singer Ferrarese had taken or composed a poem featuring popular characters from the literature of chivalry and recycled it into print and performance. In 1532, he published a pamphlet entitled *New Work about the Proud King of Sarza Rodomonte*, which was in fact a section of Pietro Aretino's *Marfisa* (Figure 9). The borrowing from Aretino's text was unattributed and a few cuts and additions 'of a *canterino* style' were made.[22] Despite Aretino's efforts to secure papal and imperial privileges for the text, and to arm it with a carefully targeted dedication, cheap and incorrect versions such as this one continued to do the rounds. On this occasion, Aretino may not have been so pleased to hear his text in the mouths of charlatans.[23] As in the case of the *First Canto*, it is possible to follow a tale rooted in the piazza tradition of chivalric balladry, as it is transformed into print at the hands of a professional writer with greater literary aspirations. But the journey does not end there. From the printed version it is picked up by a performer, who cuts and adapts it to suit the short publications that he peddles and, probably, the attention span of a public audience to whom he recited it. And so the story returns to the piazza. When Niccolò Zoppino published the *Marfisa* again in 1535, attributed to its rightful author, the publisher still emphasised that it was the kind of work which would 'nourish at once the ears and the mind with new and varied things … as much for listeners as for readers'.[24]

Aretino also turned his hand to parodies of the *Furioso* and the genre of chivalry. For example, his *Orlandino* began with a subversion of Ariosto's opening stanza, promising to sing of 'the lies about battles and love affairs, / with which the foolish world is so intoxicated'.[25] Like a large echo chamber of influence and subversion, this kind of parodying and rewriting of texts was another common characteristic of Italian Renaissance literary culture again reflected clearly in Venetian cheap print. Here, too, piazza entertainers played a role: not only repackaging and disseminating parts or continuations of the *Furioso*, but also subverting and parodying the poem and indeed the entire

9 Recycling Aretino: Ferrarese's *Opera nova del superbo Rodamonte re de Sarza* …

chivalric genre. An example of this which spoke to a specifically Venetian audience was the buffoon Zuan Polo's *Book of Rado Stizoso*, about the adventures of a Slav called Rado whose wife is kidnapped by Orlando and the knights of Charlemagne.[26] In 1533, Zuan Polo performed and sold the text from a platform in Piazza San Marco.[27] The work was written in the mock Slavic dialect that was the buffoon's stock-in-trade, a favourite with Venetian audiences, and spoken in the character of 'Ivan Paulovichio' of Ragusa, a quack doctor with pretensions to learning.[28] Thus the buffoon used Ariosto's poem as a springboard for a new text that in turn poked fun at the conventions of the chivalric genre, the pretensions of learned scholars, the boasting of medical charlatans and the attempts of Slavic migrants in Venice to speak Italian. While this was a larger and more expensive work than the *First Canto* pamphlets, it represents another example of oral performance interacting with print dissemination in the public spaces of Venice to communicate a text to a diverse audience.

The chivalric genre was looked on with increasing disapproval by the Catholic Reformation Church and the *Orlando furioso* itself came close to being banned. Echoing medieval preachers like San Bernardino of Siena, sixteenth-century churchmen continually complained that their parishioners preferred to listen to or read the tales of battles and love rather than more morally beneficial works.[29] Nevertheless, chivalric tales, parodies, translations and continuations of Ariosto's poems continued to be produced in the later part of the century and itinerant performers and publishers still played a role in their production and dissemination.[30] Some prudently adapted to the spirit of the post-Tridentine period, as when the blind poet Cristoforo 'il cieco da Forlì' published the first canto of the *Furioso* translated into 'spiritual verse' in 1593.[31] However, on the whole, the climate of the Catholic Reformation discouraged contemporary authors from experimenting further with the chivalric tales and performers largely followed the same lead.[32] Looking at catalogues of cheap print in later centuries, one is struck by how many of the chivalric poems, first transposed into print in the late fifteenth or early sixteenth centuries, continued to be reprinted. While the tales remained remarkably popular for centuries – continuing to be recited and sung by Italians of all classes, from rural peasants to Venetian gondoliers in the canals of the city – the tradition largely ossified, with less creative interaction between contemporary literary and print production and that which was recited and performed on the streets.[33]

The news in verse

Many of the same features that characterised the circulation of chivalric poems in Renaissance Venice applied also to the related genre of news-poems. These texts display a similar continuity of literary form from the pre-print era, and likewise exemplify the important role of performers and the continued interaction of the oral and written. However, here we can note more distinct development across the sixteenth century as other news forms came to predominate in print; performers and their renditions in verse and song were pushed towards the sidelines, particularly in the provision of news about war and politics.

Before the appearance of the press, the most diffuse and most accessible news medium was the spoken word and, unsurprisingly, the connections between news dissemination and oral culture remained very strong in the early years of printing. As discussed in the Introduction, from as early as the 1470s, reports of important current events such as the fall of the Venetian colony of Negroponte to the Ottomans were composed in verse, printed and performed. These verse renditions employed traditional structures such as the lament and the *cantare* in octaves and probably were sung to familiar tunes, so that they carried on a long tradition of rendering current events quickly into verse. In this easily memorised form, they could be performed by entertainers for a profit, later repeated by listeners, and thus transmitted rapidly from place to place. These accounts typically played on the dramatic and the emotional aspects of events, such as the opening of the *Loss of Negroponte* which invoked God's mercy on a suffering people and promised to recount the cruelty of the Ottoman invaders.[34]

Printed verse news accounts truly flourished in the period of the Italian wars which lasted on and off from the arrival of Charles VIII in 1494 to the Peace of Cateau-Cambrésis in 1559. The form became known as *guerre in ottava rima*, or 'wars in octave verse'.[35] Venetians (like other Italians) clearly had an urgent, unquenchable desire for information about events taking place on the mainland that so directly threatened their state. While the first news of events probably arrived by word of mouth – sometimes announced officially by a government representative in the piazza, sometimes circulating as unlicensed rumour – the printed and performed verse accounts provided a welcome commentary on the swiftly unfolding developments of the wars. They may have helped audiences to make sense of the bewildering twists and turns of political fortunes, fitting them into familiar narrative structures and stylistic forms. Indeed, these news verses were closely related to the chivalric romances, chronicling recent events of war and politics in terms not dissimilar to those used to relate the exploits of Charlemagne and his paladins and usually exploiting the *ottava rima* metre of the medieval *cantari*. In parallel, the wars also spurred an outpouring of other texts which discussed events within prognosticatory or prophetic forms.[36]

Venice's war with the League of Cambrai may mark one of the first moments in which the new communicative medium of print was able to respond rapidly and unceasingly to developments in an ongoing conflict. Clearly, much of the material produced in Venice played to local sympathies, celebrating the victories of the Republic (sometimes prematurely) and the losses of its enemies. For example, the pamphlet *La vera nova de Bressa* ... celebrated the reclaiming of Brescia by the Venetians in early February 1512, but must have come out before the city was lost again to the French only weeks later.[37] Elsewhere, Venice's enemies celebrated the often disastrous fortunes of the Serenissima in print and in song. Street performers played a crucial role in composing and performing topical texts that could then be sold in printed form. After Venice was resoundingly defeated in battle in 1509 by the League of Cambrai, the diarist Priuli recorded how across Italy verse accounts of the rout were doing the rounds in print and 'being sung and recited on the piazzas throughout Italy by charlatans, who were making a living from this'.[38] The mobility of many of these performers likely gave them privileged access to news as it unfolded, and their accounts may have carried the stamp of authenticity because they came from afar. They were able to work at great speed, using the new typographic medium to describe a swiftly evolving present. One of the singers who described Venice's defeat at the Battle of Agnadello claimed to have composed and given his work to the presses within two days of the event.[39] But most of all their accounts were eagerly sought because they rendered the news into dramatic and memorable oral and printed renditions, which fed into people's voracious desire to hear and read about, to discuss and debate, contemporary events.[40] Professional writers followed the lead of performers and also began to produce these works; in the 1530s, a character in a dialogue by Niccolò Franco resolved to pen a news verse ('componere ... un bel libro di guerre in ottava rima') in order to achieve his dream of literary fame ('Harrò per questa via il favore di tutte le genti').[41]

There is little evidence that the Venetian government sponsored such works in this period, as appears to have been the case in the papal states under Julius II.[42] However, for a local printer or an itinerant publisher or performer in Venice there was little to be gained from printing, selling or reciting a work that was not complimentary to the Venetians and derogatory of their enemies of the moment, as Niccolò Zoppino learned after his run-in with the Venetian authorities.[43] Italian rulers, including the patricians of Venice, had to live among the people that they governed in a confined urban environment, even if these people had no say in government. Permitting performers, and now printers, to stir up local patriotism in favour of the existing regime was – perhaps increasingly – considered useful to maintaining concord.[44]

However, it is interesting to speculate about what kind of political consciousness such texts may have promoted in their Venetian readers and listeners. Certainly, many were crude and simple, and unquestioningly pro-Venice, for example, a song celebrating the successful recapture of Brescia by Venice and France repeated the refrains 'Viva Franza col Leone' (i.e., the Lion of St Mark) and 'Marco Marco Marco Marco', reminiscent of a football chant (Figure 10).[45] However, with events changing so rapidly, reversals of fortune and the making and breaking of alliances, these poems may have helped to emphasise just how unstable were the fortunes of the famously serene Republic. Possibly, they also made Venetians feel more connected to people elsewhere in Italy, promoting a sense of a common Italian fate, as in a work by Ippolito Ferrarese which invoked pity for 'Poor Lady Italy afflicted and sad / once garden, chief and queen of the world' ('Poverella Italia afflitta e mesta, / del mondo già giardin, capo e regina').[46] The genre of the *lamento* in the voice of a ruler, another staple of the medieval *canterino*, is also worth highlighting, as it seemed to offer ordinary people

La noua de Bressa con vna Barzelleta in laude del Re de Franza e de san Marco Stampata nouamente.

PVrificata virgo che nel tempio
volesti presentar il tuo figliolo
sol p nostra salute:e nr̄o exēpio
che in te non si trouo fallacia o dolo
aspira al seruo tuo ignorāte e sempio
da quel tuo venerādo e sacro polo
chio possa dir vna felice noua
di tua virtu chel bel Leon rinoua,

Era si Italia gemitosa e stancha
opressa da nemici in ogni parte
che mai pensossi ritrouarsi francha
ne piu ricuperar le antiche parte
ma ecco il bel Leon alza la brancha
con tēpo:e lassa pax marce e le carte
dando de piglio a Bressa si potente
fazendola al suo stato obediente.

10 A patriotic news song: *La nova de Bressa con una barzelletta in laude del Re de Franza e de San Marco* a window into the minds and consciences of the powerful as they suffered at the hands of fate or regretted the results of their own hubris. Thus the military leader Piero Strozzi, defeated in the fight for Sienese independence in 1554, was made to lament the comeuppance accorded to those like himself who 'seek and desire to have too much', bringing great ruin upon themselves and others.[47]

Surviving examples of these news verses provide some evidence of the oral performance of the works and their sale in printed form in the streets. Indeed, they often specifically evoked these occasions, suggesting that the link to an actual performance was part of the appeal to consumers. The *guerre in ottava rima* usually featured the oral salutations of the Medieval *cantari*, and occasionally gave explicit indication of the performative context, in which the entertainer first called for the support of Christian or pagan deities in their artistic endeavour, asked for the audience's attention, then concluded his 'set' by selling the related pamphlet. Zoppino's poem about the Venetians' war with Ferrara concluded with the call to whoever wished to buy the pamphlet to 'reach into [your] purse / and take two *quattrini* from it / to put in the hands of Zoppino'.[48] The performer of an account of the lament of Rome at the time of the descent of Charles VIII into Italy in 1494–95 called on divine aid so he could tell his tale in verse and begged his audience 'that everyone might deign to listen, / open your ears attentively to my plight'.[49]

The news-poems were presented in a way that communicated to readers both the novelty and accuracy of the account (as in titles like *The True News of Brescia, Point by Point as it Happened*)[50] and its emotional impact (words like *orrendo, orribile, crudele, miserando* recur often). Furthermore, as one study has emphasised, sometimes these texts were published with evocative, topical woodcut illustrations, employing iconography potent and familiar to a broad Venetian audience, such as the lion of Saint Mark straddling the sea and land, representing Venetian domination of its *stato da mar* and *stato da terra* (Figure 10).[51] At other times, printers re-employed the same woodcut images of battles, kings and warriors used to illustrate chivalric tales, reaffirming the genre's 'amphibious state' in between the relation of current events and the narrative style of epic tales and the literature of chivalry.[52] Framing recent events within the narrative and iconographic structures of such fictional tales patently seemed an effective way to capture the interest of the audience.

Printers and performers recognised that the news-poems held many of the same attractions as chivalric and epic tales, with which they shared many stylistic similarities. They offered excitement and emotion, coupled with the pleasures of hearing, reading or singing them out loud. Readers do not seem to have been troubled by the close proximity of fact and fiction in these works, as presumably they were not when they crowded into the piazza for a *cantastorie*'s performance of material of both kinds. It was not uncommon to find both types of poetic work printed in the same compilation, as in the edition published by Ippolito Ferrarese that included a composition about the travails of Italy in the 1520s alongside a chivalric poem about the Saracen King Rodomonte.[53] It would seem that audiences and readers of war poems were content to receive news in a familiar form founded on archetypal tropes and stories. Hence many of these poems were published without the name of an author, and thus a verifiable source. Certain poems retained their appeal for a long time after the event they related as they continued to speak to contemporary interests and anxieties. For example, the enduring preoccupation with the threat of the Ottomans was expressed in works like the repeatedly reprinted *Lament of Rhodes* about the 1522 siege of the island.[54] On the other hand, when in 1515 Hernan Colòn bought a copy of a poem about the 1509 defeat of the Venetians by the Ferrarese, he paid half a *quattrino* for the two-leaf quarto, a drop in price from the three *quattrini* suggested by the singer who performed the work soon after the event. Probably 'new' news was more highly valued.[55]

Over time, however, new forms of news proliferated and the market for information became more variegated and stratified. The later sixteenth and the seventeenth centuries saw a boom in news productions of many kinds, with increasing quantities of international news reaching Venetian audiences in printed form. Readers sought a more instantaneous and detailed delivery of the news, rapid and straightforward accounts of crucial developments such as the Republic's continuous wars with the Ottomans in the Morea, including maps and images of battles.[56] Newsletters or *avvisi* began to appear which gathered together short prose descriptions of contemporary events across Europe or described particular episodes such as a noble wedding or birth, a form which would ultimately prove more durable than the verse accounts. A two-tiered market developed, with relatively expensive manuscript *avvisi* providing more recondite political and financial news to a more restricted, elite public and printed *avvisi* offering a watered-down version – news that could make it past the censors – to a broader audience.[57]

Nevertheless, news dissemination did not lose its association with oral culture. Major events in Venice like the victory against the Ottomans at Lepanto in 1571, the visit to the city of the French King Henry III in 1573 and the liberation from a great plague in 1577 occasioned celebratory songs and poems as well as prose accounts.[58] Into the seventeenth century, news works continued to be hawked by pedlars in the streets, and read aloud in public spaces like piazzas and barbershops, as testified by the prints of the Bolognese artist Giuseppe Maria Mitelli.[59] Even in the mid-eighteenth century, the Venetian authorities still exerted themselves to control the circulation of topical songs and verses, as in 1757 when they fruitlessly pursued a number of vendors 'crying' (*gridando*) a song for sale about the recent defeat of the Prussian army by the Austrians in various locations around the city, including the Rialto Bridge.[60]

Even as other, more 'modern', forms of news developed, the cheap printed news-poems of the late fifteenth and the first half of the sixteenth century occupy an important place in the history of the evolving news market. Often disseminated by the familiar figure of the *cantastorie*, and closely associated with oral recitation and performance, they played a transitional role, helping to introduce ordinary people to the concept of *buying* the news instead of simply hearing and discussing it. Although the news-poems were rough and cheap, typically offering more in the way of sensationalism and diversion than accurate and sober news reporting, they were an effective form of communication that obviously appealed to a broad audience. They fed into the urban culture of information and communication, combining novel and traditional elements, making news a more prominent feature of everyday life and a new commodity in the marketplace.

These works also seem to have played a role in fuelling public debate in which the classes who were not meant to be interested in or able to comprehend politics participated actively. Thus, from their first appearances, they raised alarm about their potential power to nurture antipathy towards the government or Venice's allies and enemies, or to whip the people up into a patriotic frenzy that could be destabilising particularly as events see-sawed rapidly.[61] In other words, they raised the spectre of a more informed and critical populace which would materialise fully in the early seventeenth century during the Interdict controversy between Venice and Rome, at which point the Venetian government realised it would have to respond by developing a more open 'media strategy' in relation to its inquisitive subjects.[62]

Secrets and lies

Pamphlets and fliers containing practical, medical or scientific knowledge were another new element on the urban scene in this period that Venetian governing authorities sometimes found troubling. Like the genres previously examined, these texts were widely available, and closely linked to oral cultural practices. They also combined a commercialist drive for profit with a recurring rhetoric about altruistically opening up to the masses certain branches of knowledge, previously the preserve of a learned elite. This was the rhetoric parodied in Franco's dialogue, discussed in Chapter 1, in which the street seller Sannio advertised his 'wonderful, new, useful and admirable invention' which could instil in anyone the key tenets of knowledge in a matter of days, 'the true way to learn any mystery, and the path to ascend to any level. And all taught for ten *scudi*'.[63] Certainly, as in the case of the news-poems, the knowledge peddled in cheap printed form often was not as new or as accurate as it purported to be. But even if driven by the desire to attract audiences and buyers, this rhetoric and the advent of cheap and accessible works on the streets, containing information that ranged from the arcane to the banal, was a development with significant social and cultural implications.

This phenomenon began to emerge clearly in the first decades of the sixteenth century, with the appearance of 'books of secrets' and instructional manuals containing a variety of medical remedies, cosmetic recipes and household hints. Venetian printers like Francesco Bindoni and Maffeo Pasini were among the first to produce such collections, as in the case of the much-reprinted *Edifice of Recipes* (*Dificio di ricette*), published in small octavo and quarto editions of twenty to thirty leaves. Frequently the compilers of these works were performers or hack writers with no particular medical or scientific knowledge, cashing in on a lucrative and relatively uncritical market. For instance, the performer Giovan Maria Lirico, who also published satirical works about courtesans and an account of the 1530 flood of Rome in Venice and Bologna in these years, produced a humble collection of recipes that addressed everyday problems (remedies for knee or tooth pain, gum decay or to improve the appearance of the hands and face) and more fanciful ones (such as how to make a woman urinate against her will).[64] The street singer and soap seller Baldassare Faentino offered a similar pamphlet of simple recipes to make hair grow or fall out, get rid of freckles, turn the hair blond 'so that it seems like golden thread', and even 'to make a cock sing when it is half roasted' (which promised to be 'a good laugh' – *una bella festa da ridere*).[65] The prolific and versatile *poligrafo* Eustachio Celebrino issued numerous pamphlets containing advice and instruction to address other pressing concerns, such as how to cure syphilis (based on his own experiences of the disease) and survive the plague (Figure 5).[66]

Celebrino also contributed to a significant sub-genre of cheap print which promised to unveil the secrets of reading, writing and basic accounting. Such works drew on the models of the chief schoolbooks for basic instruction such as the *Salterio* and the *Babuino*, printed in huge numbers in these years. One more qualified to offer this kind of instruction was Giovan Antonio Tagliente, a former teacher of handwriting in the Venetian chancery who exploited his repute in a series of popular manuals.[67] But lack of experience did not stop the charlatan Leonardo Furlano producing *A New Work in which You Will Be Able to Learn by Yourself to Write Seven Sorts of Letters, and Counting*, which commenced with a printed alphabet such as typically appeared in the *Babuino* and very simple instructions for preparing and holding a pen.[68] Such a text appears to have been pitched at artisans and small-time merchants with basic literacy skills, who could read but perhaps not write competently. It offered useful information such as the conversion of currency between Venice and other cities and a table of tariffs 'of great benefit to those who are good account-keepers as also to artisans, or to others who have no understanding of accounting'.[69] In this short pamphlet, Furlano also included a section on basic pharmacy in order to 'instruct those who do not know, to comprehend how to buy and how to recognise' the qualities of various spices and herbs.[70]

As the sixteenth century progressed, however, more specialised purveyors of medical and scientific knowledge became an increasingly common sight on the piazzas of Venice and other Italian cities and made a greater contribution to the market for cheap print.[71] Unlike the *cantastorie* or *cantimbanchi*, who had existed in one form or another throughout the late Middle Ages, medical charlatans were a newer phenomenon. These protean figures were some of the pioneers of printed advertising and of the use of entertainment to sell commercial goods.[72] The examples of cheap (or free) print that they produced reached a very wide range of people, as evidenced by the concerns of the medical authorities about the charlatans' deception of the gullible masses. The sixteenth-century records of the Venetian Health Board (the Provveditori alla Sanità) contain ever more frequent references to charlatans who sold or gave away printed recipes of the remedies they peddled, such as Latino de' Grassi who was banished from the city in 1551 for exaggerating the benefits of his electuary against venoms, which he sold along with its printed recipe.[73]

As Gentilcore comments, such prints (or the written records of them) tell us something about the effectiveness of the charlatan's oral performance on the piazza. They illustrate clearly how these figures made use of hyperbole and high rhetoric to amaze and impress their audiences, and their ability to adapt their performances to publics in different places.[74] However, governing bodies like the Venetian Sanità took it upon themselves to protect the ignorant masses from the false promises of the charlatans, just as other authorities in this period sought to prevent the spread of 'erroneous' ideas of religious reform via print and the spoken word. The Sanità, for example, expressed particular alarm that Latino de' Grassi's false advertising would bring 'great harm to the poor' and others who bought his wares.[75]

The career of Iacopo Coppa illustrates further the shrewd ways in which such figures combined performance, selling and publishing medical recipes and other works, all while playing on the idea of opening up knowledge to all. Coppa was 'one of the first charlatans of the world', according to Aretino, and one of the most prominent on the Venetian scene in the sixteenth century, although he also frequented other Italian cities, including Naples, Rome and Ferrara, where he performed Aretino's works in the piazza.[76] He was a popular cultural figure, not only winning the praise of Aretino but also deriving authority from his powerful clients (including the Duchess of Florence) and patrons (including a Venetian patrician, Caterina Barbaro). He collaborated with eminent printers to produce a number of literary publications including the first edition of some of Ariosto's poetry, proving again the numerous connections with print shop and piazza that were so fundamental to the vibrancy of Renaissance literary culture.[77]

Coppa also knew how to evoke the admiration of the crowd in the piazza, presenting himself in a flamboyant doctor's costume on a stage elaborately decked out with his licences to practice from various authorities and promising to treat the poor for free, for 'amor di Dio'.[78] In Venice in 1560, Coppa had printed up recipes of his famous electuary, written in the vernacular 'for the greater ease of the people' ('per più facilità ai populi'), which he sold or gave away when he was selling from his *banco*.[79] His recipe, which does not survive but which was transcribed in the Sanità registers, gives the ingredients of the remedy which promises to 'comfort the brain … gladden the heart and, taken as specified, bring easy digestion, dispel sadness and melancholy, purify the blood, strengthen the limbs, aid women in all of those discomforts and sicknesses that come from the womb'.[80]

However, Coppa's example also demonstrates the hostility that such characters, who slipped between social worlds and cultural registers, might encounter from official regulating bodies. The Florentine guild of doctors and the Venetian College of Physicians opposed Coppa's requests to operate in their cities, attempting to brand his form of empirical knowledge illegitimate and even dangerous.[81] Furthermore, he repeatedly encountered trouble for his blasphemous outbursts and potentially heretical opinions. In 1548, he was banished from Venice for five years for having 'many times blasphemed the most holy name of God'.[82] In the late 1560s, he was denounced, again for blasphemy, but also for reading prohibited books and holding heretical opinions, by a rival, the herbalist Leone Tartaglini.[83] Despite these obstacles, Coppa continued to show persistence and flexibility, repeatedly returning to Venice and finding new ways to adapt to the changing climate of the city.

The tension and controversy that surrounded such figures encouraged a long tradition of popular parody aimed at their hyperbolic promises and overheated rhetoric.[84] Nevertheless, the proliferation of such works along with a range of other instructional manuals in print suggests that they were still sought after and appreciated by ordinary people. Much of the knowledge they purported to contain may have been spurious, copied from elsewhere or easily available by other means (for example, family or neighbourhood wisdom, transmitted orally), but owning a copy in print evidently was still appealing. Having physical access to a printed recipe (or oration or spell), carrying it on the body or keeping it within the household, was considered more potent than simply hearing or remembering it.[85] There was something quietly revolutionary about this; from the simple implication, however erroneous, that knowledge was something that could be bought by anyone who had a few spare coins for a printed pamphlet (regardless of their gender, status or level of education). The majority seem to have embraced the promise of new, useful or 'secret' knowledge and information accessible in the form of cheap printed recipes and instructional manuals. However, as discussed in Chapter 1, a number of contemporary writers recorded conflicted reactions to the new accessibility of various brands of knowledge in print, as when a character in Doni's *Dialogue on Printing* muttered with disapproval about the 'ease and paltry effort required to be a man of learning nowadays'.[86]

The word on the street

While the various genres of cheap print offering a range of information and entertainment surveyed so far might still be considered an expendable luxury for most people, devotional and religious material could be regarded as a necessity for one's spiritual well-being. If a person bought or owned one printed item, it was likely to belong to this category, which was probably the most common type of cheap print for sale on the streets of Renaissance Venice.[87] Papal bulls and indulgences on single sheets were among the first works to flow from European presses, often in enormous quantities. But there was also already an established commercial market, from the early fifteenth century, for religious woodblock images, and thus a public for cheap religious print already existing by the time the press arrived in Venice.[88] Despite their mass produced nature, it is evident that images, broadsheets and pamphlets of a pious nature often were used in very intimate and intensive ways by consumers: stuck to walls, pasted into boxes or onto furniture, folded into amulets or pockets. One pamphlet of religious works promised on the back cover that whoever carried it on the body would be protected from danger, and any woman who could not give birth would now be able to.[89] Given this intimate use, it is little surprise that these works are among the least likely to survive, and, if they did, they often lack the author and printer's name and place of publication which makes it very difficult to get a sense of the output of any one city. The efforts of censors also were responsible for the destruction of much cheap religious print.[90]

This is an area where we must rely more on auxiliary evidence in addition to the texts themselves. And this evidence again demonstrates the role of pedlars and performers, in collaboration with printers, in opening up the trade in cheap religious print. The Ripoli logbook shows that the charlatans and pedlars who frequented the press commonly sought devotional works to take out with them onto the streets of Florence. Pedlars who bought works from the press targeted such texts precisely to moments when they were likely to sell, such as the verse *Oration to Saint Roch* sold in large quantities around the saint's feast day, and similar publications began to appear in Venice around the same time.[91] Printers in Venice, and elsewhere in Italy, quickly perceived and targeted a market for cheap religious print, for example with texts including the Credo, the Ten Commandments and the confessional manual of Saint Antoninus of Florence translated into *ottava rima*.[92] This verse form meant they may have been performed publicly but also allowed them to be easily recited and memorised by readers, particularly those with limited literacy skills.

As the sixteenth century progressed, an ever greater array of cheap religious works made its way onto the market. Much of this output comprised very familiar and traditional works of established popularity, such as religious plays (*sacre rappresentazioni*), and lives of Jesus, Mary and the saints in verse. A great deal was reprinted from city to city across Italy in more or less the same form, such as Giuliano Dati's account of a performance of Christ's passion which took place in the Coliseum in Rome.[93] However, some was more specifically targeted to appeal to the spirituality of Venetians and local religious sites and occasions. For example, Eustachio Celebrino's *ottava rima* composition, *The Stupendous and Marvellous Miracles of the Glorious Christ of Saint Roch*, described the miracles, involving ordinary Venetians in familiar locations like Rialto, associated with a painting of Christ and his tormenters installed in the Church of San Rocco in Venice in the early sixteenth century. The title page of the pamphlet featured a woodcut copy of the painting (which is attributed to Giorgione or Titian) and the work itself may have acted as a kind of souvenir for visitors to the church (Figure 11).[94]

11 A religious work in verse with a woodcut copy of a famous painting: Celebrino, *Li stupendi et maravigliosi miracoli del Glorioso Christo de Sancto Roccho Novamente Impressa*

It is not known if Celebrino himself performed his works, although he often adopted the address of the singer to his audience.[95] Certainly, there were a number of writers in this period, such as the Franciscan friar Giovanni da Firenze and the well-educated cleric Giuliano Dati, who wrote short vernacular religious works designed for public recitation and then sale in print. Dati was one of those who believed that these kinds of simple devotional works were crucial to the spiritual health of the broader populace, being much more within reach of ordinary people who might not afford an entire printed Bible, for instance.[96] But religious works had been another feature of the repertoires of late medieval street singers and there is reason to believe that performers remained directly involved in composing and publishing such works in print, as we have seen was the case with other genres in the late fifteenth and sixteenth centuries.[97] This period also saw an explosion of cheap printed prophetic works, associated with the public performances of wandering preachers and prophets. Like the more strictly religious works, prophetic poems and prognostications were disseminated to a large and eager audience by intersecting and overlapping paths – oral, written and printed.[98]

As the market for cheap religious print developed, these links with oral performance became less predominant and other forms of prose work addressed themselves to the less educated consumer. Frequently, such publications adopted a similar rhetoric to that examined above, advertising themselves as practical manuals or guidebooks to devotional practice. A pamphlet instructing how to read and write in code by the charlatan Leonardo Furlano, for instance, included some basic tenets of Christian living. The intended readership seems to have been of a relatively low educational level, including the illiterate who might be exposed to the work via reading out loud in the home or workshop. For example, on saying prayers, the work instructs

> who knows how to read should say the Office of the Madonna every day, and also say the seven psalms with the following orations and the litanies. That is, who has the opportunity to be able to do it should do it, and more or less according to the quality and condition of the person, but who does not know how to read should say the rosary of the Madonna, and the rosary of Christ, and three Paternosters, and three Ave Marias, and five Paternosters.[99]

Around the same time, Furlano published another pamphlet offering simple moral and religious instruction in the form of easily memorised tercets, distilling the wisdom of the Bible and other moral authorities, such as: 'Love God purely, O Christian / do not take his name in vain / Make sure to sanctify holy days' (Figure 1).[100] As with the other genres already examined, these works were reprinted and repackaged in various ways to maximise consumer appeal, and did not always deliver what they promised on the title page. For example, the singer Ippolito Ferrarese published a devotional manual which he attributed – wrongly – to the friar Cherubino of Spoleto, seemingly hoping to cash in on the popularity of this established author of similar works.[101]

In search of sales, printers, pedlars and performers also sometimes strayed into less conservative, and increasingly dangerous, religious territory. As discussed in Chapter 1, there were strong associations between those who championed the use of the vernacular, cheap print and religious reform. In the 1520s and 1530s, some of the chief producers of cheap print brought reformist ideas, including the works of Luther and Erasmus, into the Venetian marketplace in affordable editions. One of the first Italian translations of a Lutheran work was published by Niccolò Zoppino in 1525, even though the German reformer's writings had been prohibited in 1521.[102] Zoppino and the Bindoni brothers also published small editions of the sermons of the reformist Capuchin friar Bernardino Ochino, who caused a sensation when he preached in Venice in 1539 and in 1542 had to flee to safety in Switzerland.

The flight of Ochino and other leading figures at this moment has been seen as a turning point in the Italian reform movement, after which it was much more dangerous to express openly reformist opinions.[103] In the decades prior to this, however, cheap print played an important role in spreading reformist ideas in Italy, even if it was never permitted to do so to the same extent as in northern Europe. Although there is more work to be done on this question, there are hints that what did circulate was particularly effective because it was so closely entwined with forms of oral communication such as preaching and singing. This is suggested by a case of 1534, when the papal nuncio in Venice reported how a female food seller was imprisoned for having listened to a translation of a Lutheran work in a group 'where it was read [aloud] like a tale of Orlando [i.e., a chivalric tale] with applause from the listeners'.[104] A few months earlier, the concerned nuncio had arrested a 'French scoundrel', an uneducated glove maker later banished from the city, who was going around preaching Lutheran ideas and selling a vernacular heretical booklet.[105] And there continued to be apprehension specifically about the role of performers and pedlars in transmitting unorthodox texts to the urban public, by voice and in print. At the Council of Trent in 1546, for example, the Bishop of Senigallia railed against the indiscriminate and uncontrolled use of Scripture by 'many who should in no way be dealing with it', including 'charlatans who sing it and sell it in the piazza from their benches, introducing superstitions, and earning a living from it as they do from their other foolish words'.[106]

But cheap print and performance also were used as vehicles to promote orthodoxy. One example of this is a verse composition in the traditional performative genre of the lament in *ottava rima* published around 1530 as an eight-leaf octavo: this counselled the rulers of the peninsula and the rest of Europe to unite against the threat of Lutheranism and advised the common people against listening to and discussing Luther's ideas and hoping for them to triumph in Italy.[107] In the second half of the sixteenth century cheap religious print proliferated, encouraged by the heightened spiritual fervour of the period and by the belief of some leading religious figures such as Carlo Borromeo, archbishop of Milan, in the benefits of this medium for spreading the word of God to the masses.[108] However, as a result of the censorship mechanisms extended from the middle of the century, described more fully in the next chapter, this kind of religious ephemera was more likely to come with an institutional stamp of approval, demonstrating that it followed the official line of the post-Tridentine Church, rather than being composed according to the fancy of a printer or performer according to what he thought would sell.[109]

In this chapter, I have examined a few of the most prominent sub-genres of cheap print sold in the streets of Renaissance Venice. However, as mentioned, it was not uncommon to find works of different kinds mixed together indiscriminately in a single pamphlet, or in the performance of a street singer or charlatan. Some performers and occasional publishers, like Ippolito Ferrarese or Iacopo Coppa, produced a great variety of works, from contemporary poetry to medical recipes to traditional chivalric tales. All of these works, as well as other commercial products, came together in the multi-purpose space of the piazza, and in other urban spaces such as streets, bridges, shops and stalls. Aside from their physical form and modes of diffusion, many of these publications, even the most seemingly anodyne, had in common a propensity to trample over boundaries: between learned and unlearned cultures, between oral, written and printed, public and private, licit and illicit. This promiscuous tendency troubled many people, and we have begun to see how some boundaries progressively were redefined and reinforced in the sixteenth century, so that by the latter part of the period there was less possibility for creative interaction, while a more circumscribed, distinct corpus of 'popular' literature intended for the masses emerged.

Nevertheless, particularly in the first century of printing in Venice, city dwellers had access to a growing and extremely diverse body of cheap literature. While many of the kinds of texts surveyed would become enshrined in the corpus of cheap pamphlet literature for centuries, a good proportion were much more resistant to categorisation. They reflect a period when the literary canon had not been firmly delineated, and publishers experimented liberally with works for various audiences. Some of the texts published in cheap editions and sold on the streets were pillaged from established classics of Italian literature, as in one pamphlet published by the singer Francesco Faentino which adapted a story from Boccaccio's *Decameron* into *ottava rima*, probably allowing its performance.[110] Similarly, the story of two star-crossed lovers that is the earliest known source for the tale of Romeo and Juliet was extracted from Masuccio Salernitano's *Novellino* and published by the performer Fortunato in a pamphlet of eight leaves, as simply *A Delightful Story of Two Lovers*.[111] However, these cheap publications also delivered some of the most recent efforts of the leading lights of Renaissance Italian literary culture, including works by Aretino, Ariosto and Vittoria Colonna.[112]

In other words, these small editions contain a remarkable intermingling of themes, tropes, genres and styles, and confirm the ceaseless interaction between the exclusive milieux of the ecclesiastical and princely courts, and the urban patriciates of cities like Venice and Florence, and a more inclusive urban culture that encompassed the 'middling' sorts and penetrated even further down, into the ranks of the illiterate and poor. In many ways, they anticipate the famous chapbooks of the *Bibliothèque bleue* that flourished in France from the seventeenth century, which one scholar has described as literature that 'becomes popular' by virtue of being published in an affordable form and sold in an accessible way, rather than being popular from the beginning.[113]

In the Venetian case, interchange occurred not just between social groups in one city but between urban centres in the Italian peninsula. The works printed and sold in Venice included material from all over Italy, and sometimes beyond. This was not exclusively a Venetian culture; the mobility of printers, performers and pedlars ensured the transmission of texts between Italian urban centres, sometimes with adaptations to suit the local audience. Certainly, some works were created specifically with a Venetian audience in mind, for example those that satirised the immigrant Bergamasks, Germans or Slavs who were so numerous in the lagoon city (see, for example, Figure 4).[114] But above all the prints suggest how deeply Venetian urban life was permeated by outside influences – although this is not surprising in a city that was so famously cosmopolitan and which saw so much traffic with the Italian mainland in particular. Venice in turn exerted a cultural influence on other places, because of its leading role in the production and distribution of print.

Performers, publishers and pedlars played a singular role in the elaboration and dissemination of this culture. As well as communicating texts via recitation or song, these individuals created and adapted works to feed the growing market for cheap print. Unlike the printers and *poligrafi* with whom they collaborated, however, they also made the crucial step of taking the works out into the piazza, transforming them into multimedia performances for the urban public, feeding the material of Renaissance literature back into the ephemeral culture of everyday life.

Notes

1 'Avisami M. Francesco de gli Albizi da la Mirandola, il come Tiziano e egli furono isforzati dal grido desto de la vostra isvegliata eloquenza di fermarsi a udire lo in che foggia di favella mi metteste in cielo in su la piazza di Ferrara, cantando in banca. Del che mi laudo non altrimenti che mi lauderei, caso che Apollo avesse tanto di me detto ne i chiostri di Parnaso poetizando improviso'; 'mi rallegro d'essere in bocca de i ceretani' (Aretino, *Lettere*, vol. 3, pp. 325–7 (October 1545)). On Francesco Faentino's arrest, see the Introduction; on Coppa's, see below.
2 'Quale è quello infacendato, quale è quel bisognoso, e quale è quello avaro, che al primo tocco de la lor lira, al primo verso de la lor voce, e al primo isciorinar de la lor merce, non si fermi, non s'impegni, e non si scagli nel conto del comperare le ricette, i bossoletti, e le leggende, ch'essi donano con la vendita sino a quegli che son certi che

niente vagliano, che niente importano, e che niente dicono?' (*ibid.*, p. 326). *Bossoletti* were little boxes used for selling medicines.

3 See Chapter 1.
4 See for example the passage in his *Ragionamenti* in which he compared the skills of courtesans and charlatans (P. Aretino, *Aretino's* Dialogues, trans. R. Rosenthal (New York: Marsilio, 1994), pp. 178–9).
5 See Greenblatt, *Cultural Mobility*, esp. pp. 250–3.
6 Because of the itinerant nature of many of these publishers, pamphlets not explicitly identified as having been printed in Venice, and some printed elsewhere, are considered also.
7 A. Quondam, 'La tipografia e il sistema dei generi. Il caso del romanzo cavalleresco', in K. W. Hempfer (ed.), *Ritterepik der Renaissance. Akten des deutsch-italienischen Kolloquiums Berlin, 1987* (Stuttgart: Franza Steiner, 1989), p. 11. See also Beer, *Romanzi di cavalleria*; M. C. Cabani, *Le forme del cantare epico-cavalleresco* (Lucca: Pacini Fazzi, 1988); M. Villoresi, *La fabbrica dei cavalieri. Cantari, poemi, romanzi in prosa fra medioevo e rinascimento* (Rome: Salerno, 2005); B. Barbiellini Amidei, 'I cantari tra oralità e scrittura', in Picone and Rubini, *Il cantare italiano*, pp. 19–28.
8 Villoresi, *La fabbrica dei cavalieri*, p. 183.
9 D. Javitch, *Proclaiming a Classic: The Canonisation of* Orlando furioso (Princeton, NJ: Princeton University Press, 1991).
10 Beer, *Romanzi di cavalleria*, p. 210. See also Grendler, 'Form and function', 482–3.
11 See the works cited in Chapter 3, n. 75.
12 J. Haar, 'Arie per cantar stanze ariotesche', in M. A. Balsano (ed.), *L'Ariosto, la musica, i musicisti* (Florence: Olschki, 1981), p. 33. See also G. Fumagalli, 'La fortuna dell'*Orlando furioso* in Italia nel secolo XVI', *Atti e memorie della deputazione ferrarese di storia patria*, 20:3 (1912), 396–400; J. Haar, 'From "cantimbanco" to court: the musical fortunes of Ariosto in Florentine society', in M. Rossi and F. G. Superbi (eds), *L'Arme e gli amori. Ariosto, Tasso and Guarini in Late Renaissance Florence. Atti del convegno (Firenze, 27–29 giugno 2001)* (Florence: Olschki, 2004), vol. 2, pp. 179–80; Cavicchi, 'Musici, cantor e "cantimbanchi"'.
13 Grendler, *Schooling in Renaissance Italy*, pp. 288–9.
14 M. Roggero, 'I libri di cavalleria', in Braida and Infelise, *Libri per tutti*, p. 35.
15 Haar, 'Arie per cantar', p. 34; Haar, 'From "cantimbanco" to court'.
16 The attribution to Oriolo is made by Fumagalli, 'La fortuna dell'*Orlando furioso*', p. 260. The first Venetian edition presents the text as the work of Ippolito Ferrarese, who was also its publisher: *Canto primo del cavalier dal leon d'oro, d'Hippolito Ferrarese, qual seguita Orlando furioso* (Venice: V. Ruffinelli, 1538), BEM ALPHA Y 007 030 005. Ferrarese also published an edition in Brescia in the same year: *Canto primo del cavalier dal leon d'orro [sic] qual seguita Orlando furioso non mai più visto* (Brescia: D. Turlino, 1538), BNCF Palat. D. 4.7.77.1.
17 'E la risposta felli si com'io / narrar io vi prometto in l'altro mio'. *Canto primo del cavalier dal leon d'oro*, c. Di^v (I cite from the Venetian edition).
18 On Faentino, see Chapter 3, n. 52. Ferrarese was the first to commission publication of the work, in 1538. Petrella, '"Ad instantia d'Hippolito Ferrarese"', 48, suggests that the Venetian edition preceded the Brescian one. Editions of the work were published 'ad instantia del Romano detto il Faentino' in 1541 and 1542. The first

edition by Faentino was the *Canto primo del cavalier dal leon d'oro qual seguita Orlando furioso non mai più visto al presente* (Venice: F. Bindoni and M. Pasini), BBM RARICAST.039; the second carried the same title but no indication of where it was printed, although it seems to have been from Venice (copy in Biblioteca padre Clemente Benedettucci, Recanati). The 1541 edition is again an almost exact copy of the earlier Venetian edition of 1538.

19 The 1538 Venetian edition employed the 'Instruments' border that later was redeployed for the *Operetta nuoua di auree sententie …* and the *Stanze trasmutate del Ariosto con una canzone bellissima*, both published by Leonardo Furlano around 1545 in Venice. Both the 1541 and 1542 editions of the *Canto primo* published by Faentino employ a title page woodcut border patterned with vines and heads, the same used in several other pamphlets by Bindoni and Pasini, as well as in the 1534 edition of *Sonetti e strambotti, non mai più posti in luce* published by Ferrarese. The same border appears in Ferrarese's 1536 pamphlet: *Stanze bellissime de uno gentilhuomo …*, attributed to Bindoni and Pasini (copy in BL VOYN.18).

20 Grendler, 'Form and function', 478.

21 Performers also were active as publishers of other works by Ariosto, besides the evergreen *Furioso*. Publications included Ippolito Ferrarese's first edition of some of Ariosto's lyric poems under the title *Forze d'amore* in 1537. For this and other publications, see Bongi, *Annali di Gabriel Giolito*, vol. 2, p. 30; Fatini, 'Su la fortuna', esp. 137-60; Agnelli and Ravegnani, *Annali delle edizioni Ariostee*, vol. 2, pp. 39-40, 199-200. For other publications of Ariosto's works by the charlatan Iacopo Coppa, see below, n. 77.

22 D. Romei, Introduction to P. Aretino, *Poemi cavallereschi*, ed. D. Romei (Rome: Salerno, 1995), p. 29. On the publication of the *Marfisa*, both original and pirate editions, see *ibid.*, pp. 29-30.

23 *Ibid.*, pp. 15-24. There is no surviving privilege for this work in Venice. It should be noted that Aretino had been circulating versions of the poem in manuscript from at least 1527.

24 *Tre primi canti di Marfisa del diuino Pietro Aretino*, cited in Severi, *Sitibondo nel stampar de' libri*, p. 328. Zoppino added that readers should be grateful for his efforts to reunite the three cantos of the poem in one edition 'che tal canto non andassi solo da gli altri vagando … essendo da voi visti et uditi con allegro animo' (*ibid.*, p. 329).

25 'Le menzogne de l'armi e de gli amori, / di che il mondo coglion s'inebria tanto' (quoted in A. Luzio, 'L'*Orlandino* di Pietro Aretino', *Giornale di filologia romanza*, 3:6 (1880), 73). Aretino's text in turn was subjected to various repackagings and parodies (*ibid.*, 76-84).

26 *Libero del Rado Stixoso* (Venice: B. de' Vitali, 1533), BL 1161.i.22.1. Zuan Polo followed up this work with a sequel of sorts, the *Libero de le vendette che fese i fioli de Rado Licca Micula de Stizosi* (Venice: 1533), BL 1161.i.22.2. See G. Vidossi, 'La cantata del Rado stizzoso', *Lares* 26:3-4 (1960), 123-8.

27 See Chapter 2.

28 On the vogue for comedic dialect works growing from the 1520s and 1530s, see M. Cortelazzo, 'Esperienze ed esperimenti plurilinguistici', in Arnaldi and Pastore Stocchi (eds), *Storia della cultura veneta*, vol. 3, pt 2, pp. 183-213; and B. Richardson, 'Dialects and standard language in Renaissance printing and editing', *Journal of*

the Institute of Romance Studies, Supp. 1: *Italian Dialects and Literature from the Renaissance to the Present* (1996), 7–22.

29 Beer, *Romanzi di cavalleria*, pp. 25–6; M. Chiesa, 'Poemi biblici fra Quattro e Cinquecento', *Giornale storico della letteratura Italiana*, 586:2 (2002), 161–92; G. Fragnito, *Proibito capire. La chiesa e il volgare nella prima età moderna* (Bologna: Il Mulino, 2005), pp. 158–9; M. Roggero, *Le carte piene di sogni. Testi e lettori in età moderna* (Bologna: Il Mulino, 2006), pp. 36–65.

30 See, for example, L. Furlano, *Opera nuova nella quale si contiene uno lamento di Bradamante verso 'l suo Ruggiero* ([Venice], 'Ad instantia di Leonardo ditt'il Furlano', n.d.), listed in C. E. Rava, *Supplement à Max Sander, Le livre à figures italien de la Renaissance* (Milan: Hoepli, 1969), no. 1242 bis.

31 *Primo canto dell'Ariosto tradotto in rime spirituali dato in luce da Cristoforo Scanello*, discussed in Fumagalli, 'La fortuna dell'*Orlando furioso*', p. 447. The celebrated *cantimbanco* of Bologna, Giulio Cesare Croce, also published a 'spiritualised' version of part of the *Furioso*, as well as a great many other works that were inspired by or parodied Ariosto's poem (*ibid.*, pp. 425–30, 447).

32 Nevertheless, Torquato Tasso's refashioning of the chivalric epic into a stirring account of the First Crusade appropriate for the post-Tridentine era (his *Gerusalemme liberata*, 1581) enjoyed some of the same popularity as Ariosto. See Roggero, *Le carte piene di sogni*.

33 For later reprints, see, for example, G. Giannini, *Le arti e le tradizioni popolari d'Italia*, 2 vols (Udine: Istituto delle Edizioni Accademiche, 1938); and B. Premoli, *Spettacolo d'attori e cantastorie. Edizioni viterbesi del Seicento tra letteratura e tradizione popolare nella biblioteca della fondazione* (Rome: Fondazione Marco Besso, 1996).

34 *La persa de Nigroponte facta per uno fiorentino* ([Milan: P. Castaldi, 1471]), reprinted in *GOR*, vol. 2, pp. 27–50. There are numerous editions of this work printed with differing titles, including at least four printed in Venice into the sixteenth century. See *GOR* vol. 1, pp. 152–62.

35 The earliest documented in *GOR* is *La guerra di Genova contro Milano* (Venice: C. Arnold, *c.*1478–79), *GOR*, vol. 1, p. 23, no. 1. See also D'Ancona, *La poesia popolare italiana*, pp. 75–85; M. Beer and C. Ivaldi, 'Poemetti bellici del Rinascimento italiano: trecento testimoni per una ricerca', *Schifanoia*, 1 (1986), 91–9; and C. Ivaldi, 'Cantari e poemetti bellici in ottava rima: la parabola produttiva di un sottogenere del romanzo cavalleresco', in Hempfer, *Ritterepik der Renaissance*, pp. 35–46.

36 See Niccoli, *Prophecy and People*.

37 K. Stermole, 'Venetian art and the war of the league of Cambrai (1509–17)' (Ph.D. dissertation, Queen's University, Ontario, 2007), p. 158.

38 See the Introduction, n. 31.

39 *La miseranda rotta de venetiani a quelli data da lo inuictissimo & christianissimo Ludouico re de Franza et triumphante duca de Milano ...* ((Milan), 1509), c. Aiv^v. BCR Vol. Misc. 2059.11.

40 On the role of *cantimbanchi* in feeding public debate about the wars, see Salzberg and Rospocher, 'Evanescent public sphere'.

41 N. Franco, *Dialogi piacevoli*, ed. F. Pignatti (Manziana: Vecchiarelli, 2003), p. 197.

42 M. Rospocher, 'Propaganda e opinione pubblica: Giulio II nella comunicazione politica europea', *Annali dell'Istituto Storico Italo-germanico in Trento*, 33 (2007),

117–57. Meserve argues, with regard to printed texts produced about the fall of Negroponte to the Turks in 1470, that rulers were not yet using the press directly for propagandistic purposes; 'News from Negroponte', 468–9.

43 See Chapter 3.
44 See L. Martines, *Strong Words: Writing and Social Strain in the Italian Renaissance* (Baltimore, MD: Johns Hopkins University Press, 2001), pp. 237–8.
45 In P. Danza, *La nova de Bressa con una barzelleta in laude del Re de Franza e de san marco* … ([Venice: P. Danza, c.1516]), reprinted in GOR, vol. 2, pp. 565–6.
46 I. Ferrarese, 'Opera nova, che tratta de li tre sacchi', in *Opera nova del superbo Rodamonte re de Sarza* … ((Venice: G. Fontaneto, 1532), BLCR 132 D 2.3, c. Civ^r).
47 'Spesse volte fortuna ingiuriosa / suole negar la vittoria a colui / che cercha e brama haver troppa gran cosa. / Son stato coraggioso e sempre fui / e hora ho conosciuto il mio destino / con mio gran danno e con morte d'altrui' (*Lamento che fa Piero Strozzi* … (Bologna: 'Adistantia di Paris Mantouano detto il Fortunato', 1554), c. Ai^v, BRF NAU 471). This pamphlet also includes a *barzelletta* in the voice of Siena lamenting its fate. The publisher of this work, Paris Mantoan, is discussed further in Chapter 5. On the lament genre, see Medin's introduction to A. Medin and L. Frati (eds), *Lamenti storici dei secoli XIV, XV e XVI*, reprint of the 1887–94 edn (Bologna: Commissione per i testi di lingua, 1969), vol. 4; and F. Alazard, *Le lamento dans l'Italie de la Renaissance* (Rennes: Presses universitaires de Rennes, 2010).
48 'Chi vorà sta frotelina / per che gli è cossa novella / com' la mente peregrina / metta mane ala scarsella / dui quatrin tragam di quella / al Zoppin li ponga in mani' (Zoppino, *Barzoletta novamente composta*, cited in Chapter 3, n. 45).
49 'Acciò chi possa in rima raccontare / Misera caput mundi el mio lamento / Prego ciacun si degni ascoltare / Apra l'orechi al mio languir si attento' (*Lamento di Roma cosa noua* ([Venice]: Bertocho [1490s?]), listed in GOR, vol. 1, pp. 30–1, and reprinted in vol. 2, pp. 57–64 (here at p. 57)).
50 *La vera nova de Bressa* … (cited in Chapter 3, n. 28).
51 Stermole, 'Venetian art', ch. 4.
52 Quondam in his Introduction to GOR, vol. 1, p. 13.
53 *Opera nova del superbo Rodamonte re de Sarza*, containing the 'Opera nova, che tratta de li tre sacchi fatti in Italia'.
54 The numerous reprinted versions of the *Lamento di Rodi* throughout the sixteenth and seventeenth centuries are listed in Medin and Frati (eds), *Lamenti storici*, vol. 3, pp. 199–211. See also Meserve, 'News from Negroponte'. For the continued appeal of ballad accounts long after the original events, see A. McShane Jones, 'The gazet in metre; or the rhiming newsmonger: the broadside ballad as intelligencer. A new narrative', in J. W. Koopmans (ed.), *News and Politics in Early Modern Europe (1500–1800)* (Leuven: Peeters, 2005), p. 146.
55 *Li horrendi e magnanimi fatti dell'illustrissimo Alfonso duca di Ferrara* … (Ferrara, 1510), listed in Wagner and Carrera, *Catalogo dei libri*, p. 34, no. 30.
56 See Infelise, *Prima dei giornali*; Minuzzi, *Il secolo di carta*, p. 28. B. Dooley argues that it is only at this time that the steady, periodic production of printed newssheets and gazettes gave people a sense of true contemporaneity with events unfolding in other places and an insatiable desire for news. See his Introduction to B. Dooley (ed.), *The Dissemination of News and the Emergence of Contemporaneity in Early Modern Europe* (Farnham, UK: Ashgate, 2010), pp. 1–19.

57 *Avvisi* were not printed at regular intervals until the seventeenth century (and in Venice, not until the later seventeenth century) but occasional printed prose newssheets were produced throughout the sixteenth century, as discussed in Chapter 5. See also Infelise, *Prima dei giornali*.
58 See the works cited in Chapter 2, n. 94.
59 Dooley, Introduction to Dooley, *Dissemination of News*, p. 3, discussing Mitelli's print 'Agli appassionati per le guerre' (1690), which is reproduced on p. 4.
60 This fascinating episode is recounted in Carnelos, 'Con libri alla mano', pp. 179–84.
61 See Salzberg and Rospocher, 'Evanescent public sphere', and the instances of censorship recounted in the Introduction.
62 De Vivo, *Information and Communication*.
63 'Invenzione, bella, nuova, utile, et admirabile ... Questo, il vero modo d'apprendere ogni mistiero, e la strada d'ascendere ad ogni grado. E tutto s'insegna per diece scudi' (Franco, *Dialogo del venditore*, pp. 26–8). On this rhetoric, see also C. Ginzburg and M. Ferrari, 'The dovecote has opened its eyes', in E. Muir and G. Ruggiero (eds), *Microhistory and the Lost Peoples of Europe* (Baltimore, MD: Johns Hopkins University Press, 1991), pp. 11–19.
64 *Recettario nouo probatissimo a molte infermita, & etiamdio di molte gentilezze vtile a chi levora prouare. Cosa noua non piu stampata* ... ((Venice: 'ad instantia di Zuan maria Lirico Venitiano', 1532), BL 1038.d.35.12).
65 B. Faentino, *Opera nvova nellaquale trouerai molti bellissimi secreti* ... ([Florence], 1546), cc. Aii^v–iii^v. BL 1071.f.47.
66 See Chapter 1.
67 Celebrino's contribution was a handwriting manual: *Il modo d'imparare di scriuere lettera merchantescha* ... On Tagliente, see Schutte, 'Teaching adults'; and Lucchi, 'La Santacroce', 613. *Edit16* lists sixty-nine editions of Tagliente's various works, reprinted throughout the sixteenth century.
68 'Quando scriver vorrai bisogna prima la persona e li membri diligentemente con gratia accommodar, tenendo la penna infra el police e l'indice digito sopra la carta' (*Opera nuovo [sic] posta in luce ne laquale potrai da te medesimo imparare di scriuere sette sorte di lettere, & abaco* ... ([Venice]: for Leonardo il Furlano, c.1547), c. Aii^r. BMCV Op. Cicogna 11.16.3). On Furlano, see Giacomello, 'Ad instantia di Leonardo il Furlano'.
69 'Laqual sarà de summo frutto sì a quelli che sono boni ragionati come etiam alli artesani, over altri che non anno alcun principio di far ragione' (*Opera nuovo posta in luce* ..., c. Di^r).
70 'Ragionevol cosa è il dovere amaestrar quelli che son sanno, a saper comprare con lo saper cognoscere la bontà de le sopradette mercantie' (*ibid.*, c. Dii^v). See below, n. 99, for Furlano's work which taught how to write in code.
71 W. Eamon traces how, from the 1550s, there was a rush of larger, more expensive but still bestselling books produced by the so-called 'Professors of Secrets' who were (or styled themselves as) educated polymaths associated with elite intellectual and scientific circles. See his *Science and the Secrets of Nature. Books of Secrets in Medieval and Early Modern Culture* (Princeton, NJ: Princeton University Press, 1994), p. 128; and the appendix: 'Secreti italiani: Italian booklets of secrets, ca. 1520–1643'. On the proliferation of instructional manuals more generally, see Bell, *How to Do It*.

72 Gentilcore, *Medical Charlatanism*, esp. ch. 10. According to Gentilcore, the first flyer advertising a charlatan's remedy appeared in Camerino in the late fifteenth century ('Il sapere ciarlatanesco', p. 379).
73 ASV, *Sanità*, Notatorio, b. 729, cc. 216^r–217^r (22 April 1551). By the first of June 1551, De' Grassi had registered as a 'medicus chyrurghus' in Florence (ASF, *AMS*, f. 12, c. 61^r). At least one example of Latino's publications survives: *Opera nvova non piu posta in luce, vniversale & salutifera a tutti li corpi humani ... Composta per me maestro Latino de Grassi venitiano* (n.p., [c.1550]), Wellcome EPB 2913/A. This contains a long remedy for venomous bites as well as several standard cosmetic recipes such as for whitening teeth. On the relations of the Sanità with charlatans, see also M. Laughran, 'The body, public health and social control in sixteenth-century Venice' (Ph.D. dissertation, University of Connecticut, 1998), ch. 4.
74 Gentilcore, 'Il sapere ciarlatanesco'.
75 'Il danno grande che potria seguir a poveri et altri nelle proprie loro persone che havesse et havessino comprato de ditto ellectuario si per dar rimedio al veneno, come alle altre sorte malatie nominiate nella sua riceta' (ASV, *Sanità*, Notatorio, b. 729, c. 216^v).
76 See Aretino's letter, quoted above, n. 1.
77 Coppa dedicated several of his publications to Barbaro and she in turn wrote the dedication letter for the edition of Ariosto's *Rime* (first published 1546), for which he must have had permission from the printer Andrea Torresani, who held a privilege for them from 1545. Coppa was the publisher of a monologue by Ariosto called *L'Erbolato* in the voice of a charlatan, as well as of an anonymous dialogue, aping Castiglione, on the behaviour of the courtier, and of his own poems in Latin. See A. Casadei, 'Sulle prime edizioni a stampa delle *Rime* ariostesche', *La Bibliofilía*, 94:2 (1992), 187–8; G. Fatini, 'L'*Erbolato* di Ludovico Ariosto', *Rassegna bibliografica della letteratura italiana*, 18 (1910): 216–38; and G. Ferroni, 'Nota sull'*Erbolato*', *La rassegna della letteratura italiana*, 79:1–2 (1975), 202–14.
78 For a description of Coppa's performances in Florence, see C. Malespini, *Ducento novelle ... Nelle quali si raccontano diversi avvenimenti così lieti, come mesti e stravaganti* (Venice: Al Segno d'Italia, 1609), vol. 2, cc. 300^v–301^r. In his supplication to the Florentine duke to practise in Florence, Coppa stressed his wish 'di giovar à ogniuno et particolarmente à poveri bisogniosi' (ASF, *OSMN*, b. 195, c. 504^r (August 1573)).
79 ASV, *Sanità*, Notatorio, b. 730, c. 287^r (17 August 1560).
80 'Conforta il cervello, ... ralegra il cuore, et procura la facile digestion tolto ut supra, scacia la tristeza, et melanconia, purifica lo sangue, fortifica li membri, aiuta le donne in tute quelli incomodi, et infermità, che procedeno dalla matrice' (ASV, *Sanità*, Notatorio, b. 730, cc. 287^{r-v}). Coppa later received a licence to print his 'Ricette in materia del mal di vermi cum li secreti' (ASV, *Reformatori*, Licenzi di stampa, b. 284, unnumbered sheet dated 26 May 1564).
81 See ASV, *Sanità*, Notatorio, b. 730, cc. 254^v–256^r, 286^v–287^v; and ASF, *OSMN*, b. 195, cc. 501^r–509^v, 532^r–534^r.
82 ASV, *ECB*, b. 61, Raspe, c. 4^v (26 September 1548): banishment of 'Jacomo Modonin solito cantar in banco, per el qual apertamente consta lui piu volte haver biastemato el santissimo nome de Dio'.

83 ASV, *SU*, b. 25, loose-leaf denunciation of 'Jacomo ditto il modanino già canta in banco et hora fa professione di medico'. I intend to explore Coppa's career and brushes with the authorities further in a future article.

84 E. Levi, 'Le paneruzzole di Niccolò Povero. Contributo alla storia della poesia giullaresca nel medio evo italiano', *Studi medievali*, 3 (1908), 81–108. For a sixteenth-century example, see *Le mirabilissime virtù di Maestro Venturino Bergamasco, protomedico, e dotto in ogni scientia, cosa piaceuolissima, & rediculosa ...* (Venice: M. Pagan, [1550s]), BL 1071.c.65.14.

85 See F. Barbierato, *Nella stanza dei circoli*. Clavicula Salomonis *e libri di magia a Venezia nei secoli XVII e XVIII* (Milan: Bonnard, 2002), ch. 2.

86 Doni, *Discussion about Printing*, p. 29.

87 Already before 1500, religious works made up 48.75 per cent of surviving Italian language incunables and it is likely that the proportion would be even higher if more cheap print had been preserved (Rozzo, *Linee per una storia*, p. 12).

88 Cobianchi, 'The use of woodcuts'; Areford, *The Viewer and the Printed Image*.

89 'Questa divota e sancta passione / per noi sostenne giesù redemptore / chi'un che la legerà con divotione / o udiràlla con divoto core / liber sarà d'ogni tribulatione' (*La passione del nostro signore in stanze* ([Venice: c. 1525?]), c. Aiii^v. BL C.57.l.7.6).

90 E. Barbieri, 'Di alcuni cantari religiosi condannati. Francesco Novati e la *Raccolta d'alcune particolari operette spirituali e profane proibite*', in Picone and Rubini, *Il cantare italiano*, pp. 475–89. For discussion and details of what does survive, see Cioni, *La poesia religiosa*; A. Jacobson Schutte, *Printed Italian Vernacular Religious Books, 1465-1550: A Finding List* (Geneva: Droz, 1983); L. Baldacchini, *Bibliografia delle stampe popolari religiose del XVI-XVII secolo. Biblioteche Vaticana, Alessandrina, Estense* (Florence: Olschki, 1980).

91 Conway, Diario *of the Printing Press*, p. 193. See also Barbieri, 'Per il *Vangelo di S. Giovanni*'.

92 R. Rusconi, '"Confessio generalis": Opuscoli per la pratica penitenziale nei primi cinquant'anni dalla introduzione della stampa', in Società internazionale di studi francescani (ed.), *I frati minori tra '400 e '500: Atti del xii convegno internazionale, Assisi, 18-19-20 ottobre 1984* (Assisi: Università di Perugia, Centro di studi Francescani, 1986), pp. 189–227.

93 G. Dati, *Incomencia la passione de Christo historiato in rima uulgari secondo che recita e representa de parola a parola la dignissima Compagnia de lo Confallone di Roma lo venerdi sancto in lo loco dicto Coliseo* (Venice: G. Rusconi, 1508). Other editions from Rome and Naples listed on *Edit16*.

94 E. Celebrino, *Li stupendi et maravigliosi miracoli del Glorioso Christo de Sancto Roccho Novamente Impressa* ([Venice, c.1525]). BGC 639. See J. Anderson, '"Christ carrying the cross" in San Rocco: its commission and miraculous history', *Arte veneta*, 31 (1977), 186–8.

95 See, for example, E. Celebrino, *Fenitio essempio d'vno giovane ricchissimo ...* (Venice: F. Bindoni and M. Pasini, 1533), c. Div^r. BMV Misc. 2333.3: 'Venti anni sono, e più ch'io cerco il mondo, / per piani, monti, e per ogni confino. / Fortuna m'ha più fiate posto al fondo, / e fatto rimaner sanza un quatrino. / Pur per virtù son qui lieto, e giocondo, / credete che non mente il mio latino, / e per mostrar che per virtù son francho, / la canto a son de lira sopra il bancho'.

96 On Dati and Giovanni da Firenze, see Chapter 1; and also D. Rhodes, 'Fra Giovanni da Firenze e i suoi tipografi veneziani', in his *Studies in Early Italian Printing* (London: Pindar Press, 1982), pp. 6–13.

97 For the presence of religious texts, including the *Epistola della Domenica* also published by the Ripoli Press, in the 'portable library' of a *cantastorie*, see Adorisio, 'Cultura in lingua volgare', p. 28.

98 See Niccoli, *Prophecy and People*, pp. 92–8; Niccoli, 'Manoscritti, oralità, stampe popolari: viaggi dei testi profetici nell'Italia del Rinascimento', *Italian Studies*, 66:2 (2011), 177–92; E. Casali, *Le spie del cielo. Oroscopi, lunari e almanacchi nell'Italia moderna* (Turin: Einaudi, 2003).

99 'Chi sa leggere debbe dire l'ufficio della Madonna ogni dì, e anchora dire li sette salmi con le orationi seguente, e le letanie, cioè chi ha la comodità di poterlo fare lo debbe fare, e più e manco secondo la qualità e condition della persona, ma chi non sa leggere debbe dire la corona della Madonna, e la corona di Christo, e i tre pater nostri, e tre ave marie, e i cinque pater nostri, e i cinque ave maria' (*Opera nova laqvale insegna scriuere e leggere in vintisette modi di zifere* ... (Brescia: D. Turlino for Leonardo il Furlano, 1546), c. Ciii^v. BMV Misc. 2369.1).

100 'Ama Iddio puramente, non giurare / In vanno, o christian suo santo nome / Vogli le feste anchor santificare' (G. Greci, *Operetta noua di auree sententie & vtilissimi documenti* ... ([Venice?, c.1545]; 'Ad instantia di Leonardo detto lo Furlano da Ciuidal di Friuli'), c. Aii^r. BMV Misc. 2231.3).

101 *All'illustre Signora Vittoria dignissima Marchesa di Pescara. Opera santissima ed utile* ... On the real author of the work, Pietro da Lucca, and its likely printing in Venice, see Petrella, '"Ad instantia d'Hippolito Ferrarese"', 49–52.

102 [M. Luther], *Vno libretto volgare, con la dechiaratione de li dieci comandamenti, del credo, del Pater noster, con una breue annotatione del uiuere christiano* ... ((Venice: Zoppino, 1525). BNCF RARI.Guicc.23.2.11). Agostino Bindoni printed another edition of the same work as late as 1556. On this, and other similar works, see S. Seidel Menchi, 'Le traduzioni italiane di Lutero nella prima metà del Cinquecento', *Rinascimento*, 17 (1977), 31–108. Another curious example is a small pamphlet containing the vernacular translation of one of Erasmus's colloquies, published in Venice in 1542 by the enigmatic figure of Damonfido Pastore, probably some kind of performer: *Dialogo erasmico di due donne maritate* ... ((Venice, 1542). BMCV Op. Cicogna 59.3.110.3). On the work, translated by the *poligrafo* Ortensio Lando under a pseudonym, see S. Seidel Menchi, *Erasmo in Italia 1520–1580* (Turin: Bollati Boringhieri, 1987), pp. 189–90, 415–16.

103 See, for example, Grendler, *Roman Inquisition*, p. 76.

104 'Una pizzocara è venuta in penitentia di haverlo ascoltato leggere più volte, dove si leggeva come cosa di Orlando con applause degli ascoltatori' (Letter of Girolamo Aleandro to Pietro Carnesecchi, 23 April 1534, in Gaeta, *Nunziature di Venezia*, p. 209). On the role of cheap print in spreading Reformation ideas in Italy, see O. Niccoli, 'Un aspetto della propaganda religiosa nell'Italia del Cinquecento: opuscoli e fogli volanti', in *Libri, idee e sentimenti*, pp. 29–37; U. Rozzo and S. Seidel Menchi, 'The book and the Reformation in Italy', in J.-F. Gilmont (ed.), *The Reformation and the Book* (Aldershot, UK: Ashgate, 1998), pp. 319–68.

105 Gaeta, *Nunziature di Venezia*, p. 202. The nuncio noted with concern that this figure 'faceva impression nelli animi del vulgo'. R. W. Scribner stressed the crucial role of

pedlars, hawkers and performers and of song and speech in 'Oral culture and the diffusion of Reformation ideas', in his *Popular Culture and Popular Movements in Reformation Germany* (London: Hambledon, 1987), pp. 49–69. See also A. Pettegree, *The Reformation and the Culture of Persuasion* (Cambridge: Cambridge University Press, 2005).

106 Quoted in O. Niccoli, *Rinascimento anticlericale. Infamia, propaganda e satira in Italia tra Quattro e Cinquecento* (Rome: Laterza, 2005), p. 129. On pedlars who smuggled heterodox works, including images of Luther, into Italy, see U. Rozzo, 'Pietro Perna colportore, libraio, tipografo ed editore tra Basilea e l'Italia', *Bibliotheca. Rivista di studi bibliografici*, 1 (2004), 46–64; L. Ceriotti and F. Dallasta, 'Lutero sulle spalle. Colportage e diffusione dell'iconografia protestante in un processo del 1558', *Aurea Parma*, 93 (2009), 405–22.

107 'Et voi gente plebea e vulgo ignaro / Non dite ognhor mille cianze e novelle … // Lassate andare tante conclusione / Ne voler più la fede disputare / Queste sue false e rie interpretatione / Non si voglion né legere né ascoltare …' (*Lamento de Italia contra Martin Lutherano. Opera nuoua* ([Bologna?, c.1530]), cc. Bi^v–Bii^r. BL 1071.g.22.10).

108 The work of K. Stevens and P. Gehl, for example, on the inventories of Milanese bookshops and stationers in the later sixteenth century, has shown huge quantities of cheap religious works in circulation. See their 'Cheap print'. More generally, see L. Baldacchini, 'Il libro popolare religioso tra Cinque e Seicento. Spunti e riflessioni', *Berichte im Auftrag der Internationalen Arbeitgemeinschaft für Forschung zum romanischen Volksbuch*, 6 (1983), 1–11; L. Baldacchini, 'Il libro popolare italiano d'argomento religioso durante la Controriforma', in P. Aquilon, H.-J. Martin, and F. Dupuigrenet Desrousilles (eds), *Le Livre dans l'Europe de la Renaissance. Actes du XXVIIIe colloque international d'études humanistes de Tours* (Tours: Promodis, 1988), pp. 434–5; Chiesa, 'Poemi biblici'.

109 On the great 'immobility' of popular religious texts after the sixteenth century, see Baldacchini, 'Il libro popolare religioso', p. 4.

110 *Opera nvova d'vn gentil'huomo florentino …*, from the seventh story of the third day of the *Decameron*, although published without the author's name.

111 *Historia dilettevole di dvoi amanti … hora dal Fortunato posti in luce* (n.p.d.), BL G 9879, attributed to the printer Giovanni Padovano in Venice, c.1540, by Rhodes, *Silent Printers*, p. 130.

112 For more examples, see Salzberg, 'In the mouths of charlatans'.

113 G. Bollème, 'Letteratura popolare e commercio ambulante del libro nel XVIII secolo', in Petrucci, *Libri, editori e pubblico*, p. 216. See also R. Chartier, 'The *bibliothèque bleue* and popular reading', in his *Cultural Uses of Print*, pp. 240–64.

114 For discussion of some of these texts, see Y. Fellner Simpson, 'Unmasking the revels: medium and message in the popular music culture of sixteenth-century Venice' (Ph.D. dissertation, Royal Holloway, University of London, 2004), ch. 2, and the works cited above, n. 28.

'Extreme disorder and confusion': policing the ephemeral city

5

In January 1549, the Council of Ten again was preoccupied with the problem of printing. While all the other trades in the city were organised into guilds, the printers and booksellers were not, and the Ten lamented that 'every one [of them] operates in their own way, with extreme disorder and confusion'. Specifically, the Ten noted that the Venetian magistrates investigating heresy repeatedly were frustrated in their investigations into the publication of 'scandalous and heretical' books, as there was no one in charge to give an account of the activity of the printers and booksellers.[1] At a moment when the Venetian secular authorities were aligning more closely with Rome in the drive to stem the dissemination of heretical ideas, this situation could be tolerated no longer. In order to maintain control over the circulation of dangerous words it was necessary to monitor the people who printed and distributed them. To achieve this, the Ten called for the establishment of what would be Venice's last trade guild, that of printers and booksellers.[2]

This decree typified a new drive to organise the printing trade – to define who belonged to it and who did not, to stem the mobility and fluidity of its membership, and to dictate what could be sold, where and when. It also gives some indication of the variety of concerns, temporal and religious, that shaped the Venetian government's attitude to the printing trade in the sixteenth century. Venice stood at a pivotal point between parts of Europe increasingly divided on confessional grounds. It had strong commercial ties with the Protestant north that the government was loath to upset for reasons of religion, but equally was intent to foster an image of itself as a well-ordered and pious Catholic state. At the same time, as suggested in Chapter 1, from the late fifteenth century there was intensifying debate about the expansion of the print market and its potentially tumultuous social effects. The circulation of print was a matter of concern to many; not just because of religious fears but also as a consequence of the wider political implications of radically expanding accessibility to many kinds of texts and allowing many more voices into the public arena. Because of these fears, both the Venetian authorities and the Roman Church realised that it was not enough to prohibit the books of notorious reformist thinkers; they needed to find some way to monitor the publication and dissemination of much more abundant and ubiquitous cheaper print, as well as the contexts in which texts and discussions circulated.[3]

Because these were unprecedented problems, and because they touched on a wide variety of concerns, sometimes reinforcing and sometimes competing with each other, a number of Venetian government organs and ecclesiastical authorities became involved in the effort to extend surveillance and control over printing and bookselling, particularly in the pivotal decades between the 1540s and 1560s. In the latter half of the century, too, the guild became more closely involved in endeavours to impose order; many of those who had benefitted from the openness of Venice to immigrants and the uncontrolled nature of the early print trade now collaborated in policing it. And since cheap print in particular was so closely tied into the ephemeral culture of city life in Venice by this point, it was also affected by a broader change of climate in the period of Catholic reform, characterised by the struggle to implement tighter control over words not just printed but also spoken, written and read, as well as over the movement and behaviour of people.[4]

This chapter explores how a variety of authorities and institutions participated in efforts to monitor the composition and output of the printing industry, and argues that, although they did not always accord with each other, their cumulative actions changed the parameters of cheap print production and distribution in Venice in significant ways. Although cheap print was rarely the primary concern of the Venetian authorities, they did attempt to grapple with its specific nature and particular forms of circulation. A more or less coherent policy developed which permitted very low-quality, cheap material to circulate with relative freedom, as long as its contents did not flout religious, moral, political or social mores too flagrantly. Instead of simply exploring the limits and divining the tastes of an expanding print market, increasingly printers, writers, booksellers, pedlars and performers now had to weigh up potential repercussions if they produced or circulated anything too provocative.

The development of control mechanisms

Up until the 1540s, attempts to exert control over the Venetian press were sporadic and somewhat desultory.[5] At the height of its economic and political power in the late fifteenth century when the printing trade took root, the Venetian government's efforts to control it were limited. After a monopoly granted to the first printer in the city, John of Speyer, lapsed soon after his death in 1470, the government interceded only to grant *privilegi*, forerunners of copyright, a sort of patent on a text or typographical innovation designed to protect the financial investment of publishers and printers and thereby promote the economic well-being of the industry. The artistic rights of authors were a secondary concern and systematic efforts to supervise the content of printed texts only came later.[6]

As this was some of the first intellectual property legislation in history, the Venetians had to experiment in order to get it right. In 1517, when the system of *privilegi* had become unwieldy, with too many printers applying and hoarding control over works, the Senate cancelled existing privileges, decreeing that henceforth it would grant them only for new works never previously printed, encouraging a more open market for print and innovation in the selection of titles. Most cheap print was printed without privileges at any rate, as it was not worth the time and expense of applying for them; eventually much of it would come under the category known as *libri comuni*, works of such perennial appeal that they could be reprinted freely by whoever wished to do so, a kind of common property of the printing trade.[7] This material was also exempted from quality controls by another Senate decree of 1537.[8]

Nevertheless, in the new and uncertain conditions of the sixteenth century, there was mounting trepidation about the power of even the most ephemeral products of the press to disseminate troubling ideas and opinions, even if some began to discern the potential benefits of this powerful form of communication as well. We have seen how, during the War of the League of Cambrai, Venetian observers noted the effects of cheap print on public opinion and morale, and how the Council of Ten stepped in to prohibit the circulation of certain works but also to encourage the circulation of others.[9] The involvement of the Council of Ten (and other powerful authorities such as the Signori di Notte) at this early date indicated that the circulation of print potentially was seen as a matter of the highest concern to state security. This sent a signal to those who wished to build a successful career for themselves in Venice that it was safer not to dabble in explicitly political material, particularly not anything that might be deemed critical of the Venetian state or its allies, as the printer and performer Niccolò Zoppino learned to his detriment in 1510.[10]

As the sixteenth century progressed, Venice's position of political and economic primacy looked less secure. The disaster of the Republic's involvement in the War of the League of Cambrai and the desperate famines of the 1520s, which provoked an influx of refugees and beggars into the city, fuelled an urgent anxiety, especially concerning the pernicious effects of sin on the state.[11] In this context, the consequences of printing on public morality and piety, more than on political stability and morale, came to the forefront. In 1527, a work containing anti-clerical comments provoked complaints by the Franciscan community at the monastery of San Francesco della Vigna and led to the Council of Ten introducing a system of imprimaturs or *licenze* to prevent the publication of 'immoral works, and [works] of an ill nature', although it was not yet mandatory to apply for one.[12]

Despite these being religious affairs, Venice still preferred to have its own secular authorities lead the charge to exert control over the press, rather than bodies associated with the Roman Church. The 1530s saw the creation of a new magistracy which was to become significant in the regulation of printing, one of a number concerned with policing social order and morality created in this period under the aegis of the Council of Ten. Pesenti suggested that the establishment of the magistrates against blasphemy, or Esecutori contro la bestemmia, in 1537, specifically was motivated by the publication and public dissemination of obscene works such as Lorenzo Venier's *Il trent'uno della Zaffetta* and *Puttana errante*; the latter text, as we have seen, seemingly published in that same year by the *cantimbanco* Ippolito Ferrarese.[13] This kind of material perhaps could be winked at when circulated in manuscript around elite circles of educated patrician men, but its appearance in the public realm of print – even being peddled cheaply and performed openly in the streets – was much more problematic.[14]

While the Esecutori were to be primarily concerned with policing blasphemy, this was interpreted widely, and progressively their remit encompassed a range of behaviour seen to threaten the morals and decorum of the Venetian populace, for example, repressing singing and dancing in the streets, and gambling and drinking at *osterie* (taverns). Public offenses of blasphemy were considered the most heinous, and much effort was expended to enforce a clearer division between sacred and profane space.[15] Horodowich argued that the activities of the Esecutori reflected the anxieties of the city undergoing rapid social change, and that they were geared towards disciplining the behaviour of immigrants and the lower classes.[16]

In other words, if the involvement of organs like the Council of Ten and the Senate earlier in the century indicated a preoccupation with print as an economic and a political issue, the participation of the Esecutori suggests that increasingly it was perceived as a dangerous new element in urban culture, with a potentially corrosive effect on Venetian public morality if not properly monitored. While the political danger of cheap print largely may have been headed off after the Cambrai crisis period, the promiscuous circulation of texts was perilous in a broader sense, as it threatened to undermine theoretically strict social divisions within the populace, concerning who was allowed to access what kinds of information.

A change of tune: the 1540s

In the 1540s, local concerns increasingly intertwined with the fears of the Roman Church for the preservation of orthodox religion in Italy. Events in northern Europe had demonstrated how quickly heterodox religious ideas could spread with the aid of the press, especially with the printing of images and cheap pamphlets in the vernacular, and particularly when allied with oral forms of communication such as preaching, singing and reading aloud.[17] By the 1540s, the Venetians, always protective of the Republic's independence and proud of its reputation for intellectual freedom, finally had to acknowledge the papacy's concerns that the city had become a nexus for heterodox opinion, and a potential gateway for Protestantism to enter the Italian peninsula.[18] In the streets, squares and workshops of the city, there were heated discussions about matters of faith by people of all classes, while preachers used the pulpit to engage candidly with ideas of religious reform. Meanwhile, the diffusion of suspicious books was occurring relatively openly, and often in the most public spaces of the city.[19] We have seen how, in these years, printers were still publishing heterodox works with relative impunity, as Zoppino did the sermons of the preacher Ochino in 1542, evidently gauging the widespread interest for the Venetian public in such texts.[20] By early 1543, the papal nuncio Minganelli complained heartily to the Signoria about the free circulation of heretical printed books, 'things most unworthy of a well-governed Republic such as this one'.[21]

Such comments clearly rankled and on 12 February, the Council of Ten responded with the law that made a pre-publication imprimatur obligatory for all works printed. They cited growing concern that many were printing and also selling books 'which are very improperly against the honour of the Lord God and of the Christian faith, setting a very bad example and [causing] universal scandal'.[22] This law extended in theory to all cheap print ('prognostications, stories, songs, letters' and other things sold on the streets and bridges), the same material largely exempt from privileges and quality control legislation. Responsibility for policing was given to the Esecutori contro la bestemmia, signalling again that the Venetian government still considered this an issue of civic order and public morality best handled by its own blasphemy magistrates.

Nevertheless, grudgingly, the Venetians stepped into line with Rome, and by the end of the 1540s, lay and ecclesiastical authorities cooperated to initiate a number of measures aimed at actively suppressing heretical practice, discussion and writings, including enacting a prohibition on the importation of heterodox books (May 1547), holding bonfires of illicit works in Piazza San Marco and Rialto (July 1548) and ordering the publication of a list of prohibited books (January 1549).[23] As mentioned earlier, the formation of a guild of printers and booksellers also was decreed at the start of 1549, to facilitate control of the trade. While these moves were encouraged by the Roman Church, Venice retained a high degree of secular control, for example with the creation of a new lay magistracy on heresy, the Tre savi all'eresia (April 1547), to sit in on trials held by the Holy Office of the Inquisition, active in Venice from 1540 after lying dormant for some time.[24] Although, in theory, state and church authorities were now working together to control the circulation of print, in practice there were conflicts and uncertainties over jurisdiction, as when the 1549 Venetian Index of Prohibited Books, drawn up by a panel including the papal nuncio Giovanni Della Casa, was not enforced due to disagreement among the Venetian rulers on the matter.[25]

Indices and prohibitions

The idea to draw up lists of prohibited books was of course one of the heralds of a new era of print censorship. However, despite the expressed intention of the Council of Ten (through the medium of the Esecutori) to police the print trade down to the smallest pamphlet, the first Venetian Index of prohibited books of

1549, although not enforced, demonstrated that the major concern of the moment was for the circulation of works by the chief reformist thinkers. To be sure, it did prohibit all works printed without notification of the author, printer or place of publication, which would have outlawed many of the sorts of cheap pamphlets described in the previous chapter.[26] But many believed that surveillance needed to be extended more broadly and to target more precisely the kinds of works that most people actually read. Bishop Pietro Paolo Vergerio in fact criticised the Venetian Index specifically for not including widely diffused popular works such as chivalric poems.[27]

When the Roman Inquisition began to promulgate its own Indices of Prohibited Books, valid for all of Catholic Europe, from 1559, it demonstrated broader preoccupation with the 'pernicious' effects of secular literature and devotional material in the vernacular. The 1559 Pauline Index included significant numbers of vernacular authors, banning the entire works of Aretino, Rabelais and others.[28] The 1564 Tridentine Index added a general rule against works 'which discuss, describe or teach lascivious or obscene things in an open manner'.[29] Slowly the censors realised that cheaper, more accessible works could be even more damaging than serious theology, as 'these were the books that everyone read', simpler and more comprehensible conveyers of unacceptable views than complicated doctrinal works.[30]

Besides the Indices, other censorial documentation shows that those involved in the process of censorship across Italy were troubled ever more by the widespread circulation of cheap vernacular print of various kinds and grappled with the problem of regulating it. However, such regulation always was hampered by the fluidity of such texts, constantly reworked and reprinted under different titles and different authors (or anonymously), produced quickly and cheaply and put out onto the streets in large quantities.[31] Initially, censors attempted to address cheap works via blanket prohibitions such as those included in a new list of prohibited material of 1574, which condemned entire popular genres such as 'immoral and lascivious songs of any kind' ('canzone dishoneste e lascive cioè in canto di nessuna sorte'), 'immoral plays of any sort' ('comedie dishoneste di nessuna sorte'), love letters ('lettere amorose'), and works of sacred scripture in verse, in Latin or vernacular ('opere in versi così latini, come volgare di sacra scrittura').[32] At a stroke, such prohibitions theoretically banned many of the staples of street pedlars and performers. Works once considered permissible, if somewhat risqué, such as the extremely popular chivalric tales, fell under suspicion or were prohibited altogether.[33]

Towards the end of the century, with the threat of Protestantism largely contained in Italy, censors became more preoccupied with the prohibition of devotional orations and stories that fell outside the newly redrawn boundaries of orthodoxy. Such things, too, were extremely hard to pin down, often printed as single-sheet *fogli volanti* and distributed by charlatans and street performers. This meant also that they were closely tied into practices of oral communication and recitation that allowed them to permeate deeply throughout the community.

In order to target works of this kind, blanket prohibitions progressively gave way to more precise articulations of condemned titles, so that readers could not claim ignorance of the rules and Inquisitors knew exactly what to pursue.[34]

Enforcing the rules: the 1550s and 1560s

The development of the Indices raises the central question of how the various mechanisms for controlling the circulation of printed items – from large books to small pamphlets – in place by the mid sixteenth century, actually worked. Recent scholarship has questioned how effective these mechanisms were in practice, particularly stressing the disconnect that often existed between central authorities and enforcement in the periphery.[35] In Venice, sure enough, there was a sizeable distance between the pronouncements of monolithic control from the top and actual enforcement on the streets. For example, the government faced a nearly impossible task when it committed itself (with the 1543 Council of Ten decree) to monitor the production of print in the city down to the smallest sheet. Given the burgeoning output of the trade, even the earlier law of 1527 regarding licences has been described as a case of 'closing the stable door after the horse has bolted'.[36]

Nevertheless, the 1550s and 1560s would see sporadic efforts from both the Esecutori contro la bestemmia and the Holy Office to police the production and circulation of cheap print. Although their respective jurisdictions were not entirely clear, the Esecutori intervened more often in cases that infringed on public order – for example, the selling and performing of immoral or unlicensed print on the streets – while the Holy Office concentrated on those that involved contravention of the Index of Prohibited Books and the licensing laws.[37] The instances of prosecution or interrogation may have been relatively infrequent and minor, but they amounted to a campaign insistent enough to encourage the more prominent producers and distributors of cheap print to adjust their behaviour and rethink some of their publication strategies. They could not act with the same freedom as earlier in the century, without fear of occasionally serious consequences.

Initially, the Esecutori contro la bestemmia were more active in pursuing cases involving cheap print that was not necessarily heretical but now was frowned upon, so that its printers and distributors thought it better not to seek the required licences. This book began with the story of the *cantimbanco* Francesco Faentino's run-in with the Esecutori in 1545, after he was caught selling an 'opera inhonesta', *Il dio Priapo*, from his bench. While this may have been a translation of the revered Virgil's poems about the phallic god, its public sale and probable performance in the streets, could not be tolerated.[38]

This will to suppress unlicensed and provocative works sold openly and cheaply was expressed in a similar case a few years later. In November 1551, the Esecutori pursued another objectionable pamphlet, this one deemed offensive to the clergy, printed by two members of the Bindoni family, Bernardino and his son Giovan Antonio.[39] The Esecutori decreed that Bernardino and his son were

> moved to such iniquity and wickedness by the diabolic spirit that they have faked a letter so that it appears to come from Ravenna ... imputing against every truth two Observant friars from Ravenna who ... killed a merchant and took his money and these friars were quartered in Ravenna, which letter is completely false and alien from every truth.[40]

This pamphlet relates the 'horrendo caso' of the murderous monks in the form of a printed prose letter from an unidentified agent to his 'Signore' (Figure 12). This form of proto-newsletter was quite common in this period; this particular letter was dated 5 October 1551 and claimed to report events that had occurred in late September, so the publication presented what purported to be up-to-date news, albeit with a sensational flavour and a moral message. It described how the friars were tempted to commit the crime by the influence of the devil and, once discovered, how they were executed 'so that they might be an example, and mirror to others, both secular and religious'.[41]

Bernardino Bindoni already was viewed with suspicion by the Venetian authorities. In 1544 he was fined ten ducats for his part in printing the provocative *Paradossi* of the *poligrafo* Ortensio Lando and the year before that he had printed the earliest surviving edition of the *Beneficio di Christo* which was to become one of the most notorious heterodox texts.[42] In 1548 he worked for a time in Padua but even there was pursued for his suspected involvement in printing inflammatory pamphlets about the imprisonment of the heretical monk Fra Baldo Lupetino, which were confiscated from ambulant vendors on the Rialto Bridge.[43] In 1551, Bernardino skipped town before the Esecutori caught up with him, but on this instance they were evidently intent on sending him a clear message, as he was banished from Venetian dominions for ten years. It is not known where he went, however he seems to have violated the decree and printed at least one work in Venice in this period,[44] before resuming printing briefly in 1562 after his banishment had ended. Bernardino's son Giovan Antonio, on the other hand, was subjected to a ritual shaming between the columns of Piazza San Marco and then banished for five years, although he too later returned to Venice and published several works in the 1560s and 1570s.

However, this work printed by the Bindoni was particularly objectionable as it was sold openly in the streets and probably read aloud in some way, or at least the most juicy particulars shouted out as a way to draw in buyers.[45] Alongside the Bindoni, the Esecutori punished a certain Paris Mantoan for 'having sold the said letters on the *piazze*, and also for having had printed other works of *mala qualità* counter to the law of the most illustrious Council of Ten'.[46] Mantoan must be identified with the itinerant publisher and probable performer, Paris Mantoan 'detto il Fortunato', who commissioned the publication of a number of popular works between the 1540s and 1560s. These editions suggest the classic profile of a performer who also published and sold cheap print. They range from

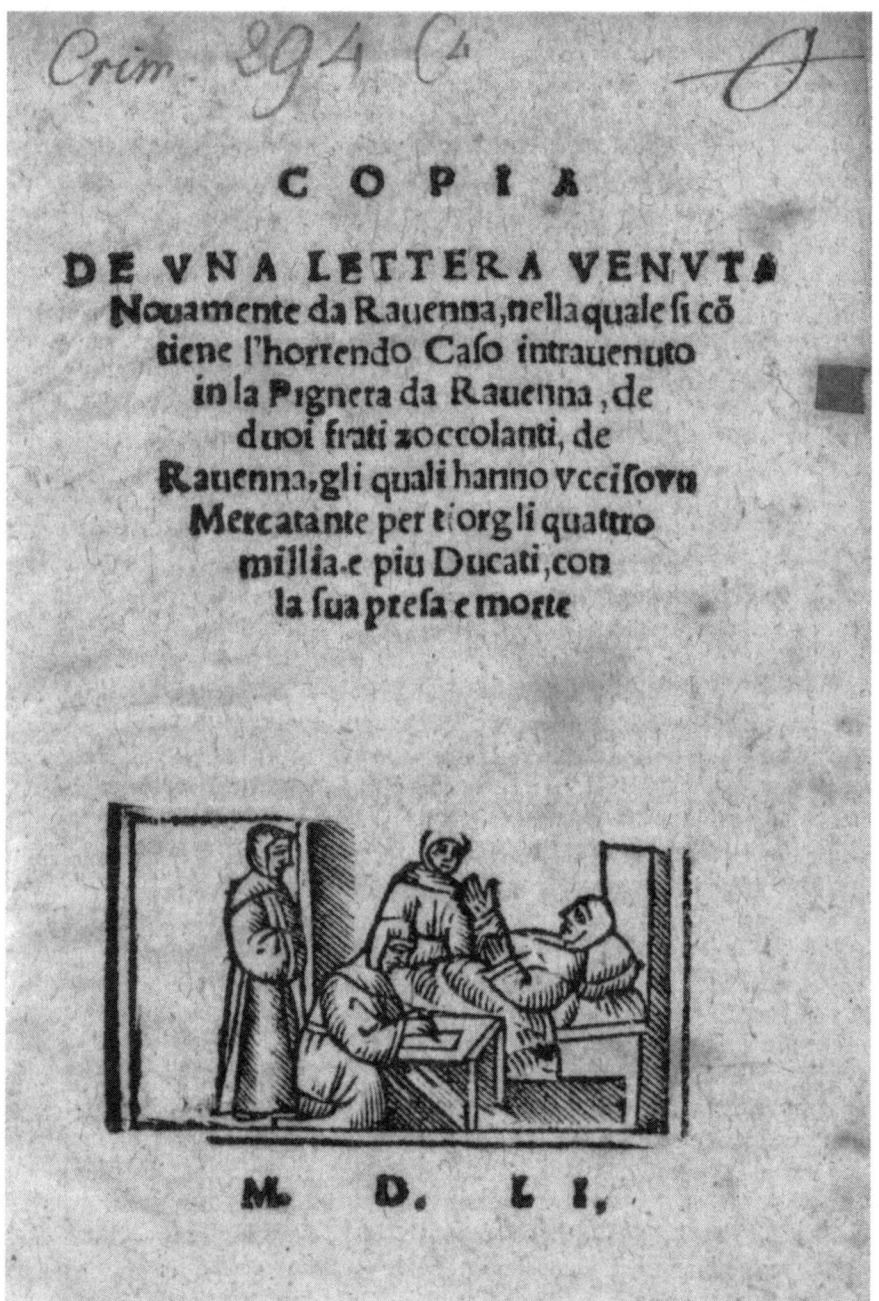

12 A horrendous case of murder: *Copia di una lettera venuta novamente da Ravenna ...*

an *ottava rima* lament in the voice of the defeated captain Piero Strozzi, another verse account of a victorious battle against the Ottomans in North Africa, a playful dialogue between the statues of Pasquino in Rome and Gobbo in Venice and several other mock letters such as one that purported to relate a series of omens that had appeared to the Turkish Sultan, warning him to convert to Christianity.[47] On this occasion Mantoan was exiled for two years, after a ritual shaming alongside Giovan Antonio Bindoni. Unlike the Bindoni, he is not known to have published another pamphlet in Venice after this time (working instead in Milan, Rome, Florence and Bologna), so the deterrence seems to have been effective. This case again shows the blasphemy magistrates particularly seeking to stop the spread of print in public spaces, which they believed could undermine the moral tone of urban life in Venice.

Whether from incompetence, lack of will or capacity, the Esecutori did not prosecute a great number of printing cases, however, and, probably to compensate, in the 1550s the Holy Office became more involved in the control of printing.[48] It targeted prominent printers above all, interrogating a number in the years 1558–59, and asking them to submit lists of their prohibited stock.[49] By focusing on those more established in Venice, with businesses to lose and a recognisable professional identity, the Inquisition must have hoped to change the culture of printing from its foundations. These figures also simply were easier to pin down than more mobile pedlars and performers. Like the blasphemy magistracy, the Holy Office was concerned not just about explicitly heterodox works but also about the unlicensed publication and sale of frivolous but morally questionable publications of the kind that would have provoked little comment in the preceding decades. Usually the penalties they handed out were not very severe (generally warnings or small fines), but they sufficed to send a message that all could not continue as before.

Domenico De' Franceschi, an immigrant from Brescia, only had his press running in the city for a short time when he was called before the Holy Office in 1558 for printing unlicensed works including one described only as an *Istoria nuova piacevole* (*A Pleasing New Story*). These words were used commonly in pamphlet titles, but the work in question was probably a four-leaf octavo which included a misogynist 'cautionary' poem about a woman who castrated her husband after he was unfaithful to her.[50] Highlighting the uncertainties surrounding cheap, commonly reprinted works of this kind, De' Franceschi defended himself by claiming that he had not sought a licence since the pamphlet was 'a thing of little importance, just something to laugh about'. Furthermore, it had been printed in the past by Agostino Bindoni and Matteo Pagan, so he did not believe it needed a new licence. De' Franceschi also excused himself as simply a poor man (*poveretto*), wanting to earn a little money.[51] As we have seen in other cases from this period, both authorities in Venice and elsewhere sometimes showed lenience towards poor printers and street sellers who they recognised were struggling to make a living. In this instance, De' Franceschi does not seem to have been fined but rather instructed to hand in the remaining copies.

Nevertheless, the warning had an effect. After this incident, his output (at least, that which survives) largely steered clear of the kinds of bawdy stories that had landed him in trouble.[52]

Agostino Bindoni died or ceased operation in this same year, but the interrogation of De' Francheschi may have led the Holy Office to look more closely at Agostino's former partner, Matteo Pagan, whom they called in a month later. Pagan is another of the mid-century printers who inherited the mantle of the Bindoni family by concentrating on small vernacular pamphlets: from verse accounts of contemporary wars to bawdy songs to popular parodies of immigrants in Venice. His shop was in the same street as that of Francesco Bindoni and Maffeo Pasini (the Frezzaria in San Moisè) and he partnered with Agostino towards the end of the latter's career. However, Pagan also was an important producer of printed maps and images that celebrated the 'myth' of Venice, including a famous woodcut of a ducal procession in Piazza San Marco which embodies the Venetian ideal of a stable and hierarchically ordered government.[53]

Despite having prudently chosen the sign of Faith (*Fede*) when he set up his *bottega* in the mid 1540s, Pagan was brought before the Holy Office in 1558, along with Zuan della Speranza 'stampador a Santa Maria Formosa', and fined three ducats for the unlicensed publication of some 'stories and other works printed against the form of the laws' ('istorie et altre opere stampati contra la forma de le leze').[54] These unspecified titles indicate the kinds of small pamphlets of secular songs and poems that were the staple of presses like those of Pagan and De' Francheschi around the middle of the century. The work that particularly may have aroused objection was the bawdy *Pronostico alla villota sopra le putane*, a parodic prophecy in a popular song form which predicted in gleeful detail the miserable fates of the prostitutes (poor, drunken, syphilitic and publicly shamed) of different Venetian neighbourhoods (Figure 13). Again, this must have been performed publicly, since it closed with an offer from the performer-composer of the work for sale.[55] Although such editions long had been printed without licences, times were changing; Del Col suggests that cases like those against Pagan and Franceschi must have 'have sounded ... as a clear and unequivocal warning to the booksellers: the Holy Office had decided not to permit the printing of prohibited or suspected works, given that it was showing its full capacity for cautious and timely censorship even for small things'.[56] Pagan, like Franceschi, appears to have stuck with safer works after this incident.[57] Targeting several of the most prominent producers of cheap print in the city must have prompted others to proceed with greater caution, think about a change of publishing strategy, or adopt methods of subterfuge.

Reforms in the early 1560s gave the Holy Office a more secure and designated place in Venetian censorship, even if the state retained a high degree of secular control. Henceforth every book had to be examined by the Inquisitor or his designate looking for 'doctrinal and moral error', as well as by two state-appointed readers who checked for politically sensitive material, before an imprimatur could be granted. However, the process of applying for an imprimatur was

13 A bawdy pamphlet on Venice's prostitutes: *Pronostico alla villota sopra le putane* …

time-consuming (generally taking one to three months) and expensive and the authorities still struggled to enforce the requirement.[58] The surviving records of licences granted suggest that a good number of works were never submitted for this process. The majority of small, vernacular editions for which licences were obtained either were religious titles, new works by prominent authors making a career for themselves in Venice and needing to be seen to obey the rules, or accounts of politically important events such as orations to the Venetian doge.[59]

Perhaps because most cheap print was exempted from quality controls and not expected to be awarded privileges, the belief continued that printers could also get around the licensing requirements for this material. Despite the warnings issued to the likes of the Bindoni, Franceschi and Pagan, in 1565 the Esecutori were still concerned with unlicensed cheap print. In that year, they reiterated the part of the 1543 decree relating to unlicensed printing and selling of small works on the Rialto and throughout the city and added a penalty for those who printed works in Venice but made them seem as if they were printed elsewhere.[60] This was an issue of sufficient concern for the powerful overseers of the Esecutori, the Council of Ten, to be moved the following year to echo the alarm about those 'printing and selling books and stories in this city without licences' ('quelli, che senza licentia stampano, e vendono libri, e historie in questa città'), or with a false notification of licence (a fraudulent 'Con licentia' printed on the title page).[61] The Ten ordered that, henceforth, all those who obtained a licence should present it, before they commenced printing, to the office of the Esecutori contro la bestemmia, so that the magistrates could more easily identify those who infringed the rules.

It was precisely in this moment, the middle of the 1560s, that a more repressive climate was taking hold in Venice after the election of the hard-line Pope Pius V.[62] After a period of inaction, there was a flurry of activity from a number of different authorities in Venice aiming to clean up the streets of aberrant behaviour, and in particular to halt the unregulated public sale of cheap print. For example, the magistracy of the Giustizia Vecchia which dealt with small-time commerce in 1565 tried to regulate the selling of appropriate works on religious holidays in the streets of Venice, prohibiting the sale of 'dishonest and shameful things'.[63] Similarly, after targeting printers and booksellers with shops in the 1550s, the Holy Office now went to great efforts to ensure that ambulant vendors and stallholders also were kept abreast of the successive prohibitions and made to obey them.[64]

The active, if not very coordinated, participation of various governing bodies, indicates that the Venetian authorities had not given up hope of policing print down to the smallest works, even if this was practically impossible. Most often, though, it was still the Esecutori who policed the street trade in print. In 1566, they fined the printer of the *Tariffa delle puttane*, the scandalous register of Venetian whores that detailed their services and their prices, and reprimanded a certain Cesare 'who goes around selling the work' ('qual anda vendendo tal opera').[65] Nevertheless, the officers of the Esecutori could not hope to keep an eye on all the public spaces of the city, and the frenetic and constantly changing events that took place there. Production was continuing despite the repeated prohibitions and print still being peddled in the same places and by the same means. In 1568, many printers and booksellers in the city were apparently still publishing 'books, stories, *frottole*, songs, letters and prognostications without the required licences and freely selling them or else having them sold by boys and others on the Rialto Bridge and in other places'.[66] In another attempt to enforce the rules, the Esecutori elected a former printer, Alvise Zio, to diligently 'inquire and investigate such infringements', seizing the offending works and denouncing the offenders so they could be punished.[67] The few prosecutions that followed confirm that the street trade continued to operate in similar ways to earlier in the century. For example, the magistrates fined Stefano Mantovano, a charlatan or street singer selling an unidentified story about vagabonds ('alcune istorie cioè quella di vagabondi') from his *banco*.[68] Another street vendor, 'Benetto the Frenchman who sells stories around the place', was picked up with some 'immoral pictures' ('alcune figure dishoneste'), printed by the engraver Domenico Zenoi alongside some equally scandalous sonnets. These works, probably based on the infamous images of sexual positions entitled *I Modi* by Giulio Romano, accompanied by Aretino's salacious sonnets, also were discovered on sale in a bookshop in San Lio, and with two other ambulant sellers.[69] These instances suggest that, despite the efforts of the authorities, some of the most scandalous works of the earlier part of the century still were available in print in Venice and established modes of street sale and public performance continued to function, even if they now entailed greater risks.

Consequences

After the late 1560s the Holy Office and the Esecutori slackened their efforts to pursue cases of unlicensed cheap print, although it is unclear to what extent this was because they had successfully encouraged a shift in the industry, or because their interests had simply moved elsewhere. While performers and pedlars could move on to another city, printers were more likely to have equipment and rented premises in Venice and to wish to remain there if they could. It was in their interests to toe the line after an interrogation by the blasphemy magistrates or the Holy Office, to avoid further trouble, costly fines or worse. Many printers turned to safer religious works as the attitude towards bawdy or immoral secular material became more hostile, although the shrewd also discerned a lucrative opportunity to cater to the heightened spiritual fervour of the period. This was the case with the prominent and prestigious printer Gabriele Giolito, who made a noted turn away from secular vernacular literature from the 1560s.[70] Others simply chose to endlessly reissue innocuous works first published in the late fifteenth or early sixteenth centuries, which had come through the crackdown of the initial period of Catholic reform and still were permitted.

Nevertheless, many could not ignore the financial lure of producing and distributing unlicensed material for which a market remained, finding ways to get around the laws. While printers like De' Franceschi and Pagan may have taken a more prudent approach after their encounters with the authorities, a brush with the law was not always enough to ensure complete obedience to the rules. The printer, Domenico De' Farri, for example, was reprimanded several times by the Esecutori, once for printing an unlicensed account of a 'fire-breathing dragon that had appeared in Rome', and again years later by the Holy Office, while his son Pietro was also questioned in 1575 regarding the printing of 'superstitious' orations.[71]

Aside from professions of ignorance, many publishers and distributors took simple measures in order to be able to print what they liked (and what they thought would sell) without retribution, for example by printing anonymously or with false details, trusting that the local authorities were not efficient enough to catch up with them. In 1596, the Esecutori contro la bestemmia again beseeched the Prior of the printing guild to remind members at least twice a year of the prohibition to print unlicensed works, and specifically to 'sell without licence stories, and similar things on the piazzas, that are or appear to be printed outside this city'.[72] Nevertheless, such practices continued through the seventeenth and eighteenth centuries.[73]

It is worth noting, however, that Venetian printers generally remained circumspect about producing anything of an explicitly politically sensitive nature. Perhaps the efforts of the Venetian state during the Cambrai War, reinforced by the continuing threat of the feared Council of Ten, were sufficient to warn printers away from this kind of material. Occasionally, something more explicitly political did slip through the net and the authorities reacted harshly. For example, in 1553, the Esecutori prosecuted the publishers of an unlicensed edition of a letter by the King of France to the electors of the Empire which it was deemed 'could also offend the majesty of the Emperor'. To serve as an example to others who might consider publishing this kind of material, the printer and publisher were fined the unusually large sum of twenty-five ducats each.[74] Even if fines of this size made local printers hesitant to publish politically sensitive works, pedlars did still sometimes bring them in to the city. In 1579, for instance, the Esecutori acted against a humble story-seller (Antonio de Saggion 'vendi historie') found peddling in Venice 'letters printed outside of this city, which contained matters of great importance, and of state' ('materia di grande importantia, et di stado') which had been prohibited by the Captains of the Council of Ten. The penalty applied to this street seller, who presumably could never have come up with a sum like twenty-five ducats, was a prohibition from selling his usual stock ('historie, libri, ne altre sorte de lettere stampate') for a year, and a fifty *lire* fine were he to reoffend.[75] At least until the explosion of printed pamphlets occasioned by the Interdict crisis of the early seventeenth century, political material was more likely to circulate in manuscript, although this did not prevent widespread discussion about political affairs throughout Venetian society.[76]

The role of the guild

As well as the actions of government or church authorities, it is important to consider the role of the guild in bringing a greater degree of order and control to the printing trade in the later sixteenth century. The guild was particularly active in policing participation in the trade and this impinged on the dissemination of cheap print and street selling in several ways. However, the interests of the guild on certain occasions conflicted with those of the higher authorities, exposing tensions and gaps between laws and decrees and everyday practice.

As we have seen, the printing industry in sixteenth-century Venice was underpinned by a web of familial and business relationships even before the masters of the trade were organised into a guild, at least among those who settled down in Venice and did not move on elsewhere. In the face of the many obstacles imposed by the new censorship laws, evidently there was some sense of group solidarity, strengthened by ties of kinship, neighbourhood and friendship. Even before the Council of Ten ordered the establishment of the guild in January 1549, a core group gathered to protest the order (of July 1548) for them to hand in any heretical works that they held.[77] Again, in January 1559, the printers and booksellers gathered in the *bottega* of one of the guild Priors, Tomaso Giunta, to discuss the Index and agree to disobey the orders of the authorities to booksellers to submit lists of their prohibited stock.[78] One of the other Priors, Melchiore Sessa, reportedly called the bookseller Zacharia Zenaro a 'traitor' for advising obedience to the Holy Office's instructions that the other booksellers had vowed to resist.[79] As Sessa was an important patron figure in the community of printers and booksellers, there would have been strong incentive for the less powerful and wealthy to follow his lead. Vincenzo Valgrisi explained that he had submitted his list late in order 'not to cut myself off from the other booksellers', but that 'for this obedience they do not speak to me'.[80] Hence, there was a sense of solidarity and professional identity among the more stable, settled group of printers already by the mid-sixteenth century, which sometimes united them against the wishes of the authorities.

Although the leading guildsmen strongly opposed some of the dictates regarding their freedom to print and sell certain works, they were more willing to accede to the desires of the Venetian government on the matter of participation in the trade. One of the Council of Ten's aims in ordering the creation of the guild was to counter the growing reputation of Venetian printed editions for poor quality, by exerting control over who could practice the trades of printing and bookselling. Many of the men elected to positions of power within the guild came from families that only had come to Venice, and sometimes only to the print trades, in the early sixteenth century. Yet it was now in their interests to make entry into the trade more difficult, effectively closing the gates behind them. The masters sought to augment their own status and to distance themselves from some of the lowly figures who took a chance in the trade, while monopolising the profits. In 1572, the Prior, Francesco Rampazetto, consequently voiced the guild's concern about the many who, 'stupidly believing that the art of printing requires little intelligence, dare to enter into the practice of it with little knowledge, and less experience'.[81] Henceforth, no one was to work in Venice as a printer or bookseller if they were not matriculated in the guild, which required serving at least five years as a registered apprentice (*garzone*) and three years as a journeyman (*lavorante*) in a print or bookshop in the city, and then being judged worthy of entrance by senior members of the trade, plus a matriculation fee of five ducats. Foreigners had to pay ten ducats, and serve the same period of time, while the children or heirs of masters were exempted from any payment.[82]

The acts of the guild surviving from the last two decades of the century and beyond show how the leading guildsmen strove to prevent the intrusion of unlicensed outsiders into the trade, the repeated rejection of the kind of 'multi-tasking' individuals considered in previous chapters. Street sellers were not banned per se, if they demonstrated experience in the industry and a fixed location of sale, such as Nicolò Furlan who held a stall in the parish of San Basso, at the northern corner of Piazza San Marco, admitted to the guild in April 1578.[83] In contrast, the guild leaders rejected Pasqualin Savioni, 'cornet player and musician in the churches, and for feast days, a new beginner in our trade', who was told that 'since this our art of printing is of great importance, he, being of a very different profession, should not practise it'.[84] The charlatan Domenico di Francesco of Florence pleaded that the guild should leave him in peace as he only sold a small amount of printed merchandise, but he was ordered to hand in his works within three days, or expect further action.[85]

The illiterate and untrained also were refused entry. Biagio at the *bottega* of the Three Hats was called for examination then told to desist from practicing the art after he admitted he did not know how to read.[86] In 1578, the masters reviewed the case of Rimondo di Zuan of Bergamo, who applied for admittance to the guild on the basis of having married the widow of the street seller Bartolomeo da Sabbio and taken over his business, and needing to support the widow and her children. However, Rimondo was a former dyer (*tintor*) with little experience in print selling, and his application was rejected.[87] By trying to exclude outsiders from their business, the Venetian masters acted like their counterparts in other Italian cities. In Bologna, printers and booksellers joined forces very early in the sixteenth century to try to limit the activity of outsiders who came to the city for brief periods and cut in on their trade; similar efforts were made by the *cartolai* of Ferrara in the 1470s, the printers and booksellers in Milan in 1589 and in Rome around 1600.[88] In the case of Venice, the desire to control entry to the guild and prevent unlicensed competition probably was sharpened by the notable decline of the printing trade in the years after the 1575–77 plague, and thus the wish to preserve the diminishing profits for themselves.[89]

As much as the interests of the government and the leading printers and booksellers coalesced in the establishment of the guild, at certain points those interests diverged in ways that reveal the preoccupations of both parties.

For example, the musician Pasqualin Savioni, in the year before he was rejected by the guild, had been declared able to participate in the art of printing by the Senate, taking measures to restart the economy after the plague.[90] Likewise, in 1586, the guild again sought to ban all those non-members of the Arte who 'print, and sell, or have books printed, or sold, from printing shops, workshops, stores and stalls, in large or small quantities'. These unlicensed outsiders 'usurp the bread from our hands, since it is primarily we who bear the burdens [i.e., taxes] of our trade'. To strengthen their argument, the masters insisted that the books that incurred the disapproval of the Inquisition or the blasphemy magistrates were 'nearly always … printed and sold by people outside of our guild, and not matriculated, who do not know or understand our profession'.[91] (In fact, this was far from true; there is ample evidence that some of the city's most prominent bookmen were involved in the clandestine trade.)[92] But again, the government disagreed on this count; the Provveditori di Comun who oversaw the Venetian guilds were not prepared to enforce the ban completely, later affirming this act of 1586 with the condition that ambulant sellers of cheap print be exempt.[93] Such vendors were of too little importance and too poor to be forced to fulfil the necessary requirements and pay the enrolment fee for the guild.

As well as divergence between government and guild, there were also always competing motives at play within the guild on the matter of outsiders participating in the trade. Non-masters who wished to cooperate in publishing, printing or selling remained useful sources of capital and labour, or outlets for sale. Repeatedly in the last decades of the sixteenth century and the early decades of the seventeenth, the guild called for the need to impose a fine for works printed by or for a *non matricolato*. While it is clear that these outsiders were collaborating with masters to have works printed, the frequent repetition of the rule suggests that the guild had trouble enforcing it.[94] Connections with outsiders continued because they were mutually beneficial, even if there was increasing incentive to disavow them publicly. At the same time, the guildsmen strove to present an image of themselves as obedient, solid and reliable businessmen; as stable, settled and valuable contributors to the Venetian economy. The rules regarding membership of the trade allowed the printers to classify themselves as professionals with distinct (and valuable) skills and know-how, in contrast to the common depiction of them as unqualified, rapacious blow-ins from other trades, discussed in Chapter 1.

The beginnings of decline in the Venetian printing industry in the last quarter of the sixteenth century contributed to a widening division between the matriculated masters in control of shops and the guild, and the small-time street sellers or stallholders who found themselves increasingly marginalised.[95] In 1598, the guild attempted to prohibit the activity of vendors of books on holy days, who cut in on the business of guildsmen who were not supposed to operate on those days. They complained that vendors 'that have not matriculated in this Arte' could thereby 'enjoy the fruits belonging to it, without sharing in its burdens and expenses, besides that they are permitted against human and divine laws to sell prohibited books, and other things that are quite against God, and to the shame of this Arte'.⁹⁶ There were so many poor bookmen, however, that the masters later relented to their pleas and permitted them to apply for a limited number of licences to sell on these days.⁹⁷ While this activity continued to occupy central city spaces in the early seventeenth century, it did so under greater restrictions regarding who could participate in it, when, and what could be sold to the Venetian public. The guild had helped the government and the Inquisition to extend some degree of control over the street trade and erect more rigid boundaries around those permitted to produce and distribute print. The new rules favoured those settled in the city with experience in the trade and thus with social connections and a local reputation, and marginalised the mobile outsiders and multi-taskers.

Policing the piazza

Finally, it is worth emphasising that the actions of the guild and the secular and ecclesiastical authorities in the later sixteenth century took place in the context of – and to some degree reinforced – broader efforts to circumscribe the spaces occupied by mobile figures like performers and pedlars in urban life. In literal terms, there were escalating attempts to limit their freedom of movement. No longer free to set themselves up where they liked, a law promulgated in early 1543, within weeks of the Council of Ten's printing regulation, strictly demarcated the places in which entertainers were allowed to operate in Piazza San Marco.⁹⁸ However, the number of performers and pedlars continued to proliferate, and later in the century, further action was taken to circumscribe their presence in the square and other public spaces of the city. In 1563, the Health Board appointed the well-known writer of books of secrets Leone Tartaglini 'l'Herbolario' to oversee the growing numbers of 'charlatans and others who sell on the piazzas various sorts of oils, powders, electuaries and other remedies, both with recipes and without, whether on benches or stalls'. In 1575, however, the raging plague spurred them to prohibit altogether the activity of those who might help spread the plague by gathering an audience, including charlatans.⁹⁹ As well as enforcing order and decorum in the streets, there were direct attempts to separate, in a concrete, spatial sense, the sacred from the profane, as in 1589, when the Procurators of San Marco who oversaw the Piazza decreed that mountebanks could only perform in the evenings 'after the closing of the church of San Marco at the completion of vespers', but not at all on Wednesdays, Fridays and Saturdays, on the important religious holidays, and during Lent.¹⁰⁰

Endeavours to control performers and pedlars reflected a wider suspicion of, even hostility towards, mobile and marginal people, characteristic of a period of crisis when factors such as war and famine pushed many more people onto the roads and towards cities such as Venice. Venice was not the only Italian city to respond to the situation with new laws that sought to restrict or stop the flow of such people into the capital, and to create a sharper distinction between locals and foreigners.[101] Notably, print itself was often used to control these mobile figures, as in the numerous *bandi* (printed decrees) expelling vagabonds and beggars from state territories, or the *bollettini* (passes) issued to street sellers with permission to work on feast days. As argued throughout this book, the mobility of printers, publishers, pedlars and performers was a major feature of the Venetian printing trade in this period, but it was an aspect that some found threatening. The Esecutori contro la Bestemmia in particular displayed a kneejerk suspicion of travelling performers because they were usually foreigners without fixed residence in the city, and because they associated with other travellers in suspect places of gathering such as *osterie*. Thus they summoned one Antheo, a street performer ('solito cantar in banco, et far bagatelle'), to testify regarding blasphemous curses overheard while playing cards in a lodging house, and banished the singer and charlatan Iacopo Coppa for five years. The Holy Office also received denunciations of several such figures, including Coppa, and had one street musician drowned as an unrepentant heretic.[102] The foreignness and experience of travel that marked out itinerant performers and pedlars as an appealing source of news and novelty were the very things that made them increasingly suspicious to the governors of Venetian society at this time. Such figures occupied a tenuous space on the margins of city life, lacking the security of tight-knit local connections that settled vendors enjoyed.

Given the conflicts between the different authorities, between those authorities and the guild, and within the guild itself, it is not surprising that the regulation of the Venetian printing trade, and particularly of the dissemination of cheap print, proceeded in fits and starts. The struggle to control the flood of print was complicated by competing motives, as economic interests clashed with political, religious and civic concerns. The Venetian authorities in particular were half-hearted in their enforcement of measures that could impinge on the success of one of the city's most flourishing industries. Their hard line could also be softened by concern for the poor and vulnerable. The guildsmen, too, were ambivalent about this matter, protesting against measures which restricted their freedom to print and sell particular works but willing to aid the extension of control – for example, over unlicensed participants in the trade – when it served their own economic and social interests. The proliferation of different prohibitions, sometimes contradictory; the complex and competing jurisdictions between different authorities; the difficulties of communication between centre and periphery, between palace and street – all of these opened up spaces and uncertainties within which members of the print trades could manoeuvre, and still get away with some technically prohibited behaviour.[103] In addition, the fleeting nature of cheap printed material, its flexible modes of production and distribution, and its numerous connections into the circuit–system of oral communication, made it almost impossible to monitor entirely.

Nevertheless, there is no doubt that the cultural space open to the producers and disseminators of cheap print was hemmed in from various angles across the course of the sixteenth century. The combination of the Indices of Prohibited Books and other inquisitorial decrees prohibited large parts of the popular vernacular corpus that frequently appeared in cheap printed form. Bursts of prosecuting activity by Venetian government authorities and the local branch of the Holy Office resulted in fines, banishments, ritual punishment or confiscation of illicit works, which encouraged many to adjust their publishing strategies, at least superficially. The guild as an organ to a certain extent fulfilled its function of restricting access to the trade. These efforts, by the end of the century, brought about distinct changes in the place of cheap print in Venetian urban culture. Even if the prevalence of anonymous and false printing makes it very hard to assess precisely how the range of offerings in the streets changed, we can conclude that, after the middle of the sixteenth century, many producers and distributors of cheap print chose to tread a safer path and to avoid more provocative material.

Notes

1 'Una delle principal arte di questa cità et delle più importante per molti rispetti è quella della stamparia; la qual nondimeno essendo quasi tute l'altre ben ordinate, et con le soe fraggie, et matricola, sola si ritrova senza ordine alcuno, di modo che essendo occorso più fiate alli tre deputati sopra li heretici di esser informati dalli authori et stampatori d'alcuni libri scandalosi et heretici per le cose pertinente al loro officio, non si ha ritrovato chi li habbi saputo render conto; et medesimamente occorendo di giorno in giorno molti inconvenienti circa le stampe, che hano bisogno de emendatione, con difficultà per l'istessa cagione si può venir in cognitione della verità, non vi essendo alcuno che rappresenti la ditta arte, nè chi risponda per quella, onde aviene, che tutti fano à modo loro, con estremo disordine e confusione' (ASV, CX, Parti comuni, f. 47, fasc. 66 (from the preamble to the law decreeing the establishment of the guild of printers and booksellers, 18 January 1549)).
2 The guild also encompassed book binders (*ligadori*). Although the minute book of the Arte only begins in 1571, members of the trade gathered and acted together as a body for some time before this, as discussed below. On a more pragmatic note, gathering together and identifying those involved in printing and bookselling also made it easier to collect taxes from them (Mattozzi, '"Mondo del libro"', 744).
3 Grendler's important study *Roman Inquisition* does not accord much space to ephemeral print and only recently have historians begun to focus on the censorship of this material. See M. Infelise, *I libri proibiti da Gutenberg all'Encyclopédie* (Rome and Bari: Laterza, 1999), pp. 49–55; U. Rozzo, 'I fogli volanti a stampa e censura libraria nel secolo XVI', in V. Bonani, G. G. Cicco and A. M. Vitale (eds), *Dal torchio alle fiamme. Inquisizione e censura: nuovi contributi dalla più antica biblioteca provinciale d'Italia (Atti del Convegno Nazionale di Studi, Salerno 2004)* (Salerno: Biblioteca provinciale di Salerno, 2005), pp. 65–6; U. Rozzo, 'La letteratura italiana all'indice', in his *La letteratura italiana negli Indici del Cinquecento* (Udine: Forum, 2005), pp. 11–71, an expanded version of his 'Italian literature on the Index', published in G. Fragnito (ed.), *Church, Censorship and Culture in Early Modern Italy*, trans.

A. Belton (Cambridge: Cambridge University Press, 2001), pp. 194–222. See also Baldacchini, 'Il libro popolare italiano d'argomento religioso'.

4 This broader view of censorship is reflected in recent historiography, which has focused less on its obscurantist legacy and more on how it came to play a part in the process of publication, shaping literary culture not only in negative ways (Landi, *Stampa, censura, opinione pubblica*, p. 71).

5 On early initiatives to control the press, see Grendler, *Roman Inquisition*, pp. 71–6; and Witcombe, *Copyright in the Renaissance*, chs 1 and 2. Texts of the major laws are reprinted in Brown, *Venetian Printing Press*, appendix 1.

6 Witcombe, *Copyright in the Renaissance*, p. 53.

7 Carnelos, 'Con libri alla mano', p. 22. The 1517 law is in ASV, ST, r. 20, fol. 58^v–59^r.

8 Law excluding works sold for less than ten *soldi*, cited above, Chapter 1, n. 33.

9 See the Introduction.

10 Discussed in Chapter 3.

11 R. Derosas, 'Moralità e giustizia a Venezia nel '500–'600: gli esecutori contro la bestemmia', in G. Cozzi (ed.), *Stato, società e giustizia nella repubblica veneta (sec. XV–XVIII)* (Rome: Jouvence, 1980), p. 438. See also Gilbert, 'Venice in the crisis of the League of Cambrai', in J. R. Hale (ed.), *Renaissance Venice* (London: Faber & Faber, 1973), pp. 274–92.

12 'Opere dishoneste, et de mala natura' (ASV, CX, Parti Comuni, f. 4, fasc. 162 (29 January 1527)). From 1544, responsibility for granting imprimaturs was granted to a body associated with the nearby University of Padua, the Riformatori dello studio di Padova.

13 G. Pesenti, 'Libri censurati a Venezia nei secoli XVI–XVII', *La Bibliofilía*, 58:1 (1956), 15–16. On the *Puttana errante*, see above (Chapter 3, n. 71). On the creation of the Esecutori, see Derosas, 'Moralità e giustizia'.

14 On attitudes to the publication of pornography, see P. Findlen, 'Humanism, politics and pornography in Renaissance Italy', in L. Hunt (ed.), *The Invention of Pornography: Obscenity and the Origins of Modernity, 1500–1800* (New York: Zone, 1993), pp. 49–108; S. F. Matthews-Grieco, 'Satyrs and sausages: Erotic strategies and the print market in Cinquecento Italy', in S. F. Matthews-Grieco (ed.), *Erotic Cultures of Renaissance Italy* (Farnham, UK and Burlington, VT: Ashgate, 2010), pp. 19–60.

15 Derosas, 'Moralità e giustizia', pp. 446–53. See also G. Cozzi, 'Religione, moralità e giustizia a Venezia: vicende della magistratura degli Esecutori contro la bestemmia (secoli XVI–XVII)', *Ateneo veneto*, 29 (1991), 7–96.

16 E. Horodowich, *Language and Statecraft in Early Modern Venice* (Cambridge: Cambridge University Press, 2008), esp. ch. 2.

17 See, for example, Scribner, *For the Sake of the Simple Folk*; Scribner, 'Oral culture'; M. U. Edwards Jr, *Printing, Propaganda and Martin Luther* (Berkeley, CA and London: University of California Press, 1994); Pettegree, *Reformation*.

18 Grendler, *Roman Inquisition*, pp. 76–8. On the relationship with Rome in this period, see A. Del Col, 'Organizzazione, composizione e giurisdizione dei tribunali dell'Inquisizione romana nella repubblica di Venezia (1500–1550)', *Critica storica*, 25:2 (1988), 244–94; A. Del Col, 'L'inquisizione romana e il potere politico nella repubblica di Venezia (1540–1560)', *Critica storica*, 28:2 (1991), 189–250.

19 See Martin, *Venice's Hidden Enemies*, pp. 89–95; Cavazza, 'Libri in volgare'.

20 See Chapter 4.

21 'De la religione et del capo [i.e., the Pope] andavano atorno cose molte indegne di una republica bene instituta come questa' (Letter of Minganelli quoted in B. Nicolini, 'Il frate osservante Bonaventura de Centi e il nunzio Fabio Minganelli. Episodio di vita religiosa veneziana', in his *Aspetti della vita religiosa, politica e letteraria del Cinquecento* (Bologna: Tamari, 1963), p. 68). See also Cavazza, 'Libri in volgare', pp. 10–11. Already in 1534, an earlier nuncio noted regarding illicit books: 'impossibile è guardare che non ci venghino per esser Venetia senza porte e che solo con le bisacche e valiggi ve ne potrebbono venire quantità grande di ogni sorte' (Letter of Girolamo Aleandro to Pietro Carnesecchi, 29 February 1534, in Gaeta, *Nunziature di Venezia*, p. 174).

22 'Sono fatti cossì licentiosi li stampadori e li botegieri de questa cità che … stampano et etiam vendeno libri et opere stampati altrove publicamente, molte delle qual sono molte inhonestissime contra l'honor del Signor Dio e della fede Christiana cum tanto mal exemplo e scandalo universal' (ASV, CX, Parte comuni, f. 32, fasc. 234).

23 Grendler, *Roman Inquisition*, pp. 80–6.

24 P. F. Grendler, 'The Tre savii sopra eresia 1547–1605: a prosopographical study', *Studi veneziani*, 3 (1979), 283–340.

25 Grendler, *Roman Inquisition*, pp. 88–9. In theory, the secular tribunal of the Esecutori was subordinate to the Holy Office, however, the Esecutori were given more power and responsibilities later in the century. See Witcombe, *Copyright in the Renaissance*, p. 68, and below.

26 The Index is reprinted in J. M. De Bujanda (with the assistance of R. Davignon and E. Stanek), *Index de Venise, 1549. Venise et Milan, 1554*, vol. 3 of De Bujanda, *Index des livres interdits* (Sherbrooke, Québec: Centre d'études de la Renaissance, Editions de l'Université de Sherbrooke; Geneva: Droz, 1987), pp. 383–93.

27 Rozzo, 'Italian literature on the Index', p. 195.

28 Grendler, *Roman Inquisition*, p. 116. More generally, see V. Frajese, *Nascita dell'Indice. La censura ecclesiastica dal Rinascimento alla Controriforma* (Brescia: Morcelliana, 2006).

29 'Qui res lascivas, seu obscoenas ex professo tractant, narrant aut docent' (J. M. De Bujanda, *Index de Rome, 1557, 1559, 1564. Les Premiers index romains et l'index du Concile de Trente*, vol. 7 of De Bujanda, *Index des livres interdits*, p. 151).

30 Rozzo, 'Italian literature on the Index', p. 205. See also G. Fragnito's contention that the Inquisition's campaign against literature in the vernacular in the sixteenth century progressed from 'iniziali scaramucce … ad una vera e propria guerra' ('"Li libbri non zo'rrobba da cristiano": la letteratura italiana e l'Indice di Clemente VIII (1596)', *Schifanoia*, 19 (1999), 123).

31 M. P. Fantini, 'Censura romana e orazioni: modi, tempi, formule (1571–1620)', in *L'inquisizione e gli storici: un cantiere aperto (Tavola rotonda nell'ambito della conferenza annuale della ricerca, Roma, 24–25 giugno 1999)* (Rome: Accademia nazionale dei Lincei, 2000), p. 234.

32 *Aviso alli librari, che non faccino venire l'infrascritti libri, e ritrovandosene havere, che non li vendino senza licenza*, emanating from Rome, reprinted in J. M. De Bujanda, U. Rozzo et al., *Index de Rome, 1590, 1593, 1596. Avec étude des Index de Parme 1580 et Munich 1582*, vol. 9 of De Bujanda, *Index des livres interdits*, pp. 746–47. On this list, see G. Fragnito, *La bibbia al rogo. La censura ecclesiastica e i volgarizzamenti della scrittura (1471–1605)* (Bologna: Il Mulino, 1997), pp. 140–1.

Another list from the Parma Office of the Inquisition prohibited 'historie tutte che non apportano giovamento né alla fede, né a buoni costumi' (Rozzo, 'I fogli volanti a stampa', pp. 63–4). M. P. Fantini, 'Saggio per un catalogo bibliografico dai processi dell'Inquisizione: orazioni, scongiuri, libri di segreti (Modena 1571–1608)', *Annali dell'Istituto storico italo-germanico in Trento*, 25 (1999), 601–2, also mentions another list of 'cose prohibite da vendere et da stampare', probably sent to Rome in the early 1570s and now preserved in the archive in Milan, that includes many titles of 'orationi, historie, legende, frottole, commedie, lamenti, proverbi', probably a synthesis of works being distributed by ambulant sellers.

33 On changing attitudes to chivalric tales, see the previous chapter.
34 Fantini, 'Saggio per un catalogo bibliografico'. In the process, Inquisitors left records of great use to modern bibliographers, helping to identify numerous editions of ephemeral works now for the most part lost (*ibid.*, 603). For other examples of this process, see Caravale, 'Censura e pauperismo'.
35 See, for example, G. Fragnito, 'The central and peripheral organization of censorship', in Fragnito, *Church, Censorship and Culture*, pp. 13–49.
36 P. Negrin, 'Licenze e privilegi di stampa a Venezia (1527–1550)' (*tesi di laurea*, Università degli studi di Venezia, 1990–1), p. 72.
37 See Frajese, *Nascita dell'Indice*, p. 342.
38 On the possible identity of the work as Niccolò Franco's translation of Virgil's *Priapea*, see the Introduction.
39 ASV, *ECB*, Notatorio, b. 56, vol. 1, cc. 123^{r-v} and Raspe, b. 61, cc. 33^{r-v}.
40 'Esser stati di tanta iniquità e sceleragine mossi da spirito diabolico che hanno fenta una lettera che par sia venuta da Ravena ... imputando contra ogni verità doi frati zoccolanti da Ravena che habbino ... amazato un marcadante e toltoli li danari, e loro frati siano stati squartati in Ravena, la qual lettera è in tutto falsissima e aliena da ogni verità' (ASV, *ECB*, Raspe, b. 61, c. 33^{r}).
41 'Acciòche siano essempio, e specchio à li altri, tanto seculari, quanto spirituali'. *Copia di una lettera venuta novamente da Ravenna, nellaquale si contiene l'horrendo caso ... de duoi frati zoccolanti, de Ravenna ...* ([Venice: B. and G. A. Bindoni], 1551), c. Aiv^{r}. BSM Crim. 294.4.
42 C. Fahy, 'Le edizioni veneziane dei *Paradossi* di Ortensio Lando', in his *Saggi di bibliografia testuale* (Padua: Antenore, 1988), pp. 169–211. Surviving records of the *Paradossi* case are in ASV, *ECB*, Notatorio, b. 56, vol. 1, cc. 41^{v}–42^{r} (2 August 1544).
43 See above, Chapter 2, n. 95. The Holy Office interrogated several Venetian printers to try to identify the producer of the pamphlet. One of the suspected was Bernardino, although no clear resolution of the question seems to have been reached.
44 *Historia di m. Bernardo Giustiniano gentilhuomo vinitiano, dell'origine di Vinegia ...* (Stampata in Vinegia: per Bernardino Bindoni milanese, 1555).
45 Public reading of newletters was not unknown. In 1596 the government of Bologna received a petition from an enterprising individual who wished to set up regular readings (upon payment) of newsletters from abroad. See P. Bellettini, 'Pietro Vecchi e il suo progetto di lettura pubblica, con ascolto a pagamento, delle notizie periodiche di attualità (Bologna 1596)', in P. Bellettini, R. Campioni and Z. Zanardi (eds), *Una città in piazza. Comunicazione e vita quotidiana a Bologna tra Cinque e Seicento* (Bologna: Editrice Compositori, 2000), pp. 68–76. Public reading of newsletters is also the subject of the Mitelli print cited in Chapter 4, n. 59.

46 'Per haver venduto ditte lettere sopra le piaze, ac etiam per haver fatto stampar altre opere de mala qualità contra le parte d'il illustrissimo Consilio di X' (ASV, *ECB*, Raspe, b. 61, c. 33^v).
47 For his publications, see *Edit16* under 'Paride Mantovano'.
48 See Grendler, *Roman Inquisition*, p. 116.
49 *Ibid.*, pp. 122–5; and the documents collected in ASV, *SU*, b. 14 and b. 156.
50 An earlier edition of this work is held in Venice: *Historia noua piaceuole da intendere: laquale tratta de le malicie de le donne ... & como una donna taglio il membro al suo marito per dispetto perche seguiua le altre donne* ([Venice: *c*.1530]). BGC 297.
51 'Non ho havuti licentia da alguno ma vedendo esser cosa de poco importanza anzi cose da rider mi per guadagnar et cavarne qualche bezo perche son poveretto le ho fatto stampir ... le ho trovate stampate per Agustin Bindon et Mathio Pagan et vedendole cusse stampati io le feci stampar et quando fussero sta apenna et non stampiti io non l'averra fatti stampar senza licenzia' (ASV, *SU*, b. 14, fasc. 1 (9 July 1558)). De' Franceschi seems also to have bought or inherited printing materials from the Bindoni.
52 See *Edit16*.
53 [*Procession of the Doge and Patriarch of Venice*] ('In Venetia per Mathio pagano in Frezzaria al segno della Fede', s.d.), reproduced in Bury, *Print in Italy*, pp. 184–5. Domenico De' Franceschi again followed Pagan in publishing a copy of this image in 1561 (*ibid.*, p. 184).
54 ASV, *SU*, b. 14, fasc. 1 (20 August 1558).
55 'Sa ghin voli comprare / cha me porte i danari / e non sie cosi avari / a posta d'un bezetto, / d'haver tanto diletto / e così bel solazzo' (*Pronostico alla villota sopra le putane. Composto per lo eccellente dottore M. Saluaor, cosa molto bellissima, et piaceuole. Et da ridere, con vna barcelletta nouamente aggiunta* (Venice: M. Pagan, 1558), c. Aiii^v–Aiiii^r. BMV Misc. 2213.7).
56 Del Col, 'Il controllo della stampa', 482.
57 See *Edit16*.
58 Grendler, *Roman Inquisition*, pp. 151–2.
59 See ASV, *CCX*, Notatorio, r. 18–31, covering the years 1560–1601.
60 'Se alcuno stampasse, over facesse stampar alcuna opera in questa città, e facesse parer, che fusse stampata altrove, sia condennato à star anno uno in pregion, e pagar ducati cento, e in bando perpetuo di questa città, e del destretto' (Proclamation of 10 October 1565, included in a printed collection of laws relating to printing in ASV, *Riformatori*, b. 364).
61 ASV, *CX*, Parti comuni, r. 74, c. 136 (17 September 1566).
62 Martin, *Venice's Hidden Enemies*, ch. 7.
63 Cited above, Chapter 2, n. 66.
64 As indicated by the 1567 list of booksellers, which listed at least a dozen who operated outdoor stalls, cited in Chapter 2, n. 45. See also the intimation to several street sellers of another prohibition of 1573, this one instructing not to print or sell Boccaccio's *Decameron*, in ASV, *SU*, b. 156. On the Holy Office's cautioning of two poor stallholders, see Chapter 3.
65 ASV, *ECB*, Notatorio, b. 56, vol. 2, c. 24^v (23 July 1566).
66 Cited in Chapter 2, n. 55.

67 'Con ogni debita diligentia et modestio el debba inquirer et indagar delle contrafation prefate et tuor li libri istorie, canzon, frotole, lettere, o pronostichi ch'el troverà …, denontiando li nomi delli contrafacenti acciò possiamo [dar]gli quel castigo et pena che dalle legi è patuite' (ASV, *ECB*, Notatorio, b. 56, vol. 2, c. 38^v (2 March 1568)).

68 *Ibid.*, c. 40^v (2 August 1568). I have not been able to identify this work, but literature about vagabonds saw a resurgence in this period. See P. Camporesi (ed.), *Il libro dei vagabondi. Lo* Speculum cerretanorum *di Teseo Pini,* Il vagabondo *di Rafaele Frianoro e altri testi di 'furfanteria'* (Milan: Garzanti, 2007; first published 1973).

69 ASV, *ECB*, Notatorio, b. 56, vol. 2, c. 41^v (9 September 1568). Zenoi had received a privilege to print 'devote figure, et ritratti' and geographical prints two years earlier, on condition that he obeyed the printing laws and showed a copy of each work to the Captains of the Council of Ten, to prove it contained no obscenities (ASV, *CCX*, Notatorio, r. 21, cc. 56^v, 65^v (December 1566–January 1567)).

70 See Quondam, '"Mercanzia d'onore"'. Requests for imprimaturs in this period also indicate a decline in the production of secular vernacular literature and an increase in religious material, although, as mentioned above, many works were not submitted for approval (Grendler, *Roman Inquisition*, pp. 131–3).

71 On Domenico, see ASV, *ECB*, Notatorio, b. 56, vol. 2, c. 33^r (28 May 1567) c. 126^v (22 December 1575); ASV, *SU*, b. 65 (18 January 1590). The work in question was probably Baldassare Pisanelli, *Discorso sopra il dragone di fuoco apparso in Roma. L'anno 1575* … (Stampata in Bologna, and ristampata in Venetia, 1575). BMV Misc. 2088.049. Piero's case is discussed in the Conclusion. Domenico's other son, Onofrio, was fined for another press offence in 1597. ASV, *ECB*, Notatorio, b. 61, c. 27^r.

72 'Vender senza licenza historie, et cose simili per le piazza, che sono o apparono stampate fuori di questa città' (ASV, *ECB*, Notatorio, b. 57, b. 278v (19 March 1596)). Much cheap religious print produced in this period lacked a date or the author's name, despite the requirement that these be present (Baldacchini, 'Il libro popolare italiano d'argomento religioso', pp. 435, 438).

73 Carnelos, 'Con libri alla mano', ch. 3.

74 'Una lettera del Re excellentissimo drezada alli elettori del Imperio … la qual lettera poteva etiam offender la maestà del Imperator' (ASV, *ECB*, Notatorio, b. 56, vol. 1, c. 130^v (11 April 1553)). The work in question was probably the eight-leaf quarto *Epistola regis christianissimi ad amplissimos sacri imperii ordines* (Venice: G. Griffo, [1553?]). However, a vernacular edition of this work was printed in the same year in Lyons, so it is likely that an Italian version also circulated in Venice which does not now survive.

75 ASV, *ECB*, Notatorio, b. 56, vol. 2, c. 147^r (29 April 1579).

76 De Vivo, *Information and Communication*, p. 201. More generally on the censorship of political works, see Grendler, *Roman Inquisition*, pp. 156–60.

77 M. Jacoviello, 'Proteste di editori e librai veneziani contro l'introduzione della censura sulla stampa a Venezia (1543–1555)', *Archivio storico italiano*, 151:1 (1993), 34–5. As Dondi notes in 'Printers and guilds', 230, the guild's record book or *mariegola* refers back to dates from 1517 on, so the printers and booksellers probably congregated in some form from this date.

78 This episode is mentioned in Grendler, *Roman Inquisition*, pp. 118–19.

79 'Marchio Sessa qual mi disse che io era sta traditor de l'arte per haver obedito' (ASV, SU, b. 14, fasc. labelled 'Constituto contra Vincentium Valgrisum librarium 1559 9 Agosto', c. 3ʳ).

80 'La causa del tardar fo per non desmembrarmi da li altri librari ... per questa obedientia non mi parlano' (*ibid.*, cc. 1ᵛ–2ʳ). On Sessa's role as a patron to other printers, see Chapter 3.

81 'Quanti suscitano di continuo in essa arte, in quali grossamente credendo che l'essercito della stamparia sia cosa de poca intelligentia, si fanno lecito entrar al maneggio di essa per poca cognitione, et manco esperienza che ne habbiano' (BMCV, *Matricola dell'Arte dei stampatori e librari di Venezia*, c. 18ᵛ (27 April 1572)). Rampazetto added that the same applied to bookselling.

82 *Ibid.*, cc. 18ᵛ–19ʳ.

83 The admission of 'Nicolo Furlan ... sta a San Basso, in corte del balloner, banchetto', can be found in ASV, ALS, Atti, b. 163, r. 1, cc. 5ʳ⁻ᵛ (20 April 1578).

84 'Pasqualin Savioni, sonador di cornetto, et musico per le chiese, et feste, di nuovo principiante nell'arte nostra ... [G]li fu risposto, che per esser questa nostra arte di stampador di grande importanza, non devea egli, d'altra professione lontana, esercitarla' (*ibid.*, c. 7ʳ (25 April 1578)).

85 'Domenico di ser Francesco fiorentino, cerettano' claimed that 'io vendo poco, e per ciò le signori vostri mi ponno [possono] lasciar star' (*ibid.*, c. 10ʳ (4 June 1578)). 'Gabriel di Anzoli maestro da scola' who was told to desist from selling books 'con banchetti nella Piazza di San Marco' and refused entry to the Arte (see *ibid.*, r. 2, c. 28ᵛ (27 September 1601)).

86 *Ibid.*, r. 1, c. 35ʳ (21 September 1583). In the seventeenth century, even more stringent exams were introduced for entrants to block the illiterate and untrained (see Mattozzi, '"Mondo del libro"', 756).

87 See ASV, ALS, Atti, b. 163, r. 1, cc. 10ʳ⁻ᵛ (4 June 1578), application of 'Rimondo de Zuan bergamasco, vende libri con un banchetto sotto li portici a Rialto'. The fate of this bookselling operation is somewhat unclear. In 1591, an 'Oratio di maestro Bortolameo da Sabio' was accepted into the guild, presumably as a legitimate heir to Bortolomeo, while Rimondo seems also to have stayed in the trade, as in 1599 he was given permission, as a poor bookseller, to sell on *feste* (*ibid.*, c. 19ʳ; r. 2, c. 15ʳ).

88 On Bologna, see G. Cencetti, 'Alcuni documenti sul commercio libraio bolognese al principio del secolo XVI', *L'Archiginnasio*, 30:14 (1935), 355–62; on Ferrara, A. Nuovo, *Il commercio libraio a Ferrara tra XV e XVI secolo. La bottega di Domenico Sivieri* (Florence: Olschki, 1998), pp. 15–16; on Milan, K. M. Stevens, 'Printers, publishers and booksellers in Counter-Reformation Milan: a documentary study' (Ph.D. dissertation, University of Wisconsin-Madison, 1992), pp. 44–5; and on Rome, Palazzolo, 'Banchi, botteghe, muricciuoli', pp. 8–10.

89 See Grendler, *Roman Inquisition*, p. 226.

90 Carnelos, 'La corporazione e gli esterni', 6.

91 'Stampano, et vendeno, seu fanno stampar, et vender libri in stamparie, botteghe, magazeni, et banchetti, in grosso, et à minuto ... Né è conveniente ch'altri ne usurpi il nostro pane dalle mani, essendo massime noi quelli, che portamo le gravezze dell'arte nostra ... Molte volte occorre, che dalla Santa Inquisitione, dalli illustrissimi Signori capi, dal clarissimo Officio della Biastema, o da qualche altro magistrato vien

domandato alli capi dell'arta nostra d'alcuna cosa stampata, o libro venduto, né da essi nostri capi si sa che cosa responderseli, essendono quasi sempre libri stampate et venduti da gente fuor dell'arte nostra, et non matricolati, liquali non intendono, né sanno il nostro mestiero' (ASV, ALS, Atti, b. 163, r. 1, c. 74^r (4 September 1586)). The Roman guild of booksellers made similar claims about ambulant booksellers in the seventeenth century; see Palazzolo, 'Banchi, botteghe, muricciuoli', p. 10. J. Salman, 'Peddling in the past: Dutch itinerant bookselling in a European perspective', *Publishing History*, 53 (2003), 12, notes that Dutch pedlars were often the 'first victims of censorship', before established booksellers.

92 For an overview of the main cases, see C. De Frede, 'Tipografi, editori, librai italiani del Cinquecento coinvolti in processi di eresia', *Rivista di storia della chiesa in Italia*, 23:1 (1969), 21–53; Grendler, *Roman Inquisition*, pp. 105–15.

93 Cited above, Chapter 3, n. 84.

94 The first reference I have found to this fine is in ASV, ALS, Atti, b. 163, r. 1, c. 16^r (31 May 1580); however, it was affirmed again several times in the following years.

95 Mattozzi, '"Mondo del libro"', 749–53. This process continued into the seventeenth century, according to P. Ulvioni, 'Stampatori e librai a Venezia nel Seicento', *Archivio veneto*, 108 (1977), 93–124.

96 'Fa lecito a quelli, che non sono di essa Arte matricolati, goder li frutti di essa, senza concorrer alli gravami, et spese di esse, oltra ché si fanno lecito contra le leggi divine, et humane vender libri prohibiti, et altro, che non stà bene contra Dio, et vergogna di essa Arte' (ASV, ALS, Atti, b. 163, r. 2, cc. 2^{r-v} (16 July 1598)).

97 *Ibid.*, c. 8^r (5 November 1598).

98 Cited above, Chapter 2, n. 79.

99 'Li zaratani et altri che sopra le piaze vendono diverse sorte di oglie, polvere, letuarii et altri remedii si con recette come senza, si in bancho come sopra scagni, stuoie et etiam alle case loro' (ASV, *Sanità*, b. 731, c. 4^r (5 July 1563)). On the plague prohibition, see B. Pullan, *Rich and Poor in Renaissance Venice* (Oxford: Blackwell, 1971), pp. 316–17.

100 'Monta in banco non habbino à montar niun giorno della settimana né festivo, né ferial la mattina, ma sibene sia lor permesso il montarlo il doppo disnar doppo serrata la chiesa di San Marco per il vespero compito, adoperando un sol banco ordinario. Eccettuando le feste di Natal, Epiffania, Pasqua di Resurretione, Ascensione, Pentecoste, Corpo di Cristo, et tutte di Nostra Donna, Ogni Santi, et di San Marco, ne quali tempo non debbano montar à modo alcuna à niun hora. Né similmente possino montar tutte le domeniche di Quadragesima' (ASV, *PSM*, Discipline – Terminationi, b. 4, fasc. 2, c. 89^v (24 August 1589)). For another example of the Procuratori regulating the presence of a piazza performer, see *ibid.*, c. 48^v (14 February 1571). For more on the regulation of performers in this period, see Salzberg and Rospocher, 'Street singers'; Carnelos, *'Con libri alla mano'*, pp. 186–7.

101 B. Pullan, 'Poveri, mendicanti, e vagabondi (secoli XIV–XVII)', in *Storia d'Italia. Annali*, vol. 1: *Dal feudalismo al capitalismo* (Turin: Einaudi, 1978), esp. pp. 1008–20.

102 For Antheo, see ASV, *ECB*, Notatorio, b. 56, vol. 1, cc. 64^v–65^r (September 1546). On Coppa's banishment and denunciation, see Chapter 4. The musician is mentioned in Martin, *Venice's Hidden Enemies*, pp. 145–6. See also the case of Giacomo Angelo

degli Urani, a pedlar who worked on the Rialto Bridge, forced to abjure heretical opinions (ASV, *SU*, b. 21, fasc. 4: 'Massimo de' Massimi').
103 Cf. A. Brundin, 'Literary production in the Florentine Academy under the first Medici dukes: reform, censorship, conformity?', in A. Brundin and M. Treherne (eds), *Forms of Faith in Sixteenth-Century Italy* (Aldershot, UK and Burlington, VT: Ashgate, 2009), p. 73.

Conclusion

This work began with one pedlar apprehended on the streets of Venice, and it ends with another. The incident occurred in November 1575, with Venice in the middle of the most devastating plague since the Black Death. This time it was a lame street vendor, Battista Furlano, who was discovered peddling problematic printed fliers – right underneath the noses of the authorities, by the gate of the Palazzo Ducale in Piazza San Marco. The work he sold was a flimsy octavo sheet, the size of an open hand, containing a short Latin oration and its vernacular translation. However, the humble object announced itself to be a thing of great importance:

> THIS IS THAT GREAT SECRET FOR STAYING SAFE IN A TIME OF PLAGUE. You should carry with you, and recite the following words in praise of OUR LORD JESUS CHRIST and of the virgin MARY his most glorious mother, every morning with faith and devotion. [original capitals][1]

In the hope of protecting oneself from a plague in which one-third of the population of the city perished, one could purchase a flier from Battista for the small sum of one *bezzo* (Figure 14).[2]

While these modest slips of paper might have offered a tempting promise of protection to Venetian consumers, the Holy Office deemed such orations superstitious and potentially dangerous, and called in for questioning those involved in printing and distributing them.[3] First was the street seller, Furlano, who had worked from a *banco* in the piazza since at least 1567.[4] He led the Inquisitors to the printer, Pietro De' Farri, who, notably, had not put his name or mark on the sheets. De' Farri belonged to a printing family already established in Venice with long experience producing printed ephemera marking events such as the Venetian victory at Lepanto in 1571.[5] He claimed not to have applied for a licence for the work because it had been printed in the past – a common excuse, as we have seen.[6] And, indeed, De' Farri got off relatively lightly, instructed only to stop printing the fliers and to hand in the remaining copies.

This case shows the publishing industry operating in by now well-tested ways, printed matter flowing through established channels of distribution, even during

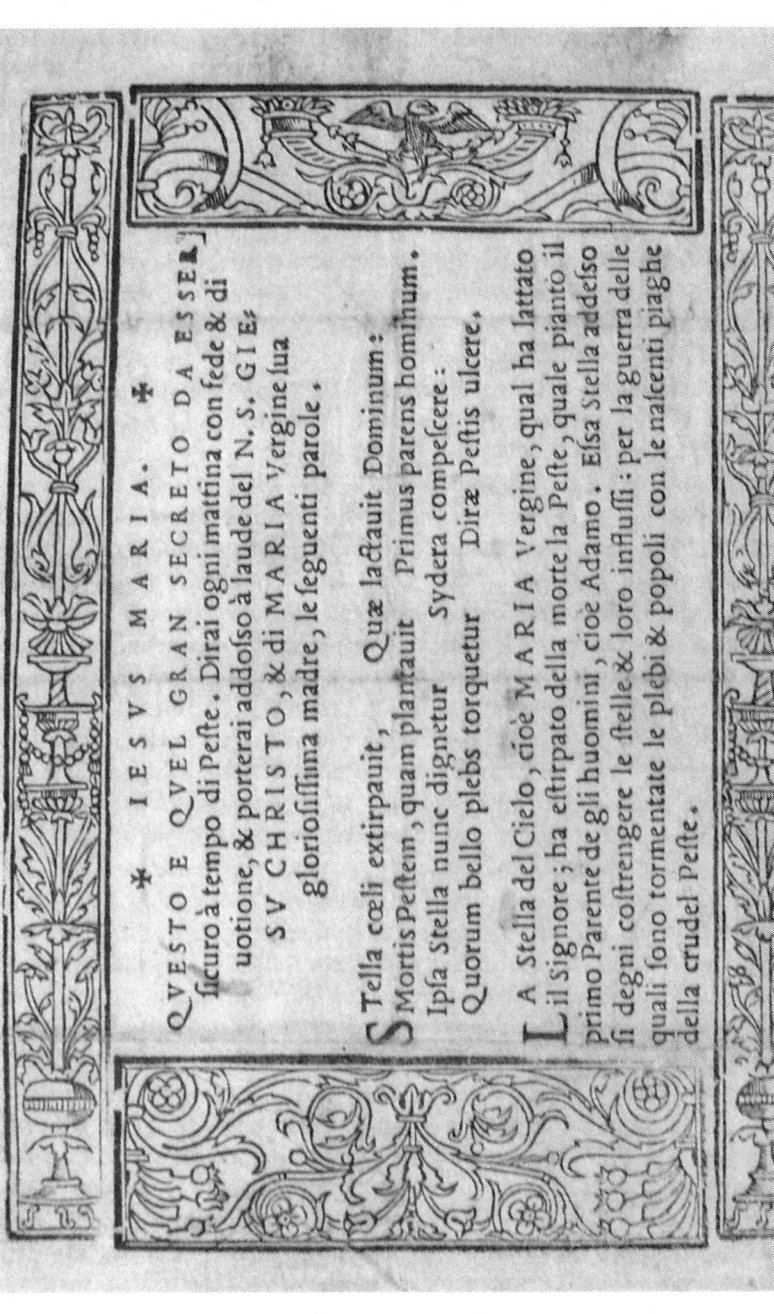

14 An oration offering protection from plague: Questo è quel gran secreto da esser sicuro à tempo di peste ....

a crisis. In the midst of the epidemic, the printer and his peddling associates identified a potential market for cheap printed items that offered some hope of protection, and set about catering to it. De' Farri claimed only to have printed the fliers at the request of 'certain noblewomen', but, whether this was true or not, he evidently perceived a wider market as well.[7] He sent the works out not only with Battista, but also with another vendor, Iseppo Mantelli, who operated on the Rialto Bridge. Both Furlano and Mantelli took about 200 copies of the octavo flier, although Battista passed his on to another vendor called Paolo Lauto, effectively subcontracting him and presumably taking a cut.[8] Rapidly, via this small network of distribution, several hundred copies were channelled onto the streets of Venice, particularly hawked around the two busiest hubs of Rialto and San Marco. Furthermore, the Holy Office collected other works doing the rounds at the same time, offering similar solutions, such as another flier including orations to Saints Roch and Martha and an assurance that the person who faithfully recited them 'will be liberated from every pestiferous ill, and from sudden death, even if he himself has the disease'.[9]

As in the opening case of Francesco Faentino and his run-in with the blasphemy magistrates, these ephemeral items and their transaction on the streets would have left little trace were it not for the efforts of the Holy Office – they were not designed to last. But in fact a miscellany preserved in the Vatican Library demonstrates conclusively how these little fliers were just a trickle in a larger torrent of cheap print associated with the plague.[10] Despite the unexpected ferocity of the epidemic, much of the printed material produced concerning it would have been comfortably familiar to Venetians, as traditional forms and genres were deployed to provide information about the disease, instructions on how to cope with it or distraction from its terrors. Within the palimpsest of plague literature included in the miscellany one encounters: a prognostication instructing its readers on the safest days to travel to avoid the disease;[11] small fliers offering religious and medical remedies for protection;[12] the vernacular translation of a papal brief informing Venetians of an indulgence that could be gained by helping the suffering;[13] and printed decrees from the Venetian Health Board that instructed how to minimise the spread of the disease.[14] Even in the darkest of moments, some writers and printers saw a market for more humorous or satirical texts. For example, one *foglio volante* recorded all of the signs that people had posted up on their shops explaining why they had closed them during the plague, ranging from the prosaic ('Because of the contagion', 'Because no one comes to buy anything', 'So as to live as long as I can') to the more whimsical ('Gone to the land of Cockaigne').[15] Others parodied the ridiculous claims and promises of medical charlatans.[16] And the collection also suggests how the ephemeral textual culture of the plague was intertwined with a visual culture, including single-sheet images of Christ and the plague patron Saint Roch which, like the textual orations, were meant to possess healing powers for those who carried them.[17]

As in the texts produced during the Cambrai War, discussed in the Introduction, officially commissioned print could be hard to distinguish from the unofficial. Laws were reprinted in seemingly pirate copies; one decree from the Health Board reused a woodcut illustration of the Lion of Saint Mark that had appeared, decades before, on a news-poem about the Cambrai War (Figure 10); the reports of plague doctors sanctioned by the government were collected alongside the rival publications of other healers and charlatans. Indeed, Domenico De' Farri (the father of Pietro, who was questioned regarding the anti-plague orations) worked as an official printer for the Health Board in this period, so the same families could produce both officially commissioned and unlicensed works.[18]

While Venetians devoured this array of printed matter during the epidemic, afterwards they turned to other genres for consolation and explanation. Echoing the celebration of earlier events like the victory at Lepanto, printed verses and songs rejoiced in the liberation of Venice from the plague and recounted the festivities and thanksgiving that took place there in its wake. Examples of a newer genre, the *Successo della peste*, traced the spread of the disease in the hope of understanding it and preventing recurrences.[19] Despite the mechanisms of censorship in place, a plethora of cheap print rapidly issued onto the streets in this period. This was also part of a wider conversation that extended across the *terraferma*; including, for example, poems and songs printed in the Venetian mainland cities that discussed the terrible plague in the capital.[20]

Much of this print was highly conservative, for example an oration that encouraged people to pray for their governors and lords who would save them from the crisis.[21] But a good deal of what was produced was unlicensed and some of it explicitly disapproved of, as in the case of the orations sequestered by the Holy Office.[22] In this moment of utmost fear and panic, the Venetian people looked to cheap print to be informed, saved, comforted, amused, distracted. While their government and official authorities like the College of Physicians and the church provided some material, opportunistic and commercially minded printers, poets and *cantastorie*, astrologers, doctors and charlatans stepped in to offer a much wider selection.

If the plague, like other crisis points throughout the period, produced an *acqua alta* of cheap print, it also highlights how much had changed in the century or so since foreign printers established the first presses in Venice. Examining the surviving sales register of the bookseller Francesco de Madiis from the 1480s, Martin Lowry observed 'an unshaken continuity not only in the intellectual matter of the books themselves, but in the institutions which dictated their use, and in the people who bought them' – still predominantly clerics, nobles and professionals. Rather than an opening up of literature and learning to the masses, Lowry found it difficult to see 'anything except massive consolidation of the intellectual establishment' taking place in Venice at that moment.[23] Nearly a century later, by the mid 1570s, the initial explosion of print had penetrated much more deeply. Over the period surveyed in this book, Venetians of all social levels became accustomed to encountering a great variety of print on their streets, hearing it hawked and performed on the piazza, the streets and bridges.

Every major event in urban life now occasioned a printed response, and manifold forms of print, alongside more traditional modes of communication, sought to cater to the needs, desires and interests of the populace. Print had become part of the temporary architecture of the city – ubiquitous enough to be taken for granted, for huge quantities of it to be produced, recycled or disposed of without much thought.

In many ways, this tide of cheap print would only continue to rise. One scholar has dubbed the seventeenth century in Venice a 'century of paper', characterised by the escalating production of ephemeral works following ever more closely and quickly on contemporary events, and by the appearance of new genres of disposable literature such as opera *libretti*.[24] Even as the Venetian printing industry ebbed in importance from the late sixteenth century, and then recovered somewhat from the late seventeenth, the established structures of dissemination which allowed print to permeate urban space so effectively remained intact. Stallholders, pedlars and print-selling charlatans and performers continued to be a fixture of city life. Yet printed matter also filtered further out into the peripheral areas of the city, reaching city dwellers who ventured less often into the central zones, such as women and children, and surfaced in new spaces like the emerging coffeehouses, vital hubs of discussion and debate.[25] Beyond Venice, the rising production of *libri da risma* and expanding networks of long-range pedlars facilitated the capillary transmission of cheap printed chapbooks and images ever deeper into rural areas, and even across the Alps into the rest of Europe.[26]

Nonetheless, the flood of cheap printed matter, partly surveyed in this book, did not wash down the foundational structures of power and authority, neither in Venice, nor in the Italian peninsula more broadly, as some sixteenth-century commentators feared, or hoped. When print helped bring about more dramatic change elsewhere in Europe (most obviously, in the German states during the Protestant Reformation), this was because powerful factional interests employed the press to marshal public opinion to their side.[27] In Venice, the most receptive of environments, the press on its own was not enough to cause cataclysmic shifts in religious, political, social life.

And yet, this was in part because the Venetian government was ever vigilant of the mood in the city, and especially keen to control the evanescent spheres of public opinion that surfaced at crisis moments.[28] At climactic junctures such as during the Cambrai War, or the religious turmoil of the 1540s, they experimented with mechanisms to tame the flood of print, initially ad hoc but progressively more extensive and established. Aided by the church and the guild when their interests coalesced, the government attempted to channel the flood of print into more acceptable streams, block the production of risqué works and encourage self-censorship among printers and writers. Nonetheless, when the Interdict controversy erupted in 1606 and Venice entered a war of words (and nearly an actual war) with the papacy, the Venetian government found itself unable to halt the flood of pamphlets that discussed and debated the crisis, many of them extremely cheap and accessible. Eventually, though, they responded to the new circumstances, finally forced to acknowledge that the circulation of news, information and political commentary in print was impossible to control entirely, and that it was better to counter by publishing their own version of events than to pretend that their subjects would not be interested in political affairs.[29] Ultimately, seeking stability above all things, the Venetian ruling regime retained a largely united front and the foundations of its power remained firmly in place, even if slowly they were being eroded by successive waves of change.

Surveying the cultural landscape of Venice from the later sixteenth century, we can see that, in reaction to the sense of unrestrained proliferation and declining literary standards charted in Chapter 1, a clearer division was emerging between printed works sanctioned for reading by the general public and those that could be handled only by the more educated. From the mid-seventeenth century, for example, the Veneto-based Remondini press churned out reams of relatively innocuous, sanctioned cheap material. Compared to the English or French chapbooks produced in the same period, which shared a similar form and methods of dissemination, a very high proportion of this output was of a religious nature (74.5 per cent in the case of the surviving Remondini editions).[30] Illicit and semi-pornographic works that might once have been found as cheap pamphlets on the streets now had to be sought in manuscript, generally more expensive and harder to obtain.[31]

Traditionally, it has been argued that the cumulative effects of censorship smothered the most vibrant aspects of Venetian culture from the late sixteenth century, making that culture 'an elite phenomenon' and stifling the circulation of ideas between different social groups.[32] More recently, however, some scholars have insisted on a more varied, vibrant vision of Venice in the era of Catholic Reformation, not simply one of decadence and intellectual stagnation. Forms of communication were diverted into often very fertile underground channels, or flowed around the obstacles erected before them, as in the production of clandestine print and manuscripts, and the almost irrepressible forces of song and speech.[33] Nonetheless, the changes of the sixteenth century undoubtedly generated, at least for a time, a more restricted cultural environment, dampening the heady sense of creative change and growth registered earlier in the century. This was aided by the evolution of the printing industry, as it emerged out of its 'pioneer phase' and printers, publishers and booksellers settled down into a more established and respectable professional body, with greater vested interests and occasionally with significant wealth and power.[34]

If the Venetian case study does not provide an example of rapid, revolutionary change following the introduction of the printing press, it does illustrate especially clearly the kinds of hopes and fears aroused within early modern Europeans by the spread of this new technology for communication. It provides a particularly vivid instance of how print could infiltrate the heart of urban life, mingling with existing modes of communication, percolating into established cultural itineraries, and rapidly becoming vital to the way that information and knowledge circulated, that authority was constructed, and that Venetians thought about themselves and others. It also demonstrates how the ruling authorities were able to manage that flow more or less from its very beginning, allowing it to spread and flourish but never letting it run entirely out of control. Yet again, the skilful management of an equilibrium between change and continuity, mobility and stasis, were crucial to the maintenance of Venice's stability.

In this process, I have insisted on the significance of the cheapest, most ephemeral products of the press. These flimsy items did not only sustain the businesses of printers and deliver a much-needed source of income for indigent pedlars. They also opened a threshold for many consumers into the world of print, and were a most rapid and effective way to communicate particular kinds of messages. Designed, in most cases, not to endure, when they do survive they constitute an extremely precious source for historians interested in reconstructing forgotten aspects of urban life in early modern cities. If we listen carefully to these paper echoes, we can hear something of the shifting, stimulating experience of life in the ephemeral city.

Notes

1 'Questo è quel gran secreto da esser sicuro à tempo di peste. Dirai ogni mattina con fede e divotione, e porterai addosso à laude del Nostro Signore Giesù Christo, e di Maria Vergine sua gloriosissima madre, le seguenti parole'. A copy of the oration is preserved with the trial records in ASV, *SU*, b. 39, fasc. 7.
2 On the devastation of this plague, particularly in Venice, see S. K. Cohn Jr, *Cultures of Plague: Medical Thinking at the End of the Renaissance* (Oxford: Oxford University Press, 2010), p. 21.
3 On the censorship of orations in the 1570s, see Fantini, 'Censura romana e orazioni', 227.
4 On Furlano, see Chapter 2, n. 45.
5 On De' Farri, who seems only to have begun printing in this year, see *DTEI*, s.v. On his father Domenico's brushes with the law, see Chapter 5.
6 ASV, *SU*, b. 39, fasc. 7, c. 1^v.
7 *Ibid.*, c. 2^r: 'ad instantia di certe gentildonne, et non per venderle, se non da cento'.
8 ASV, *SU*, b. 39, fasc. 7, c. 1^r. It is unclear whether Mantelli had his own shop at Rialto or a street-based operation. He acted as a publisher of two works in 1567 (see Ascarelli and Menato, *La tipografia del '500*, p. 417).
9 'Chi dirà questo versetto con pura fede, et bona divotione, sarà liberato da ogni mal pestifero, e da morte subitanea, etiam se fusse con il mal addosso (che Dio ne guardi ciascuno) facendosi tre volte il segno della santa Croce, sparirà via subito'. This is also preserved in the Holy Office file, and reproduced in *Venezia e la peste, 1348–1797* (Venice: Marsilio, 1979), p. 137.
10 BV Misc. MAG. R I IV 1551. It is rare to find such an array of ephemeral print concerning one single event gathered together in this way. Manuscript annotations at the end of the volume in what appears to be a sixteenth-century hand suggest that this collection was gathered at the time of, or soon after, the plague. The notes, which seem

to record death statistics in different parts of Venice, would suggest that the collector was perhaps someone associated with the Health Board. Cohn, *Cultures of Plague*, argues that this plague in particular unleashed a whole new wave of printed literature. For further examples, see *Venezia e la peste*.

11 *Pronostico delleccellente M. Adamo Manderio medico, e matematico* ... (n.p.d.) (BV Misc. MAG. R I IV 155.42).

12 See, for example, *Otimi remedi per mantenersi sani nel tempo della peste* ... (n.p.d.) (BV Misc. MAG. R I IV 1551.83); *Queste sonle vere et esperimentate ricette per guarir giandusse, et carboni con molta faciltà* ... (n.p.d) (*ibid.*, no. 86); *Probatissima medicina contra la peste* (n.p.d.), unnumbered sheet in the volume, between nos 43 and 44. This last flier parodies the style of a charlatan's medical recipe but instead counsels faith, hope and charity as the best remedies against the plague (no. 77 in the same volume is a Latin version of the same text).

13 *Copia del breve mandato da sua santità allillustrissimo dominio* ... (n.p.d.) (BV Misc. MAG. R I IV 1551.49). No. 50 is another shorter version of the same text.

14 See, for example, BV Misc. MAG. R I IV 1551 nos 84, 88 and 89. No. 78 in the same volume is entitled *Copia del rimedio contra la pesta qual è descritto nella parte presa nelleccellentissimo Conseglio di X* ... but may not be an official publication by this office.

15 'Per il contagio', 'Per voler viver fin che poderò', 'Perché nissun no vien a comprar', 'Per esser andà in Cucagna' (*Scelta de i più belli, e bizari motti che si sono veduti scritti sopra le botteghe serrate di Venetia* (n.p.d.). BV Misc. MAG. R I IV 1551.67).

16 See the *Sonetto sopra tutti gli rimedii che si usano contra la peste* (n.p.d.) (BV Misc. MAG. R I IV 1551.98a). See also nos 98c, e and f in the same volume.

17 BV Misc. MAG. R I IV 1551.43, is an engraving of Christ on the cross with Saints Roch and Sebastian signed by the engraver Luca Bertelli, which promises at the bottom that 'Con questo santo segno, e con devote orationi à questi due santi nostri advocati, ci libererà il Signore come liberò già il suo popolo, dalla pestilenza' (reproduced in Cohn, *Cultures of Plague*, p. 36). See also no. 77 in the same volume.

18 BV Misc. MAG. R I IV 1551.89, which appears to be a decree from the Health Board, lists De' Farri as official printer, although no. 84 notes that Pietro De' Franceschi (brother of Domenico, discussed in the previous chapter) was the official printer of this office. No. 88, is a decree from the Health Board which appears to reuse exactly the same woodcut illustration of the Lion of Saint Mark as used in Danza, *La nova de Bressa*. Some official publications by De' Farri and De' Franceschi are reproduced in *Venezia e la peste*, pp. 130–1.

19 Cohn, *Cultures of Plague*, ch. 4.

20 See, for example, the *Barcelletta sopra il lamento di Venetia, del mal contagioso. Di Francesco Cieco, Veronese* (Brescia, [1575–76]). BV Misc. MAG. R I IV 1551.40, which used the traditional lament form (in the voice of *Venetia poverina*) to describe the suffering of the city. See also no. 41: *La canzone sopra la citta di Venetia liberata da la peste* ... (Verona: S. and G. dalle Donne, 1577).

21 See, for example, the single-sheet *Oratione al Signore Iddio, per la liberatione del male contagioso* (n.p.d.) (BV Misc. MAG. R I IV 1551.46), which instructs people to pray for 'quelli che hai constituito sopra di noi superiori, e governatori ... per tutti i Principi e Signori, e i quali tu hai commesso il governo della tua giustitia, e particolarmente per questi nostri Signori di Venetia'.

22 Licences for the years 1575–77 are recorded in ASV, *CCX*, Notatorio, r. 24, and include only a few of the works discussed in the Vatican miscellany.
23 Lowry, *Nicholas Jenson*, pp. 192, 199.
24 Minuzzi, *Secolo di carta*, esp. pp. 35, 252 (on *libretti*, see p. 79).
25 Carnelos, 'Con libri alla mano', ch. 7. On the vicissitudes of the industry in the seventeenth and eighteenth centuries, see also Ulvioni, 'Stampatori e librai'; Mattozzi, '"Mondo del libro"'; M. Infelise, *L'editoria veneziana nel '700* (Milan: FrancoAngeli, 1989).
26 See M. Infelise, *I Remondini di Bassano. Stampa e industria nel Veneto del Settecento*, 2nd edn (Bassano del Grappa: Ghedina & Tassotti, 1990); Carnelos, *Libri da risma*; A. Milano, 'Selling prints for the Remondini': Italian pedlars from the Tesino and Natisone Valleys travelling through Europe during the eighteenth century', in Raymond *et al.*, *Not Dead Things*, pp. 75–96; and, more broadly, Fontaine, *History of Pedlars*. The diffusion of print also was aided by the rise of regional printing centres from the later sixteenth century, discussed in P. Bellettini, 'Publishing in the Provinces: Printing Houses in Romagna in the Seventeenth Century', in Reidy, *Italian Book*, pp. 291–322.
27 See, for examples, Scribner, *For the Sake of the Simple Folk*; Edwards Jr, *Printing, Propaganda*; Pettegree, *Reformation*.
28 See, in particular, Salzberg and Rospocher, 'Evanescent public sphere'.
29 De Vivo, *Information and Communication*. See too the Italian edition of De Vivo's work, with an exhaustive analytical bibliography of pamphlets produced during the Interdict: *Patrizi, informatori, barbieri. Politica e comunicazione a Venezia* (Milan: Feltrinelli, 2012).
30 Carnelos, 'Con libri alla mano', p. 66. See also Minuzzi, *Secolo di carta*, pp. 223–4, 233.
31 In 1579, the son of Agostino Bindoni was punished by the Holy Office for commissioning a manuscript copy of the *Ragionamenti*. See ASV, *SU*, b. 56, fasc. marked 'Stefano Bindoni'. See also Barbierato, *Nella stanza dei circoli*, pp. 175, 191–2.
32 G. Cozzi, 'Books and society', *Journal of Modern History*, 51:1 (1979), 95. See also P. Ulvioni, 'Stampa e censura a Venezia nel Seicento', *Archivio veneto*, 104 (1975), 93; Niccoli, 'Italy', p. 193. On the broader separation of 'high' and 'low' cultures from this period, see also the works cited in the Introduction, n. 56.
33 See, for example, Barbierato, *Nella stanza dei circoli*; F. Barbierato, *The Inquisitor in the Hat Shop. Inquisition, Forbidden Books and Unbelief in Early Modern Venice* (Farnham, UK, Ashgate, 2012); E. Muir, *The Culture Wars of the Late Renaissance: Skeptics, Libertines and Opera* (Cambridge, MA and London: Harvard University Press, 2007).
34 See, for example, the Baglioni family of printers, who became wealthy enough to buy their way into the patriciate in the early eighteenth century (Ulvioni, 'Stampatori e librai', 122).

Bibliography

Manuscript and archival sources

Archivio di Stato, Florence
    Arte dei medici e speziali
    Ospedale di Santa Maria Nuova

Archivio di Stato, Venice
    Archivio delle arti, Arte dei librai, stampatori, e ligatori
        Atti
    Avogaria di Comun
        Notatorio
    Capi del Consiglio dei dieci
        Notatorio
    Consiglio dei dieci
        Parte Comuni
    Dieci savi sopra la Decime
        Condizioni
    Esecutori contro la bestemmia
        Notatorio
        Raspe
    Notarile
        Atti
        Testamenti
    Provveditori di San Marco de supra
        Affitanza
        Discipline – Terminazioni
    Provveditori alla Sanità
        Notatorio
    Reformatori dello studio di Padova
        Licenze di stampa
    Sant'Uffizio
        Processi

Scuola Grande di San Marco
    Libro di morti
Senato Terra

Biblioteca del Museo Correr, Venice
MS. Cicogna 1650/XV: *Articoli estratti dai Diarii di Marino Sanudo concernenti notizie storiche di Commedie, Mumarie, Feste e Compagnie della Calza*.
MS. Cicogna 3044/Mariegola no. 119: *Matricola dell'Arte dei stampatori e librari di Venezia*.
MS. Prov. Div. 252-c: Girolamo Priuli. *Diarii*.

Published primary sources (including modern editions)

All'illustre Signora Vittoria dignissima Marchesa di Pescara. Opera santissima ed utile a qualunque fidel christiano de trenta documenti di frate Cherubino da Spoliti heremita. Donato per il detto a Hyppolito detto Ferrarese e stampata novamente ad instantia sua. [Venice?]; for Ippolito Ferrarese, 1538. BUP 112.b.147/2.
Aretino, P. *La Cortigiana*. Turin: Einaudi, 1970.
— *Aretino's Dialogues*. Translated by R. Rosenthal. New York: Marsilio, 1994. This translation first published 1971.
— *Poemi cavallereschi*. Edited by Danilo Romei. Rome: Salerno, 1995.
— *Lettere*. Edited by Paolo Procaccioli. 5 vols. Rome: Salerno, 1999.
Ariosto, L. *Forze d'amore. Opera nova nella quale si contiene sei capitoli di messer Ludouico Ariosto* ... [Brescia]: Turlini for Ippolito Ferrarese, 1537. BMV Misc. 1900.1.
— *Herbolato ... nel quale figura Mastro Antonio Faentino*. Venice: G. A. Nicolini for Iacopo Coppa, 1545. BL 1071.g.4.
— *Stanze transmutate del Ariosto con una canzone bellissima pastorale. Et uno sonetto in laude dela beltà de le donne, e secondo i costumi di paesi*. [Venice: B. l'Imperatore], for Leonardo il Furlano, 1545. BL 239.c.41.2.
Barzoletta novamente composta de la mossa facta per Venetiani contra alo illustrissimo Signore Alphonso duca terzo de Ferrara. [Ferrara?: N. Zoppino, c.1510]. BL 11426.c.93.
Bianco, N. *Viaggio da Venetia al Santo Sepolcro, et al monte Sinai* ... Venice: A. De' Vecchi, 1606. Getty Institute Library, Los Angeles, 2951–716.
Britti, P. *Canzoneta nova nella qual se intende li auisi, che manda Paolo Briti à i suoi confederati amici dandoli noua come non è vero che lui sia morto* ... Treviso, 1641. BMV 95.C.278.18.
Canto primo del cavalier dal leon d'oro, d'Hippolito Ferrarese, qual seguita Orlando Furioso. Venice: V. Ruffinelli for Ippolito Ferrarese, 1538. BEM alfa.Y.7.30/5.
Canto primo del cavalier dal leon d'oro qual seguita Orlando Furioso non mai più visto al presente. Venice: F. Bindoni and M. Pasini for il Romano Faentino, 1541. BBM RARICAST.039.
Canto primo del cavalier dal leon d'orro qual seguita Orlando furioso non mai più visto al presente. Brescia: D. Turlino for Ippolito Ferrarese, 1538. BNCF Palat. D. 4.7.77.1.
Canto primo del cavalier del leon d'oro qual seguita Orlando Furioso non mai più visto al presente. [Venice]: for il Romano Faentino, 1542. Biblioteca padre Clemente Benedettucci, Recanati.

Canzon nuoue dal Fortunato nuouamente poste in luce. Venice, D. De' Franceschi, 1568. BMV Misc. 2208.026.

La canzone sopra la citta di Venetia liberata da la peste ... Verona: S. and G. dalle Donne, 1577. BV Misc. MAG. R I IV 1551.41.

Canzonetta delle massarette, cosa piaceuole da ridere, con la brauata del signor Hieronymo... Venice: M. Pagan, n.d. BMV Misc. 2213.13.

Celebrino, E. *Fenitio, essempio d'vno giovane ricchissimo* ... Venice: F. Bindoni and M. Pasini, 1533. BMV Misc. 2333.3.

— *Formulario de lettere amorose, intitulato Chiaue damore.* Venice: F. Bindoni and M. Pasini, 1527.

— *Il modo d'imparare di scriuere lettera merchantescha ... composto per lo ingenioso maistro Eustachio Cellebrino* ... [Venice], 1525.

— *Opera noua che insegna a parecchiar una mensa a vno conuito ... Intitulata Refetorio* ... Cesena, [1527].

— *Opera noua piaceuole la quale insegna di far varie compositioni odorifere per far bella ciascuna dona et etiam agiontoui molti secreti necessarij alla salute humana* ... Venice: F. Bindoni and M. Pasini, 1526.

— *Questo e lo modo da guarir del mal francioso novo, & vechio ... cosa excellentissima, & piu volte experimentata* ... Venice: G. A. Niccolini da Sabbio, 1526. BGC998.

— *Regimento mirabile, et verissimo a conseruar la sanita in tempo di peste ... intitulato Optimo remedio de sanita.* Cesena: H. Soncino, 1527.

— *Li stupendi et maravigliosi miracoli del Glorioso Christo de Sancto Roccho Novamente Impressa.* [Venice, c.1525]. BGC 639.

La congivra che fanno le massare, contra coloro che cantano la sua canzone ... Venice: A. Facol, [c.1600]. BL 1071.a.37.

Copia del breve mandato da sua santità all'illustrissimo dominio ... [Venice, 1575–77]. BV Misc. MAG. R I IV 1551.49.

Copia del rimedio contra la pesta qual è descritto nella parte presa nell'eccellentissimo Conseglio di X ... [Venice, 1575–77]. BV Misc. MAG. R I IV 1551.78.

Copia de vna lettera venvta da Constantinopoli ...Venice: for Paris Mantoan, 1551. BMV Misc. 1486.007.

Copia di una lettera venuta novamente da Ravenna, nellaquale si contiene l'horrendo caso ... de duoi frati zoccolanti, de Ravenna ... [Venice: Bernardino and G. A. Bindoni], 1551. BSM Crim. 294.4.

Coryate, T. and G. Coryate. *Coryate's Crudities.* 2 vols. Glasgow: J. MacLehose, 1905. Reprint of 1611 edn.

Croce, G. C. *Indice uniuersale della libraria, o studio del celebratiss. eccellentiss. eruditiss. et plusquam opulentiss. arcidottor Gratian Furbson da Francolino* ... Ferrara, 1600.

— *La libraria, conuito uniuersale doue s'inuita grandissimo numero di libri, tanto antichi, quanto moderni* ... Ferrara and Bologna, [1592?].

Damonfido detto il Pastore. *Opera nuova, nella quale si contiene un capitolo in laude della città di Fiorenza.* Florence: for Damonfido il Pastore, n.d. BNCF Palat. E.6.6.119.

Da Porto, L. *Lettere storiche di Luigi da Porto vicentino dall'anno 1509 al 1528,* ed. B. Bressan. Florence: Le Monnier, 1857.

Dati, G. *Incomencia la passione de Christo historiato in rima uulgari secondo che recita e representa de parola a parola la dignissima Compagnia de lo Confallone di Roma lo venerdi sancto in lo loco dicto Coliseo.* Venice: G. Rusconi, 1508.

De Grassi, L. *Opera nvova non piu posta in luce, vniversale & salutifera a tutti li corpi humani* ... *Composta per me maestro Latino de Grassi venitiano*. N.p., [c.1550]. Wellcome EPB 2913A.

De Strata, Fra F. *Polemic against Printing*. Translated by S. Grier. Edited by M. Lowry. Birmingham: Hayloft Press, 1986.

Di Cori, B. *La obsidione di Padua*. Venice: Alessandro Bindoni, 1515. BTM Inc. C.257.1.

Diluuio di Roma che fu a dì sette di ottobre lanno del mille cinquecento e trenta ... Venice: for Giovanni Maria Lirico, 1530. BL 1073.i.40.

Domenichi, L. *Dialoghi di m. Lodouico Domenichi* ... Venice: G. Giolito, 1562. BMV C068C197.

Doni, A. F. *La seconda libraria del Doni*. Venice: F. Marcolini, 1555. BL 271b23.

— *A Discussion about Printing Which Took Place at I Marmi in Florence*. Translated by D. Brancaleone. Turin: Tallone, 2003.

Dragoncino, G. B. [*Lugubris est titulus, lacrimosaque carmina*]. Venice: [M. dei Vitali], 1526. BMV Misc. 2147.7.

Egloga pastorale di Lylia ... [Venice], for Francesco Faentino and partner, 1538. BMV Rari 810.5.

[Erasmus, D.]. *Dialogo erasmico di due donne maritate, in nel quale luna mal contenta del marito si duole, altra la consiglia* ... *Tradotta per Andronico Collodio di latino in vulgare* ... Venice: for Damonfido il Pastore, 1542. BMCV Op. Cicogna 59.3.110.3.

Erasmus, D. *Erasmus on His Times: A Shortened Version of the 'Adages' of Erasmus*. Edited by M. Mann Phillips. Cambridge: Cambridge University Press, 1967.

— 'Penny-pinching (*Opulentia sordida*)'. In his *Colloquies*, translated and annotated by C. R. Thompson. In *The Collected Works of Erasmus*. Toronto: University of Toronto Press, 1997. Vol. 40, pp. 979–95.

Fioravanti, L. *Dello specchio di scientia universale* ... Venice: A. Ravenoldo, 1567.

Folengo, T. *Baldo*. Translated by A. E. Mullaney. 2 vols. Cambridge, MA and London: Harvard University Press, 2007.

Francesco cieco. *Barcelletta sopra il lameto di Venetia, del mal contagioso. Di Francesco Cieco, Veronese*. Brescia, [1575–76]. BV Misc. MAG. RII 1551.40

Franco, N. *Dialogi piacevoli*. Edited by F. Pignatti. Manziana: Vecchiarelli, 2003.

— *Dialogo del venditore di libri (1539–1593)*. Venice: Marsilio, 2005.

Frottole nuoue di Lazaro da Cruzola. Con vna barzelletta, & alcune stanze ala schiauonescha ... [Venice], 1547. BMV Misc. 2231.4.

Garzoni, T. *La piazza universale di tutte le professioni del mondo*. Edited by G. B. Bronzini. 2 vols. Florence: Olschki, 1996.

Giovanni di Giorgio, il cieco. *Lamento di meloni, in barcelletta. Et vn capitulo in lode de l'vua* ... Venice: M. Pagan, 1557. BL 1071.c.65.18.

— *il pianto, e'l lamento che fa il famoso censor mastro Pasquino, per la morte de la Signora Lucretia Milanese ditta Romana* ... *Composta per Giouanni di Georgi cieco Venetiano*. Venice: 1550. BNR 69.7.C.19.3.

Greci, G. *Operetta noua di auree sententie & vtilissimi documenti* ... [Venice?, c.1545], for Leonardo il Furlano. BMV Misc. 2231.3.

Guerre in ottava rima. 4 vols. Ferrara: Istituto di Studi Rinascimentali; Modena: Edizioni Panini, 1989.

Herbolario volgare. Nel quale le virtu delle herbe e molti altri simplici se dechiarano con alcune belle aggionte novamente de latino in volgare tradotto. Venice: Alessandro Bindoni, 1522. BL 453.c.8.

Historia dilettevole di dvoi amanti ... hora dal Fortunato posti in luce. [Venice: G. Padovano] for 'il Fortunato' [c.1540]. BL G 9879.

Historia noua piaceuole da intendere: laquale tratta de le malicie de le donne ... & como una donna taglio il membro al suo marito per dispetto perche seguiua le altre donne. [Venice: c.1530]. BGC 297.

Lamento che fa Piero Strozzi ... Bologna: for Paris Mantoan [c.1554–55]. BRF NAU 471.

Lamento de Italia contra Martin Lutherano. Opera nuoua. [Bologna?, c.1530]. BL 1071.g.22.10.

Il lamento della femena di pre Augustino, qual si duol di esser viua vedendolo in tante angustie ... [Venice:1520s?]. BMV 2231.5.

Lamento d'Hyppolito detto il Ferrarese che cantaua in bancha. N.p.d. BMV Misc. 2231.8.

[*Lamento di Firenze*]. Pesaro: for Ippolito Ferrarese, 1531. BMV Misc. 2405.6.

Lamento dun Bergamasco venuto in pouerta per la carestia, con diuerse altre canzoni alla bergamasca, Cosa nuoua da ridere, & pigliarsi piacere. N.p., 1554. BL 11427.b.20.

de' Leonardis, C. *Lunario nouo perpetuo al modo de Italia ...* Venice: Ippolito Ferrarese, 1532. BL 1395.a.29.

[Luther, M.]. *Vno libretto volgare, con la dechiaratione de li dieci comandamenti, del credo, del Pater noster, con una breue annotatione del uiuere christiano ...* Venice: N. Zoppino, 1525. BNCF RARI.Guicc.23.2.11.

Malespini, C. *Ducento novelle ... Nelle quali di raccontano diversi avvenimenti così lieti, come mesti e stravaganti.* 2 vols. Venice: Al Segno d'Italia, 1609.

Le mirabilissime virtù di Maestro Venturino Bergamasco, protomedico, e dotto in ogni scientia, cosa piaceuolissima, & rediculosa ... Venice: M. Pagan, [1550s]. BL 1071.c.65.14.

La miseranda rotta de venetiani a quelli data da lo invictissimo et christianissimo Ludovico re de Franza et triumphante duca de Milano ... Milan, 1509. BCR Vol. Misc. 2059.11.

Vna morte finta d'amore. [Venice: F. Bindoni and M. Pasini] for Francesco Faentino, 1543.

Vna morte finta d'amore, nella quale si veggono sette nobili donne romane piangendolo come morto. [Venice]: for Francesco Faentino, 1542. BMV Misc. 2213.23.

La nova de Bressa con una barzelletta in laude del Re de Franza e de San Marco. Venice: P. Danza, [c.1516]. BL C.20.c.22.55.

Opera nova del superbo Rodamonte re de Sarza ... Venice: G. Fontaneto for Ippolito Ferrarese, 1532. BLCR 132 D 2.3.

Opera nova laqvale insegna scriuere e leggere in vintisette modi di zifere ... Brescia: D. Turlini for Leonardo il Furlano, 1546. BMV Misc. 2369.1.

Opera nuova de le malitie che usa ciascheduna arte ... Novamente Stampata ... Venice: P. Danza, [c.1525]. BL 11426.e.

Opera nvova d'vn gentil'huomo florentino chiamato Tibaldo Eliseo ... Venice: [V. Ruffinelli] for Francesco Faentino, [c.1540]. BL C.62.a.13.

Opera nvova nellaquale trouerai molti bellissimi secreti ... [Florence]: for Baldassare Faentino, 1546. BL 1071.f.47.

Opera nuova posta in luce ne laquale potrai da te medesimo imparare di scrivere sette sorte di lettere, e abaco. [Venice]: for Leonardo il Furlano, [c.1547]. BMCV Op. Cicogna 11.16.3.

Opera nuovo [sic] posta in luce ne laquale potrai da te medesimo imparare di scriuere sette sorte di lettere, & abaco ... ([Venice]: for Leonardo il Furlano, c.1547). BMCV Op. Cicogna 11.16.3.

Oratione al Signore Iddio, per la liberatione del male contagioso. [Venice, 1577?]. BV Misc. MAG. R I IV 1551.46.

Gli orrendi e magnanimi fatti del duca Alfonso. [Ferrara,1510]. BMV 1945.50.

Otimi remedi per mantenersi sani nel tempo della peste ... [Venice, 1575–77]. BV Misc. MAG. R I IV 1551.83.

La passione del nostro signore in stanze. [Venice: c.1525?]. BL C.57.l.7.6.

Il pianto e gran lamento fatto per il Ferrarese, in Luca, un giorno auanti la sua morte ... N.p.d. BL 1071.g.22.5.

Il pianto e lamento fatto per Hippolito Ferrarese in Luca vn giorno auanti la morte sua ... N.p.d. BMV Misc. 2208.14.

Probatissima medicina contra la peste. [Venice, 1575–77]. BV Misc. MAG. R I IV 1551.43b.

Pronostico alla villota sopra le putane. Composto per lo eccellente dottore M. Saluaor, cosa molto bellissima, et piaceuole. Et da ridere, con vna barcelletta nouamente aggiunta. Venice: M. Pagan, 1558. BMV Misc. 2213.7.

Pronostico dell'eccellente M. Adamo Manderio medico, e matematico ... [Venice, 1575–77]. BV Misc. MAG. R I IV 155.42.

Queste sonle vere et esperimentate ricette per guarir giandusse, et carboni con molta faciltà ... [Venice, 1575–77]. BV Misc. MAG. R I IV 155.86.

Questo e quel gran secreto da esser sicuro à tempo di Peste ... [Venice: P. de' Farri, 1575]. Copy in ASV, *SU*, b. 39, fasc. 7.

Recettario nouo probatissimo a molte infermita, & etiamdio di molte gentilezze vtile a chi levora prouare. Cosa noua non piu stampata ... Venice: for Giovanni Maria Lirico, 1532. BL 1038.d.35.12.

Sanudo, M. *I diarii (1496–1533).* Edited by R. Fulin *et al.* 58 vols. Venice: Visentini, 1879–1903.

— *De origine, situ et magistratibus urbis venetae ovvero la città di Venetia (1493–1530).* Milan: Cisalpino-La Goliardica, 1980.

— 'Praise of the city of Venice'. In D. Chambers and B. Pullan (eds), *Venice: A Documentary History: 1450–1630.* Oxford: Blackwell, 1992.

Savonarola, G. *Triumpho della croce di Christo volgare* ... Venice: F. Bindoni and M. Pasini, 1535. BL 3901aaa71.

Scelta de i più belli, e bizari motti che si sono veduti scritti sopra le botteghe serrate di Venetia. [Venice, 1575–77]. BV Misc. MAG. R I IV 1551.67.

Sonetti e strambottti [sic], non mai più posti in luce ... *Con quattro triumphi de lussuria sopra le cortegiane antiche de Roma.* [Brescia: D. Turlini] for Ippolito Ferrarese, 1534. BNCF Palat. E.6.6.153 II n. 18.

Stanze bellissime de uno gentilhuomo qual essendo inamorato, acorazossi con la sua diva. [Venice: F. Bindoni and M. Pasini] for Ippolito Ferrarese, 1536. BL VOYN.18.

Tagliente, G. A. *Lo presente libro insegna la vera arte de lo Excellente scrivere* ... *Con la presente opera ognuno le potra imparare impochi giorni per lo amaistramento ragioni, essempi, come qui seguente vedrai.* [Venice], 1525. BL C.31.f.7.

Venier, L. *La puttana errante.* Edited by N. Catelli. Milan: Unicopli, 2005.

— *La Zaffetta.* Catania: Guaitolini, 1929.

Venier, M. *Canzoni e sonetti.* Venice: Corbo e Fiore, 1993.

La vera nova de Bressa de punto in punto come andata. [Venice: Alessandro Bindoni, *c.*1512]. BL C.20.c.22.17.

Viaggio de Zan Padella, cosa ridiculosa e bela, dond es descrif tug le cose ches vende sul punt de Rialt in Venesia. Modena, [*c.*1580]. BL 1071.c.63.20.

Zuan Polo. *Libero de le vendette che fese i fioli de Rado Licca Micula de Stizosi.* Venice, 1533. BL 1161.i.22.2.

— *Libero del Rado Stixoso.* Venice: B. de' Vitali, 1533. BL 1161.i.22.1.

Secondary sources

Adorisio, A. M. 'Cultura in lingua volgare a Roma fra Quattro e Cinquecento'. In G. de Gregori and M. Valenti (eds), *Studi di biblioteconomia e storia del libro in onore di Francesco Barberi*, pp. 19–36. Rome: Associazione Italiana Biblioteche, 1976.

Agnelli, G. and G. Ravegnani. *Annali delle edizioni Ariostee.* 2 vols. Bologna: Zanichelli, 1933.

Alazard, F. *Le lamento dans l'Italie de la Renaissance.* Rennes: Presses universitaires de Rennes, 2010.

Amidei, B. Barbiellini. 'I cantari tra oralità e scrittura'. In Picone and Rubini (eds), *Il cantare italiano*, pp. 19–28.

Anderson, J. '"Christ carrying the cross" in San Rocco: its commission and miraculous history'. *Arte veneta*, 31 (1977), 186–8.

Aquilecchia, G. 'Pietro Aretino e altri poligrafi a Venezia'. In Arnaldi and Pastore Stocchi (eds), *Storia della cultura veneta.* Vol. 3, pt. 2, pp. 61–98.

Areford, D. S. *The Viewer and the Printed Image in Late Medieval Europe.* Burlington, VT: Ashgate, 2010.

Arnaldi, G. and M. Pastore Stocchi, eds. *Storia della cultura veneta: dal primo Quattrocento al concilio di Trento.* Vol. 3, pt 2. Vicenza: Neri Pozza, 1981.

Ascarelli, F. and M. Menato. *La tipografia del '500 in Italia.* Florence: Olschki, 1989.

Asor Rosa, A., ed. *Letteratura italiana.* Vol. 2: *Produzione e consumo.* Turin: Einaudi, 1983.

Baldacchini, L. *Bibliografia delle stampe popolari religiose del XVI–XVII secolo. Biblioteche Vaticana, Alessandrina, Estense.* Florence: Olschki, 1980.

— 'Il libro popolare religioso tra Cinque e Seicento. Spunti e riflessioni'. *Berichte im Auftrag der Internationalen Arbeitgemeinschaft für Forschung zum romanischen Volksbuch*, 6 (1983), 1–11.

— 'Il libro popolare italiano d'argomento religioso durante la controriforma'. In P. Aquilon, H.-J. Martin and F. Dupuigrenet Desrousilles (eds), *Le Livre dans l'Europe de la Renaissance. Actes du XXVIIIe colloque international d'études humanistes de Tours*, pp. 434–45. Tours: Promodis, 1988.

— 'I centri di produzione del libro nell'Italia del Cinquecento'. In M. Guerrini (ed.), *Il linguaggio della biblioteca. Scritti in onore di Diego Maltese*, pp. 492–504. Milan: Editrice Bibliografica, 1996.

— 'Chi ha paura di Nicolò Zoppino? Ovvero: la bibliologia è una "coraggiosa disciplina"?' *Bibliotheca. Rivista di studi bibliografici*, 1 (2002), 187–99.

— *Alle origini dell'editoria in volgare: Niccolò Zoppino da Ferrara a Venezia. Annali (1503–1544).* Manziana: Vecchiarelli, 2011.

Barbierato, F. *Nella stanza dei circoli*. Clavicula Salomonis e libri di magia a Venezia nei secoli XVII e XVIII. Milan: Bonnard, 2002.
— *The Inquisitor in the Hat Shop. Inquisition, Forbidden Books and Unbelief in Early Modern Venice*. Farnham, UK: Ashgate, 2012.
Barbieri, E. 'Tradition and change in the spiritual literature of the Cinquecento'. In Fragnito (ed.), *Church, Censorship and Culture*, pp. 111–33.
— 'Per il *Vangelo di San Giovanni* e qualche altra edizione di San Jacopo a Ripoli'. *Italia medioevale a umanistica*, 43 (2002), 383–400.
— 'Di alcuni cantari religiosi condannati. Francesco Novati e la *Raccolta d'alcune particolari operette spirituali e profane proibite*'. In Picone and Rubini (eds), *Il cantare italiano*, pp. 475–89.
Baron, S. A., E. N. Lindquist and E. F. Shevlin, eds. *Agent of Change. Print Culture Studies after Elizabeth L. Eisenstein*. Amherst, MA: University of Massachusetts Press and the Center for the Book, Library of Congress, 2007.
Barry, J. and C. Brooks, eds. *The Middling Sort of People. Culture, Society and Politics in England, 1550–1800*. London: Macmillan, 1994.
Beer, M. *Romanzi di cavalleria. Il Furioso e il romanzo italiano del primo Cinquecento*. Rome: Bulzoni, 1987.
Beer, M. and C. Ivaldi. 'Poemetti bellici del Rinascimento italiano: trecento testimoni per una ricerca'. *Schifanoia*, 1 (1986), 91–9.
Behringer, W. 'Communications revolutions: a historiographical concept'. *German History*, 24:3 (2006), 333–74.
Belfanti, C. M. 'Guilds, patents and the circulation of technical knowledge: northern Italy during the early modern age'. *Technology and Culture*, 45:3 (2004), 569–89.
Bell, R. M. *How to Do It: Guides to Good Living for Renaissance Italians*. Chicago, IL and London: University of Chicago Press, 1999.
Bellavitis, A. *Identité, mariage, mobilité sociale. Citoyennes et citoyens à Venise au XVIe siècle*. Rome: École Française de Rome, 2001.
Bellettini, P. 'Publishing in the Provinces: Printing Houses in Romagna in the Seventeenth Century', in Reidy (ed.), *The Italian Book*, pp. 291–322.
— 'Pietro Vecchi e il suo progetto di lettura pubblica, con ascolto a pagamento, delle notizie periodiche di attualità (Bologna 1596)'. In Bellettini, Campioni and Zanardi (eds), *Una città in piazza*, pp. 68–76.
Bellettini, P., R. Campioni and Z. Zanardi, eds. *Una città in piazza. Comunicazione e vita quotidiana a Bologna tra Cinque e Seicento*. Bologna: Editrice Compositori, 2000.
Beltrami, D. *Storia della popolazione di Venezia dalla fine del secolo XVI alla caduta della Repubblica*. Padua: Cedam, 1954.
Bernicoli, S. 'Librai e tipografi in Ravenna a tutto il secolo XVI'. *L'Archiginnasio*, 30:14 (1935), 170–88.
Bertoli, G. 'Librai, cartolai e ambulanti immatricolati nell'Arte dei medici e speziali di Firenze dal 1490 al 1600'. Pts 1 and 2. *La Bibliofilía*, 94:2, 125–64; 94:3, 227–62 (1992).
Bertolo, F. M. *Aretino e la stampa. Strategie di autopromozione a Venezia nel Cinquecento*. Rome: Salerno, 2003.
Bianchi, M. L. and M. L. Grossi. 'Botteghe, economia e spazio urbano'. In F. Franceschi and G. Fossi (eds), *Arti fiorentine. La grande storia dell'artigianato*, pp. 26–63. Florence: Giunti, 1999.

Blair, A. M. *Too Much to Know: Managing Scholarly Information Before the Modern Age*. New Haven, CT and London: Yale University Press, 2010.
Boerio, G. *Dizionario del dialetto veneziano*. Venice: Cecchini, 1867.
Bollème, G. 'Letteratura popolare e commercio ambulante del libro nel XVIII secolo'. In Petrucci (ed.), *Libri, editori e pubblico*, pp. 203–47.
Bonazzi, N. *Il carnevale delle idee: l'antipedanteria nell'età della stampa, Venezia, 1538–1553*. Bologna: Gedit, 2007.
Bongi, S. *Annali di Gabriel Giolito de' Ferrari da Trino di Monferrato, stampatore in Venezia*. 2 vols. Rome: Ministero della Pubblica Istruzione, 1890.
Botrel, J.-F. 'Les aveugles colporteurs d'imprimés en Espagne'. *Mélanges de la casa de Velázquez*, 9–10 (1973–74), 417–82, 233–71.
Bradbury, J. D. 'Anton Francesco Doni and his *Librarie*: bibliographical friend or fiend?'. *Forum for Modern Language Studies*, 45:1 (2009), 90–107.
Braida, L. *Le guide del tempo. Produzione, contenuti e forme degli almanacchi piemontesi nel settecento*. Turin: Deputazione subalpina di storia patria, 1989.
— 'Gli studi italiani sui "libri per tutti"'. In Braida and Infelise (eds), *Libri per tutti*, pp. 326–44.
Braida L. and M. Infelise, eds. *Libri per tutti. I generi editoriali di larga circolazione tra antico regime ed età contemporanea*. Turin: Utet, 2010.
Braunstein, P. 'Cannaregio, zona di transito?' In Calabi and Lanaro (eds), *La città italiana e i luoghi degli stranieri*, pp. 52–62.
Brayman Hackel, H. 'Rhetorics and practices of illiteracy or the marketing of illiteracy'. In I. F. Moulton (ed.), *Reading and Literacy in the Middle Ages and the Renaissance*, pp. 169–83. Turnhout, Belgium: Brepols, 2004.
Brown, H. F. *The Venetian Printing Press*. London: Nimmo, 1891.
Brown, P. F. '"Not one but many separate cities": Housing diversity in Renaissance Venice'. In N. Howe (ed.), *Home and Homelessness in the Medieval and Renaissance Worlds*, pp. 13–56. Notre Dame, IN: University of Notre Dame Press, 2004.
Brundin, A. 'Literary production in the Florentine Academy under the first Medici dukes: Reform, censorship, conformity?' In A. Brundin and M. Treherne (eds), *Forms of Faith in Sixteenth-Century Italy*, pp. 57–76. Aldershot, UK and Burlington, VT: Ashgate, 2009.
Bruni, R. L. 'Le tre edizioni cinquecentesche delle *Rime contro l'Aretino* e la *Priapea* di Nicolò Franco'. In *Libri, tipografi, biblioteche: ricerche storiche dedicate a Luigi Balsamo*, pp. 123–43. Florence: Olschki, 1997.
Burke, P. 'Oral culture and print culture in Renaissance Italy'. *ARV: Scandinavian Yearbook of Folklore* (1998), 7–18.
— 'Early modern Venice as a center of information and communication'. In J. Martin and D. Romano (eds), *Venice Reconsidered: The History and Civilization of an Italian City-State, 1297–1797*, pp. 390–408. Baltimore, MD: Johns Hopkins University Press, 2000.
— *Popular Culture in Early Modern Europe*. 3rd edn. Farnham, UK: Ashgate, 2009; first published 1978.
Bury, M. *The Print in Italy, 1550–1620*. London: British Museum, 2001.
Cabani, M. C. *Le forme del cantare epico-cavallaresco*. Lucca: Pacini Fazzi, 1988.
Cairola, A. *Le monete del rinascimento*. Rome: Editalia, 1973.
Calabi, D. 'Il rinnovamento urbano del primo Cinquecento'. In Tenenti and Tucci (eds), *Storia di Venezia*. Vol. 5, pp. 101–63.

— 'Gli stranieri e la città'. In Tenenti and Tucci (eds), *Storia di Venezia*. Vol. 5, pp. 913–46.
Calabi, D. and P. Lanaro, eds. *La città italiana e i luoghi degli stranieri. XIV–XVIII secolo*. Rome: Laterza, 1998.
Calabi, D. and P. Morachiello. *Rialto: le fabbriche e il ponte (1514–1591)*. Turin: Einaudi, 1987.
Camporesi, P. 'Cultura popolare e cultura d'élite fra medioevo ed età moderna'. In C. Viviani (ed.), *Storia d'Italia: Annali*. Vol. 4: *Intellettuali e potere*, pp. 81–157. Turin: Einaudi, 1981.
— *Bread of Dreams: Food and Fantasy in Early Modern Europe*. Translated by D. Gentilcore. Chicago, IL: University of Chicago Press, 1989; paperback edn, 1996.
— *Camminare il mondo: Vita e avventure di Leonardo Fioravanti, medico del Cinquecento*. Milan: Garzanti, 1997.
—, ed. *Il libro dei vagabondi. Lo* Speculum cerretanorum *di Teseo Pini,* Il vagabondo *di Rafaele Frianoro e altri testi di 'furfanteria'*. Milan: Garzanti, 2007; first published 1973.
Canepari, E. *Stare in compagnia. Strategie di inurbamento e forme associative nella Roma del Seicento*. Soveria Mannelli: Rubettino Università, 2008.
— 'Immigrati, spazi urbani e reti sociali nell'Italia d'antico regime'. In Corti and Sanfilippo (eds), *Storia d'Italia: Annali 24, Migrazioni*, pp. 55–74.
Cannata, N. *Il canzoniere a stampa (1470–1530). Tradizione e fortuna di un genere fra storia del libro e letteratura*. Rome: Bagatto, 2000.
Caravale, G. 'Censura e pauperismo tra Cinque e Seicento. Controriforma e cultura dei "senza lettere"'. *Rivista di storia e letteratura religiosa*, 38:1 (2002), 39–77.
Cardona, G. R. 'Culture dell'oralità e culture della scrittura'. In Asor Rosa (ed.), *Letteratura italiana*, vol. 2, pp. 25–101.
Carnelos, L. *I libri da risma. Catalogo delle edizioni Remondini a larga diffusione (1650–1850)*. Milan: FrancoAngeli, 2008.
— 'La corporazione e gli esterni stampatori e librai a Venezia tra norma e contraffazione (XVI–XVIII)'. *Società e storia*, 33:130 (2010), 657–88.
— '*Con libri alla mano*'. *L'editoria di larga diffusione a Venezia tra Sei e Settecento*. Milan: Unicopli, 2012.
Carter, T. 'Music-printing in late sixteenth- and early seventeenth-century Florence: Giorgio Marescotti, Cristofano Marescotti and Zanobi Pignoni'. *Early Music History*, 9 (1990), 27–72.
Casadei, A. 'Sulle prime edizioni a stampa delle *Rime* ariostesche'. *La Bibliofilía*, 94:2 (1992), 187–95.
Casali, E. *Le spie del cielo. Oroscopi, lunari e almanacchi nell'Italia moderna*. Turin: Einaudi, 2003.
Catoni, G. 'Processi a librai senesi del Cinquecento'. In *Studi di storia medievale e moderna per Ernesto Sestan*, vol. 2, pp. 519–28. Florence: Olschki, 1980.
Cavaciocchi, S., ed. *Produzione e commercio della carta e del libro, secc. XIII–XVIII*. Prato: Le Monnier, 1992.
Cavazza, S. 'Libri in volgare e propaganda eterodossa: Venezia 1543–47'. In *Libri, idee e sentimenti*, pp. 9–28.
Cavicchi, C. 'Musici, cantor e "cantimbanchi" a corte al tempo dell'*Orlando Furioso*'. In G. Venturi (ed.), *L'uno e l'altro Ariosto in corte e nelle delizie*, pp. 263–89. Florence: Olschki, 2011.

Cencetti, G. 'Alcuni documenti sul commercio libraio bolognese al principio del secolo XVI'. *L'Archiginnasio*, 30:14 (1935), 355–62.
Ceriotti, L. and F. Dallasta, 'Lutero sulle spalle. Colportage e diffusione dell'iconografia protestante in un processo del 1558'. *Aurea Parma*, 93 (2009), 405–22.
Chartier, R. 'Culture as appropriation: Popular cultural uses in early modern France'. In S. L. Kaplan (ed.), *Understanding Popular Culture: Europe from the Middle Ages to the Nineteenth Century*, pp. 229–53. Berlin: Mouton, 1984.
— 'The *bibliothèque bleue* and popular reading'. In his *Cultural Uses of Print*, pp. 240–64.
— *The Cultural Uses of Print in Early Modern France*. Translated by L. G. Cochrane. Princeton, NJ: Princeton University Press, 1987.
— 'Publishing strategies and what the people read, 1530–1660'. In his *Cultural Uses of Print*, pp. 145–82.
— *The Order of Books*. Stanford, CA: Stanford University Press, 1994.
Chartier, R. and H.-J. Lüsebrink, eds. *Colportage et lecture populaire. Imprimés de large circulation en Europe XVIe–XIXe siècles (Actes du colloque des 21–24 avril 1991, Wolfenbüttel)*. Paris: Institut mémoires de l'édition contemporaine/Maison des Sciences de l'Homme, 1996.
Chauvard, J.-F. 'Scale di osservazione e inserimento degli stranieri nello spazio veneziano tra XVII e XVIII secolo'. In Calabi and Lanaro (eds), *La città italiana e i luoghi degli stranieri*, pp. 85–107.
Cherubini, P. 'Note sul commercio libraio a Roma nel '400'. *Studi romani*, 33:3–4 (1985), 212–21.
Chiesa, M. 'Poemi biblici fra Quattro e Cinquecento'. *Giornale storico della letteratura Italiana*, 586:2 (2002), 161–192.
Cioni, A., ed. *La poesia religiosa. I cantari agiografici e le rime di argomento sacro*. Florence: Sansoni antiquariato, 1963.
Cobianchi, R. 'The use of woodcuts in fifteenth-century Italy'. *Print Quarterly*, 23:1 (2006), 47–54.
Cohn Jr, S. K. *Cultures of Plague: Medical Thinking at the End of the Renaissance*. Oxford: Oxford University Press, 2010.
Connell, S. 'Books and their owners in Venice, 1345–1480'. *Journal of the Warburg and Courtauld Institutes*, 35 (1972), 163–86.
Conway, M. *The Diario of the Printing Press of San Jacopo di Ripoli, 1476–1484: Commentary and Transcription*. Florence: Olschki, 1999.
Cortelazzo, M. 'Esperienze ed esperimenti plurilinguistici'. In Arnaldi and Pastore Stocchi (eds), *Storia della cultura veneta*, vol. 3, pt 2, pp. 183–213.
Corti, P. and M. Sanfilippo (eds). *Storia d'Italia: Annali 24, Migrazioni*. Turin: Einaudi, 2009.
Cowan, A. '"Not carrying out the vile and mechanical arts": touch as a measure of social distinction in early modern Venice'. In A. Cowan and J. Steward (eds), *The City and the Senses: Urban Culture since 1500*, pp. 39–59. Aldershot, UK: Ashgate, 2007.
Cozzi, G. 'Books and society'. *Journal of Modern History*, 51:1 (1979), 86–98.
— 'Religione, moralità e giustizia a Venezia: vicende della magistratura degli Esecutori contro la bestemmia (secoli XVI–XVII)'. *Ateneo veneto*, 29 (1991), 7–96.
Cresswell, T. *On the Move: Mobility in the Modern Western World*. New York: Taylor & Francis, 2006.
D'Ancona, A. *La poesia popolare italiana*. 2nd edn. Leghorn: Giusti, 1906.

Davis, N. Zemon. 'Beyond the market: books as gifts in sixteenth-century France'. *Transactions of the Royal Historical Society*, 33 (1983), 69–88.

Davis, R. C. *Shipbuilders of the Venetian Arsenal. Workers and Workplace in the Preindustrial City*. Baltimore, MD: Johns Hopkins University Press, 1991.

De Bujanda, J. M. *Index de Rome, 1557, 1559, 1564. Les Premiers index romains et l'index du Concile de Trente*. Vol. 7 of De Bujanda, *Index des livres interdits*.

—, ed. *Index des livres interdits*. 11 vols. Sherbrooke, Québec: Centre d'études de la Renaissance, Editions de l'Université de Sherbrooke; Geneva: Droz, 1984–93.

De Bujanda, J. M., with the assistance of R. Davignon and E. Stanek. *Index de Venise, 1549. Venise et Milan, 1554*. Vol. 3 of De Bujanda, *Index des livres interdits*.

De Bujanda, J. M., U. Rozzo et al. *Index de Rome, 1590, 1593, 1596. Avec étude des Index de Parme 1580 et Munich 1582*. Vol. 9 of De Bujanda, *Index des livres interdits*.

De Frede, C. 'Tipografi, editori, librai italiani del Cinquecento coinvolti in processi di eresia'. *Rivista di storia della chiesa in Italia*, 23:1 (1969), 21–53.

Degl'Innocenti, L. *I Reali dell'Altissimo: Un ciclo di cantari tra oralità e storia*. Florence: Società Editrice Fiorentina, 2008.

Del Col, A. 'Organizzazione, composizione e giurisdizione dei tribunali dell'Inquisizione romana nella Repubblica di Venezia (1500–1550)'. *Critica storica*, 25:2 (1988), 244–94.

— 'L'inquisizione romana e il potere politico nella Repubblica di Venezia (1540–1560)'. *Critica storica*, 28:2 (1991), 189–250.

Delancey, J. '"In the streets where they sell colors': placing *vendecolori* in the urban fabric of early modern Venice'. *Wallraf-Richartz-Jahrbuch*, 72 (2011), 193–232.

Derosas, R. 'Moralità e giustizia a Venezia nel '500–'600: gli Esecutori contro la bestemmia'. In G. Cozzi (ed.), *Stato, società e giustizia nella Repubblica veneta (sec. XV–XVIII)*, pp. 431–528. Rome: Jouvence, 1980.

De Vivo, F. *Information and Communication in Venice: Rethinking Early Modern Politics*. Oxford: Oxford University Press, 2007.

— 'I luoghi della cultura a Venezia nel primo Cinquecento'. In A. De Vincentiis (ed.), *Atlante della letteratura italiana*, vol. 1: *Dalle origini al Rinascimento*, pp. 708–18. Turin: Einaudi, 2010.

— *Patrizi, informatori, barbieri. Politica e comunicazione a Venezia*. Milan: Feltrinelli, 2012.

Di Filippo Bareggi, C. *Il mestiere di scrivere. Lavoro intellettuale e mercato librario a Venezia nel Cinquecento*. Rome: Bulzoni, 1988.

Dionisotti, C. 'La letteratura italiana nell'età del Concilio di Trento'. In his *Geografia e storia della letteratura italiana*, pp. 227–54. Turin: Einaudi, 1967.

Dizionario biografico degli italiani. Rome: Istituto della Enciclopedia italiana, 1960–

Donato, M. P. and X. von Tippelskirch. '"Il tanto leggere mi fa doler la testa". Appunti sulle lettrici alla soglia del pubblico'. In B. Borello (ed.), *Pubblico e pubblici di antico regime*, pp. 1–20. Pisa: Pacini, 2009.

Dondi, C. 'Printers and guilds in fifteenth-century Venice'. *La Bibliofilía*, 106:3 (2004), 229–65.

Dooley, B., ed. *The Dissemination of News and the Emergence of Contemporaneity in Early Modern Europe*. Farnham, UK: Ashgate, 2010.

Eamon, W. 'Markets, piazzas, and villages'. In K. Park and L. Daston (eds), *The Cambridge History of Science*, vol. 3, *Early Modern Science*, pp. 206–23. Cambridge: Cambridge University Press, 2008.

— *Science and the Secrets of Nature. Books of Secrets in Medieval and Early Modern Culture.* Princeton, NJ: Princeton University Press, 1994.

Edwards Jr, M. U. *Printing, Propaganda and Martin Luther.* Berkeley, CA and London: University of California Press, 1994.

Eisenstein, E. L. *The Printing Press as an Agent of Change: Communications and Cultural Transformations in Early Modern Europe.* 2 vols. Cambridge: Cambridge University Press, 1979.

— 'An unacknowledged revolution revisited'. In *American Historical Review*, 107:1 (2002), 87-105.

— *Divine Art, Infernal Machine: The Reception of Printing in the West from First Impressions to the Sense of an Ending.* Philadelphia, PA: University of Pennsylvania Press, 2011.

Eisermann, F. 'Mixing pop and politics. Origins, transmission, and readers of illustrated broadsides in fifteenth-century Germany'. In K. Jensen, ed. *Incunabula and Their Readers. Printing, Selling and Reading Books in the Fifteenth Century*, pp. 159-77. London: British Library, 2003.

Fahy, C. 'Le edizioni veneziane dei *Paradossi* di Ortensio Lando'. In his *Saggi di bibliografia testuale*, pp. 169-211. Padua: Antenore, 1988.

Fantini, M. P. 'Censura romana e orazioni: modi, tempi, formule (1571-1620)'. In *L'Inquisizione e gli storici: un cantiere aperto (Tavola rotonda nell'ambito della conferenza annuale della ricerca, Roma, 24-25 Giugno 1999)*, pp. 221-43. Rome: Accademia nazionale dei Lincei, 2000.

— 'Saggio per un catalogo bibliografico dai processi dell'Inquisizione: orazioni, scongiuri, libri di segreti (Modena 1571-1608)'. *Annali dell'Istituto Storico Italo-Germanico in Trento*, 25 (1999), 587-668.

Fatini, G. 'L'*Erbolato* di Ludovico Ariosto'. *Rassegna bibliografica della letteratura italiana*, 18 (1910), 216-38.

— 'Su la fortuna e l'autenticità delle liriche di Lodovico Ariosto'. *Giornale storico della letteratura italiana*. Supplement 22-23 (1924), 193-296.

Fattori, D. 'Incunaboli sconosciuti ed incunaboli semisconosciuti all'Archivio di Stato di Venezia'. *La Bibliofilía*, 102:3 (2000), 253-64.

Febvre, L. and H. J. Martin. *The Coming of the Book: The Impact of Printing 1450-1800.* Edited by G. Nowell-Smith and D. Wootton. Translated by D. Gerrard. New edn. London: NLB, 1976.

Fenlon, I. *The Ceremonial City. History, Memory and Myth in Renaissance Venice.* New Haven, CT: Yale University Press, 2007.

Ferguson, R. 'Staging scripted comedy in Renaissance Venice (1500-1560): A survey of the evidence'. In B. Richardson, S. Gilson and C. Keen (eds), *Theatre, Opera, and Performance in Italy from the Fifteenth Century to the Present. Essays in Honour of Richard Andrews*, pp. 39-54. London: Society for Italian Studies, 2004.

Ferroni, G. 'Nota sull'*Erbolato*'. *La rassegna della letteratura italiana*, 79:1-2 (1975), 202-14.

Findlen, P. 'Humanism, politics and pornography in Renaissance Italy'. In L. Hunt (ed.), *The Invention of Pornography: Obscenity and the Origins of Modernity, 1500-1800*, pp. 49-108. New York: Zone, 1993.

Firpo, M. 'Riforma religiosa e lingua volgare nell'Italia del '500'. *Belfagor*, 57:5 (2002), 517-39.

Flood, J. L. 'The printed book as a commercial commodity in the fifteenth and early sixteenth centuries'. *Gutenberg Jahrbuch*, 76 (2001), 72–82.

Fontaine, L. 'Gli studi sulla mobilità in Europa nell'età moderna: Problemi e prospettive di ricerca'. *Quaderni storici*, 93:3 (1996), 739–56.

— *History of Pedlars in Europe*. Translated by V. Whittaker. Cambridge: Polity, 1996.

Fox, A. *Oral and Literate Culture in England, 1500–1700*. Oxford: Oxford University Press, 2000.

Fragnito, G. *La bibbia al rogo. La censura ecclesiastica e i volgarizzamenti della scrittura (1471–1605)*. Bologna: Il Mulino, 1997.

— '"Li libbri non zo'rrobba da cristiano": la letteratura italiana e l'indice di Clemente VIII (1596)'. *Schifanoia*, 19 (1999), 123–35.

— 'The central and peripheral organization of censorship'. In Fragnito (ed.), *Church, Censorship and Culture*, pp. 13–49.

—, ed. *Church, Censorship and Culture in Early Modern Italy*. Translated by A. Belton. Cambridge: Cambridge University Press, 2001.

— *Proibito capire. La chiesa e il volgare nella prima età moderna*. Bologna: Il Mulino, 2005.

Frajese, V. *Nascita dell'Indice. La censura ecclesiastica dal Rinascimento alla controriforma*. Brescia: Morcelliana, 2006.

Frasso, G. 'Una poeta improvvisatore nella "familia" del Cardinale Francesco Gonzaga: Francesco Cieco da Firenze'. *Italia medioevale e umanistica*, 20 (1977), 395–400.

Fulin, R. 'Documenti per servire alla storia della tipografia veneziana'. *Archivio veneto*, 12 (1882), 84–212.

Fumagalli, G. 'La fortuna dell'*Orlando furioso* in Italia nel secolo XVI'. *Atti e memorie della deputazione ferrarese di storia patria*, 20:3 (1912), 135–497.

Fumerton, P. *Unsettled: The Culture of Mobility and the Working Poor in Early Modern England*. Chicago, IL and London: University of Chicago Press, 2006.

Gaeta, F., ed. *Nunziature di Venezia. Vol. 1 (12 marzo 1533–14 agosto 1535)*. Rome: Istituto storico italiano per l'età moderna e contemporanea, 1958.

Gentilcore, D. *Medical Charlatanism in Early Modern Italy*. Oxford: Oxford University Press, 2006.

— 'Il sapere ciarlatanesco. Ciarlatani, "fogli volanti" e medicina nell'Italia moderna'. In M. P. Paoli (ed.), *Saperi a confronto nell'Europa dei secoli XIII–XIX*, pp. 375–93. Pisa: Edizioni della Normale, 2009.

Giacomello, A. 'Ad instantia di Leonardo il Furlano. I libri di un editore del XVI secolo'. In *Cultura in Friuli. Omaggio a Giuseppe Marchetti*, pp. 133–56. Udine: Società Filologica Friulana, 1988.

Giannini, G., ed. *Le arti e le tradizioni popolari d'Italia*. 2 vols. Udine: Istituto delle Edizioni Accademiche, 1938.

Gilbert, F. 'Venice in the crisis of the League of Cambrai'. In J. R. Hale (ed.), *Renaissance Venice*, pp. 274–92. London: Faber & Faber, 1973.

Ginzburg, C. *The Cheese and the Worms. The Cosmos of a Sixteenth-Century Miller*. Translated by J. Tedeschi and A. Tedeschi. London: Routledge & Kegan Paul, 1980. First published in Italian 1976.

Ginzburg, C. and M. Ferrari. 'The dovecote has opened its eyes'. In E. Muir and G. Ruggiero (eds), *Microhistory and the Lost Peoples of Europe*. Translated by E. Branch, pp. 11–19. Baltimore, MD: Johns Hopkins University Press, 1991.

Grafton, A. 'Introduction: How revolutionary was the print revolution?'. *American Historical Review*, 107:1 (2002), 84–6.

Greenblatt, S., ed., *Cultural Mobility: A Manifesto*. Cambridge: Cambridge University Press, 2010.

Grendler, P. F. *Critics of the Italian World, 1530 – 1560: Anton Francesco Doni, Nicolò Franco and Ortensio Lando*. Madison, WI and London: University of Wisconsin Press, 1969.

— 'Form and function in Italian Renaissance popular books'. *Renaissance Quarterly*, 46:3 (1993), 451–85.

— *The Roman Inquisition and the Venetian Press, 1540-1605*. Princeton, NJ: Princeton University Press, 1977.

— *Schooling in Renaissance Italy: Literacy and Learning, 1300-1600*. Baltimore, MD: Johns Hopkins University Press, 1989.

Grubb, J. S. 'When myths lose power: four decades of Venetian historiography'. *Journal of Modern History*, 58:1 (1986), 43–94.

Guarino, R. *Teatro e mutamenti. Rinascimento e spettacolo a Venezia*. Bologna: Il Mulino, 1995.

Haar, J. 'Arie per cantar stanze arioteshe'. In M. A. Balsano (ed.), *L'Ariosto, la musica, i musicisti*, pp. 31–46. Florence: Olschki, 1981.

— 'From "*cantimbanco*" to court: the musical fortunes of Ariosto in Florentine society'. In M. Rossi and F. G. Superbi (eds), *L'Arme e gli amori. Ariosto, Tasso and Guarini in Late Renaissance Florence. Atti del convegno (Firenze, 27-29 giugno 2001)*, vol. 2, pp. 179–97. Florence: Olschki, 2004.

Halasz, A. *The Marketplace of Print. Pamphlets and the Public Sphere in Early Modern England*. Cambridge: Cambridge University Press, 1997.

Harris, N. 'L'avventura editoriale dell'*Orlando innamorato*', in *I libri di* Orlando innamorato, pp. 35–100. Ferrara and Modena: Panini, 1987.

— *Bibliografia dell'*Orlando innamorato. 2 vols. Ferrara: Istituto di Studi Rinascimentali; Modena: Panini, 1988.

— 'Marin Sanudo, forerunner of Melzi. Parte I'. *La Bibliofilía* 95 (1993), 1–37.

— Review of L. Baldacchini. *Alle origini dell'editoria in volgare: Niccolò Zoppino da Ferrara a Venezia. Annali (1503-1544)* (2011). In *The Library: The Transactions of the Bibliographical Society*, 14:2 (2013), 213–17.

Hempfer, K. W., ed. *Ritterepik der Renaissance. Akten des deutsch-italienischen Kolloquiums Berlin, 1987*. Stuttgart: Franza Steiner, 1989.

Henke, R. 'Towards reconstructing the audiences of the commedia dell'arte'. *Études théâtrales / Essays in Theatre*, 15:2 (1997), 207–20.

— *Performance and Literature in the Commedia dell'Arte*. Cambridge: Cambridge University Press, 2002.

— 'Representations of poverty in the commedia dell'arte'. *Theatre Survey*, 48:2 (2007), 229–46.

Horodowich, E. *Language and Statecraft in Early Modern Venice*. Cambridge: Cambridge University Press, 2008.

Houston, R. A. *Literacy in Early Modern Europe: Culture and Education 1500-1800*. 2nd edn. Harlow, UK: Pearson Education, 2002.

Hufton, O. H. *The Poor of Eighteenth-Century France, 1750-1789*. Oxford: Clarendon, 1974.

Infelise, M. *L'editoria veneziana nel '700*. Milan: FrancoAngeli, 1989.
— *I libri proibiti da Gutenberg all'Encyclopédie*. Rome and Bari: Laterza, 1999.
— *I Remondini di Bassano. Stampa e industria nel Veneto del Settecento*. 2nd edn. Bassano del Grappa: Ghedina and Tassotti, 1990.
— *Prima dei giornali. Alla origine della publica informazione (secoli XVI e XVII)*. Rome and Bari: Laterza, 2002.
Ivaldi, C. 'Cantari e poemetti bellici in ottava rima: la parabola produttiva di un sottogenere del romanzo cavalleresco'. In Hempfer (ed.), *Ritterepik der Renaissance*, pp. 35–46.
Jacoviello, M. 'Proteste di editori e librai veneziani contro l'introduzione della censura sulla stampa a Venezia (1543–1555)'. *Archivio storico italiano*, 151:1 (1993), 27–56.
Jardine, L. *Erasmus, Man of Letters: The Construction of Charisma in Print*. Princeton, NJ: Princeton University Press, 1993.
Javitch, D. *Proclaiming a Classic: The Canonization of* Orlando furioso. Princeton, NJ: Princeton University Press, 1991.
Johns, A. *The Nature of the Book: Print and Knowledge in the Making*. Chicago, IL and London: University of Chicago Press, 1998.
— 'How to acknowledge a revolution'. *American Historical Review*, 107:1 (2002), 106–25.
Judde de Larivière, C. and R. Salzberg. 'Le peuple est la cité. L'idée de popolo et la condition des popolani à Venise (XVe–XVIe siècles)'. *Annales ESC*, 68:4 (2013): 1113–40.
Kallendorf, C. *Virgil and the Myth of Venice. Books and Readers in the Italian Renaissance*. Oxford: Clarendon Press, 1999.
Kohler, H.-J. (ed.). *Flugschriften als Massenmedium der Reformationszeit: Beiträge zum Tübinger Symposion 1980*. Stuttgart: Ernst Klett, 1981.
Lanaro, P. 'Corporations et confréries: les étrangers et le marché du travail à Venise (XVe–XVIIIe siècles)'. *Histoire urbaine*, 21 (2008), 31–48.
Landau, D. and P. Parshall. *The Renaissance Print, 1470–1550*. New Haven, CT: Yale University Press, 1994.
Landi, S. *Stampa, censura e opinione pubblica in età moderna*. Bologna: Il Mulino, 2011.
Levi, E. 'Le paneruzzole di Niccolò Povero. Contributo alla storia della poesia giullaresca nel medio evo italiano'. *Studi medievali*, 3 (1908), 81–108.
Libri, idee e sentimenti religiosi nel Cinquecento italiano. Ferrara: Istituto di Studi Rinascimentali; Modena: Panini, 1986.
Lowry, M. *The World of Aldus Manutius: Business and Scholarship in Renaissance Venice*. Ithaca, NY: Cornell University Press, 1979.
— 'The social world of Nicholas Jenson and John of Cologne'. *La Bibliofilía*, 83:3 (1981), 193–218.
— '"Nel beretin convento": the Franciscans and the Venetian press (1474–78)'. *La Bibliofilía*, 85 (1983), 27–40.
— 'Venetian capital, German technology and Renaissance culture in the later fifteenth century'. *Renaissance Studies*, 2:1 (1988), 1–13.
— *Nicholas Jenson and the Rise of Venetian Publishing in Renaissance Europe*. Oxford: Blackwell, 1991.
— 'La produzione del libro'. In Cavaciocchi (ed.), *Produzione e commercio*, pp. 365–87.
Lucas, C. 'Vers une nouvelle image de l'écrivain: *Della dedicatione de' libri* de Giovanni Fratta'. In C. A. Fiorato and J.-C. Margolin (eds), *L'écrivain face a son public en France et en Italie a la renaissance*, pp. 85–104. Paris: J. Vrin, 1989.

Lucchi, P. 'La Santacroce, il Salterio e il Babuino. Libri per imparare a leggere nel primo secolo della stampa'. *Quaderni storici*, 38 (1978), 593–630.

Luzio, A. 'L'*Orlandino* di Pietro Aretino'. *Giornale di filologia romanza*, 3:6 (1880), 68–84.

Mackenney, R. *Tradesmen and Traders. The World of the Guilds in Venice and Europe, c.1250–c. 1650*. London: Croom Helm, 1987.

McKenzie, D. F. 'The economies of print, 1550–1750: scales of production and conditions of constraint'. In Cavaciocchi (ed.), *Produzione e commercio*, pp. 389–425.

— 'Speech–manuscript–print'. First published 1990. Reprinted in *Making Meaning. Printers of the Mind and Other Essays*. Edited by P. D. McDonald and M. F. Suarez, pp. 237–58. Amherst and Boston, MA: University of Massachusetts Press, 2002.

McKitterick, D. *Print, Manuscript and the Search for Order, 1450–1830*. Cambridge: Cambridge University Press, 2003.

McShane Jones, A. 'The gazet in metre; or the rhiming newsmonger: the broadside ballad as intelligencer. A new narrative'. In J. W. Koopmans (ed.), *News and Politics in Early Modern Europe (1500–1800)*, pp. 131–50. Leuven: Peeters, 2005.

Marsh, C. 'The sound of print in early modern England: The broadside ballad as song'. In J. Crick and A. Walsham (eds), *The Uses of Script and Print, 1300–1700*, pp. 171–90. Cambridge: Cambridge University Press, 2004.

Martin, J. *Venice's Hidden Enemies: Italian Heretics in a Renaissance City*. Berkeley, CA: University of California Press, 1993.

Martin, J. and D. Romano. 'Reconsidering Venice'. In J. Martin and D. Romano (eds), *Venice Reconsidered: The History and Civilisation of an Italian City-State, 1297–1799*, pp. 1–38. Baltimore, MD: Johns Hopkins University Press, 2000.

Martines, L. *Strong Words: Writing and Social Strain in the Italian Renaissance*. Baltimore, MD: Johns Hopkins University Press, 2001.

Marzo, A. 'Pasquino e il Gobbo di Rialto'. In C. Damianaki, P. Procaccioli and A. Romano (eds), *Ex marmore. Pasquini, pasquinisti, pasquinate nell'Europa moderna*, pp. 121–34. Manziana: Vecchiarelli, 2006.

Masetti Zannini, G. L. *Stampatori e librai a Roma nella seconda metà del cinquecento: documenti inediti*. Rome: Palombi, 1980.

Matthews-Grieco, S. F. 'Satyrs and sausages: erotic strategies and the print market in Cinquecento Italy'. In S. F. Matthews-Grieco (ed.), *Erotic Cultures of Renaissance Italy*, pp. 19–60. Farnham, UK and Burlington, VT: Ashgate, 2010.

Mattozzi, I. '"Mondo del libro" e decadenza a Venezia (1570–1730)'. *Quaderni storici*, 72:3 (1989), 743–86.

Medin, A. and L. Frati, eds. *Lamenti storici dei secoli XIV, XV e XVI*. Reprint of 1887–94 edn. 4 vols. Bologna: Commissione per i testi di lingua, 1969.

Melograni, A. 'The illuminated manuscript as a commodity: Production, consumption and the *cartolaio*'s role in fifteenth-century Italy'. In M. O'Malley and E. Welch (eds), *The Material Renaissance*, pp. 71–84. Manchester: Manchester University Press, 2007.

Melzi, G. and P. A. Tosi. *Bibliografia dei romanzi e poemi cavallereschi italiani*. 2nd edn. Milan: Tosi, 1838.

Menato, M., E. Sandal and G. Zappelli, eds. *Dizionario dei tipografi e degli editori italiani. Il Cinquecento*. Vol. 1: A–F. Milan: Editrice Bibliografia, 1997.

Menis, I. 'I Bindoni: materiali storico-documentari per una ricostruzione biografica e annalistica'. *Tesi di laurea*, Università degli studi di Udine, 1992–93.

Meserve, M. 'News from Negroponte: politics, popular opinion, and information exchange in the first decade of the Italian press'. *Renaissance Quarterly*, 59:2 (2006), 440–80.

Milani, M. *Piccole storie di stregoneria nella Venezia del '500*. Verona: Essedue, 1989.

Milano, A. '"Selling prints for the Remondini": Italian pedlars from the Tesino and Natisone Valleys travelling through Europe during the eighteenth century'. In Raymond, Salman and Harms (eds), *Not Dead Things*, pp. 75–96

Milner, S. J. '"... Fanno bandire, notificare, et expressamente comandare". Town criers and the information economy of Renaissance Florence'. *I Tatti Studies* 16:1–2 (2013), 107–51.

Minuzzi, S. *Il secolo di carta: Antonio Bosio artigiano di testi e immagini nella Venezia del Seicento*. Milan: FrancoAngeli, 2009.

Moatti, C. and W. Kaiser. 'Mobilità umana e circolazione culturale nel mediterraneo dall'età classica all'età moderna'. In Corti and Sanfilippo (eds), *Storia d'Italia. Annali 24: Migrazioni*, pp. 5–20.

Molà, L. and R. C. Mueller. 'Essere straniero a Venezia nel tardo medioevo: accoglienza e rifiuto nei privilegi di cittadinanza e nelle sentenze criminali'. In S. Cavaciocchi (ed.), *Le migrazioni in Europa, secc. XIII–XVIII*, pp. 839–51. Florence: Le Monnier, 1994.

Moro, G. 'Insegne librarie e marche tipografiche in un registro veneziano del '500'. *La Bibliofilía*, 91:1 (1989), 51–80.

Moschetti, A. 'Il Gobbo di Rialto e le sue relazioni con Pasquino'. *Nuovo archivio veneto*, 5:1 (1893), 5–93.

Motta, E. 'Uno stampatore del Lago Maggiore a Venezia'. *Bollettino storico della svizzera italiana*, 14:9–10 (1892), 199–200.

Mueller, R. C. *Immigrazione e cittidinanza nella Venezia medievale*. Rome: Viella, 2010.

Muir, E. *Civic Ritual in Renaissance Venice*. Princeton, NJ: Princeton University Press, 1981.

— *The Culture Wars of the Late Renaissance: Skeptics, Libertines and Opera*. Cambridge, MA and London: Harvard University Press, 2007.

Mussell, J. 'The passing of print'. *Media History*, 18:1 (2012), 77–92.

Myers, R., M. Harris and G. Mandelbrote, eds. *Fairs, Markets and the Itinerant Book Trade*. London: British Library, 2007.

Negrin, P. 'Licenze e privilegi di stampa a Venezia (1527–1550)'. *Tesi di laurea*, Università degli studi di Venezia, 1990–1.

Neerfeld, C. *Historia per forma di diaria: la cronachistica veneziana contemporanea a cavallo tra il Quattro e il Cinquecento*. Venice: Istituto Veneto di Scienze, Lettere ed Arti, 2006.

Niccoli, O. 'Un aspetto della propaganda religiosa nell'Italia del Cinquecento: opuscoli e fogli volanti'. In *Libri, idee e sentimenti religiosi*, pp. 29–37.

— *Prophecy and People in Renaissance Italy*. Translated by L. G. Cochrane. Princeton, NJ: Princeton University Press, 1990. First published in Italian 1987.

— *Rinascimento anticlericale. Infamia, propaganda e satira in Italia tra Quattro e Cinquecento*. Rome: Laterza, 2005.

— 'Italy'. In Raymond (ed.), *The Oxford History of Popular Print Culture*, pp. 187–95.

— 'Manoscritti, oralità, stampe popolari: viaggi dei testi profetici nell'Italia del Rinascimento'. *Italian Studies*, 66:2 (2011), 177–92.

Nicolini, B. 'Il frate osservante Bonaventura de Centi e il nunzio Fabio Minganelli. Episodio di vita religiosa veneziana'. In his *Aspetti della vita religiosa, politica e letteraria del Cinquecento*, pp. 59–83. Bologna: Tamari, 1963.

Noakes, S. 'The development of the book market in late Quattrocento Italy: Printers' failures and the role of the middleman'. *Journal of Medieval and Renaissance Studies*, 11:1 (1981), 23–55.

'Notizie: sul famoso libraio veneziano Gaspare Bindoni'. *La Bibliofilía*, 35:8–9 (1933), 359–60.

Novati, F. *Scritti sull'editoria popolare nell'Italia di antico regime*. Edited by E. Barbieri and A. Brambilla. Rome: Archivio Guido Izzi, 2004.

Nuovo, A. *Il commercio librario a Ferrara tra XV e XVI secolo. La bottega di Domenico Sivieri*. Florence: Olschki, 1998.

— *Il commercio librario nell'Italia del Rinascimento*. Milan: FrancoAngeli, 1998.

Nuovo, A. and C. Coppens. *I Giolito e la stampa nell'Italia del XVI secolo*. Geneva: Librairie Droz, 2005.

Ogborn, M. and C. W. J. Withers. 'Introduction: Book geography, book history'. In M. Ogborn and C. W. J. Withers (eds), *Geographies of the Book*, pp. 1–25. Farnham, UK and Burlington, VT: Ashgate, 2010.

Padoan, G. 'La commedia rinascimentale a Venezia dalla sperimentazione umanistica alla commedia "regolare"'. In G. Arnaldi and M. Pastore Stocchi (eds), *Storia della cultura veneta*, vol. 3, pt 2, pp. 377–465.

Page Moch, L. *Moving Europeans. Migration in Western Europe since 1650*. Bloomington, IN: Indiana University Press, 1992.

Palazzolo, M. I. 'Banchi, botteghe, muricciuoli. Luoghi e figure del commercio del libro a Roma nel Settecento'. In her *Editoria e istituzioni a Roma tra Settecento e Ottocento*, pp. 3–27. Rome: Archivio Guido Izzi, 1994.

Parker, D. 'Women in the book trade in Italy, 1475–1620'. *Renaissance Quarterly*, 49:3 (1996), 509–41.

Passavant, J. D. *Le peintre-graveur*. 6 vols. Leipzig: Weigel, 1864.

Pastorello, E. *Tipografi, editori, librai a Venezia nel secolo XVI*. Florence: Olschki, 1924.

Pavanini, P. 'Abitazioni popolari e borghesi nella Venezia cinquecentesca'. *Studi veneziani*, 5 (1981), 63–126.

Pesenti, G. 'Libri censurati a Venezia nei secoli XVI–XVII'. *La Bibliofilía*, 58:1 (1956), 15–30.

Petrella, G. '"Ad instantia d'Hippolito Ferrarese". Un cantimbanco editore nell'Italia del Cinquecento'. *Paratesto*, 8 (2011), 23–79.

— *Fra testo e immagine. Edizioni popolari del Rinascimento in una miscellanea ottocentesca*. Udine: Forum, 2009.

Petrucci, A. 'Alle origini del libro moderno. Libri da banco, libri da bisaccia, libretti da mano'. *Italia medioevale e umanistica*, 12 (1969), 295–313.

—, ed. *Libri, editori e pubblico nell'Europa moderna. Guida storica e critica*. Bari: Laterza, 1977.

Pettegree, A. *The Book in the Renaissance*. New Haven, CT and London: Yale University Press, 2010.

Picone, M. and L. Rubini, eds. *Il cantare italiano fra folklore e letteratura. Atti del convegno internazionale, Landesmuseum Zürich, 23–25 Giugno 2005*. Florence: Olschki, 2007.

Picot, É. 'La raccolta di poemetti italiani della Biblioteca di Chantilly'. *Rassegna bibliografica della letteratura italiana*, 2 (1894), 114–23, 154–67.

Pizzorusso, G. 'Le migrazioni degli italiani all'interno della penisola e in Europa in età moderna'. In A. Eiras Roel and D. L. González Lopo (eds), *Movilidad y migraciones internas en la Europa latina*, pp. 55–85. Santiago de Compostela: Universidad de Santiago de Compostela, 2002.

Plebani, T. *Il 'genere' dei libri. Storie e rappresentazioni della lettura al femminile e al maschile tra medioevo e età moderna*. Milan: FrancoAngeli, 2001.

— 'Voci tra le carte. Libri di canzone, leggere per cantare'. In Braida and Infelise (eds), *Libri per tutti*, pp. 56–75.

Pon, L. *Raphael, Durer and Marcantonio Raimondi: Copying and the Renaissance Print*. New Haven, CT: Yale University Press, 2004.

Potter, J. M. 'Nicolò Zoppino and the book-trade network of Perugia'. In Reidy (ed.), *The Italian Book*, pp. 135–59.

Premoli, B. *Spettacolo d'attori e cantastorie. Edizioni viterbesi del Seicento tra letteratura e tradizione popolare nella Biblioteca della Fondazione*. Rome: Fondazione Marco Besso, 1996.

Pullan, B. *Rich and Poor in Renaissance Venice*. Oxford: Blackwell, 1971.

— 'Poveri, mendicanti, e vagabondi (secoli XIV–XVII)'. In *Storia d'Italia. Annali. Vol. 1: Dal feudalismo al capitalismo*, pp. 981–1047. Turin: Einaudi, 1978.

Quondam, A. '"Mercanzia d'onore", "mercanzia d'utile". Produzione libraria e lavoro intellectuale a Venezia nel Cinquecento'. In Petrucci (ed.), *Libri, editori e pubblico*, pp. 51–104.

— 'Nel giardino dei Marcolini: un editore veneziano tra Aretino e Doni'. *Giornale storico della letteratura italiana*, 157 (1980), 75–116.

— 'La letteratura in tipografia'. In Asor Rosa (ed.), *Letteratura italiana*, vol. 2, pp. 555–686.

— 'La tipografia e il sistema dei generi. Il caso del romanzo cavalleresco'. In Hempfer (ed.), *Ritterepik der Renaissance*, pp. 1–13.

Rava, C. E. *Supplement à Max Sander*, Le Livre à figures italien de la Renaissance. Milan: Hoepli, 1969.

Raymond, J. *Pamphlets and Pamphleteering in Early Modern Britain*. Cambridge: Cambridge University Press, 2003.

— 'The origins of popular print culture'. In Raymond (ed.), *The Oxford History of Popular Print Culture*, pp. 1–14.

—, ed. *The Oxford History of Popular Print Culture*, vol. 1. Oxford: Oxford University Press, 2011.

Reidy, D. V. (ed.). *The Italian Book, 1465–1800. Studies Presented to Dennis E. Rhodes on His 70th Birthday*. London: British Library, 1993.

Reynolds, A. *Renaissance Humanism at the Court of Clement VII. Francesco Berni's Dialogue against Poets in Context*. New York and London: Garland, 1997.

Rhodes, D. 'Francesco detto il Faventino'. *Gutenberg Jahrbuch*, 52 (1977), 144–5.

— 'Fra Giovanni da Firenze e i suoi tipografi veneziani'. In his *Studies in Early Italian Printing*, pp. 6–13. London: Pindar, 1982.

— *Silent Printers: Anonymous Printing at Venice in the Sixteenth Century*. London: British Library, 1995.

— 'La battaglia di Lepanto e la stampa popolare a Venezia. Studio bibliografico'. *Miscellanea marciana*, 10–11 (1995–96), 9–63.

Richardson, B. 'Dialects and standard language in Renaissance printing and editing'. *Journal of the Institute of Romance Studies*. Supplement 1: *Italian Dialects and Literature from the Renaissance to the Present* (1996), 7–22.

— 'The debates on printing in Renaissance Italy'. *La Bibliofilía*, 100 (1998), 135–55.

— 'Print or pen? Modes of written publication in sixteenth-century Italy'. *Italian Studies*, 59 (2004), 39–64.
— *Print Culture in Renaissance Italy: The Editor and the Vernacular Text, 1470–1600*. Cambridge and New York: Cambridge University Press, 2004.
— *Manuscript Culture in Renaissance Italy*. Cambridge: Cambridge University Press, 2009.
Roggero, M. *L'alfabeto conquistato. Apprendere e insegnare nell'Italia tra sette e ottocento*. Bologna: Il Mulino, 1999.
— *Le carte piene di sogni. Testi e lettori in età moderna*. Bologna: Il Mulino, 2006.
— 'I libri di cavalleria'. In Braida and Infelise (eds), *Libri per tutti*, pp. 23–41.
Rollison, D. 'Exploding England: the dialectics of mobility and settlement in early modern England'. *Social History* 24:1 (1999), 1–16.
Romano, D. *Patricians and* Popolani: *The Social Foundations of the Venetian Renaissance State*. Baltimore, MD: Johns Hopkins University Press, 1987.
— 'The gondola as a marker of station in Venetian society'. *Renaissance Studies*, 8:4 (1994), 359–74.
Rospocher, M. 'Propaganda e opinione pubblica: Giulio II nella comunicazione politica europea'. *Annali dell'Istituto Storico Italo-germanico in Trento*, 33 (2007), 117–57.
— 'Versi pericolosi? Controllo delle opinioni e ricerca del consenso nelle guerre d'Italia'. In D. Ramada Curto *et al.* (eds), *From Florence to the Mediterranean and Beyond: Essays in Honour of Anthony Molho*, vol. 1, pp. 394–402. Florence: Olschki, 2009.
— '"Non vedete la libertà di voi stessi essere posta nelle proprie mani vostre?" Guerre di scritture e cambi di regime al tempo di Cambrai'. In M. Bonazza and S. Seidel Menchi (eds), *Dal leone all'aquila. Comunità, territori e cambi di regime nell'età di Massimiliano I* (Rovereto: Accademia roveretana degli Agiati-Edizioni Osiride, 2012), pp. 127–47.
Rossi, V. 'Su, su, su chi vuol la gatta'. *Giornale storico della letteratura italiana*, 5 (1885), 504–7.
— 'Di un cantastorie ferrarese del secolo XVI'. *Rassegna emiliana*, 2 (1890), 435–46.
Rossini, G. 'Ulteriori notizie su la cartiera, i librai e le prime stampe faentine'. *Studi romagnoli*, 7 (1956), 283–92.
Rothstein, M. 'Disjunctive images in Renaissance books'. *Renaissance and Reformation*, 14:2 (1990), 101–20.
Rouse, M. A. and R. H. Rouse. Cartolai, *Illuminators, and Printers in Fifteenth-Century Italy*. Los Angeles: Department of Special Collections, University Research Library, University of California, 1988.
Rozzo, U. *Linee per una storia dell'editoria religiosa in Italia (1465–1600)*. Udine: Arti Grafiche Friulane, 1993.
— 'Il presunto "omicidio rituale" di Simonino di Trento e il primo santo tipografico'. *Atti dell'Accademia Udinese di Scienze, Lettere e Arti*, 90 (1997), 185–223.
— 'La battaglia di Lepanto nell'editoria dell'epoca e una miscellanea fontaniniana'. *Rara volumina*, 1–2 (2000), 41–69.
— 'Italian literature on the Index'. In Fragnito (ed.), *Church, Censorship and Culture*, pp. 194–222.
— 'Pietro Perna colportore, libraio, tipografo ed editore tra Basilea e l'Italia'. *Bibliotheca. Rivista di studi bibliografici*, 1 (2004), 46–64.
— 'I fogli volanti a stampa e censura libraria nel secolo XVI'. In V. Bonani, G. G. Cicco and A. M. Vitale (eds), *Dal torchio alle fiamme. Inquisizione e censura. Atti del convegno*

    nazionale di studi (Salerno 2004), pp. 51–80. Salerno: Biblioteca provinciale di Salerno, 2005.
— *La letteratura italiana negli indici del Cinquecento*. Udine: Forum, 2005.
— 'La letteratura italiana all'indice'. In Rozzo, *La letteratura italiana negli indici*, pp. 11–71.
— *La strage ignorata: I fogli volanti a stampa nell'Italia dei secoli XV e XVI*. Udine: Forum, 2008.
Rozzo, U. and S. Seidel Menchi. 'The book and the Reformation in Italy'. In J.-F. Gilmont (ed.), *The Reformation and the Book*, pp. 319–68. Aldershot, UK: Ashgate, 1998.
Rubini, L. 'Fiabe in ottava rima: il cantare fiabesco a stampa (1475–1530)'. In Picone and Rubini (eds), *Il cantare italiano*, pp. 413–40.
Rusconi, R. '"Confessio generalis": Opuscoli per la pratica penitenziale nei primi cinquant'anni dalla introduzione della stampa'. In Società internazionale di studi francescani (ed.), *I frati minori tra '400 e '500: Atti del xii convegno internazionale, Assisi, 18-19-20 ottobre 1984*, pp. 189–227. Assisi: Università di Perugia, Centro di studi Francescani, 1986.
— 'Pratica culturale ed istruzione religiosa nelle confraternite italiane del tardo medioevo: "libri di compagnia" e libri di pietà'. In *Le mouvement confraternel au Moyen Age: France, Italie, Suisse*, pp. 133–53. Geneva: Droz, 1987.
Salman, J. 'Peddling in the past: Dutch itinerant bookselling in a European perspective'. *Publishing History*, 53 (2003), 5–21.
— 'Watching the pedlar's movements: Itinerant distribution in the urban Netherlands'. In Myers, Harris and Mandelbrote (eds), *Fairs, Markets and the Itinerant Book Trade*, pp. 137–58.
Salzberg, R. 'In the mouths of charlatans: street performers and the dissemination of pamphlets in Renaissance Italy'. *Renaissance Studies*, 24:5 (2010), 638–53.
— 'Masculine republics: Establishing authority in the early modern Venetian printshop'. In S. Broomhall and J. Van Gent (eds), *Governing Masculinities in the Early Modern Period*, pp. 47–64. Farnham, UK: Ashgate, 2011.
— '"Selling stories and many other things in and through the city": Peddling print in sixteenth-century Florence and Venice'. *Sixteenth Century Journal*, 42:3 (2011), 737–59.
Salzberg, R. and M. Rospocher. 'The evanescent public sphere: voices, spaces, and publics in Venice during the Italian wars'. In M. Rospocher (ed.), *Beyond the Public Sphere: Opinions, Publics, Spaces in Early Modern Europe (XVI–XVIII)*, pp. 93–114. Bologna and Berlin: Il Mulino/Duncker & Humblot, 2012.
— 'Street singers in Italian Renaissance culture and communication'. *Cultural and Social History*, 9:1 (2012), 9–26.
San Juan, R. M. *Rome: A City Out of Print*. Minneapolis, MN: University of Minnesota Press, 2001.
Sandal, E. '"Folli da papir" e "merchantia de libri". Il caso della Riviera di Salò'. In A. Nuovo and E. Sandal (eds), *Il libro nell'Italia del Rinascimento*, pp. 163–95. Brescia: Grafo, 1998.
—, ed. *Il mestier de le stamperie e dei libri. Le vicende e i percorsi dei tipografi di Sabbio Chiese tra Cinque e Seicento e l'opera dei Nicolini*. Brescia: Grafo, 2002.
Sander, M. *Le Livre à figures italien depuis 1467 jusqu'à 1530: essai de sa bibliographie et de son histoire*. 5 vols. Nendeln, Liechtenstein: Kraus Reprint, 1969.

— 'La mobilità dei mestieri del libro: caratteristiche e valenze'. In Santoro and Segatori (eds), *Mobilità dei mestieri del libro*, pp. 285–97.
Santoro, M. and S. Segatori, eds. *Mobilità dei mestieri del libro tra Quattrocento e Seicento: Convegno internazionale, Roma, 14–16 marzo 2012*. Pisa and Rome: Fabrizio Serra, 2013.
Sapori, G. 'Giuliano de' Ricci e la polemica sulla stampa nel Cinquecento'. *Nuova rivista storica*, 56 (1972), 151–64.
Scholderer, V. 'Printing at Venice to the end of 1481'. In his *Fifty Essays in Fifteenth- and Sixteenth-Century Bibliography*. Edited by D. E. Rhodes, pp. 74–89. Amsterdam: Hertzberger, 1966.
Schulz, A. M. 'Giovanni Andrea Valvassore and his family in four unpublished testaments'. In *Artes atque humaniora. Studia Stanislao Mossakowski sexagenario dicata*, pp. 117–25. Warsaw: Instytut Sztuki Polskiej Akademii Nauk, 1998.
Schutte, A. J. *Printed Italian Vernacular Religious Books, 1465–1550: A Finding List*. Geneva: Droz, 1983.
— 'Teaching adults to read in sixteenth-century Venice: Giovanni Antonio Tagliente's *Libro maistrevole*'. *Sixteenth Century Journal*, 17:1 (1986), 3–16.
Scribner, R. W. 'Oral culture and the diffusion of Reformation ideas'. In his *Popular Culture and Popular Movements in Reformation Germany*, pp. 49–69. London: Hambledon, 1987.
— *For the Sake of the Simple Folk: Popular Propaganda for the German Reformation*. Oxford: Clarendon Press, 1994; first published 1981.
Segarizzi, A, ed. *Bibliografia delle stampe popolari italiane della R. Biblioteca nazionale di San Marco di Venezia*. Bergamo: Istituto Italiano d'Arti Grafiche, 1913.
— 'Un calligrafo milanese'. *Ateneo veneto*, 3:1 (1909), 63–77.
Seidel Menchi, S. 'Le traduzioni italiane di Lutero nella prima metà del Cinquecento'. *Rinascimento*, 17 (1977), 31–108.
— *Erasmo in Italia, 1520–1580*. Turin: Bollati Boringhieri, 1987.
Serra-Zanetti, A. *L'arte della stampa in Bologna nel primo ventennio del Cinquecento*. Bologna: Alle spese del Comune, 1959.
Severi, L. *Sitibondo nel stampar de' libri: Niccolò Zoppino tra libro volgare, letteratura cortigiana e questione della lingua*. Manziana: Vecchiarelli, 2009.
Shaw, J. E. *The Justice of Venice. Authorities and Liberties in the Urban Economy, 1550–1700*. Oxford: Oxford University Press for the British Academy, 2006.
Shemek, D. 'Books at banquet: Commodities, canon and culture in Giulio Cesare Croce's *Convito universale*'. *Annali d'italianistica*, 16 (1998), 85–101.
Short-Title Catalogue of Books Printed in Italy and of Italian books Printed in Other Countries from 1465 to 1600 Now in the British Library. London: British Library, 1958.
Simpson, Y. F. 'Unmasking the revels: medium and message in the popular music culture of sixteenth-century Venice'. Ph.D. dissertation, Royal Holloway, University of London, 2004.
Spini, G. *Tra Rinascimento e Riforma: Antonio Brucioli*. Florence: La Nuova Italia, 1940.
Spufford, M. *Small Books and Pleasant Histories: Popular Fiction and Its Readership in Seventeenth-Century England*. Cambridge: Cambridge University Press, 1985; first published 1981.
Stallybrass, P. '"Little Jobs": broadsides and the printing revolution'. In Baron, Lindquist and Shevlin (eds), *Agent of Change*, pp. 315–41.

Stermole, K. K. 'Venetian art and the war of the League of Cambrai (1509–17)'. Ph.D. dissertation, Queen's University, Ontario, 2007.

Stevens, K. M. 'Printers, publishers and booksellers in Counter-Reformation Milan: a documentary study'. Ph.D. dissertation, University of Wisconsin-Madison, 1992.

— 'Vincenzo Girardone and the popular press in Counter-Reformation Milan: A case study (1570)'. *Sixteenth Century Journal*, 26:3 (1995), 639–59.

Stevens, K. M. and P. F. Gehl. 'Cheap print: a look inside the Lucini–Sirtori stationary shop at Milan (1597–1613)'. *La Bibliofilía*, 92:3 (2010), 281–327.

Sullivan, G. and L. Woodbridge. 'Popular culture in print'. In A. Kinney (ed.), *The Cambridge Companion to English Literature 1500–1600*, pp. 265–86. Cambridge: Cambridge University Press, 2000.

Tafuri, M., ed. *'Renovatio urbis'. Venezia nell'eta di Andrea Gritti (1523–1538)*. Rome: Officina edizioni, 1984.

Tassini, G. *Curiosità veneziane, ovvero origini delle denominazioni stradali di Venezia*. Revised edn. Edited by L. Moretti. Venice: Filippi, 1970.

Tenenti, A. and U. Tucci, eds. *Storia di Venezia dalle origini alla caduta della Serenissima. Vol. 5: Il Rinascimento: società ed economia*. Rome: Istituto della Enciclopedia Italiana, 1996.

Von Tippelskirch, X. 'Lettrici e lettori sospetti davanti al tribunale dell'Inquisizione nella Venezia post-tridentina'. *Mélanges de l'école française de Rome: Italie et méditerranée* 115:1 (2003), 315–44.

Ulvioni, P. 'Stampa e censura a Venezia nel Seicento'. *Archivio veneto*, 104 (1972), 45–93.

— 'Stampatori e librai a Venezia nel Seicento'. *Archivio veneto*, 108 (1977), 93–124.

Valenti, C. *Comici artigiani. Mestiere e forme dello spettacolo a Siena nella prima metà del Cinquecento*. Ferrara: Panini, 1992.

Van den Heuvel, D. 'Selling in the shadows: peddlers and hawkers in early modern Europe'. In M. van der Linden and L. Lucassen (eds), *Working on Labour: Essays in Honour of Jan Lucassen*, pp. 125–51. Leiden and Boston, MA: Brill, 2012.

Van der Sman, G. J. 'Print publication in Venice in the second half of the sixteenth century'. *Print Quarterly*, 17 (2000), 235–47.

Venezia e la peste, 1348–1797 (Venice: Marsilio, 1979).

Vianello, D. *L'arte del buffone. Maschere e spettacolo tra Italia e Baviera nel XVI secolo*. Rome: Bulzoni, 2005.

Vidossi, G. 'La cantata del Rado Stizzoso'. *Lares*, 26:3–4 (1960), 123–8.

Villoresi, M. *La fabbrica dei cavalieri. Cantari, poemi, romanzi in prosa fra medioevo e Rinascimento*. Rome: Salerno, 2005.

— 'Zanobi della Barba, canterino ed editore del rinascimento'. In Picone and Rubini (eds), *Il cantare italiano*, pp. 461–73.

Waddington, R. B. *Aretino's Satyr: Sexuality, Satire, and Self-Projection in Sixteenth-Century Literature and Art*. Toronto: University of Toronto Press, 2004.

Wagner, K. and M. Carrera. *Catalogo dei libri a stampa in lingua italiana della Biblioteca Colombina di Siviglia / Catalogo de los impresos en lengua italiana de la Biblioteca Colombina de Sevilla*. Ferrara: Panini, 1991.

Watt, T. *Cheap Print and Popular Piety 1550–1640*. Cambridge: Cambridge University Press, 1991.

Welch, E. *Shopping in the Renaissance: Consumer Cultures in Italy 1400–1600*. New Haven, CT: Yale University Press, 2005.

— 'Lotteries in early modern Italy'. *Past and Present*, 199:1 (2008), pp. 71–111.
Wilhelm, R. *Italienische flugschriften des cinquecento (1500–1550). Gattungsgeschichte und sprachgeschichte*. Tübingen: Niemeyer, 1996.
Wilson, Blake. *Singing Poetry in Renaissance Florence: The* Cantasi come *Tradition (1375–1550)*. Florence: Olschki, 2009.
Wilson, Bronwen. *The World in Venice: Print, the City and Early Modern Identity*. Toronto: University of Toronto Press, 2005.
Wiseman, S. '"Popular culture": a category for analysis?'. In M. Dimmock and A. Hadfield (eds), *Literature and Popular Culture in Early Modern England*, pp. 15–28. Farnham, UK: Ashgate, 2009.
Witcombe, C. L. C. E. *Copyright in the Renaissance: Prints and the* Privilegio *in Sixteenth-Century Venice and Rome*. Leiden: Brill, 2004.
— *Print Publishing in Sixteenth Century Rome: Growth and Expansion, Rivalry and Murder*. Turnhout: Brepols, 2008.
Woodward, D. *Maps as Prints in the Italian Renaissance: Makers, Distributors and Consumers*. London: British Library, 1996.
Würzbach, N. *The Rise of the English Street Ballad, 1550–1650*. Translated by G. Walls. Cambridge: Cambridge University Press, 1990. First published in German 1981.
Yachnin, P. and B. Wilson, eds. *Making Publics in Early Modern Europe: People, Things, Forms of Knowledge*. New York: Routledge, 2009.
Zannini, A. 'Il "pregiudizio meccanico" a Venezia in età moderna. Significato e trasformazione di una frontier sociale'. In M. Meriggi and A. Pastore (eds), *Le regole dei mestieri e delle professioni (secoli XV–XIX)*, pp. 36–51. Milan: FrancoAngeli, 2000.
— 'L'identità multipla: Essere popolo in una capitale (Venezia, sec. xvi–xviii)'. *Ricerche storiche*, 32:2–3 (2002), 247–62.
— *Venezia, città aperta. Gli stranieri e la Serenissima XIV–XVIII sec*. Venice: Marcianum, 2009.
Zorzi, M. 'Stampatori tedeschi a Venezia'. In his *Venezia e la Germania*, pp. 115–40. Milan: Electa, 1986.
— 'La circolazione del libro a Venezia nel Cinquecento: biblioteche private e pubbliche'. *Ateneo veneto*, 28 (1990), 117–90.
—, ed. *La vita nei libri. Edizioni illustrate a stampa del Quattro e Cinquecento dalla Fondazione Giorgio Cini*. Venice: Edizioni della Laguna, 2003.

Index

Note: 'n.' after a page reference indicates the number of a note on that page. Literary works can be found under author's name.

Aleandro, Girolamo (nuncio) 46n.85, 117, 151n.21
Altissimo (street singer) 83, 94n.58, 96n.76
Ancona 79
anonymous printing *see* cheap print, anonymity of
Aretino, Pietro 18, 33, 43n.61, 56, 63, 98, 112, 118, 134, 142
    author of *Marfisa* 102, *103*
Ariosto, Ludovico 83, 85, 101, 102, 104, 112, 118, 121n.21
    author of *Orlando Furioso*
        imitations of 23, 100–1
        parodies of 102, 104
        performance of 100–1
Arte dei medici e speziali (Florentine guild) 82
avvisi see news, *avvisi*

Baldacchini, Lorenzo 92n.40
Ballarin, Tomaso (printer) 68n.37
Bartolomeo da Sabbio (street seller) 56, 87, 145
barzellette see songs and singing
Bergamo 7
Bernardino of Siena 104
Bianchino del Leone, Cosimo (printer) 94n.58
Bibliothèque bleue 119

Bindoni family (printers) 75, 76–8, 89, 117, 136
Bindoni, Agostino 53, 77, 127n.102, 138, 139
Bindoni, Agostino the younger 78
Bindoni, Alessandro 36, 77, 80
Bindoni, Benedetto 53, 77
Bindoni, Bernardino 67n.31, 77, 78, 136
Bindoni, Francesco 53, 77, 78, 83, 110, 121n.19
Bindoni, Francesco the younger 78
Bindoni, Gaspare 78
Bindoni, Giovan Antonio 136, 138
Bindoni, Orsia (widow of Alessandro) 77
Bindoni, Stefano 166n.31
Bini, Luca (printer) 94n.58
blasphemy *see* Esecutori contro la bestemmia
blind singers 59, 82, 88, 104, 165n.20
    see also street singers
Boccaccio, Giovanni 118, 153n.64
Bologna 79, 85, 111, 138, 145
Bongi, Salvatore 93n.48
bookselling 31, 32, 34–5, 49–50, 55
    see also manuscripts, trade in; street selling of print
books of secrets 110–12
    see also cheap print, medical or scientific

Bordogna, Sigismondo (publisher and bookseller) 55
Borromeo, Carlo 117
Brescia 75, 85, 91n.28, 105, 106, *107*, 120n.16, 138
Britti, Paolo (street singer) 88
Brucioli, Antonio 37
bulls *see* papal bulls

cantastorie see street singers
cantimbanco see street singers
cartolai 42n.29, 50, 145
  see also manuscripts, trade in
Catholic Reformation
  impact on print production 10–11, 104, 117–18, 130, 142–3, 163
  use of press to support 117–18
  see also censorship
Celebrino, Eustachio 24, *27*, 36, 111, 114, *115*, 116
censorship
  calls for increased 37, 117, 129, 133
  involvement of Roman Church in 132–3, 139, 162
  of anti-clerical works 131, 135–6
  of bawdy or risqué works 1–2, 37, 57, 132, 134, 135, 138–9, 141, 142, 162, 163
  of political material and news 6–7, 80, 109, 131, 143
  of religious material 114, 117–18, 129–30, 133–5, 136, 141–2, 158, 160
  see also Catholic Reformation; Esecutori contro la bestemmia; Holy Office; Indices of Prohibited Books; licensing of print; news-poems, control of; printers and publishers, questioning of; street selling of print, control of
charlatans, medical *22*, 33–4, 35, 61, 86, 98, 112–13, 116, 145, 161
  and promotional use of print 61, 62, 111–12
  parodies of 104, 113, 160, 165n.12
  supervision of 112, 113, 147–8
  see also cheap print, medical or scientific; street performance; street singers

Chartier, Roger 64
cheap print
  advertising of 21, 24, 33–4, 36, 49, 56, 57, 58, 62, 98, 110, 116
  anonymity of 82–3, 134, 143
  as *libri comuni* 131
  common genres of 19, 99
  debates about 8, 19, 29–38 *passim*
  definition of 19–20
  illustration of 21, 24, 102, 110, 114
  importance in business strategies 3, 5, 77
  in Europe 7, 162
  language of 86
  material form of 21, 28
  medical or scientific 24, 36, 110–12, 113, 160, 161
  performance of 6, 24, 58–9, 61, 64, 79, 98–9, 100–2, 104, 105–6, 108, 109, 116, 135, 139
  poverty as theme of 88
  prices of 20, 28
  print runs of 40n.20
  public for 9, 13n.14, 20, 21, 24, 36, 64, 118–19, 161, 163
  religious or devotional 5, 21, *22*, 36–7, 57, 77, 113–14, *115*, 116–18, 134, 158, *159*, 160, 163
  sources for studying 8
  survival of 3, 126n.87, 164
  see also Bibliothèque bleue; books of secrets; chivalric tales; indulgences; *libri da risma*; news-poems; orations, printed; papal bulls; street selling of print
chivalric tales 23, 100–2, *103*, 104
  close relation to news-poems 105
  suspicion of 104, 134
  see also Ariosto, Lodovico
Church, Roman *see* Catholic Reformation; censorship, involvement of Roman Church in; Holy Office; indulgences; papal bulls
Clario, Benedetto (street singer) 94n.52
Colòn, Hernan 9, 20, 109
Colonna, Vittoria 85, 118
Comin da Trino (printer) 75

commedia dell'arte 83, 88
confraternities *see* printers and publishers, membership of confraternities
Coppa, Iacopo (charlatan) 83, 98, 112, 113, 118, 148
copyright legislation 7, 130–1
  see also licenses to print
Coryate, Thomas 61
Council of Ten 6, 7, 19, 55, 57, 64, 129, 131, 133, 135, 141, 143, 144
Council of Trent 117
courtesans *see* prostitutes
crime *see* murder
Cristoforo, 'il cieco da Forlì' (poet) 104
Croce, Giulio Cesare (street singer) 38, 122n.31
cultural mobility 99

Danza, Paolo 63, 81, 90n.12, 91n.20–1, *107*
Da Porto, Luigi 74
Dati, Giuliano 37, 114, 116
De' Barbari, Jacopo 47, *48*
De' Farri family (printers) 78
  De' Farri, Domenico 143, 161
  De' Farri, Pietro 143, 158, *159*
De' Franceschi family (printers) 53, 78, 139
  De' Franceschi, Domenico 75, 83, 138, 153n.53
  De' Franceschi, Pietro 165n.18
Degli Agostini, Nicolò 93n.44
De' Grassi, Latino (charlatan) 112
Della Barba, Zanobi (publisher and street singer) 81
Della Casa, Giovanni (nuncio) 133
Della Rotonda, Perosino (street singer) 63
Della Speranza, Zuan (printer) 139
De' Madiis, Francesco (bookseller) 20, 161
De' Ricci, Giuliano 32, 41n.45
De Saggion, Antonio (street seller) 143
De Strata, Filippo 29, 33, 74
De Vivo, Filippo 40n.19
Domenichi, Lodovico 37
Domenico di Francesco (charlatan) 145
Doni, Anton Francesco 31, 32, 34, 35, 37, 38, 44n.68, 77, 113

Dooley, Brendan 123n.56
Dragoncino, Giovan Battista 33
Dürer, Albrecht 56

Eamon, William 124n.71
Eisenstein, Elizabeth 4, 28
Erasmus of Rotterdam 30–1, 32, 73, 117, 127n.102
Esecutori contro la bestemmia 1, 56, 98, 132, 133, 135, 136, 138, 141, 142, 143, 148

Faelli, Giovan Battista (printer) 94n.58
Faentino, Baldassare (street singer) 83, 94n.52, 102, 111
Faentino, Francesco (street singer) 1, 2, 37, 83, 118, 135
Faentino, Romano *detto il* (street singer) 120n.18
Farina, Antonio (singer) 82
Ferrara 7, 79, 80, 84, 96n.77, 98, 112, 145
Ferrarese, Ippolito (street singer) 16n.51, *23*, 24, *25*, 83, 84–6, 89, 94n.58, 101, 102, *103*, 106, 108, 116, 118, 121n.19, 121n.21, 132
Fioravanti, Leonardo 35
Florence 49, 55, 79, 82, 96n.77, 113, 114, 125n.78, 138
Folengo, Teofilo, author of *Baldo* 80
Fondaco dei Tedeschi 51
Fontaneto da Monferrato, Guglielmo (printer) 2, 53, 75, 76, 83
Fortunato (performer) 118
Francesco da Firenze (singer) 82
Franco, Niccolò 1, 18, 33, 34–5, 37, 38, 106, 110
Fratta, Giovanni 42n.54
frottole see songs and singing
Furlan, Nicolò (street seller) 145
Furlano, Battista (street seller) 55, 158
Furlano, Leonardo (charlatan) *22*, 83, 85, 94n.58, 111, 116, 120n.19

Garzoni, Tomaso 31, 32, 35, 54, 61
Gentilcore, David 112
Giacomo da Trino (street seller) 55, 87

Giolito, Gabriele 74, 90n.12, 142
Giovanni da Firenze 36, 116
Giovanni di Giorgio *veneto* (street singer) 88
Giunta, Giovan Maria 91n.21
Giunta, Luc'Antonio 77
Giunta, Tomaso 2, 91n.21, 144
Giustinian, Leonardo 20
Giustiniani family 53
Giustizia Vecchia 57, 94n.53, 141
Gobbo (statue at Rialto) 63, 138
Grendler, Paul F. 20, 21, 102
guerre in ottava rima see news-poems
guild of printers and booksellers, Venice 10, 78, 82, 87, 129, 144–7, 148
   and attempts to control street selling 58, 82, 87, 145–6
   restriction of membership 145
   see also Arte dei medici e speziali (Florentine guild)
Gutenberg, Johannes 3, 5

hawking *see* cheap print, advertising of; street selling of print
Health Board *see* Provveditori alla Sanità
Henry III, King of France 64, 109
Holy Office (Venetian branch) 51, 55, 57, 64, 87, 135, 138, 139, 141, 142, 148, 149, 158, 160
   see also censorship
Horodowich, Elizabeth 132

illustration *see* cheap print, illustration of; printed images
imprimaturs *see* licenses to print
Indices of Prohibited Books 38, 87, 133–4, 135
indulgences 3, 5, 40n.20, 63, 113, 160
Inquisition *see* Holy Office
Interdict crisis (1606–7) 40n.19, 110, 162–3
Italian Wars 5, 105
   see also War of the League of Cambrai

Jenson, Nicholas 5, 74
John of Speyer 29, 76, 130
Julius II, pope 5, 106

lamenti 25, 57, 84, 85, 86, 88, 95n.70, 97n.87, 105, 106–7, 108, 109, 117, 138, 165n.20
Landi, Giovanni (printer) 94n.58
Lando, Ortensio 127n.102, 136
Lauto, Paolo (street seller) 160
Lepanto, Battle of (1571) 64, 109, 161
libels *see* pasquinades
libri comuni see cheap print, as *libri comuni*
libri da risma 28, 162
licenses to print (imprimaturs) 1, 56, 78, 131, 133, 135, 138, 139, 141, 142–3, 158, 161
Lion, Angelo (scribe) 51
Lirico, Giovan Maria (performer) 111
literacy 9–10, 64, 116
   works instructing in 111
Lowry, Martin 82, 161
Lupetino, Fra Baldo 64, 136
Luther, Martin 117

mal francese see syphilis
Mantelli, Iseppo (street seller) 160
Mantoan, Paris *detto il Fortunato* (performer) 123n.47, 136, *137*
Mantovano, Stefano (charlatan) 142
manuscript circulation
   interaction with print 7, 50, 64
   of illicit material 63, 132, 143, 163
   of political material and news 6, 53, 109, 143
   social aspects of 24, 33
   see also news, *avvisi*
manuscripts, trade in 49–50
   see also bookselling; *cartolai*
Manuzio, Aldo 5, 30, 31, 74
maps *see* printed images
Marcolini, Francesco 33
Marescotti, Giorgio (printer) 55
massare (housekeepers) 59, *60*
Maximilian I, Holy Roman Emperor 6
medical works *see* books of secrets; cheap print, medical or scientific
Menocchio (Domenico Scandella) 9
migrants, parodies of language *26*, 104, 119, 139

migration
    and citizenship 75
    and mobility 73, 79
    control of 74–5, 147–8
    to Venice 8–9, 18, 47, 51–2, 74–5, 87
    see also printers and publishers, migration of; street singers, mobility of
Milan 7, 79, 85, 138, 145
Minganelli, Fabio (nuncio) 133
Mitelli, Giuseppe Maria 109
mountebanks see charlatans, medical; street singers
murder 5, 88, 136, *137*
music see songs and singing; street performance; street singers

Naples 18, 112
Negroponte 5, 105
news
    avvisi (newssheets) 53, 109, 136
    circulation of 5, 62–4
    -poems (*guerre in ottava rima*) 77, 104–6, *107*, 108–10
    control of 109–10
    see also censorship of political material and news; manuscript circulation of political material and news
Nicolini da Sabbio family (printers) 53, 80, 90n.12
Nicolini da Sabbio, Niccolò 91n.21
Novati, Francesco 93n.48
Nuovo, Angela 50

Ochino, Bernardino 117, 133
oral culture
    and spread of religious reform 132
    interaction with print 4, 6, 64, 84, 99, 104
    see also cheap print, performance of; songs and singing; street performance
orations, printed 20, 28, 82, 84, 114, 116, 134, 141, 143, 158, *159*, 160, 161
    see also cheap print, religious or devotional
Oriolo, Bartolomeo 101

Padovano, Giovanni (printer) 2, 80, 83, 128n.111
Padua 6, 52, 91n.28, 136
Pagan, Matteo (printer) 67n.31, 138, 139, *140*
Paganini, Paganino (printer) 76
Paganino, Alessandro (printer) 76
Paganino, Anna (sister of Alessandro) 76
Paola (widow of John of Speyer) 76
papal bulls 5, 6, 113
Parma 85
parody see migrants, parodies of language
Pasini, Maffeo (printer) 53, 77, 78, 83, 110, 121n.19
pasquinades 63
Pasquino (statue in Rome) 138
Pastore, Damonfido (performer) 96n.76, 127n.102
pedlars, peddling see street selling of print
Perugia 79
Pesaro 75, 79, 85
Piazza San Marco see Venice, Piazza San Marco
Pincio, Aurelio (printer) 68n.37
Pius V, pope 141
plague (of 1575–77) 109, 145, 147, 158, *159*, 160–1
poligrafi 35, 100, 106
political communication see censorship of political material and news; manuscript circulation of political material and news; news
poverty see cheap print, poverty as theme of; street selling of print, and poverty
printed images 5, 12n.14, 47, 53, 56, 63–4, 114, 139, 142, 160
printers and publishers
    attitudes towards 31–2
    collaboration with street singers and sellers 2, 55, 82, 83, 145, 158
    locations of shops 51–4, 75
    membership of confraternities (*scuole*) 76
    migration of 51–2, 53, 73–6, 77, 79
    questioning of 138–9

social networks of 54, 75–6, 80–1, 144
status of 30, 31
women in families 76, 77
see also guild of printers and booksellers, Venice
Priuli, Girolamo 6, 74, 106
privilegi see copyright legislation
Procurators of San Marco 83, 147
prognostication and prophecy 19, 54, 57, 105, 116, 139, *140*, 160
prostitutes 56, 63, 98, 111, 139, *140*, 141
Protestant Reformation 10, 132, 162
 and spread of reformist ideas in Italy 36–7, 78, 81, 112, 117, 129–30, 132–4
 see also censorship; oral culture and spread of religious reform; vernacular translations, and religious reform
Provveditori alla Sanità 61, 83, 112, 147, 160, 161
Provveditori di Comun 87, 146

Raimondi, Marc'Antonio 56
Rampazetto, Francesco (printer) 145
Ravenna 79, 136, *137*
Raymond, Joad 4
readers
 appeals to less experienced 36
 attitudes towards less experienced 32, 34
 women as 35, 36
 see also cheap print, public for
recipe books *see* books of secrets; cheap print, medical or scientific
religious reform *see* Catholic Reformation; oral culture and spread of religious reform; Protestant Reformation; vernacular translations, and religious reform
religious works *see* cheap print, religious or devotional; indulgences; orations, printed; papal bulls
Remondini press 28, 163
Rialto *see* Venice, Rialto Bridge and market area
Richardson, Brian 34

Riformatori dello studio di Padova 150n.12
Rimondo di Zuan of Bergamo (street seller) 145
Ripoli press, Florence 40n.20, 82, 83, 84, 114
Riviera di Salò 75
Rocca, Francesco (bookseller) 55
Romano, Giulio 142
Rome 18, 56, 111, 112, 138, 145
Ruffinelli, Venturino (printer) 11n.5, 83
Rusconi, Daria (daughter of Giorgio) 76
Rusconi, Giorgio (printer) 53, 76, 80

Sabellico, Marc'Antonio 50
Salernitano, Masuccio 118
Sansovino, Jacopo 52
Santoro, Marco 89n.4
Sant'Uffizio *see* Holy Office
Sanudo, Marin 9, 20, 50, 52, 56, 62, 63, 71n.74, 96n.76
satire *see* migrants, parodies of language
Savioni, Pasqualin 145, 146 (musician)
Savonarola, Girolamo 36
Scribner, Robert W. 127n.105
scuole (confraternities) *see* printers and publishers, membership of confraternities
Senate, Venetian 6, 28, 130, 146
Sensa (Ascension fair) 57, 63
servants *see massare* (housekeepers)
Sessa, Melchiore 2, 53, 75, 76, 144
Simon of Trent 5
Sommariva, Giorgio 6
songs and singing 1, 6–7, 9, 19, 20, *26*, 56, 57, 58–9, *60*, 61, 63, 67n.29, 79–80, 85–6, 88, 98, 101, 105–6, 108–9, 117, 132, 133, 134, 139, 142, 161, 163
stallholders *see* street sellers; street selling of print
Stallybrass, Peter 3
stationers *see cartolai*
street performance
 control of 61, 83, 112, 147
 locations of 59, 61, *62*
 times of 59

street performance (*cont.*)
  see also charlatans, medical; cheap print, performance of; songs and singing; street singers
street performers see blind singers; charlatans, medical; street singers
street sellers see street selling of print
street selling of print 1, 6, 7–9, 21, 24, 28, 33, 50–1, 54–9, 61, 64, 65, 81–2, 84, 86–9, 108, 109, 114, 119, 142, 143, 145–8, 158–9, 160, 162
  alongside other goods 81
  and poverty 58, 78, 86–8
  and spread of religious reform 117
  attitudes towards 33–4
  by young boys 56, 142
  control of 57–8, 87, 135, 136, 141–2, 145, 146–7
  locations of 55–7
  on feast days (*feste*) 55, 57–8, 87, 141
  times of 57–8
  see also bookselling; cheap print, advertising of
street singers 1–2, 25, 34, 42n.48, 59, 61, 62, 79–81, 94n.52, 96n.76, 98, 117, 142
  as authors and publishers 6, 9, 23, 61, 63, 80–6, 88, 93n.48, 100–2, 104–6, 111, 112, 114, 116, 118, 136, 138–9
  cultural role of 84, 119
  language used by 86
  mobility of 84–5
  partnerships between 80–1, 83
  suspicion of 148
  see also blind singers; charlatans, medical; printers and publishers, collaboration with street singers and sellers
Strozzi, Piero 108, 138
syphilis 24, 27, 36, 111

Tagliente, Giovan Antonio 36, 111
Tariffa delle puttane 141
Tartaglini, Leone 113, 147
Tasso, Torquato 122n.32

Torresani d'Asola, Andrea 31, 125n.77
translations see vernacular translations
Tre savi all'eresia 133

Valgrisi, Vincenzo 90n.14, 144
Valvassore, Giovan Andrea (printer and engraver) 53, 91n.20
Varisco, Giovanni (bookseller) 76
Venice
  Campo San Polo 57
  Frezzaria 52, 53, 67n.31, 77, 139
  government, use of print 6, 63, 106, 160, 161
  Merceria 50, 51, 53, 54, 56, 57
  myth of 2, 139
  Parishes
    San Bartolomeo 52
    San Basso 145
    San Fantin 53, 79
    San Giuliano 51, 53
    San Lio 142
    San Luca 53, 78
    San Moisè 52, 53, 75, 77
    San Paternian 30, 51, 53
    San Polo 55
    San Salvador 56
    Santa Maria Formosa 50
    Santa Marina 67n.31
  Piazza San Marco 2, 6, 7, 47, 49, 51, 52, 55, 56, 57, 58, 59, 61, 62, 63, 80, 104, 133, 136, 147, 158
  Ponte dei Fuseri 53
  printing industry 5, 18, 29, 30, 50, 129, 162
  Rialto Bridge and market area 6, 7, 19, 20, 50, 51, 52, 54, 55, 56, 57, 58, 59, 62, 63, 64, 88, 109, 114, 133, 136, 141, 142, 160
  San Rocco, church of 114, *115*
  social organisation 47, 74
  see also Council of Ten; Esecutori contro la bestemmia; Procurators of San Marco; Provveditori di Comun; Riformatori dello studio di Padova; Senate; Tre savi all'eresia
Venier, Lorenzo
  author of *La puttana errante* 85, 132

author of *Il trent'uno della Zaffetta* 56, 132
Venier, Maffio 57
Vergerio, Pietro Paolo 134
vernacular translations 5, 24, 29, 34–7, 79, 116, 158, 160
and religious reform 36–7, 117, 127n.102, 134
Vincenzo di Paolo (street singer and publisher) 80, 83
Virgil 1, 135

War of the League of Cambrai (1509–17) 5, 74–5, 77, 105, 131
see also Italian Wars
Welch, Evelyn 55

women *see* printers and publishers, women in families; readers, women as
woodcuts *see* cheap print, illustration of; printed images

Zannini, Andrea 76
Zenaro, Zacharia (bookseller) 144
Zenoi, Domenico (engraver) 142
Zio, Alvise (printer) 142
Zoppini, Agostino and Fabio (printers) 93n.46
Zoppino, Niccolò (printer and performer) 35, 36, 53, 77, 78–81, 82, 83, 89, 102, 106, 108, 117, 131, 133
Zoppino, Sebastiano (son of Niccolò) 79
Zuan Polo (buffoon) 40n.25, 61, 83, 104